To Marie, Melody, Adam, Jared, Joseph, and Rebekah
To Andrew, Ashley, and Kimberly

2ND EDITION

STRATEGIC MANAGEMENT OF ORGANIZATIONS AND STAKEHOLDERS

CONCEPTS

Jeffrey S. Harrison
University of Central Florida

Caron H. St. John
Clemson University

SOUTH-WESTERN College Publishing

An International Thomson Publishing Company

Publishing Team Director: John Szilagyi
Sponsoring Editor: John Szilagyi
Developmental Editor: Katherine Pruitt-Schenck
Production Editor: Kara ZumBahlen
Marketing Manager: Steve Scoble
Production: WordCrafters Editorial Services, Inc.
Text Composition: Maryland Composition Co., Inc.
Art: Miyake Illustration/Design and Maryland Composition
Text and Cover Designer: Michael H. Stratton
Cover Illustration: ©Photonica

23456789 WCBS 654321098

Printed in the United States of America

I⒯P®
International Thomson Publishing
South-Western College Publishing is an ITP Company.
The ITP trademark is used under license.

Library of Congress Cataloging-in-Publication Data

Harrison, Jeffrey S.
    Strategic management of organizations and stakeholders :   concepts
and cases / Jeffrey S. Harrison, Caron H. St. John. — 2nd ed.
        p.   cm.
    Includes bibliographical references and index.
    ISBN 0-538-87839-8 (comprehensive : hardcover : alk. paper). —
ISBN 0-538-87843-6 (concepts : pbk. : alk. paper). — ISBN
0-538-87842-8 (cases : pbk. : alk. paper)
    1. Strategic planning.   2. Industrial management.   I. St. John,
Caron H.   II. Title.
HD30.28.H3774   1998
    658.4'012—dc21   97-20328
                                                                                              CIP

BRIEF CONTENTS

CONTENTS

PREFACE

THE STAKEHOLDER APPROACH TO STRATEGIC MANAGEMENT

The stakeholder model of strategic management offers a level of integration that makes it highly relevant for firms moving into the next century. It combines perspectives from other traditional models such as industrial organization economics, resource-based theory, cognitive theory, and the institutional view of the firm. The stakeholder model provides a useful tool for students and managers as they deal with an increasingly complex and interconnected environment.

The first edition of *Strategic Management of Organizations and Stakeholders* was a response to the outcry for more responsible management. A stakeholder approach to strategic management results in a broader view of the organization and its environment than that afforded by other approaches. One possible outcome from such broadening is an increase in the likelihood that organizational decisions will be viewed as socially responsible. In other words, organizations who are "tuned in" to their key stakeholders may be able to avoid situations that can damage their reputations. History has demonstrated that an excellent reputation can be a source of sustainable competitive advantage. However, a stakeholder approach encompasses much more than just socially responsible behavior. A stakeholder approach provides a partnering mentality.

Increasing global competition has made it almost impossible for one organization to perform all business functions on its own. Most organizations are reaching outside their own pools of resources and creating alliances with customers, suppliers, communities, unions, and even rivals. The best run companies have found ways to successfully and efficiently manage the diverse interests of these and other stakeholders. In the process, they have developed competitive advantages and discovered and exploited opportunities that were previously unimaginable. Many of these opportunities represent unmet needs of stakeholders or new combinations of resources they provide to the organization.

First Edition Success

We were delighted by the way our first edition was received. Over 100 universities and colleges adopted *Strategic Management of Organizations and Stakeholders,* including some of the best business schools in the country. Since the printing of the first edition, we have had time to explore the stakeholder approach in even more depth. Some of this research was published in a recent issue of the *Academy of Management Executive.*

A FOCUS ON LEARNING

If you are engaged in a typical business program, you are already familiar with the functional business disciplines such as marketing, finance, accounting, production, and human resource management. However, few of your classes have attempted to integrate these disciplines into a meaningful whole. That is one of the purposes of the class you are now taking and this book—to conceptually pull together the tasks of an organization. As you study strategic management, we encourage you to constantly consider the needs, desires, demands, and opportunities presented by important stakeholders such as shareholders, competitors, employees, governments, technology leaders, and many others. This type of treatment will help keep the material relevant to real organizations and will help you avoid the folly of developing plans that "look good on paper" but will not work in a real organization.

Most of you will not become chief executive of a major corporation in the near future; however, the decision-making tools you will develop during this course are relevant at all levels in an organization and in your own career planning. You will also discover that techniques such as stakeholder analysis and industry analysis are highly relevant in all types of organizations, including small entrepreneurial firms and nonprofit organizations.

A FOCUS ON TEACHING

Many existing strategy texts include sections or chapters on social responsibility, stakeholder analysis, or ethics, which is a reflection of the importance of these topics to modern strategic management. However, these issues are often treated as additions to the theory and practice of strategic management. As we see it, all strategic decisions are "ethical" decisions because they are directly linked to the way the organization interacts with its stakeholders. Stakeholders develop expectations concerning organizational behavior and outcomes. It is the strategic manager's job to balance the needs and demands of key stakeholders and incorporate knowledge gained through interactions with stakeholders into the mission, goals, strategies, and plans of the organization. In this book, we develop the idea that responsiveness to stakeholders can lead to a socially responsible reputation for the organization *and* higher performance.

The process of integrating the traditional theory of strategic management with stakeholder analysis and management was not difficult. Everything fits. In fact, we discovered that many of the best run organizations have already integrated comprehensive stakeholder analysis and management processes into their organizational planning.

A COMPREHENSIVE CASE SELECTION

The second edition of *Strategic Management of Organizations and Stakeholders* offers a selection of thirty new, comprehensive cases. These cases were chosen with special emphasis on a wide range of stakeholder themes. Topics include global competitiveness, small business management, higher education, and the strategic management of highly technical industries. These cases were selected on the basis of their currency, depth, and relevance in providing a comprehensive study of the role of stakeholders and organizations in strategic management. Included with the cases for the instructor are a set of comprehensive case notes. These provide detailed information on each case, instructions for how to teach it, and questions that can be asked to better understand and analyze the case materials.

Strategic Management of Organizations and Stakeholders: Cases, 2e can be purchased separately as an entire casebook. Adopters also have the option to select a combined text/casebook or a separate text on the "Concepts" portion of the main text, or order customized cases from the casebook. Additional cases to accompany the text can be ordered at ITP's exclusive on-line case service, Casenet, at http://casenet.thomson.com.

NEW TO THIS EDITION

Based on reviewer response and current teaching needs and trends in the field, we have incorporated a wealth of important new material into the second edition. In addition, we have restructured and improved upon the presentation of the material in the first edition to better serve our readers and instructors.

- *New Chapter 2*: A new chapter was created on environmental scanning, strategic surveillance, and development of corporate intelligence systems.
- *Streamlining of Chapter 3*: The material on external stakeholders (formerly Chapter 2) has been streamlined, drawing from the most important elements of the field.
- *Restructuring of the Corporate-Level Chapters*: The first edition broke corporate-level strategy into the traditional corporate-level strategy process and strategy implementation. However, much of the material included in this last chapter also applies to business-level strategy. Thus, a new sequence was created to accommodate the cross-functional nature of implementation.
- *New Chapter 9*: As a result of these changes, a new Chapter 9 was created called "Corporate Restructuring." This chapter draws from material in both Chapters 7 and 9 of the first edition.
- *Expanded Topics*: Coverage is expanded in the areas of restructuring, downscoping, and rightsizing. In addition, more material is included on resource-based theory and the creation of a sustainable competitive advantage. The international strategy section has also been expanded.

DIFFERENTIATING FEATURES

Stakeholder Approach. Each stakeholder group is given detailed treatment. The book provides information concerning what each group wants from the organization, the type of influence it can have on organizational processes, how each group can contribute to achieving organizational goals, and how managers can manage relationships with each group. This feature brings reality into the classroom. Other approaches don't ignore stakeholders, but they tend to deemphasize stakeholder management as a means of creation of a sustainable competitive advantage.

Integrative Examples. Although the book contains examples from hundreds of companies to illustate theory, three or four of these companies are used regularly throughout the book. These are well-known companies such as Disney, Toys 'R' Us, Marriott, and Rubbermaid. Frequent use of the same companies not only offers the advantage of familiarity, but also provides students with an ability to see how pieces of an organization fit together.

Global Issues and Examples Woven into Each Chapter. Instead of including one big global chapter, the assumption here is that, to be competitive, firms must quickly become global players.

Ethics Given More Treatment Than in Any Other Text. Ethics are at the heart of a stakeholder approach to strategic management. As the organization deals with its stakeholders, ethical issues emerge with regularity. Instead of sweeping these issues to the side and depending on rational and nonpolitical models as a basis for discussion—the approach that most texts use—we build stakeholder implications directy into everything we do in the text.

Student-Friendly Style. Students who used the first edition found it to be written in an easy-to-understand style with clear examples. This edition is written in the same flowing style, but also benefits from three more years of in-class experience and feedback from students.

PEDAGOGICAL FEATURES

Opening Vignette. Each chapter begins with a description of an actual company situation, with an emphasis on the chapter topic. The vignettes create student interest and provide an excellent vehicle for instructors to begin their lectures.

Margin Definitions. Major terms are defined in the margins. This helps students get familiar with and remember the terminology of the field, and it helps them study for exams. For the instructor, the definitions provide a quick glance at the chapter to determine what is covered.

In-Text Examples. These are detailed examples that are set off from the rest of the textual material but are not in boxes. Since they are a part of the flow of the material, there is a high likelihood that students will not skip them. The examples reinforce the points that are being taught. They are drawn from a combination of domestic and global, large business and small business, manufacturing and service, for-profit and nonprofit firms.

"Strategic Insights." These boxes are detailed examples of companies and industries. They are longer than the in-text examples. They also are drawn from a combination of domestic and global, large business and small business, manufacturing and service, for-profit and nonprofit firms. Approximately four insights are provided per chapter.

"Strategic Applications." These boxes are provided in nearly every major section in the book (about two to three per chapter). They provide techniques that can be used by students to apply textual material to the cases. Instructors can assign students to apply an application to an actual company and then devote class time to discussing it.

Figures. Figures are used to demonstrate the relationships that exist among stakeholders inside and outside the organization. Many of them deal with influences one group has on another group or on an organizational process. They also provide information concerning the flow of activities or processes in organizations and the flow of textual material.

Instructional Aids for Instructors. A complete instructor's manual is provided. Materials include: (1) answers to discussion questions; (2) detailed outlines of the chapter material; (3) comprehensive test bank with multiple choice, true/false, and essay questions for all chapters; (4) overhead transparency masters for tables, figures, and outlines of chapter sections; and (5) suggestions for course sequence.

ACKNOWLEDGMENTS

We would like to acknowledge the excellent work of the following reviewers who helped us develop this text into its present form:

Gary Aitchison, Iowa State University

Kenneth Auperlee, University of Akron

Inga Baird, Ball State University

Bruce R. Barringer, University of Central Florida

Sidney Barton, University of Cincinnati

Reginald Beal, University of Wisconsin–Whitewater

Joseph E. Benson, New Mexico State University

Donald Bergh, Pennsylvania State University

William Boulton, Auburn University

Gary Bruten, University of Tulsa

Paul Buller, Gonzaga State University

Lavon Carter, Harding University

Gary J. Castrogiovanni, University of Houston

Marian Clark, New Mexico State University

Roy A. Cook, Fort Lewis College

Karen A. Froelich, North Dakota State University

Paul C. Godfrey, Brigham Young University

Arthur Goldsmith, University of Massachusetts–Boston

Peter Goulet, University of Northern Iowa

Ernest H. Hall, Jr., University of Southern Indiana

Phil Hall, University of Nebraska

W. Harvey Hegarty, Indiana University

Don Huffmire, University of Connecticut

Jon G. Kalinowski, Mankato State University

Robert Keating, University of North Carolina–Wilmington

Dan Kopp, Southwest Missouri State University

Charles R. Kuehl, University of Missouri–St. Louis

James Lang, Virginia Polytechnic Institute and State University

Cynthia Lengnick-Hall, Wichita State University

Joseph G. P. Paolillo, University of Mississippi

Douglas Polley, St. Cloud State University

Rhonda Kay Reger, Arizona State University

Michael Russo, University of Oregon

Dwaine Tallent, St. Cloud State University

Melanie Trevino, University of Texas–El Paso

Frank Winfrey, Kent State University

We hope you will find our approach to the field of strategic management refreshing and relevant. You and your students are *our* most important stakeholders. As you use this text, if you have any comments, criticisms, or suggestions, we welcome them.

Jeffrey S. Harrison
Department of Management
University of Central Florida
Orlando, FL 32816
(407) 823-2916

Caron H. St. John
Department of Management
Clemson University
Clemson, SC 29634
(803) 656-2011

part
1

Strategic Management and Environmental Analysis

1

Stakeholders and the Strategic Management Process

Can Disney Tame 42nd Street?

"Can Disney Tame 42nd Street?" This headline from a recent *Fortune* article announces another of Disney's many ambitious projects. The Walt Disney Company is pouring millions of dollars into the development of one of the most crime-ridden areas in New York City—42nd Street between Times Square and Eighth Avenue in Manhattan. The area will feature a live production theater, a Disney Store, cinemas, hotels, game parlors, and restaurants. Michael Eisner, Disney's chief executive officer, announced, "I think the Disney brand is going to be enhanced by being on Forty-Second Street. It's a magic word and a magic place."

Why not? Under Eisner's leadership, the sleeping giant that was once Disney has been transformed into a worldwide entertainment superpower. Investors are delighted. In fact, during the past ten years an investment in Disney stock returned an average 28% per year, compared to 16% for the Standard and Poor's 500 companies. Disney has major theme parks in the United States, Europe, and Asia and owns several movie production companies, which have turned out major motion picture successes such as *The Lion King, The Hunchback of Notre Dame, While You Were Sleeping,* and *Father of the Bride.* With the success of its live Broadway version of *Beauty and the Beast*, Disney plans to release a new Broadway production every year. Its television shows, such as *Home Improvement*, have also enjoyed great success. Disney merchandise is sold in a large and growing network of Disney Stores. Finally, in a move that shocked the entertainment industry, Disney acquired Capital Cities/ABC, one of the three largest broadcast networks in the United States.

Disney's successes are attributable to masterful management of the organization as well as the creation of a tangled web of strategic alliances with external constituencies. On the inside, Eisner holds regular "synergy" meetings comprised of top managers from each division. The purpose of the meetings is to plan how each division can promote other divisions. Innovation, perhaps Disney's key competitive advantage, is managed through Walt Disney's Imagineering Division. From an external perspective, few companies rival Disney's ability to create profitable alliances. Tokyo Disneyland, the best attended theme park in the world, is a joint venture with Oriental Land Company Ltd. An alliance with McDonald's makes the fast food giant the primary promotional partner in the restaurant business. Another deal with Canada's Royal Mounties allows Disney to sell officially licensed Mounties souvenirs. Indeed, the project on 42nd Street is being financed largely through local government loans at only 3% interest.[1]

Why are companies like Disney successful, while so many businesses fail? Some organizations may just be lucky. They may have the right mix of products and/or services at the right time. But often that is not enough. Even if luck works for a while, it probably will not last long. Most highly successful companies are both keenly aware of and successful in managing relationships with a wide range of organizations, groups, and people that have a stake in their organizations. These important constituencies are called stakeholders. **Stakeholders** are groups or individuals who can significantly affect or are significantly affected by an organization's activities.[2] They have (or believe they have) a legitimate claim on some aspect of the organization or its activities because they are involved with or are influenced by the organization.[3] While these relationships are typically defined from the perspective of the stakeholder, they are not unidirectional. Just as stakeholders have a stake in the organization, the organization depends on its stakeholders to survive and prosper.

Successful organizations also possess resources and capabilities that provide competitive advantages. For example, Disney enjoys almost unparalleled brand recognition, world-class human resource management, and an unequaled ability to create. These resources and capabilities are carefully fostered and applied to all of Disney's business areas.

This book focuses on how organizations like Walt Disney, whether they are competing in the for-profit or nonprofit domain, satisfy their most important stakeholders through successful execution of the strategic management process. **Strategic management** is the process through which organizations analyze and learn from the stakeholders inside and outside of the organization, establish strategic direction, create strategies that are intended to help achieve established goals, and execute those strategies, all in an effort to satisfy key stakeholders. Twenty years of experience has shown us that organizations practicing strategic management processes will outperform their counterparts that do not.[4] Strategic Insight 1.1 contains a brief narrative that describes the increasing importance of strategic management.

THE STRATEGIC MANAGEMENT PROCESS

In general, firms pass through four phases in their planning processes, in response to increasing size, diversity, and environmental complexity:

Phase 1: *Basic Financial Planning.* In this phase, organizations are internally oriented, with a focus on meeting budgets and developing financial plans.

Phase 2: *Forecast-Based Planning.* Organizations begin to look outward to the external environment for trends and developments that may impact the future.

Phase 3: *Externally Oriented Planning.* At this point organizations begin to think strategically; that is, they devise strategies in response to markets and competitors.

Phase 4: *Strategic Management.* In the final phase, organizations manage all of their resources in an attempt to develop sustainable competitive advantages and "create the future."[5]

In this framework, organizations move from an internal to an external focus in their planning, first by responding to the environment and ultimately by attempting to control it. Responding to the environment is often referred to as **adaptation**, while the processes associated with attempting to control the environment to make

Stakeholders
Groups or individuals who can significantly affect or be affected by an organization's activities.

Strategic Management
The process through which organizations analyze and learn from their internal and external environments, establish strategic direction, create strategies that are intended to help achieve established goals, and execute those strategies, all in an effort to satisfy key organizational stakeholders.

Adaptation
The process of responding to the environment.

BUSINESS

STRATEGY

The Increasing Importance of Strategic Management

Prior to the twentieth century, most of the human race was engaged in producing the basic necessities of life. However, during the Industrial Revolution, many family-run farms and businesses were replaced by professionally managed firms. International trade increased with advances in transportation. Communications became a major global industry. Service industries such as entertainment and travel flourished. These trends accelerated during the post–WWII era. Prosperity during the Industrial Revolution also resulted in the creation of large and diversified business organizations. By the middle of the twentieth century, approximately 40% of the business-related assets in the United States were controlled by the largest 200 companies.

In the immediate post–WWII era, U.S. companies dominated the global economy due to technological superiority and because the infrastructures of many countries were badly damaged during the war. However, these countries, most notably Japan and Germany, gradually but consistently improved their standing in the world economy. In particular, the United States lost its dominance in industries such as automobiles and electronics. Changes in the global and domestic business environments during the twentieth century gave rise to the need for new management techniques, especially from the perspective of the top manager. The dual tasks of efficiently running a large, often multinational firm and guiding its course became too difficult for any one leader to handle alone. New organizational forms emerged, with new divisions of managerial labor and new managerial techniques. Also, while the large organizations that formed during the early part of the century were internally focused on efficiency (a management science approach combined with basic financial planning), they soon learned that effective management in a rapidly changing business environment required more of an outward orientation.

Business schools responded to changing top management needs by offering a course on business policy. The business policy course applied general administrative principles to a variety of business situations through cases, which described real-world businesses and the challenges they faced. Competitiveness problems in U.S. firms also gave rise to substantial growth in consulting firms that specialized in top management issues and questions. Additionally, the topics of strategy and strategic management became major research topics in many business schools across the United States and elsewhere. By the early 1970s, teachers and researchers of business policy began meeting to discuss changes that were taking place in the field of business policy and how they should respond to them. Then, in May 1977, a major conference was held at the University of Pittsburgh. This conference confirmed the birth of a field that is now known as strategic management.

Since that critical meeting in 1977, the field of strategic management has continually grown in importance as researchers in almost every country in the world attempt to discover the strategies and strategic management techniques that differentiate successful from unsuccessful organizations. Strategic management processes are widely recognized for their value to organizations. Most large corporations in the United States and abroad have staffs dedicated to strategic management activities. Smaller organizations have also found the tools and techniques of strategic management helpful.

Sources: D. E. Schendel and C. W. Hofer, eds., *Strategic Management: A New View of Business Policy and Planning* (Boston: Little, Brown and Company, 1979); L. W. Weiss, "The Extent and Effects of Aggregate Concentration," *Journal of Law and Economics* 26 (1983), pp. 429–455.

Enactment
The process of influencing the environment to make it less hostile and more conducive to organizational success.

it less hostile and more conducive to organizational success are called **enactment**.[6] Organizations that have reached phase 4 in their planning efforts engage in significant amounts of both adaptation and enactment, as opposed to organizations in earlier phases that focus primarily on adaptation.

A simple model of the strategic management process is contained in Figure 1.1. The typical sequence of activities begins with (1) analysis of the broad and operating environments of the organization and (2) the organization itself, followed by the (3) establishment of strategic direction, reflected in missions, visions, and/or long-term goals, (4) formulation of specific strategies, (5) implementation of those strategies, and (6) development of control systems to ensure that they are both successfully carried out and still appropriate for the firm in its current environment. Finally, strategic restructuring may occur as a firm makes major changes to its strategic direction, strategies, and/or the way those strategies are implemented, usually in response to inconsistencies between expected and actual performance. While these activities may occur in the order specified, especially if a firm is engaging in a formal strategic planning program, they may also be carried out in some other order or simultaneously. Also, the dashed lines in Figure 1.1 indicate that organizations often cycle back to earlier activities during the strategic management process, as new information is gathered and assumptions change. For instance, an organization may attempt to develop strategies consistent with its long-term goals and, after a trial period, discover that the goals were too ambitious or too easy to obtain. Also, an organization may discover rather quickly (or over a longer period of time) that a proposed strategy cannot be implemented feasibly. As a result, the organization may have to cycle back to the formulation stage to fine-tune its strategic approach. In other words, organizations may learn from their own past actions and from environmental forces, and may modify their behavior in response.

Start-up firms seldom exhibit the sophisticated planning processes associated with phase 4 planning. They rarely engage in all of the processes depicted in Figure 1.1. Start-ups often begin with an entrepreneur who has an idea for a product or service that he or she believes will lead to market success. Venture capital is raised through a variety of public or private sources and a new business is born. The entrepreneur may establish an informal sense of direction and a few goals, but the rest of the formal strategy process may be overlooked. If the organization is successful, it will typically expand in both sales and personnel until it reaches a critical point at which the original entrepreneur feels a loss of control. At this point the entrepreneur may attempt to formalize various aspects of strategic planning, either by hiring outside consultants, by creating planning positions within the firm, or by involving other managers in planning activities. This same process is typical of nonprofit start-ups as well, except that the nature of the cause (i.e., humanitarian, educational) may place tighter constraints on the way the firm is financed and organized.

Consequently, the model in Figure 1.1 is not intended to be a rigid representation of the strategic management process in all organizations as they currently operate. Nevertheless, the progression of activities—from analysis to plan to action and control—provides a logical way to study strategic management. Furthermore, the activities relate equally well to for-profit, nonprofit, manufacturing, and service organizations, although some of the differences in the way these organizations approach strategic management are described throughout the text.

Now that the strategic management process has been introduced, each of its components will be described in more detail—environmental analysis, organiza-

Figure 1.1 *The Strategic Management Process*

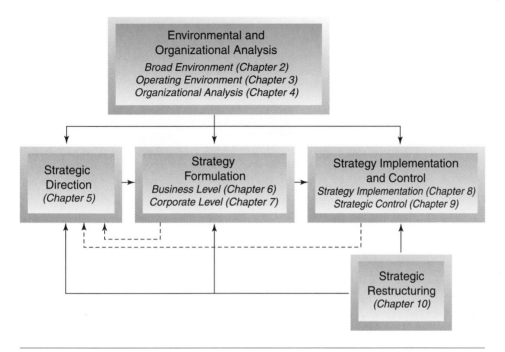

tional analysis, strategic direction, strategy formulation, strategy implementation and control, and strategic restructuring.

Environmental and Organizational Analysis

This book utilizes a stakeholder approach to strategic management. Just as the chief aim of an organization is the satisfaction of its key stakeholders, these stakeholders form the basis for analysis of the environment and the organization. For the purposes of this book, an organization's **environment** includes groups, individuals, and forces outside of the traditional boundaries of the organization that are significantly influenced by or have a major impact on the organization.[7] The **organization** includes all of the stakeholders, resources, and processes that exist within the boundaries of the firm.

Many of the stakeholders and forces that have the potential to be most important to organizations are shown in Figure 1.2. Examples of key stakeholders within the organization are managers, employees, and owners. Organizational analysis, the subject of Chapter 4, also includes a broader evaluation of all of the organization's resources and capabilities. External stakeholders, which are a part of an organization's **operating environment**, include competitors, customers, suppliers, financial intermediaries, local communities, unions, activist groups, and government agencies and administrators. These groups are discussed in Chapter 3. The **broad environment** forms the context in which the organization and its operating environment exist, and includes sociocultural forces, global economic forces, technological change, and global political and legal forces. One organization, acting independently, can have very little influence on the forces in the broad environment; however, the forces in this environment can have a tremendous

Environment
Groups, individuals, and forces outside of the traditional boundaries of the organization that are significantly influenced by or have a major impact on the organization.

Organization
All of the stakeholders, resources, and processes that exist within the traditional boundaries of the firm.

Operating Environment
An organization's external stakeholders: competitors, customers, suppliers, financial intermediaries, local communities, unions, activist groups, and government agencies and administrators.

Broad Environment
Sociocultural forces, global economic forces, technological change, and global political/legal forces.

Figure 1.2 *The Organization and Its Primary Stakeholders*

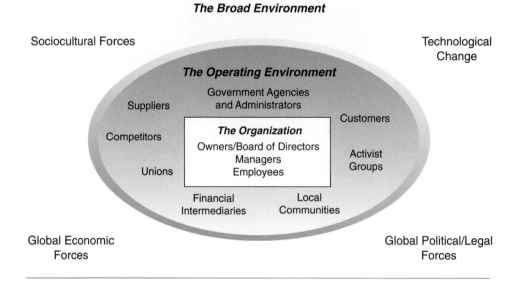

impact on the organization. The major components of the broad environment are discussed in Chapter 2.

All of the stakeholders inside and outside of the organization should be analyzed at both the domestic and international levels. In all of the countries in which a company operates, managers must interact with government agencies, employees, competitors, and activist groups. In addition, the global perspective certainly applies to sociocultural, political, economic, and technological forces. Thus, Figure 1.2 contains both a global and a domestic dimension.

As illustrated by the downward-pointing arrows in Figure 1.1, analyzing the environment and the organization can assist the organization in all of the other tasks of strategic management. For example, an organization's managers should formulate strategies based on organizational strengths and weaknesses and in the context of the opportunities and threats found in its environment. In addition, strategic direction is an outcome of melding the desires of key organizational stakeholders with environmental realities.

Strategic Direction

Strategic direction pertains to the longer term goals and objectives of the organization. At a more fundamental level, strategic direction defines the purposes for which an organization exists and operates. This direction is often contained in **mission** and **vision** statements. Unlike shorter term goals and strategies, the mission is an enduring part of planning processes within the organization. Often missions also describe the areas or industries in which an organization operates. For example, the mission of the New York Stock Exchange is as follows:

> *Support the capital-raising and asset-management processes by providing the highest-quality and most cost-effective, self-regulated marketplace for the trading of financial instruments; promote confidence in and understanding of that process; and serve as a forum for discussion of relevant national and international policy issues.*[8]

Mission Statement
Statement describing the organization's overall purpose, broad goals, and the scope of its operations.

Vision Statement
Statement expressing management's view of what the organization can or should become in the future.

A vision statement expresses what the organization wants to be in the future, which may involve a fundamental change in its business. For example, a start-up firm may have a mission to provide software design and support for its clients, but its long-range vision may be to become a fully integrated Internet provider. Although the mission directs the business for now, the mission will gradually change as the organization moves over time toward fulfillment of its vision. A well-established strategic direction provides guidance to the stakeholders inside the organization who are largely responsible for carrying it out. A well-defined direction also provides external stakeholders with a greater understanding of the organization and its activities. Strategic direction is the central topic of Chapter 5. The next logical step in the strategic management process is strategy formulation.

Strategy Formulation

A **strategy** can be thought of in two ways: (1) as a pattern that emerges in a sequence of decisions over time and (2) as an organizational plan of action that is intended to move an organization toward the achievement of its shorter term goals and, ultimately, toward the achievement of its fundamental purposes. In some organizations, particularly small businesses and those experiencing rapidly changing environments, strategies are not "planned" in the formal sense of the word. Instead, managers seize opportunities as they come up, but within guidelines or boundaries defined by the firm's strategic direction or mission. In those cases, the strategy reflects the insight and intuition of the strategist or business owner and becomes clear over time as a pattern in a stream of decisions.

> **Strategy**
> An organizational plan of action intended to move an organization toward the achievement of its goals and mission.

Strategies as "plans" are common in most organizations, however. Strategy formulation—the process of planning strategies—is often divided into three levels: corporate, business, and functional.

Corporate-level strategy formulation refers primarily to domain definition, or the selection of business areas in which the organization will compete. Although some firms, such as McDonald's, are involved in one basic business, diversified organizations are involved in several different businesses and serve a variety of customer groups. Corporate-level strategy formulation is the topic of Chapter 7. **Business-level strategy formulation**, on the other hand, pertains to domain direction and navigation, or how businesses compete in the areas they have selected. Business-level strategy formulation is covered in Chapter 6. **Functional-level strategy formulation** contains the details of how the functional areas such as marketing, operations, finance, and research should work together to achieve the business-level strategy. Thus, functional-level strategy is most closely associated with strategy implementation, which is treated in Chapter 8.

> **Corporate-level Strategy Formulation**
> Selection of business areas in which the organization will compete.
>
> **Business-level Strategy Formulation**
> How organizations will compete in the areas they have selected.
>
> **Functional-level Strategy Formulation**
> How an organization's functional areas should work together to achieve the business-level strategy.

Another way to distinguish among the three levels is to determine the level at which decisions are made. Corporate-level decisions are typically made at the highest levels of the organization by the chief executive officer (CEO) and/or board of directors, although these individuals may receive input from managers at other levels. If an organization is only involved in one area of business, then business-level decisions tend to be made by the same people. However, in organizations that have diversified into many areas, which are represented by different operating divisions or lines of business, business-level decisions are made by division heads or business unit managers. Functional-level decisions are made by functional managers, who represent organizational areas such as operations,

Figure 1.3 *Strategy Formulation in a Multibusiness Organization*

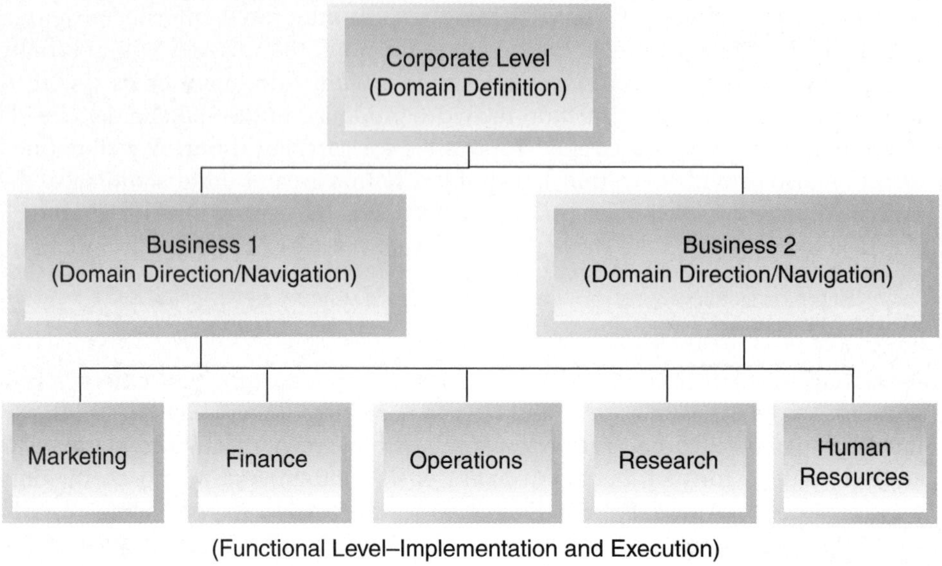

(Functional Level–Implementation and Execution)

finance, personnel, accounting, research and development, or information systems. Figure 1.3 shows the levels at which particular strategy decisions are made within a multibusiness firm.

Strategy Implementation and Control

Strategy formulation, as described in the last section, results in a plan of action for the organization and its various levels. Strategy implementation, on the other hand, represents a pattern of decisions and the actions needed to carry out the plan. **Strategy implementation** involves creating the functional strategies, systems, structures, and processes needed by the organization to achieve strategic ends. Functional strategies outline the specific actions that each function must undertake to convert business- and corporate-level strategies into actions. Organizational systems are developed to train and compensate employees, assist in planning efforts, reinforce organizational values, and gather, analyze, and convey information. Structures reflect the way people and work are organized, which includes reporting relationships and formation into work groups, teams, and departments. Processes, such as standard operating procedures, are developed to create uniformity across the organization and promote efficiency. Strategy implementation, which is discussed in depth in Chapter 8, may require changes to any of these factors as the organization pursues new strategies over time.

Good control is also critical to organizational success. **Strategic control** refers to the processes that lead to adjustments in strategic direction, strategies, or the implementation plan, when necessary. Thus, managers may collect information that leads them to believe that the organizational mission is no longer appropriate or that its strategies are not leading to the desired outcomes. On the other hand, the strategic control system may tell managers that the mission and strategies are appropriate, but they have not been well executed. In such cases, adjustments should be made to the implementation process. Strategic control is the subject of Chapter 9.

Strategy Implementation
Creating the functional strategies, systems, structures, and processes needed by the organization to achieve strategic goals.

Strategic Control
Ongoing evaluation and appropriate adjustments of the mission, goals, strategies, or implementation plan.

STRATEGIC APPLICATION 1.1

IDENTIFYING THE STRATEGIC MANAGEMENT PROCESS

Think of an organization with which you are familiar. Can you bring to mind any evidence that the organization engages in any of the following strategic management activities?

Environmental Analysis

Does the organization make any efforts to assess the needs or desires of its key stakeholders through surveys, interviews, or direct contact?

How does the organization use information about key stakeholders?

Is the organization systematically engaged in collecting information about social trends, financial trends, or advances in technology?

Strategic Direction

Does the organization have a formal mission statement? How is it communicated to employees and other stakeholders?

If no formal mission statement exists, have organizational managers provided a sense of corporate direction? Do employees know what the organization is trying to achieve? Do members of the external environment under-

stand the organization and its purposes? How is this direction communicated?

Strategy Formulation

Does the organization apply a consistent approach to the way products and services are produced and marketed? How would you describe this approach?

Does the organization stress low cost and efficiency, customer satisfaction, high quality, innovation, or flexibility?

Does the organization seem to focus on one particular type of customer or client?

Strategy Implementation and Control

Is there a formal reporting structure or line of communication in the organization?

How does each of the functional areas (i.e., finance, marketing, manufacturing, etc.) contribute to the overall organization? Are there any functional plans?

Does the organization hold groups and individuals accountable for their performance?

What reporting mechanisms are used to measure performance?

As a reinforcement of the concepts discussed thus far, Strategic Application 1.1 provides an opportunity to identify various components of the strategic management process in a familiar organization.

Strategic Restructuring

At some point in the life of almost every organization, growth will slow and some stakeholders will begin to feel dissatisfied. Wal-Mart is an excellent example of this phenomenon. After two decades of incredible growth in sales, earnings, and stock value, Wal-Mart has begun to level off. In fact, Wal-Mart stock recently has been listed as a poor investment by some major financial advisors. Some assert that Sam Walton's death triggered the decline. Others argue that Wal-Mart is suffering from market saturation.

Regardless of the reason, many organizations eventually feel the need to reevaluate, in a major way, their strategies and how they are executing them.

Restructuring
Streamlining and reorienting an organization's current format of operations to place it in a position in which it is better able to compete; often involves reducing the scope of the business at the corporate level combined with refocusing efforts on the things the organization does well.

Restructuring typically involves a renewed emphasis on the things an organization does well, combined with a variety of tactics to revitalize the organization and strengthen its competitive position. Current popular restructuring tactics include refocusing on a more limited set of activities by divesting parts of the business, retrenchment (scaling back of growth efforts), Chapter XI reorganization, leveraged buyouts, and changes to the organizational structure. Restructuring is the topic of Chapter 10.

Now that the strategic management process has been described and the outline of the book presented, we next establish a foundation on which the rest of the book will rest. We first describe the various theoretical perspectives that underlie the field of strategic management. Then we briefly outline stakeholder analysis and the ethics associated with working with stakeholders. Finally, we turn our attention to the trends that are accelerating organizational movement toward a global playing field.

ALTERNATIVE PERSPECTIVES ON STRATEGY DEVELOPMENT

Situation Analysis
Analyzing the internal and external environments of the organization to arrive at organizational strengths, weaknesses, opportunities, and threats (SWOT).

Environmental Determinism
The view that good management is associated with determining which strategy will best fit environmental, technical, and human forces at a particular point in time and then working to carry it out.

The traditional process for developing strategy consists of analyzing the internal and external environments of the organization to arrive at organizational strengths, weaknesses, opportunities, and threats (SWOT). The results from this **situation analysis**, as this process is sometimes called, are the basis for developing missions, goals, and strategies.[9] In general, an organization should select strategies that (1) take advantage of organizational strengths and environmental opportunities or (2) neutralize or overcome organizational weaknesses and environmental threats.

The traditional approach to strategy development is conceptually related to **environmental determinism**. According to this view, good management is associated with determining which strategy will best fit environmental, technical, and human forces at a particular point in time, and then working to accomplish that strategy.[10] From this perspective, the most successful organization will be the one that best *adapts* to existing forces. In other words, the environment is the primary determinant of strategy. After a critical review of environmental determinism, a well-known researcher once argued:

> *There is a more fundamental conclusion to be drawn from the foregoing analysis: the strategy of a firm cannot be predicted, nor is it predestined; the strategic decisions made by managers cannot be assumed to be the product of deterministic forces in their environments . . . . On the contrary, the very nature of the concept of strategy assumes a human agent who is able to take actions that attempt to distinguish one's firm from the competitors.*[11]

The principle of enactment, which we discussed earlier, assumes that organizations do not have to submit to existing forces in the environment—they can, in part, create their environments through strategic alliances with stakeholders, investments in leading technologies, advertising, political lobbying, and a variety of other activities.[12] Of course, smaller, independent organizations are somewhat limited in their ability to influence some components of their environments, such as national government agencies and administrators; however, they typically have more influence on forces in their local operating environments.

It is not necessary to reject completely determinism and the view that organizations should adapt to their environments or the more modern view that organizations can determine their environments through enactment. The stakeholder view is a realistic compromise between the two theoretical extremes of choice and determinism. Evaluation of organizational and environmental stakeholders, and forces in the broad environment, can result in the identification of organizational strengths and weaknesses as well as environmental opportunities and threats. Such an analysis can be used to help the organization identify strategies that will lead to success in the existing environment. For example, Disney recently applied its expertise in staging dramatic presentations (developed in its theme parks and movie making) to Broadway musicals.

There is some evidence that the ability to align the skills and other resources of the organization with the needs and demands of the environment can itself be a source of competitive advantage.[13] However, stakeholder analysis can also lead to the identification of opportunities that can alter an organization's environment. For instance, Disney acquired a major customer of its television programs and movies when it bought Capital Cities/ABC.

The traditional school of thought concerning strategy formulation also supports the view that managers respond to the forces discussed thus far by making decisions that are consistent with a preconceived strategy. In other words, strategy is deliberate. **Deliberate strategy** implies that managers *plan* to pursue an *intended* strategic course. On the other hand, in some cases, as we noted earlier, strategy simply emerges from a stream of decisions. Managers learn as they go. An **emergent strategy** is one that was not planned or intended. According to this perspective, managers *learn* what will work through a process of trial and error.[14] Supporters of this view argue that organizations that limit themselves to acting on the basis of what is already known or understood will not be sufficiently innovative to create a sustainable competitive advantage.[15]

The story of the small Honda motorcycle offers support for the concept of emergent strategy. When Honda executives decided to market a small motorcycle, they had no idea it would be so successful. In fact, the prevailing wisdom was that small motorcycles would not sell very well. But Honda executives broke the rules and made the decision to market a small motorcycle. As sales expanded, they increased marketing, and ultimately captured two-thirds of the American motorcycle market. In another example, General Motors had a minivan on the drawing boards long before Chrysler. On the basis of rational analysis, GM decided that the minivan would probably not sell.[16] In spite of the strength of these examples concerning emergent strategy, it is not a good idea to reject deliberate strategy either. One of the strongest advocates of learning and emergent strategy recently confessed, "we shall get nowhere without emergent learning alongside deliberate planning."[17] Both processes are necessary if an organization is to succeed.

Finally, in recent years another perspective on strategy development has been gaining wider acceptance. It is called the **resource-based view of the firm** and has its roots in the work of the earliest strategic management theorists.[18] According to this view, an organization is a bundle of resources, which fall into the general categories of (1) financial resources, including all of the monetary resources from which a firm can draw; (2) physical resources such as plants, equipment, locations, and access to raw materials; (3) human resources, which pertains to the skills, background, and training of individuals within the firm; and (4) general organizational resources, including the formal reporting structure, management techniques, systems for planning and controlling, culture, reputation, and relationships within the organization as well as relationships with external stakeholders.[19]

From a resource-based perspective, **strengths** are the firm's resources and capabilities that can lead to a competitive advantage. **Weaknesses** are resources

Deliberate Strategy
An intended strategic course planned and pursued by managers.

Emergent Strategy
A strategy not planned or intended, but which emerges from a stream of managerial decisions.

Resource-based View of the Firm
A perspective on strategy development that views the organization as a bundle of financial, physical, human, and general organizational resources.

Strengths
A firm's resources and capabilities that can lead to a competitive advantage.

Weaknesses
Resources and capabilities that the firm needs but does not possess, resulting in a competitive disadvantage.

Opportunities
Conditions in the broad and operating environments that allow a firm to take advantage of organizational strengths, overcome organizational weaknesses, and/or neutralize environmental threats.

Threats
Conditions in the broad and operating environments that may stand in the way of organizational competitiveness or the achievement of stakeholder satisfaction.

Sustainable Competitive Advantage
An advantage that is difficult to imitate by competitors, leading to higher-than-average organizational performance over a long time period.

and capabilities that the firm does not possess but that are necessary, resulting in a competitive disadvantage. **Opportunities** are conditions in the broad and operating environments that allow a firm to take advantage of organizational strengths, overcome organizational weaknesses, and/or neutralize environmental threats. **Threats** are conditions in the broad and operating environments that may stand in the way of organizational competitiveness or the achievement of stakeholder satisfaction.

If a resource that a firm possesses allows the firm to take advantage of opportunities or neutralize threats, if only a small number of firms possess it, and if it is costly or impossible to imitate, then it may lead to a **sustainable competitive advantage**. A sustainable competitive advantage is an advantage that is difficult to imitate by competitors and thus leads to higher than average organizational performance over a long time period.[20] For example, the success of Marriott is largely attributable to advantages created by resources that have been difficult to duplicate by other companies in the hotel industry. The first is financial controls. Marriott can determine and anticipate construction and operating costs with nearly exact precision. Second, Marriott has developed a distinctive competence in customer service, or "becoming the provider of choice." Looking to the future, Marriott is actively engaged in creating a third organizational capability as the "employer of choice." Marriott executives reason that with fewer people entering the labor force in the 18- to 25-year-old age group, good workers will become increasingly difficult to attract. Also, good workers are especially important in a service business like hotels because they interact directly with customers.[21]

Many scholars of strategy believe that effective development of organizational resources is the most important reason that some organizations are more successful than others. Most of the resources that a firm can acquire or develop are directly linked to an organization's stakeholders. For example, financial resources are closely linked to establishing good working relationships with financial intermediaries. Also, the development of human resources is associated with effective management of organizational stakeholders. Finally, organizational resources reflect the organization's understanding of the expectations of society and the links it has established with stakeholders. The next two sections introduce stakeholder analysis and management.

STAKEHOLDER ANALYSIS AND MANAGEMENT

Stakeholder Analysis
Identifying and prioritizing key stakeholders, assessing their needs, collecting ideas from them, and integrating this knowledge into strategic management processes.

Stakeholder Management
Communicating, negotiating, contracting, and managing relationships with stakeholders and motivating them to behave in ways that are beneficial to the organization and its other stakeholders.

Stakeholder analysis involves identifying and prioritizing key stakeholders, assessing their needs, collecting ideas from them, and integrating this knowledge into strategic management processes such as the establishment of strategic direction and the formulation and implementation of strategies (refer to the arrows pointing down from environmental and organizational analysis in Figure 1.1). **Stakeholder management**, on the other hand, includes communicating, negotiating, contracting, and managing relationships with stakeholders and motivating them to behave in ways that are beneficial to the organization and its other stakeholders. Whereas stakeholder analysis tends to be most closely associated with efforts on the part of organizations to adapt to their environments, stakeholder management is more closely linked to enactment. In reality, the two processes overlap. The importance of effective stakeholder analysis and management is demonstrated in Strategic Insight 1.2.

STRATEGIC INSIGHT 1.2

BUSINESS

STRATEGY

Stonyfield Farm Saved from Demise Through Innovative Use of Stakeholders

In 1987, the Londonderry yogurt manufacturer named Stonyfield Farm, Inc. (Londonderry, New Hampshire) did not have a plant of its own. In October of that year, the company that manufactured under contract for Stonyfield declared bankruptcy, leaving Stonyfield with no ability to continue production. Faced with this loss, the company developed and implemented an innovative recovery plan that involved several key stakeholders, including employees, suppliers, a government agency, a new bank, stockholders, managers, and customers.

First, the company turned its product development plant into a full-scale production operation until a permanent facility could be built. Because the prototype plant was so small, a seven-day, three-shift schedule was implemented to maintain volume. This required the support and patience of employees, which management fostered through weekly meetings. Financial resources were strained throughout the entire recovery period due to the cost of the new manufacturing facility, and employees were asked to accept lower pay for future bonuses. Low-wage hourly workers were scarce in the region because of an abundance of high paying, "high tech" jobs. To attract and retain workers, the company instituted flexible time scheduling, an improved benefits program, increased training, and participative decision making. In spite of the stress, employee relations were excellent.

Due to its weakened financial condition, Stonyfield established creative partnerships with several suppliers and engineers, who agreed to provide up-front service and products without pay for exclusive supply and service agreements. Stonyfield also obtained the assistance of a government agency, the Small Business Administration, in the form of a loan guarantee. An emergency meeting of stockholders yielded commitments for bridge loans, which would help the company meet its financial obligations while long-term financing was being arranged. Finally, the company secured construction financing from a major lender.

The company was eventually able to create a permanent manufacturing facility, which opened in 1989, and along with it a management structure to prevent the crisis from recurring. The next task was to bring the company to the position of operating stability. This involved a series of management changes that strengthened the company, including a three-tiered management structure. Still faced with a tiny marketing budget, the company developed some creative ways to reach its customers. They created a "Moo Patrol" program, complete with a "Moos from the Farm" newsletter and an "Adopt-a-Cow" program, in which children received a picture of their adopted cow and periodic letters indicating how many calves they had or how much milk they were producing.

Now squarely on its feet, sales have grown to more than $6 million, with an annual growth rate of more than 60% in several of the region's largest chains. The company also opened several major national new product lines.

Source: Adapted from "Stonyfield Farm, Inc.," *Strengthening America's Competitiveness: The Blue Chip Enterprise Initiative* (New York: Warner Books on behalf of Connecticut Mutual Life Insurance Company and the U.S. Chamber of Commerce, 1991), pp. 56–57.

Figure 1.4 *Typical Roles of Various Stakeholders*

		Formal (Contractual or Regulatory)	Economic	Political
STAKE	Ownership	Managers Who Own Stock in Organization Directors Who Own Stock in Organization Stockholders in General Sole Proprietors	Other Companies That Own Stock in the Organization	
	Economic Dependence	All Paid Managers and Directors of For-Profit and Nonprofit Firms Joint Venture Partners Creditors Internal Revenue Service	Employees Customers Suppliers Creditors Competitors	Competitors Foreign Governments Local Communities
	Social	Regulatory Agencies (e.g., EPA, OSHA, and SEC) Unpaid Trustees or Managers of Nonprofit Organizations	Financial Community at Large (e.g., large brokerage houses, fund managers, and analysts)	Activist Groups (e.g., Nader's Raiders) Government Leaders The Mediaw

INFLUENCE ON BEHAVIOR

Source: Adapted from R.E. Freeman, *Strategic Management: A Stakeholder Approach* (Boston: Pittman, 1984), p. 63. Reprinted with permission of the author.

Stakeholder Analysis

Figure 1.4 demonstrates that stakeholders can be classified based on their stakes in the organization and the type of influence they have on the organization. Such an analysis can help managers understand both the needs and the potential power of their key stakeholders. In Figure 1.4, groups and individuals can have an ownership stake, an economic stake, or a social stake. An ownership stake means that the value of the organization has a direct impact on their own wealth. Stakeholders also can be economically dependent without ownership. For example, employees receive a salary, debt holders receive interest payments, governments collect tax revenues, customers may be dependent on what they purchase to produce their own products, and suppliers receive payments for goods and services provided to the organization. Finally, a social stake describes groups that are not directly linked to the organization, but are interested in ensuring that the organization behaves in a manner that they believe is socially responsible. These are the "watchdogs" of our modern social order.

On the influence side, groups and individuals may enjoy formal power, economic power, or political power. Formal power means stakeholders have a legal or contractual right to make decisions for some part of the organization, such as regulatory agencies and the Internal Revenue Service. Economic power, on the other hand, is derived from the ability to withhold services, products, capital, revenues, or business transactions that the organization values. Finally, political power comes from the ability to persuade lawmakers, society, or regulatory agencies to influence the behavior of organizations. Notice that some stakeholders have more than one source of power. For example, creditors sometimes have both economic and formal influence because they have formal contracts and may also have a seat on the board of directors.

Stakeholders should be prioritized so that the more important stakeholders are given ample attention during strategy formulation and implementation. Important external stakeholders are those with the greatest impact on the ability of the firm to survive and prosper. In for-profit organizations, the most important stakeholders typically include customers, employees, and shareholders or owners.[22] For example, according to Tony Anderson, CEO of H. B. Fuller Company, a *Fortune* 500 company that makes glue, "Customers are first, employees second, shareholders third, and the community fourth."[23] At Fuller, satisfaction of customers is the key to satisfying other stakeholders.

In nonprofit organizations, there are no shareholders. Consequently, donors, customers (i.e., clients or beneficiaries of services), employees, and sometimes regulatory bodies are typically given highest priority. Chapter 3 contains more detail on how to determine the priority of external stakeholders.

Analysis of stakeholders is even more complicated when organizations are significantly involved in countries other than their home countries. There are several ways to respond to this situation. First, an organization can conduct an analysis of all stakeholders in all countries simultaneously. The resulting combined influences provide the organization with a global picture that helps managers craft missions, goals, strategies, and implementation plans that are applicable in a broad global setting. On the other hand, managers can deliberately segment organizational stakeholders by global region to assist in the creation of custom-tailored or modified approaches to missions, goals, strategies, and implementation plans.

Stakeholder Management

Traditionally, at least in the United States, the focus in management has been on internal (e.g., employees) rather than external stakeholders, with organizational boundaries drawn around the individuals and groups over which managers had direct supervisory control. An inherent assumption in the drawing of organizational boundaries was that external stakeholders could not be "managed," in the traditional sense of the word, because they were not a part of the organization. However, two important trends have blurred the distinction between internal and external stakeholder management.[24]

The first trend is the weakening of the traditional management hierarchy in many organizations.[25] The importance of middle managers has decreased with the delegation of real decision-making authority to work teams and operating-level supervisors and employees. As one team of researchers put it, "Leadership in these new organizations seems to reflect a shift from maintaining rational control to leadership without control, at least in the traditional sense."[26] The nontraditional management techniques being developed in many organizations are also useful for management of external stakeholders, who reside outside conventional organizational boundaries. Consequently, techniques and principles associated with managing internal and external stakeholders are converging.

The second trend that is closing the gap between internal and external stakeholders is the "hollowing out" of corporations in the United States.[27] Organizations increasingly are subcontracting functions that have traditionally been performed in-house. For example, Nike subcontracts its shoe assembly operations and Liz Claiborne has all of its apparel manufactured overseas. In an extreme example of hollowing, Firestone once sold some of its radial tire operations to Bridgestone of Japan, only to buy back the tires to sell under the Firestone name. Subcontracting of vital activities requires a high level of communication and control. A company like Nike has to ensure that the quality of its shoes is maintained, especially in a global marketplace that requires high quality. After the crash of one of its airliners in the Everglades, ValuJet was sharply criticized for subcontracting its maintenance activities. The perception of the media and others, whether accurate or not, was that ValuJet was not able to exercise the same oversight over an external contractor that it could over its own operations. Therefore, organizations must manage relationships with subcontracting organizations as if they were part of their own organizations.

The result of these trends is that management of increasingly autonomous internal work groups is not all that different from management of what used to be considered purely external stakeholders. If management scholars and practitioners believe the former can be managed, then there is no reason to exclude the latter. These ideas help us understand why more and more organizations are embracing a proactive external stakeholder management approach.

Productive Stakeholder Relationships. A recent *Fortune* magazine cover story described modern business in these terms: "Business already is moving to organize itself into virtual corporations: fungible modules built around information networks, flexible work forces, outsourcing, and webs of strategic partnerships."[28] Negotiating and contracting have always been important to business. However, the trend in business is toward more strategic alliances, joint ventures, and subcontracting arrangements. Business organizations are becoming a tangled web of alliances and contracts. For example, Toyota, the automobile giant, chooses to rely on outside suppliers rather than produce supplies in-house. Only two suppliers are owned outright by Toyota, with everything else provided by more than 200 outside sources.[29]

On the other hand, Apple Computer may be an example of a company that encountered problems because of its resistance to partnering with external stakeholders. Once the king of the personal computer industry, Apple resisted the notion that it should partner with other companies through license agreements for its hardware and software. Managers within Apple believed that technical superiority would be sufficient to sustain Apple's position or, at least, a strong position, in the industry. However, after several periods of decline in market share, Apple managers realized the mistake and scrambled to create partnerships with a variety of companies. However, it was too late for Apple to regain its previous position as an industry leader.

Effective management of existing relationships with external stakeholders is an important managerial activity. Recent research indicates that effective partnerships are associated with high communication quality and participation, joint problem solving, commitment, coordination, and trust.[30] Stakeholders develop expectations concerning how an organization should behave and the outcomes they expect to receive. When stakeholders become openly dissatisfied with organizational practices or performance, the organization's ethical image and reputation are tarnished. Furthermore, this lack of consistency between the organization and its key stakeholders may result in financial losses due to legal suits, lost contracts, and lost revenues.

The increasing incidence of shareholder legal suits against top managers in recent years provides evidence that many organizations are not satisfying all of their stakeholders' expectations very well.[31] The next section provides a broad understanding of organizational ethics and social responsibility.

Ethics and Social Responsibility. Stakeholder management involves ethics. Virtually all strategic decisions contain ethical dimensions because they are directly linked to the way the organization interacts with its stakeholders.[32] As they relate to individuals, **ethics** are a personal value system that help determine what is right or good. These values are typically associated with a system of beliefs that supports a particular moral code or view.[33] **Organizational ethics** are a value system that has been widely adopted by members of an organization. For example, Wal-Mart's values emphasize the worth of customers and employees, while Motorola has values that focus on participation and patriotism. To determine what the ethics of an organization are, a student can simply study the pattern of decisions in the organization to discover what or who is given priority.[34] Sometimes the stated ethics of an organization differ from the actual values that guide organizational decisions.

For example, an organization may publish an affirmative action statement that condemns prejudice in hiring and promotion decisions on the basis of sex or race. However, that same organization may not have a single minority member or female in its top management team. Thus, studying the pattern of promotion decisions over a few years can determine whether the stated ethical position differs from the actual behavior of the organization. This approach to ethics is consistent with the stakeholder model developed in this book, since stakeholders will naturally make these types of judgments when determining how well the organization is satisfying their needs and desires.

Embedded within the application of ethics found here is the notion of social responsibility. Social responsibility contains four major components: (1) economic responsibilities such as the obligation to be productive and profitable and meet the consumer needs of society, (2) a legal responsibility to achieve economic goals within the confines of written law, (3) moral obligations to abide by unwritten codes, norms, and values implicitly derived from society, and (4) discretionary responsibilities that are volitional or philanthropic in nature.[35]

Research evidence does not unequivocally support the idea that firms that rank high on social responsibility, based on the four components just described, are necessarily any more or less profitable than firms that rank low.[36] However, social responsibility is only one part of the stakeholder-based strategic management model developed in this book. Although a stakeholder approach can help an organization maintain an untarnished reputation, it should also provide opportunities to enhance economic performance. Organizations that apply stakeholder analysis and management well, including many that are featured in this book, can achieve higher than normal economic profits by learning from stakeholders, forecasting their needs, forming alliances, and avoiding negative outcomes such as strikes, legal suits, boycotts, and stiffer government regulation.

Furthermore, firms that have an overall high rank in the four areas listed earlier (one of which is productivity and profitability) have achieved an end in itself. The old belief, espoused primarily by economists such as Milton Friedman, is that

Ethics
A personal value system used in determining what is right or good.

Organizational Ethics
A value system widely adopted by members of an organization.

Figure 1.5 *Need for and Outcomes from Ethical Behavior*

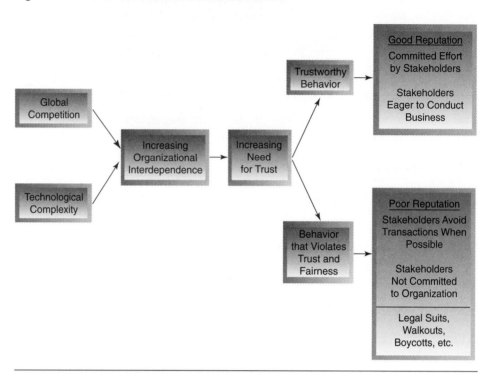

the only valid objective of a corporation is to maximize profits, within the rules of the game (legal restrictions). This view, particularly when only considered within the short term, is no longer considered acceptable by many members of modern societies. A profit maximization philosoply can lead to, at best, shortsightedness and, at worst, disaster, to the extent that organizations forget their longer term obligations to customers, employees, and other constituents in the pursuit of short-run financial rewards.

In addition, one business ethics expert argued that "there is a long-term cost to unethical behavior that tends to be neglected. That cost is to the trust of the people involved. Companies today—due to increasing global competition and advancing technological complexity—are much more dependent than ever upon the trust of workers, specialists, managers, suppliers, distributors, customers, creditors, owners, local institutions, national governments, venture partners, and international agencies. People in any of those groups who believe that they have been misgoverned by bribes, sickened by emissions, or cheated by products tend, over time, to lose trust in the firm responsible for those actions."[37] The logic continues that trust leads to commitment, which leads to increased effort on the part of everyone associated with the firm (see Figure 1.5). Committed effort is precisely what is needed to prosper in a complex world in which interdependence is increasing.

In summary, organizations that exhibit trustworthy behavior enjoy good reputations, a more committed effort by stakeholders to the organization, and an eagerness on the part of stakeholders to conduct business. On the other hand, behavior that violates trust can lead to a poor reputation, legal suits, walkouts, and

Table 1.1 *Forces Favoring Globalization*

Saturated domestic markets
Profitability of foreign markets
Falling trade barriers (e.g., EC 1992)
Newly industrialized countries (e.g., Korea, Taiwan, Spain) leading to increasing global
    competition and new market opportunities
Gorwing similarity of industrialized nations
Shift toward market economies (e.g., East Germany)
English becoming a universally spoken language
Globalization of capital markets
Availability of lower cost resources (e.g., labor) in some foreign countries
Uniformity in technical standards
Opportunities to learn from foreign joint venture partners

Sources: Based on information contained in H. Henzler and W. Rall, ''Facing Up to the Globalization Challenge,'' *McKinsey Quarterly* (Winter 1986), pp. 52–68; T. Peters, ''Prometheus Barely Unbound,'' *Academy of Management Executive* (November 1990), pp. 70–84; M. E. Porter, ed., *Competition in Global Industries* (Boston: Harvard Business School Press, 1986), pp. 2–3.

boycotts, as well as reluctance on the part of stakeholders to participate in transactions with the organization. The case of Manville is illustrative of this point.

> *Nearly fifty years ago, employees and managers of Manville (then Johns-Manville) started to receive information that asbestos inhalation was associated with various forms of lung disease. Manville chose to ignore this information and suppress research findings. The company even went so far as to conceal chest X-rays from employees in their asbestos operations. When confronted about this tactic, a Manville lawyer was quoted as saying that they would let their employees work until they dropped dead, all in the interest of saving money. Eventually, this neglect of research findings and their own employees led to financial ruin for Manville.*[38]

Concerning ethical decision making, the approach of many business organizations seems to be to wait until someone complains before actions are taken. This is the type of attitude that resulted in the Savings and Loan crisis, the Bhopal explosion tragedy in India, and the explosion of the space shuttle *Challenger*. In each of these situations, the organizations involved could have avoided problems by being more responsive to warning signals from key stakeholders. History has taught us that many human-induced disasters and crises could be avoided if organizations were sensitive to what one or another of their stakeholders is saying.

Organizations face complex stakeholder management issues in domestic and international environments. In the following section, we discuss the increasingly global marketplace.

THE CASE FOR GOING GLOBAL

Most successful organizations find that their domestic markets are becoming saturated or that foreign markets offer opportunities for growth and profitability that are often not available domestically. Many forces are leading U.S. firms into the international arena (see Table 1.1). Several of these forces are quite remarkable. Concerning profitability, Coke makes substantially higher profits in its foreign operations than it does at home.[39] Hasbro, the toy maker, also enjoys much higher prices and higher margins in other countries than it does in the United States.

STRATEGIC INSIGHT 1.3

Management Differences Across the United States, Europe, and Japan

The following quotations are based on a recent study of differences in management perspectives and styles across the three regions of the United States, Europe, and Japan, from a European manager perspective. They are illustrative of the types of challenges American managers face when doing business abroad.

Sir Anthony Pilkington, chairman of Pilkington: "In Germany, in Sweden, in Denmark, and even in France, there are a lot of checks and balances against management freedom of actions, there are supervisors' reports, there are workers' representatives on the board and there is much more government intervention."

Jacopo Vittorelli, former deputy chairman of Pirelli: "If you have to close a plant in Italy, in France, in Spain or in Germany, you have to discuss the possibility with the State, the local communities, with the trade unions, everybody feels entitled to intervene . . . . Even the Church."

Andre Leysen, chairman of the supervisory board of Agfa Gevaert: " . . . we work for profit, but also for people. On the other hand, in the U.S., profit dominates everything, and people are considered as a resource that you can take or leave. This is a major difference. Now you could say that the European philosophy is close to the Japanese. I do not think so. There is a fundamental difference between the two. Europe is an individualistic society whereas the Japanese society is based on the collective."

Willem H. J. Guitink, corporate director of management training and education at Philips: "European business leaders are better equipped to deal with cultural diversity, geographical diversity, than most American managers. I don't think that that would necessarily hold for the Japanese."

Justus Mische, member of the board in charge of personnel of Hoechst: "Europe, at least the big international firms in Europe, have a philosophy between the Japanese, long term, and the United States, short term."

Source: R. Calori and B. Dufour, "Management European Style," *Academy of Management Executive* (August 1995), pp. 61–73. Used with permission.

McDonald's expects to see much greater growth in international markets than in U.S. markets.

Changes in European markets such as falling trade barriers are among the most significant global changes. Although the process of unification in Europe is proceeding slowly, it is expected to lead eventually to increased productivity and reduced costs for European businesses. Furthermore, strategic alliances in the sector are expected to increase.[40] Eastern Europe, despite political turmoil, still offers substantial investment opportunities, due to low labor rates and untapped consumer markets.[41] Latin America, some authors have suggested, also offers substantial business opportunities.[42] Of course, Japan is already an economic superpower. Now that Japanese consumers have gained purchasing power, the world economy is dominated by three regions, called the "Triad" regions: North America, Europe, and the Pacific Rim (led by Japan). Some researchers have suggested that in order to remain competitive, larger organizations should be involved in all three regions.[43]

Going global offers many new management challenges. The fact is that Europeans and the Japanese have different views of business and management than Americans, although management techniques around the globe are slowly converging.[44] Strategic Insight 1.3 contains quotations from European managers that demonstrate some of the differences among the Triad regions.

Summary

This chapter emphasized the important role of the strategic management process in modern organizations. The strategic management process includes (1) analysis of the stakeholders and forces in the broad and operating environments and within the organization itself, (2) the establishment of a strategic direction, (3) strategy formulation, and (4) strategy implementation and strategic control. These processes are typically ongoing, although they may also be associated with a formal planning meeting held periodically within organizations. The strategic management process outlined in this book applies to for-profit, nonprofit, manufacturing, and service organizations.

Managers, employees, and owners are the key stakeholders inside the organization. Important stakeholders outside of the organization include competitors, customers, suppliers, financial intermediaries, local communities, unions, activist groups, and government agencies. All of these stakeholder groups can be domestic or global in their scope. In addition, all of these stakeholders operate within a broad environment, which consists of the global societies in which organizations operate, the global technological environment, the global political and legal environment, and the worldwide economy.

Stakeholder analysis processes include identifying stakeholders, prioritizing them, assessing their needs, collecting their ideas, and integrating this knowledge into strategic management processes. Stakeholder management involves communicating with stakeholders, negotiating and contracting with them, managing relationships with them, and motivating them to behave in ways that are beneficial to the organization. Ethics are a part of all of these processes.

Organizational ethics are the values that guide decisions made within organizations. Almost all strategic decisions contain ethical dimensions because they are directly linked to the way the organization interacts with its stakeholders. When stakeholders become openly dissatisfied with organizational practices or performance, the organization's ethical image and reputation are tarnished. Furthermore, this lack of consistency between the organization and its key stakeholders may also result in financial losses. Therefore, assessing the values of stakeholders and treating them with fairness should be a top priority for chief executives and other top managers. Incorporating the needs and desires of a broad group of stakeholders into strategic planning can lead to competitive advantages.

Discussion Questions

1. What are the four phases firms experience in their planning processes in response to increasing size, diversity, and environmental complexity?
2. What is the difference between adaptation and enactment? Which of these processes is more important in large, industrial firms?
3. What are some of the current trends noted by strategic management scholars? What implications do these trends have with regard to strategic management in general and stakeholder management in particular?
4. Explain each of the activities in the definition of strategic management. Which of these activities do you think is most important to the success of an organization? Why?

5. Use the model in Figure 1.4 to develop a stakeholder grid for an organization with which you are familiar. Use specific names for stakeholders (i.e., names of key managers or owners, government agencies, major competitors, etc.). Based on your grid, which stakeholders should be given the most weight in strategic decisions?

6. How can stakeholder analysis be integrated into the strategic management process?

7. What are organizational ethics? What is considered ethical behavior? Why should organizations behave in a manner that is considered ethical?

8. What are some of the forces and trends that are motivating U.S. companies to go global?

9. In what ways does stakeholder management differ from "public relations"? From political manipulation?

References

1. F. Rose, "Can Disney Tame 42nd Street?" *Fortune* (June 24, 1996), pp. 95–104; Reuter, "McDonald's, Disney, as Expected, Cinch Extensive Marketing Pact," *Investor's Business Daily* (May 24, 1996), pp. 1–10; *Annual Report*, The Walt Disney Company, 1995.

2. This is essentially the definition used by Edward Freeman in his landmark book on stakeholder management: R.E. Freeman, *Strategic Management: A Stakeholder Approach* (Marshfield, Mass.: Pitman Publishing Inc., 1984).

3. This view is explained in detail in M. B. E. Clarkson, "A Stakeholder Framework for Analyzing and Evaluating Corporate Social Performance," *Academy of Management Review* 20 (1995), pp. 92–117.

4. C. C. Miller and L. B. Cardinal, "Strategic Planning and Firm Performance," *Academy of Management Journal* 37 (December 1994), pp. 1649–1665.

5. F. W. Gluck, S. P. Kaufman, and A. S. Walleck, "Strategic Management for Competitive Advantage," *Harvard Business Review* (July/August 1980), pp. 154–161.

6. L. Smirchich and C. Stubbart, "Strategic Management in an Enacted World," *Academy of Management Review* 10 (1985), pp. 724–736.

7. Freeman, *Strategic Management: A Stakeholder Approach*; M. Pastin, *The Hard Problems of Management: Gaining the Ethics Edge* (San Francisco: Jossey-Bass, 1986).

8. *Annual Report*, New York Stock Exchange, 1990.

9. C. W. Hofer and D. E. Schendel, *Strategy Formulation: Analytical Concepts* (St. Paul, Minn.: West Publishing, 1978).

10. L. J. Bourgeois, III, "Strategic Management and Determinism," *Academy of Management Review* 9 (1984), pp. 586–596; L. G. Hrebiniak and W. F. Joyce, "Organizational Adaptation: Strategic Choice and Environmental Determinism," *Administrative Science Quarterly* 30 (1985), pp. 336–349.

11. Bourgeois, "Strategic Management and Determinism," p. 589.

12. L. Smirchich and C. Stubbart, "Strategic Management in an Enacted World," *Academy of Management Review* 10 (1985), pp. 724–736.

13. T. C. Powell, "Organizational Alignment as Competitive Advantage," *Strategic Management Journal* 13 (1992), pp. 119–134; N. Venkatraman, "Environment-Strategy Coalignment: An Empirical Test of Its Performance Implications," *Strategic Management Journal* 11 (1990), pp. 1–23.

14. H. Mintzberg and A. McHugh, "Strategy Formation in an Adhocracy," *Administrative Science Quarterly* 30 (1985), pp. 160–197.

15. H. Mintzberg, "The Design School: Reconsidering the Basic Premises of Strategic Management," *Strategic Management Journal* 11 (1990), pp. 171–196.

16. H. Mintzberg, "Learning 1, Planning 0: Reply to Igor Ansoff," *Strategic Management Journal* 12 (1991), pp. 463–466.

17. Mintzberg, "Learning 1, Planning 0," p. 465.

18. N. J. Foss, C. Knudsen, and C. A. Montgomery, "An Exploration of Common Ground: Integrating Evolutionary and Strategic Theories of the Firm," in C. A. Montgomery, ed., *Resource-Based and Evolutionary Theories of the Firm* (Boston: Kluwer Academic Publishers, 1995).

19. J. B. Barney, "Firm Resources and Sustained Competitive Advantage," *Journal of Management* 17 (1991), pp. 99–120; J. B. Barney, *Gaining and Sustaining Competitive Advantage* (Reading, Mass.: Addison-Wesley, 1997); J. S. Harrison, M. A. Hitt, R. E. Hoskisson, and R. D. Ireland, "Synergies and Post-Acquisition Performance: Differences Versus Similarities in Resource Allocations," *Journal of Management* 17 (1991), pp. 173–190; J. T. Mahoney and J. R. Pandian, "The Resource-Based View Within the Conversation of Strategic Management," *Strategic Management Journal* 13 (1992), pp. 363–380; B. Wernerfelt, "A Resource-Based View of the Firm," *Strategic Management Journal* 5 (1984), pp. 171–180.

20. Barney, "Firm Resources and Sustained Competitive Advantage"; Mahoney and Pandian, "The Resource-Based View."

21. Ulrich and Lake, "Organizational Capability: Creating Competitive Advantage," *Academy of Management Executive* (February 1991), p. 79.

22. B. Z. Posner and W. H. Schmidt, "Values and the American Manager: An Update," *California Management Review* 3 (1984), p. 206.

23. P. Sellers, "Who Cares About Shareholders," *Fortune* (June 15, 1992), p. 122.

24. These arguments are also found in J. S. Harrison and C. H. St. John, "Managing and Partnering With External Stakeholders," *Academy of Management Executive* (May 1996), pp. 46–60.

25. R. E. Miles and C. C. Snow, "Organizations: New Concepts for New Forms," *California Management Review* 28 (1986), pp. 62–73.

26. R. L. Daft and A. Y. Lewin, "Where are the Theories for the 'New' Organizational Forms? An Editorial Essay" *Organization Science* 4 (1993), pp. ii–iii.

27. M. Pastin and J. S. Harrison, "Social Responsibility in the Hollow Corporation," *Business and Society Review* (Fall 1987), pp. 54–58.

28. J. Huey, "The New Post-Heroic Leadership," *Fortune* (February 21, 1994), p. 44.

29. G. G. Dess, A. M. A. Rasheed, K. J. McLaughlin, and R. L. Priem, "The New Corporate Architecture," *Academy of Management Executive* (August 1995), pp. 7–20.

30. J. Mohr and R. Spekman, "Characteristics of Partnership Success: Partnership Attributes, Communication Behavior and Conflict Resolution Techniques," *Strategic Management Journal* 15 (1994), pp. 135–152.

31. I. F. Kesner, "Crisis in the Boardroom: Fact and Fiction," *Academy of Management Executive* (February 1990), pp. 23–35.

32. R. E. Freeman and D. R. Gilbert, Jr., *Corporate Strategy and the Search for Ethics* (Englewood Cliffs, N.J.: Prentice Hall, 1988), p. 20.

33. L. T. Hosmer, *The Ethics of Management*, 2nd ed. (Homewood, Ill.: Irwin, 1991), p. 103.

34. This entire discussion of ethics as ground rules was strongly influenced by Pastin, *The Hard Problems of Management*, pp. 40–42.

35. A.B. Carroll, "A Three Dimensional Model of Corporate Social Performance," *Academy of Management Review* 4 (1979), pp. 497–505.

36. K. E. Aupperle, A. B. Carroll, and J. D. Hatfield, "An Empirical Examination of the Relationship Between Corporate Social Responsibility and Profitability," *Academy of Management Journal* 28 (1985), pp. 446–463.

37. L. T. Hosmer, "Response to `Do Good Ethics Always Make For Good Business,'" *Strategic Management Journal* 17 (1996), p. 501. See also L. T. Hosmer, "Strategic Planning as if Ethics Mattered," *Strategic Management Journal* 15 (Summer Special Issue, 1994), pp. 17–34.

38. S. W. Gellerman, "Why 'Good' Managers Make Bad Ethical Choices," *Harvard Business Review* (July/August 1986), pp. 85–90.

39. "As a Global Marketer, Coke Excels by Being Tough and Consistent," *Wall Street Journal* (December 19, 1989), p. 1.

40. H. Weihrich, "Europe 1992: What the Future May Hold," *Academy of Management Executive* (May 1990), pp. 7–18.

41. E. T. Yon, "Corporate Strategy and the New Europe," *Academy of Management Executive* (August 1990), pp. 61–65.

42. J. I. Martinez, J. A. Quelch, and J. Ganitsky, "Don't Forget Latin America," *Sloan Management Review* (Winter 1992), pp. 78–82.

43. K. Ohmae, "Becoming a Triad Power: The New Global Corporation," in H. Vernon-Wortzel and L.H. Wortzel, eds., *Global Strategic Management: The Essentials*, 2nd ed. (New York: John Wiley and Sons, 1991), pp. 62–74.

44. R. Calori and B. Dufour, "Management European Style," *Academy of Management Executive* (August 1995), pp. 61–73.

2

The Broad Environment

GM Takes Environmental Responsibility to Heart

The following excerpts are taken from a statement by John F. Smith, Jr., chief executive officer of General Motors, in a special environmental report published by the company:

"Global businesses must act responsibly in regard to their business and to the natural environments in which they operate.

As we pursue our strategies worldwide, we accept a social and environmental responsibility as well. These responsibilities include the promotion of a sustainable global economy and recognition of the accountability we have to the economies, environments, and communities where we do business around the world. It is important to work for environmental protection in balance with economic objectives and to establish national policies to foster development that can be sustained over the long term. Indeed, sustainable development is supported by the fact that economic growth and environmental protection can be collectively achieved through cooperative efforts—and that's a key philosophy at General Motors.

In January 1994, a GM representative was appointed by President Clinton to the President's Council on Sustainable Development. Through this council, GM has collaborated with government and environmental organizations to develop action plans that will foster U.S. economic vitality and support the international directives that are outlined in Agenda 21, a document adopted by participants at the United Nations Conference on Environment and Development which describes the roles and responsibilities of transnational corporations and industrial activities in a sustainable world.

We at GM have many challenges ahead in defining sustainable development within the context of the global automotive industry. One thing is certain: The managerial skills and technology that a global enterprise such as GM can mobilize provide considerable potential for sustainable development initiatives."[1]

Why would the world's largest automaker devote resources to publishing an environmental report and becoming involved in environmental initiatives, especially considering the performance problems GM has experienced in the last two decades? Top executives are thinking long term. They realize that the environmental movement that began with a few special interest groups half a century ago has become a part of mainstream social opinion, especially in the United States. GM is also establishing alliances with government and other organizations that keep them in this mainstream, and they are using public relations to promote their actions, as shown by the preceding quote. This is good stakeholder management. GM realizes, as do many other organizations, that staying aware of and responding to forces in the broad environment can provide benefits, some of which are hard to quantify. Another example is Dow Chemical, which plans to spend $1 billion on environmental initiatives over a ten-year period.[2]

This chapter describes some of the forces in the broad environment that organizations should stay aware of and how some organizations respond to them. Although typically an organization cannot directly influence forces in the broad environment, it can collect information about the broad environment and use that information to anticipate trends, which will help it buffer threats and take advantage of opportunities. In-depth discussions of forces in the operating environment and in the organization follow in Chapters 3 and 4.

ASSESSMENT OF THE BROAD ENVIRONMENT

As mentioned in Chapter 1, the broad environment can have a tremendous impact on a firm and its operating environment; however, individual firms typically have only a marginal impact on this environment. For example, it would be difficult for an independent firm to dramatically influence societal views on abortion, drug abuse, free trade with China, migration to the Sun Belt, or even the desirability of particular clothing styles. Consequently, although firms may be able to influence the broad environment to some degree, the emphasis in this book is generally on collecting information, forecasting, and responding to this segment of the environment. The most important elements in the broad environment, as it relates to a business organization and its operating environment, are sociocultural forces, global economic forces, technological trends, and global political and legal forces.

Sociocultural Forces

Society is comprised of the individuals who make up a particular geographic region. Some sociocultural trends are applicable to the citizens of an entire country. For example, a few of the major social issues currently facing the United States are shown in Table 2.1. On the other hand, attitudes and beliefs can relate to geographic areas that are larger or smaller than individual countries. For example, people refer to the South (which alludes to the Southern states of America) Western culture (globally speaking), Latin American countries, or the EC (European Community). These sociocultural groups have meaning to most well-educated people, because of the widely held beliefs and values that are a part of the culture in these areas.

Analysis of societal trends is important from at least four perspectives. *First, the values and beliefs of key stakeholders are derived from broader societal influences, which can create opportunities and threats for organizations.* For example, societal interest in fitness has led to business opportunities in home fitness, whereas concerns about

TABLE 2.1 *Major Sociocultural Issues in the United States*

Role of government in health care and child care
Declining quality of education
Legality of abortion
Increasing levels of crime
Importance and role of the military
Levels of foreign investment/ownership in the United States
Social costs of restructuring, especially layoffs
Pollution and disposal of toxic and nontoxic wastes
General increase in environmental awareness
Drug addiction
Continued migration toward the Sun Belt states
Graying of America
AIDS and other health problems
Major global issues
Immigration restrictions

teenagers who smoke cigarettes set the stage for a regulatory backlash against the tobacco companies.

The values and interests of society can vary from region to region and nation to nation. Consequently, it is important to adapt company strategy to each geographic region or country in which a firm is involved. For example, a product that will sell in Los Angeles may not sell very well in North Dakota. In addition, treatment that is offensive to an employee in Germany may be seen as fair and just in Mexico.

Second, awareness of and compliance with the attitudes of society can help an organization avoid problems associated with being a "bad corporate citizen." As mentioned previously, evidence concerning the relationship between social responsibility and financial performance is not very clear.[3] Nevertheless, it is obvious that firms may reduce the risk of gaining a bad "ethical" reputation by anticipating and adjusting for social trends. For example, Denny's was known for many years as one of America's most racist companies. However, Ron Petty, Denny's new CEO, who was hired in part to resolve the racism issue, introduced initiatives that turned the company into a model of multicultural sensitivity:

> *The percentage of minority officers, vice presidents and above, has risen from zero in 1993 to 11% today. Minorities hold 20% of the jobs directly below vice president, a category called director; there were no nonwhites in 1993. Of Denny's 512 franchises, 27 are African American, vs. one in 1993; the goal is 65 by the end of 1997. . . . "Denny's has jumped out in front and taken a positive approach to solving its problems, unlike most companies that do the minimum required by law," says Terry Demchak, a partner at Saperstein Goldstein Demchak & Baller, the California law firm that represented black customers in one of two class-action suits against the chain.*[4]

Shoney's, one of Denny's major competitors, is also involved in major initiatives to erase its racist stigma.[5]

Companies such as Coca-Cola, Procter & Gamble, Rubbermaid, and Johnson & Johnson go to great lengths to present themselves in a positive light. A recent article in *Fortune* magazine that rated corporations on the basis of their reputations began, "Each year we hear of more companies that have made an explicit corporate goal of improving their performance in *Fortune*'s annual survey of corporate reputations."[6] A corporate reputation can be a very important organizational resource, since it cannot be imitated completely. The value of this resource is discussed further in Chapter 4.

Third, correct assessment of social trends can help businesses avoid restrictive legislation. Industries and organizations that police themselves are less likely to be the target of legislative activity. Legislative activity is often in response to a public outcry against the actions of firms or industries, as has been the case with some intrusive and unethical telemarketing activity.

For international firms, the societal expectations and legal environments of business differ widely from nation to nation, which can create complex managerial problems. For example, business practices of U.S. firms in foreign countries continue to be an issue of social debate. This debate is complicated by a strict government regulation called the Foreign Corrupt Practices Act (FCPA). The FCPA was passed by Congress and signed into law by President Carter in 1977. The act was a response to social concern about bribes paid by U.S. companies to foreign government officials. The public and Congress seemed to believe that foreign governments work similarly to the government of the United States. Unfortunately, the "rules of the game" are different in many foreign countries, where payments are demanded as a regular part of business. In the United States, although these types of payments may occur, they are illegal.

Some business writers believe that the FCPA reduced the competitiveness of U.S. firms in foreign markets for two reasons. First, U.S. firms cannot compete fairly with firms from countries that do permit bribery. Second, the FCPA requires detailed record keeping and reporting, which adds another administrative expense to foreign operations and makes them less efficient. The lesson for businesses is fairly clear: "Once legislation that is supposedly ethically motivated is passed, it is almost impossible to rescind. The time to participate forcefully in discussion of ethically motivated legislation is before it is passed, no matter how difficult this appears to be at the time."[7]

Another example of avoidable legislation is the United States Sentencing Guidelines (USSG), compulsory guidelines courts must use to determine fines and penalties when corporate illegalities are proven. These guidelines, which substantially increase corporate punishments, are a direct response to social distress over the increasing incidence of white-collar crime. The guidelines also lay out recommendations for preventing crime, which can reduce the level of punishments should an infraction occur. If corporations had been more proactive in fighting white-collar crime in the first place, this costly legislation could have been avoided.[8]

The fourth reason that analysis of social values is important is that changes in society can create opportunities and threats to an organization's revenue growth and profit prospects. For example, many baby boomer couples had babies later in life than past generations, causing a demographic trend toward older couples with children. The higher levels of income of these more established "thirty-" and "forty-something" parents have led to the development of higher quality baby accessories, clothing, and supplies, and new business opportunities in child care and specialized education. Seemingly unrelated industries, such as the motion picture and television industries, have taken advantage of these trends by producing many movies and television shows that center on birth, babies, and children. Although

STRATEGIC INSIGHT 2.1

Eliminating Waste Makes Bottom-Line Sense

Valerie Sandborg, manager of corporate affairs at the health care giant Baxter International, has seen her company save millions of dollars through its pollution-prevention efforts, which eliminate or minimize pollution when it is created, instead of cleaning it up afterwards. Estimates are that in 1994 alone the company saved $21.7 million. The U.S. Environmental Protection Agency estimates that the international market for waste-abatement and other environmental technologies is worth $200 to $300 billion, and that this figure could double in the next decade. Environmental concern is a worldwide phenomenon. According to Joanna Underwood, president of the environmental research group INFORM, "The signals coming out of Europe—also Eastern Europe—and this country are that preventing waste is going to be more and more important because waste is going to cost more and more to get rid of."

In a recent meeting, representatives from large corporations such as Johnson & Johnson, Procter & Gamble, IBM, and Colgate-Palmolive met to discuss how to integrate environmental decision making into business decisions profitably. The efforts of these businesses are representative of the shift in the corporate environmental mind-set from one of compliance with regulations to one that includes environmental thinking as an overall part of strategic management activities.

In another example, one of Dexter Corporation's most profitable products was a paper used in teabags. However, one of the agents used in the paper resulted in 98% of Dexter's annual hazardous wastes. Dexter was reluctant to make any changes to its paper for fear of losing customers. However, R&D developed a substitute product and the company convinced customers that they were partners in the change to the environmentally friendly substitute. The end result was that Dexter simultaneously increased market share and virtually eliminated hazardous wastes.

Sources: H. Clifford, "Pay Dirt," *Profiles* (October 1995), pp. 47–51; K. Dechant and B. Altman, "Environmental Leadership: From Compliance to Competitive Advantage," *Academy of Management Executive* (August 1994), pp. 7–27.

---

the baby boomer parents and their children have provided growth and profit opportunities for child-related businesses, the counter cycle of the baby boomer trend, the baby bust generation, is likely to threaten the growth and profits of those child-related businesses. Strategic Insight 2.1 provides an example of how companies are saving millions and increasing market share by responding to environmental concerns through "greening" their strategies.

Demographic changes, such as the ones described, can help direct organizational planning and are often at the core of any forecast of industry demand. Annual demand for washing machines, for example, is created for the most part by the number of new household formations, which is influenced by the number of young adults in the population. Currently, the aging U.S. population is providing opportunities for companies in recreation, health care, and nursing homes. However, companies in many other industries are also taking advantage of this trend by offering special services and discounts to senior citizens.

Not only must an organization assess the potential effects of social forces on its business, it must manage its relationship and reputation with society at large. The media acts as a "watchdog" for society. It is a commanding force in managing the attitudes of the general public toward organizations. Executives have nightmares about their organizations being the victims of the next *20/20* program or some other news show. On the other hand, a well-managed media can have a significant positive impact on the image of a firm. Burger King combined local social responsibility with astute media management by announcing that after fourteen years of sponsoring a float in the Orange Bowl Parade, monies ordinarily used for the float would be used to support education (primarily scholarships) in its headquarters city of Miami.[9]

To manage relations with the media, large organizations typically employ public relations (PR) experts. The PR staff is usually active in releasing information that will place their organizations in a favorable light, while being careful not to create the impression that their organizations are withholding information from the public. President Clinton's presidential election campaign "war room" is an interesting example of media management. The room operated twenty-four hours a day in Clinton's campaign headquarters, responding instantly with fast-faxed press releases to any political attack.[10] Press releases, press conferences, individual interviews with reporters, and even seemingly social activities, such as banquets for members of the press, are some of the many efforts organizations make to cultivate the goodwill of the press.

Global Economic Forces

Economic forces can have a profound influence on organizational behavior and performance. Economic forces that create growth and profit opportunities allow organizations to take actions that satisfy many stakeholders simultaneously, particularly owners, employees, and suppliers. On the other hand, when economic trends are negative, managers face tremendous pressures as they balance potentially conflicting stakeholder interests, often between employees and owners.

Economic growth, interest rates, the availability of credit, inflation rates, foreign exchange rates, and foreign trade balances are among the most critical economic factors (see Table 2.2). Of course, many of these forces are interdependent. Organizations should constantly scan the economic environment to monitor critical but uncertain assumptions concerning the economic future and then link those assumptions to the demand pattern and profit potential for their products and services. These assumptions often form the base on which strategies and implementation plans are built.

Economic growth can have a large impact on consumer demand for products and services. Consequently, organizations should consider forecasts of economic growth in determining when to make critical resource allocation decisions such as plant expansions. However, overall economic growth should not be the only or even the most important factor in making these decisions. It is more important for the organization to understand how specific economics trends will affect its demand pattern. Although high interest rates and slow economic growth may hurt housing starts, they do not hurt demand for food.

Some organizations prosper in spite of economic downturns. For example, Novell in network software and Toys 'R' Us in retailing both prospered during the downturn in the early 1990s because other environmental trends were the primary drivers of their businesses. Novell prospered because it was operating at the leading edge of the networking technology trend. Toys 'R' Us prospered because

Table 2.2 *Examples of Types of Global Economic Forces to Monitor and Predict*

The following are a few examples of global economic forces that are worthy of monitoring and, depending on the organization and its business, possibly forecasting as well. These forces should be considered for every country or region in which a firm is involved; global trends as a whole should be tracked as well.

Force	Potential Influences
Economic growth	Consumer demand, cost of factors of production, availability of factors of production (especially labor and scarce resources)
Interest rates	Cost of capital for new projects, cost of refinancing existing debt, consumer demand (due to customer ability to finance purchases)
Inflation	Interest rates, cost of factors of production, optimism or pessimism of stakeholders
Exchange rates	Ability to profitably remove profits from foreign ventures, government policies toward business
Trade deficits	Government policies, incentives, trade barriers

the baby boomer echo (children of baby boomers) provided increasing numbers of children. When faced with an economic downturn, global organizations are able to invest differentially in a wide variety of domestic economies based on current or forecasted conditions. For example, John Deere Corporation, a major producer of farm equipment, was able to withstand the farm crisis of the 1980s because of strong sales in Europe.

Inflation and the availability of credit are among the factors that influence the interest rates paid by organizations. High interest payments can constrain the strategic flexibility of firms by making new ventures and capacity expansions prohibitively expensive. On the other hand, low interest rates can increase strategic flexibility for organizations and also influence demand by encouraging customers to purchase goods and services on credit. Volatile inflation and interest rates, such as those experienced in the United States in the 1970s and in South American and Eastern European countries, increase the uncertainty associated with making strategic decisions. Therefore, they are worthy of forecasting efforts in most organizations, but especially in those that are highly dependent on debt or have customers who finance their purchases.

Foreign exchange rates are another major source of uncertainty for global organizations. Organizations sometimes earn a profit in a foreign country, only to see the profit turn into a loss due to unfavorable currency translations. Furthermore, the organization may have billings in one currency and payables in another. An even bigger problem exists when a foreign currency is not convertible in world financial markets, such as the Russian ruble. Nevertheless, some companies have prospered by taking risks in these situations.[11]

Finally, foreign trade balances are highly relevant to both domestic and global organizations because they are an indication of the nature of trade legislation that might be expected in the future. For example, the United States has a large trade surplus with the European Community (EC). As a result, American manufacturers who export to the EC are concerned about new protectionist legislation such as high tariffs that may be enacted to reduce the trade imbalance.[12]

The social forces discussed in the last section are often interdependent with the economic forces. In the United States, birth rates (a social force) are low and, because of improved health care and lifestyles (another social force), more people are living longer. This demographic shift toward an older population is influencing the economic forces in society. For example, the older population means that the demand for premium services is high but, simultaneously, there are shortages of young workers to fill the service jobs, which drives up wage rates and can lead to inflation. So, for example, a service firm tracking these trends may project that its demand will go up as it sells its services to the older customers, but that its wage rates will go up as well, leading to lower unit profitability.

To assess the effect of the interdependent social and economic forces, organizations often model their business environments using different scenarios. The scenarios are composed of optimistic, pessimistic, and best case assumptions and interpretations of various economic and social data gleaned from the business intelligence system. Continuing with our previous example, the service firm may develop different demand and wage rate scenarios as a way of considering several different possible future business environments. These scenarios can be updated as information becomes more firm and can be used for evaluating different courses of action, such as capacity expansions or investments in labor-saving technologies.

This brief discussion of economic forces provides an indication of the importance of monitoring and forecasting events in the global economy. We now turn our attention to the role that technological forces play in the strategic management of organizations.

Technological Forces

Technological change creates new products, processes, services, and, in some cases, entire new industries. It also can change the way society behaves and what society expects. Notebook computers, compact discs and players, direct satellite systems, and cellular telephones are technological innovations that have experienced extraordinary growth in recent years, leaving formerly well-established industries stunned, creating whole new industries, and influencing the way many people approach work and leisure. Computers and telecommunications technologies, for example, have played an essential role in creating the increasingly global marketplace.

Technology refers to human knowledge about products and services and the way they are made and delivered. Technologies typically evolve through a series of steps, with each step having its own set of implications for managers. When a new idea or technology is proven to work in the laboratory, it is called an **invention**. New inventions are made every day: Corporate research laboratories, universities, and individuals invent new products, new processes, new technologies all of the time. Only a handful of those inventions, however, are ever developed past the laboratory stage.

When an invention can be replicated reliably on a meaningful scale, it is referred to as an **innovation**. Most technological innovations take the form of new products or processes, such as fax machines, airbags, cellular phones, and minimill steel technologies. A **basic innovation**, such as the microprocessor, lightbulb, superconductors, and fiber optics, impacts much more than one product category or one industry. It reverberates through society transforming existing industries and creating new ones. With basic innovations, the process of moving from the invention stage to the innovation stage involves development of component technologies and new marketing channels, which creates opportunities for new technologies and new businesses. The development of portable, notebook-sized computers, for example, required simultaneous innovations in flat-panel displays,

Technology
Human knowledge about products and services and the ways they are made and delivered.

Invention
A new idea or technology proven to work in the laboratory.

Innovation
An invention that can be replicated reliably on a meaningful scale.

Basic Innovation
An invention that impacts more than one product category or industry.

battery size and storage capability, and production processes involving miniaturized components and circuitry.

As James Utterback pointed out in his book, *Mastering the Dynamics of Innovation*, most innovations draw from the existing technologies of the time, but, through a new configuration of some type, fulfill a new need or fulfill an existing need better.[13] For example, the first personal computers were sold as do-it-yourself kits for electronics enthusiasts and made use of existing electronics technology. It was only after Apple Computer provided a user-friendly interface and appearance, and software designers provided applications, that the personal computer began to gain legitimacy as a potential home and office machine. With the entry of IBM into the market, which further signaled the importance of the innovation, the market for personal computers exploded. Since then, innovations in semiconductor and microprocessor manufacturing have led to smaller, less expensive components, which has improved affordibility and design flexibility.

This discussion of the personal computer industry illustrates a second characteristic of technological innovation. Just like the invention process, commercial innovations tend to evolve through predictable stages, from chaotic efforts to develop new and different variations on the innovation, to emergence of a *dominant design* as customer needs become clear.[14] Emergence of a dominant design has strategic implications for firms already in the industry and those considering entry into the industry. A dominant design suggests that the industry may evolve as a commodity, with customers comparing prices and firms finding fewer ways to create differences that customers will pay for. For example, when the personal computer was emerging, many firms entered the market. They each had different target applications, different keyboard configurations, different operating systems, different microprocessor capabilities, and different overall appearances. Each manufacturer was struggling to create a computer that would appeal to a largely unknown target market. Over time, however, the personal computers began to converge toward a dominant design: operating systems with pull-down menus and user-friendly icons, a standard keyboard, standard word-processing, spreadsheet, and graphics applications, and a standard microprocessor. Although computers made by different companies are not identical, they are so similar few people have trouble moving from model to model.

A third characteristic of the innovation process is that radical innovations usually originate outside of the industry boundaries, which makes monitoring of trends outside the immediate competitive group so important. For example, it was not the existing office machine companies that developed the personal computer, although office machines were ultimately displaced by personal computers. Many new innovations in electronics, telecommunications, and specialty materials have originated with space and military projects and then been adopted by other industries for use in various commercial applications. In general, when the rate of improvements with an existing technology begins to slow down, the likelihood of a new substitute innovation increases.

Technological change is difficult, but not impossible, to predict. An understanding of the three characteristics of innovation—(1) new innovations from existing technologies, (2) emergence of a dominant design, and (3) radical innovation from outside of the industry group—can help an organization develop a plan for monitoring technological change. Organizations should monitor the technological developments in industries other than their own, and conduct brainstorming sessions about the possible consequences for their own products and markets.

To help identify trends and anticipate their timing, organizations may participate in several kinds of technological forecasting efforts. In general, organizations may monitor trends by studying research journals, government reports, and patent filings. Because the U.S. government is a major sponsor of basic research, government reports and federal technology assessments are often a rich source of information on emerging technologies. Another more formal method of technological forecasting is to solicit the opinions of experts outside of the organization. These experts may be interviewed directly or contacted as part of a formal survey, such as a Delphi study. A third method is to develop scenarios of alternative technological futures, which capture different rates of innovation and different emerging technologies. Scenarios allow an organization to conduct "what if" analyses and to develop alternative plans for responding to new innovations.

In addition to forecasting, some organizations establish strategic alliances with universities to engage in joint research projects, which allows them to keep abreast of new trends. Other organizations simply donate funds to universities for research in exchange for information about findings. The Partnership Data Net, a Washington-based information center on partnerships, lists about 3,000 partnerships between schools and businesses.[15] Akzo NV, the Dutch chemical giant, with more than 11,000 employees at 161 locations in North America alone, created a massive partnership that has paid healthy dividends:

> *A few years ago, Akzo NV launched a "crash program" in research and develop-*
> *ment in the United States, in cooperation with 12 U.S. colleges. The goals for the*
> *university program were: (1) To create options for new business, either through the*
> *upgrading of present products or exploring new technologies; and (2) To identify*
> *talented people active in the academic scientific community and introduce them to*
> *Akzo for possible future recruitment.*
>
> *Within three years, the venture yielded 40 patent applications, nine of which*
> *have been approved. The first estimate of the market size for six of these devel-*
> *opments is greater than $2 billion.[16]*

The Akzo example is a fitting conclusion for this section on analysis of the technological environment. Akzo not only stayed aware of technological changes in its broad environment, but it formed partnerships with members of that environment that resulted in the creation of new technology.

Organizations also form alliances with other firms as a way to monitor technological trends and prepare their organizations for the changes. Formation of strategic alliances between firms for purposes of technology sharing is a growing trend and is discussed in detail in subsequent chapters. With a well-thought-out plan for monitoring technological trends, an organization can better prepare itself to receive some early warning about trends that will create opportunities and threats.

Now we turn our attention to a discussion of the global political and legal forces in the broad environment of organizations.

Global Political and Legal Forces

Political forces, both at home and abroad, are among the most significant determinants of organizational success. The stakes are often high. For instance, a newly revised pact among the governments of Kazakhstan, Russia, and Oman may allow Chevron to recover a $715 million investment in the Tengiz oil field.[17] In another example, Israel recently asked the White House to limit the ability of U.S. satellite companies to survey Israel from space. However, an Israeli company that is about to enter the same business would not face similar restrictions.[18] In the United States, a Supreme court ruling allows liability lawsuits against manufacturers of medical devices even though the devices are regulated by law.[19] Also, recent court rulings have made banks liable when *their customers* pollute.[20]

Governments provide and enforce the rules by which organizations operate. Even in the United States, which is considered a "free"-market economy, no organization is allowed the privilege of total autonomy from government regulations. Governments can encourage new business formation through tax incentives and subsidies, can restructure organizations, as in the case of the AT&T breakup, and can totally close organizations that do not comply with laws, ordinances, or regulations. Furthermore, alliances among governments provide an additional level of complexity for organizations with significant foreign operations. Nonprofit organizations are as subject to government intervention and regulation as for-profit organizations.

Some organizations find themselves in a situation in which they are almost entirely dependent on government regulators for their health and survival. In many countries, tight regulatory controls are found in a wide variety of industries. In communist countries, such as China or Cuba, the government has almost complete control over the economy. In the United States, utilities are a good example of a highly regulated environment.

Although all organizations face some form of regulation, the trend is toward deregulation and privatization of industries worldwide. In Portugal, for example, the previously regulated government-owned banking industry is moving toward privatization. In Eastern Europe, many industries are struggling to survive and prosper in an emerging free-market economy. In the United States, the last twenty years have brought the deregulation of the airline, banking, long-distance telephone communication, and trucking industries. The previously highly regulated utility industry is undergoing partial deregulation, which is opening up new opportunities, but creating competitive threats as well. Regulation protected these industries from competition, but required set prices and strict operating procedures. With deregulation, existing industry competitors face turbulence and unpredictability. Also with deregulation, however, new opportunities arise for new firms to enter the market.

The amount of time and effort organizations should devote to learning about regulations, complying with them, and fostering good relationships with regulatory agencies and their representatives depends, in part, on the industry. Some laws and regulations pertain to only one industry, such as nuclear energy. On the other hand, many regulations are cross-cutting, in that they apply to organizations in general. In the United States, two of the most widely known regulatory agencies are the Occupational Safety and Health Administration (OSHA) and the Environmental Protection Agency (EPA).

Monitoring and complying with laws and regulations is a good idea from a financial perspective. Fines and penalties imposed by government units can run in the millions of dollars, especially under the new mandatory sentencing guidelines. Strategic Insight 2.2 demonstrates what can happen when an organization mishandles government regulation. Some researchers have even discovered that when announcements are made that firms are involved in illegal activities, their stock prices fall.[21]

A simplified model of some of the major groups in the United States that influence the political environment of business is found in Figure 2.1. Government influences come from (1) lawmakers, (2) regulatory agencies, (3) revenue collection agencies, and (4) the courts. Notice that each of these influences can occur at the federal, state, or local level, which results in twelve major forces instead of four. Involvement in more than one country further increases the number of relevant government forces.

STRATEGIC INSIGHT 2.2

BUSINESS

STRATEGY

Golfing Conglomerate Forgets to Check with Regulators

Buying California's most famous, most beautiful, most historic golf course—the one where Crosby kidded Hope and knocked out ashes from his pipe against the cypress trees—must have seemed the coup of coups to Minoru Isutani, owner of Cosmo World, a Japanese golfing conglomerate.

True, the price he paid in September 1990—said to be somewhere between $800 million and $1 billion—seemed high. But Isutani had a plan. He would transform Pebble Beach into a private club, with memberships (at $740,000 each) sold primarily to wealthy Japanese.

Golfers of lesser means protested. Under existing rules, anybody willing to endure a waiting list and pay a $200-per-person greens fee could play the course. But if Pebble Beach went private, the best hours would be reserved for members.

Enter the California Coastal Commission, all powerful in matters of coastal access: Did the new owners have a commission permit for this conversion? Er . . . no, they didn't. They didn't think they needed one. The commission ruled they did, and withheld it.

Source: A. Farnham, "Biggest Business Goofs of 1991," *Fortune* (January 13, 1992), p. 83. Used with permission.

Lawmakers make the laws, often in response to requests and pressures from constituents. Regulatory agencies and revenue collection agencies often develop the specifics of the regulations needed to carry out new laws and they serve an enforcement role as well. The courts handle disputes, interpret laws as needed, and levy fines and penalties. Courts may also make decisions that alter the make-up or strategies of organizations, as in the case of antitrust actions. As mentioned earlier, a federal court was involved in the AT&T restructuring that resulted in spinning off of local telephone services into smaller, independent companies, sometimes called the "Baby Bells." The court's position was that AT&T held a monopoly position in phone services in the United States that made it difficult for other long-distance companies to compete.

Although one organization may not be able to dramatically alter major political forces, it may have considerable impact within its own specific industries and operating domain. Consequently, major political and legal forces are considered a part of the broad environment, whereas government agencies and administrators are considered a part of the operating environment. Political strategies for dealing with government are described in Chapter 3.

Foreign Environments

Significant changes in the global environment have created great opportunities for organizations that are willing to take a risk and wait patiently for returns. For example, the old Soviet Union may have up to a quarter of the world's undiscovered oil, about equal to the oil remaining in the Middle East. They also possess more natural gas than any other country. Dozens of companies are rushing to help bring this oil to market; however, as in the Chevron case, instability in the region makes investment recovery difficult and risky. Furthermore, OPEC, fearing that a new force in

Figure 2.1 *Government Influences on Organizations in the United States*

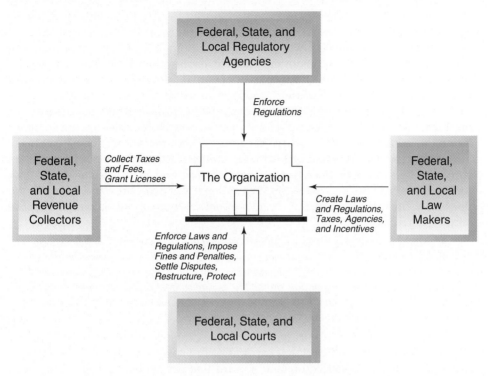

Source: Based on information contained in R. E. Freeman, *Strategic Management: A Stakeholder Approach* (Boston: Pitman, 1984).

oil will reduce its own power, is considering offering seats in its cartel to Russia, Kazakhstan, and Azerbaijan.[22] Oil is not the only risky business in Russia. Although Russia's many regions are working to attract funds from foreign investors, investments often bring unexpected problems. For example, a British steelmaker that bought Kazakhstan's largest steel plant had to negotiate for two months to get more than a dozen old KGB agents to leave their electronically sophisticated corner office in the factory.[23] Furthermore, communist ideals are still popular and some Russian officials are working to reverse business privatization.[24]

The problems associated with business ventures in Russia are similar to those found in most developing countries—an unstable government, inadequately trained workers, low levels of supporting technology, shortages of supplies, a weak transportation system, and an unstable currency. Firms also have to struggle with managing stakeholders that are typically very different—in terms of values, beliefs, ethics, and many other ways—from stakeholders found in the home country. However, firms that are "first movers" into developing countries may be able to develop stakeholder-based advantages such as long-term productive contractual and informal relationships with host-country governments and organizations that followers will not have the opportunity to develop. For example, Spanish firms took huge risks by making major investments in Latin America during the first wave of privatizations; however, they are now firmly entrenched in one of the world's fastest growing regions. According to one large Spanish bank executive with significant investments in Latin America, "It's not a new frontier for

Spanish companies because we discovered America in 1492. But it's a growth frontier. It's a financial rediscovery of the Americas."[25]

Another region with a lot of potential is Asia. The "Pacific Century" refers to a forecast that the world's growth center for the twenty-first century will shift across the Pacific Ocean to Asia. Asia is already the world's biggest consumer of steel and the second fastest growing market for automobiles. China alone has more than one billion potential consumers and television sets and beer are increasingly popular.[26] In response to the huge market potential, Motorola is doubling its stake in China. Also, Atlantic Richfield, referred to as "the lucky company" by the Chinese, just completed a $1.13 billion gas pipeline project off the southeast coast of China with very few problems. Nevertheless, many companies are not so lucky. Rampant corruption and a culture that considers counterfeiting "cool" can make business dealings difficult. Furthermore, Chinese/American relations are often strained due to China's poor human rights record and its unwillingness to conform to American policies on issues such as copyright protection and arms sales to politically unstable countries.[27] To make matters worse, anti-U.S. sentiment is surging in China:

> *According to a recent survey of youths, 90% said they feel the U.S. behaves "hegemonistically," with expansionist aims, towards China. When the romantic movie, "Bridges of Madison County," played here, film authorities were inundated with phone calls complaining about "unhealthy capitalist lifestyles" of the lead characters, who engage in adultery. Even fast-food restaurants like McDonald's have come under attack for undermining children's health.[28]*

Reforms in China are currently progressing slowly and it is hard for Westerners to forget the blood that was spilled in Tiananmen Square as prodemocracy student protesters faced off against hard-line government forces.[29] However, according to many experts, China is headed toward capitalism and it is already too late to turn back.[30] Already, money and management from Hong Kong, Taiwan, and Singapore are transforming South China.[31]

In addition to China, other Asian countries hold great potential. The newly industrialized economies (NIEs) of South Korea, Taiwan, Hong Kong, and Singapore have been experiencing growth in real gross domestic product at a level that is nearly twice that of the EC, Japan, and the United States.[32] Strategic Insight 2.3 describes the strategic role of Singapore in developing other Asian countries.

Finally, changes in Europe have made it increasingly important for U.S. companies to be involved there. The demise of some trade barriers among European countries has created a more open market of 340 million consumers.[33] Reduction in trade barriers means that companies involved in Europe can better take advantage of regional variations in wage rates and the cost of raw materials, which can lead to lower costs. Also, differentiation is easier to achieve because organizations can draw freely from the technological strengths of each nation. Organizations that have businesses in Europe already enjoy the advantages of a typically well-educated workforce, a well-developed infrastructure, a sophisticated level of technology, and high consumer demand, all factors that are associated with "first world" countries. The recent changes in Europe make the EC even more attractive for investment.

Many characteristics must be evaluated when considering a foreign country for investment. Many of them fall within the general areas of the broad environment, including the social environment, the economy, the state of technology, and the political and legal environment. Other characteristics are related to specific industries and markets. Questions concerning each of these factors are listed in Strategic Application 2.1, which is a useful tool for evaluating a potential country.

The wrong answers to any of the questions in Strategic Application 2.1 can make

STRATEGIC INSIGHT 2.3

Need a Friend in Asia? Try the Singapore Connection

Foreigners doing business in Asia have long relied on middlemen—*compradors*, as they are known in the region—to cut through red tape, hook up with the right people, get deals done, and occasionally take a small piece of the action. But these have typically been well-connected individuals. Enter the Singapore Connection— a whole nation willing to act as a comprador for Western companies expanding across Asia. In the most ambitious part of its new role, Singapore is creating what are in effect mini-Singapores. These are enclaves, generally industrial parks, that this tiny country is erecting inside its big neighbors—China, India, Indonesia, and Vietnam so far. Most of these projects are clusters of factories, roads, and power plants, but in Suzhou, China, an entire Singapore-style township is taking shape as well.

Inside those enclaves, multinational corporations can operate pretty much as they do in Singapore, a country they trust more than any other in Asia because it provides a business environment free from graft, with transparent and consistent regulations. Though only in the early stages, the enclaves have already attracted more than $2.5 billion worth of investments from nearly 200 leading companies, including Advanced Micro Devices of the United States, L'Oreal of France, and British Oxygen. The U.S.-based disk-drive maker Seagate Technology has set up a $30 million plant in Wuxi, China. The German electronics giant Siemens is putting factories into every Asian frontier that Singapore opens, to make devices ranging from hearing aids to semiconductors. "We're comfortable wherever they sell the Singaporean way of doing business," says Harmut Lueck, managing director of Siemens Component in Singapore.

Source: L. Kraar, "Need a Friend in Asia? Try the Singapore Connection," *Fortune* (March 4, 1996), p. 174.

a country less attractive. Some examples follow that demonstrate this point: (1) An unstable government can greatly increase the risk of a total loss of investment, (2) an inefficient transportation system can increase total product costs to prohibitively high levels, (3) inadequate school systems can result in poorly skilled workers, which may not have the ability to manufacture technical products, (4) a slowly growing GNP could mean that consumer demand will be sluggish, (5) high foreign tax rates can virtually eliminate profits, and (6) if the local currency is not translatable into U.S. dollars the organization will have a tough time removing profits from the country.

Answers to the questions should also be judged based on the type of activity the organization is considering. For example, a high per-capita income is favorable if the organization is only going to sell U.S. products in the foreign market (export). On the other hand, low per capita income could mean that wages are very low, which is positive if the organization is considering foreign manufacturing or assembly.

COLLECTING INFORMATION ON THE BROAD ENVIRONMENT

Information about broad environmental forces and trends is often available through public and private, published and unpublished sources, but organizations must take deliberate steps to find and make use of the information. For example,

STRATEGIC APPLICATION 2.1

EXAMPLES OF QUESTIONS TO ASK ABOUT A POTENTIAL FOREIGN MARKET

Social Forces

What are the current hot topics of debate? How well organized are special interest groups with regard to environmental, labor, and management issues? Are the current policies or behaviors of the organization likely to be offensive in the new host country? What is the attitude of potential consumers toward foreign products/services? Will there be significant cultural barriers to overcome? How difficult is the language? How old is the population? What other differences could cause difficulty for the organization?

The Economy

What is the inflation rate? How large is the gross national product (GNP)? How fast is it growing? What is income per capita? How much impact does the global economy have on the domestic economy? How high is the unemployment rate? What actions does the government take to fuel economic growth? What is the trade balance with the United States? Can the currency be exchanged for the home currency? How high are interest rates? Is the financial sector well organized? How expensive are the factors of production?

Political and Legal Environment

What is the form of government? How much influence does the government have over business? Is the government stable? What is the attitude of the government toward private enterprise and U.S. firms? What is the attitude of the home government toward the foreign government? How high are tax rates compared with the home country? How are taxes assessed and collected? How high are import and export taxes? What is the nature of the court system? Is legal protection available through incorporation or a similar form?

Technology

Is the country technologically advanced? Do schools and universities supply qualified workers? Are the required skills available in sufficient quantity? Are suitable information systems available? Is the infrastructure sound (i.e., roads, transportation systems)? Is an appropriate site available?

Industry Specific

How large is the industry? How fast is it growing? Is it segmentable? How many competitors are there? How strong are they? What is the relative position of industry participants in relation to suppliers and customers? Are substitute products available? What is the primary basis for competition? Is there a possibility of reaching the market through a joint venture?

---

information about U.S. demographic patterns, investment patterns, economic trends, technological advances, and even societal views are widely available through published sources and government reports in libraries. For local economic and sociocultural trends, census data and Chamber of Commerce reports are just a few of the sources available.

Most well-managed firms collect broad environmental information regularly and understand its value in decision making. Perception, Inc., the world's largest producer of kayaks, has identified a sociocultural trend toward "extreme sports" that is helping its kayak business. Perception can track the interests of these sports enthusiasts through sports and recreation publications and can associate the trend with a particular demographic profile. The number of individuals who fit that demographic profile provides an estimate of a target market for some of Perception's products, and can help them in identifying new product directions and marketing programs.

STRATEGIC APPLICATION 2.2

ASSESSMENT OF THE BROAD ENVIRONMENT

The following chart is a useful tool for organizations that want to track trends in their broad environments. On the left, a manager (or a student) should describe the nature of each trend. The column in the middle can be used to identify each trend as an opportunity, threat, or neutral implication to the organization. The third column should be created to describe actions the firm should take to respond to the opportunities and threats.

Force	Implication for Organization			Organizational Response
	Opportunity	*Threat*	*Neutral*	
Sociocultural Forces				
Attitude changes				
Demographic shifts				
Sensitive issues				
New fads				
Public opinions				
Emerging public opinion leaders				
Global Economic Forces				
Economic growth				
Interest rates				
Inflation				
Foreign exchange rates				
Trade deficits				
Other (depending on business)				
Technological Forces				
New production processes				
New products/product ideas				
Current process research efforts				
Current product research efforts				
Scientific discoveries that may have an impact				
Political/Legal Forces				
New laws				
New regulations				
Current administrative policies				
Government stability				
Wars				
International pacts and treaties				

Information about technological and economic trends is also widely available. Because a large portion of the technology investment in the United States is sponsored by the government, the findings of those research efforts are published through various government reports, which are available to the public. Government reports also detail economic activity, investments, and trends within different regions and states, providing a rich source of information for business organizations.

Collecting broad environmental information in an international setting is a different matter, however. Although industrialized nations will have similar sources of trend data, developing nations will not. Consequently, organizations often rely on a local firm to provide the kinds of broad environmental insights necessary for good strategic decision making.

We have concluded our discussion of the broad environment and the importance of collecting information on broad environmental trends. As a review, Strategic Application 2.2 contains a chart that can help organizational managers track trends in their broad environments. It is also helpful to students in identifying opportunities and threats as a basis for developing alternatives during case analysis.

Summary

The most important elements in the broad environment, as it relates to a business organization and its operating environment, are sociocultural forces, global economic forces, technological forces, and global political and legal forces. The broad environment can have a tremendous impact on a firm and its operating environment; however, individual firms typically have only a marginal impact on this environment.

Analysis of society is important because most of the other stakeholder groups are also members of society, which means that some of their values and beliefs are derived from broader societal influences. It is also important because awareness of and compliance with the attitudes of society can help an organization avoid problems associated with being a "bad corporate citizen," because correct assessment of social trends can help businesses avoid restrictive legislation and because changes in society can provide opportunities for organizations.

Economic forces such as economic growth, interest rates, the availability of credit, inflation rates, foreign exchange rates, and foreign trade balances are among the most critical economic factors. Economic forces play a key role in determining demand patterns and cost characteristics within industries.

Technological forces in the broad environment have the power to create and destroy entire industries. In general, (1) innovations usually arise from existing technologies, (2) most products and processes evolve toward a dominant design, and (3) radical innovations tend to come from outside the established group of competitors. An understanding of these characteristics can help a manager develop a system for monitoring technology trends.

Also, organizations should track global political and legal forces, particularly as they relate to increases and decreases in degree of regulation. Government influences come from (1) lawmakers, (2) regulatory agencies, (3) revenue collection agencies, and (4) the courts. Each of these influences can occur at the federal, state, or local level, which results in twelve major forces instead of four. Involvement in more than one country further increases the number of relevant government forces. Although one organization may not be able to alter major political forces dramatically, it may have considerable impact within its own specific industries and operating domain. Consequently, major political and legal forces are considered a part of the broad environment, whereas government agencies and administrators are considered a part of the operating environment.

Discussion Questions

1.   Why is analysis of the broad environment important for effective strategic management?
2.   What are the major components of the broad environment? Give an example of a trend in each area that could affect the welfare of a business organization.

3. Why should social forces be monitored? What are some of the current social forces in the United States?

4. What are some of the most important factors to track in the global economy? Why are these factors important to organizations?

5. Describe the roles of lawmakers, regulatory agencies, revenue collection agencies, and the courts as they relate to doing business in the United States. How are these roles likely to be different in other countries?

6. What is the difference between an invention and an innovation? Which should organizations attempt to monitor?

7. Explain the three characteristics of technological innovation and how an understanding of those characteristics can be used to develop a technological forecasting process.

8. What are some of the things an organization should know about a country before making a significant business investment in it?

References

1. *Environmental Report*, General Motors, 1995.
2. "Dow Chemical Will Spend $1 Bil on Environment Over 10 Years," *Investor's Business Daily* (April 29, 1996), p. B14.
3. J. B. McGuire, A. Sundgren, and T. Schneeweis, "Corporate Social Responsibility and Firm Financial Responsibility," *Academy of Management Journal* 31 (1988), pp. 854–872.
4. F. Rice, "Denny's Changes Its Spots," *Fortune* (May 13, 1996), pp. 133–134.
5. D. J. Gaiter, "How Shoney's, Belted by a Lawsuit, Found the Path to Diversity," *Wall Street Journal* (April 16, 1996), pp. A1, A6.
6. A. B. Fisher, "Corporate Reputations," *Fortune* (March 6, 1996), p. 90.
7. M. Pastin, *The Hard Problems of Management: Gaining the Ethics Edge* (San Francisco: Jossey-Bass, 1986), p. 123.
8. D. R. Dalton, M. B. Metzger, and J. W. Hill, "The 'New' U.S. Sentencing Commission Guidelines: A Wake-up Call for Corporate America," *Academy of Management Executive* (February 1994), pp. 7–16.
9. M. R. Moskowitz, "Company Performance Roundup," *Business and Society Review* (Spring 1985), p. 74.
10. G. F. Seib and M. K. Frisby, "As Opponents Gear Up, Clinton Prepares Pitch for His Economic Plan," *Wall Street Journal* (February 5, 1993), pp. A1, A4.
11. T. Smart, "Why Ignore 95% of the World's Market?" *Business Week Special Issue: Reinventing America* (1992), p. 64.
12. R. A. Melcher, "Europe, Too, Is Edgy About Imports—From America," *Business Week* (January 27, 1992), pp. 48–49.
13. James M. Utterback, *Mastering the Dynamics of Innovation* (Boston: The Harvard Business School Press, 1994).
14. Ibid.
15. S. A. Waddock, "Building Successful Social Partnerships," *Sloan Management Review* (Summer 1988), p. 18.
16. J. Vleggaar, "The Dutch Go Back to School for R&D," *Journal of Business Strategy* (March/April 1991), p. 8.
17. A. Reifenberg, "Caspian Pact May Bolster Chevron Effort," *Wall Street Journal* (March 11, 1996), pp. A3, A6.
18. J. J. Fialka, "Israel Asks White House to Place Curbs on 3 U.S. Satellite-Surveillance Firms," *Wall Street Journal* (June 17, 1996), p. A2.
19. "Business and Finance," *Wall Street Journal* (June 27, 1996), p. A1.
20. G. Hector, "A New Reason You Can't Get a Loan," *Fortune* (September 21, 1992), pp. 107–112.
21. W. N. Davidson III and D. L. Worrell, "The Impact of Announcement of Corporate Illegalities on Shareholder Returns," *Academy of Management Journal* 31 (1988), pp. 195–200.
22. P. Nulty, "The Black Gold Rush in Russia," *Fortune* (June 15, 1992), p. 126.
23. K. Pope, "A Steelmaker Built Up by Buying Cheap Mills Finally Meets Its Match," *Wall Street Journal* (May 2, 1996), pp. A1, A10.
24. N. Banerjee, "Russia's Many Regions Work to Attract Funds from Foreign Investors," *Wall Street Journal* (April 30, 1996), pp. A1, A13; S. Liesman, "Some Russian Officials Are Moving to Reverse Business Privatization," *Wall Street Journal* (March 20, 1996), pp. A1, A6; C. Rosett, "Communists Mount Comeback in Russia, and Mean Business," *Wall Street Journal* (March 27, 1996), pp. A1, A4.
25. T. Kamm and J. Friedland, "Spanish Firms Discover Latin America Business As New World of Profit," *Wall Street Journal* (May 23, 1996), pp. A1, A9.
26. L. Kraar, "Asia 2000," *Fortune* (October 5, 1992), p. 111.
27. J. Barnathan, "A Pirate Under Every Rock," *Business Week* (June 17, 1996), pp. 50–51; L. Kraar, "The Risks Are Rising in China," *Fortune* (March 6, 1995), pp. 179–180; K. Schoenberger, "Motorola Bets Big on China," *Fortune* (May 27, 1996), pp. 116–124; K. Schoenberger, "Arco's Surprisingly Good Fortune in China," *Fortune* (February 5, 1996), p. 32.
28. K. Chen, "Anti-U.S. Sentiment Surges in China, Putting a Further Strain on Relations," *The Wall Street Journal* (March 15, 1996), p. A11.
29. P. Steidlmeier, "China's Most-Favored-Nation Status: Attempts to Reform China and the Prospects for U.S. Business," *Business and the Contemporary World* 4 (1992), pp. 68–80.
30. B. Schlender, "China Really Is on the Move," *Fortune* (October 5, 1992), pp. 114–122.
31. L. Kraar, "A New China without Borders," *Fortune* (October 5, 1992), pp. 124–128.
32. J. Labate, "The World Economy in Charts," *Fortune* (July 27, 1992), p. 62.
33. S. Tully, "Europe 1992: More Unity Than You Think," *Fortune* (August 24, 1992), pp. 136–142.

3

The Operating Environment and External Stakeholders

AT&T Forms Alliance to Enter Credit Card Business

Bob Ranalli, president of Consumer Communications Services at AT&T, saw an opportunity to extend the traditional telephone calling card to the credit card business as a way to attract new customers and retain the old customer base. He hired Paul Kahn, a credit company executive from Wells Fargo and First Chicago, to lead this new venture. After reviewing AT&T's own ability to enter the credit card business, Kahn found the basic operating skills lacking. An alliance was found preferable to an acquisition, since credit card operations were not the core business of AT&T and earlier experiences at acquisitions were not always successful. AT&T wanted to provide credit card services that uniquely combined long-distance telephone calls that originate away from home with the purchasing capabilities of Visa and MasterCard.

An alliance was formed with Total Systems Services, Inc. (TSYS).

Under the terms of the alliance, AT&T markets and services the innovative AT&T Universal card, while TSYS issues the credit cards, handles card transactions billing, and maintains customer records. The alliance has complemented the traditional strengths of AT&T's quality service and TSYS's quality product. Within three years, this world-class alliance resulted in the issuance of more than 19 million cards to 12.5 million account holders.[1]

Successful organizations like AT&T stay in touch with their external stakeholders and the broader external environment to predict trends, anticipate concerns, and generate ideas. These activities can help managers discover external opportunities and threats, which are then considered by managers as they develop an organization's strategic direction and formulate and implement organizational strategies. As the AT&T case clearly demonstrates, formation of partnerships with external stakeholders is one way to take advantage of opportunities.

On the down side, many business declines can be traced to not listening to stakeholders. For example, for many years, Sears ignored the changing needs of their predominantly middle class customers. Many middle class consumers were forced to tighten up their finances due to a significant decline in their spending power. They switched their loyalties to lower priced stores like K-mart and Wal-Mart.[2] Of course, K-mart and Wal-Mart, as competitors, are also stakeholders of Sears. Therefore, Sears could have adjusted its strategy on the basis of information received from either of two stakeholders, customers or competitors. Instead, Sears, after more than a decade of restructuring, is just now beginning to recover its footing as a major retail chain.

Analysis and management of external stakeholders are the central topics in this chapter. An organization can have a much more significant influence on events that transpire in its operating environment than it can in its broad environment. In fact, this is one way to distinguish between the two environments. Figure 3.1 displays the relationship of an organization to its broad and operating environments. Remember that government agencies and administrators are included in the model because, although an organization can only have a minimal influence on government policy in general, within a particular business area organizations can have significant influence, especially through forming political alliances and lobbying efforts.

In Chapter 1, stakeholder analysis activities were described as identifying and prioritizing key stakeholders, assessing their needs, collecting ideas and information from them, and integrating this knowledge into strategic management processes. On the other hand, stakeholder management was defined as communicating with stakeholders, negotiating and contracting with them, managing relationships with them, and motivating them to behave in ways that are beneficial to the organization and its other stakeholders. The distinction between stakeholder analysis and stakeholder management is blurred—the processes occur simultaneously. The important point is not whether a particular activity is primarily analysis or management, but that both activities occur on an ongoing basis.

ASSESSMENT OF THE OPERATING ENVIRONMENT

The operating environment consists of stakeholders with whom organizations interact on a fairly regular basis. These stakeholders include customers, suppliers, competitors, government agencies and administrators, local communities, activist groups, unions, and financial intermediaries. Not all stakeholders are equally important to firm success. Furthermore, the importance of a particular stakeholder can change over time. Balancing the interests of a diverse set of stakeholders is one of the key difficulties of stakeholder management. The major challenge associated with satisfying stakeholders is to please one stakeholder without jeopardizing the interests of other high-priority stakeholders in the process. For example, a firm facing a cost increase from suppliers must choose whether to pass on the cost increase to customers in the form of a price increase, or absorb the cost increase,

Figure 3.1 *Primary Influence Processes*

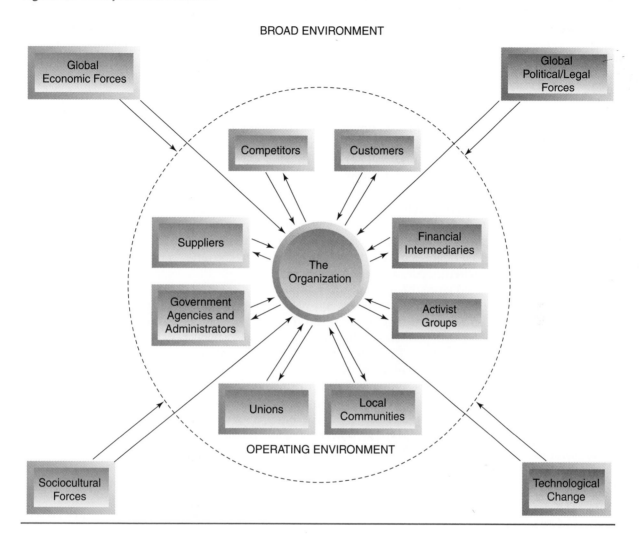

which may result in lower profits and negative consequences for stockholders, employees, and managers. The potential for conflicting stakeholder expectations is one of the reasons why it is so important to study and understand them. Consequently, for organizational planning purposes, it is useful to classify or prioritize key stakeholders so that their interests receive the proper type and degree of attention.[3] Also, for planning purposes, it is useful to obtain information from stakeholders that can be used in making strategic decisions, such as demand for products, threats from competitors, and availability of supplies.

External Stakeholders and Environmental Uncertainty

One of the key factors that determines the priority of a particular stakeholder is its influence on the **environmental uncertainty** facing the firm.[4] For example, organizations are uncertain of the level of future demand, the price elasticity of demand, the strategic moves of competitors, suppliers, activists, unions, and oth-

Environmental Uncertainty
Organizations' uncertainties regarding factors such as economic cycles, social trends, their ability to secure adequate resources, future government regulations, and the actions of external stakeholders—all adding to the difficulty of managerial decision making.

er key stakeholders, the nature of future government regulations, and the ability to secure adequate resources, whether physical, financial, or human.

One way to understand the role of environmental uncertainty is to imagine a situation in which managers knew everything that would happen with regard to customers, suppliers, unions, competitors, regulators, financial intermediaries, and every other relevant external force for the next year. In such a hypothetical situation, management of the firm would be a straightforward task of generating maximum revenues at minimum costs so that profits are maximized. Management is difficult because our hypothetical world does not exist. Managers have to make decisions without knowing how customers, suppliers, and competitors will react. Customers are particularly important because their actions have so much impact on how the firm will perform. In other words, they have a large influence on the uncertainty that the firm is facing.

Although environmental uncertainty often originates in the broad environment (e.g., economic cycles, social trends), organizations feel most of its influence through external stakeholders. For example, the Arab oil embargo was a major shock in the broad environment of U.S. automobile companies. However, they felt its influences indirectly through changes in customer expectations about the size, fuel-efficiency, and styling of new cars.

Figure 3.2 illustrates the influence of the broad environment and external stakeholders on the level and nature of uncertainty facing an organization. The arrows connecting external stakeholders to the organization are a representation of interdependence, which is a function of the stake each stakeholder has in the organization. The nature of these interdependencies can change over time. For example, a bank increases its financial stake (i.e., becomes economically dependent) and its contractual power increases when it loans a company a large sum of money. Also, a supplier, customer, or competitor increases in importance when it buys stock in a company (i.e., becomes an owner). In the latter case, the purchaser now has formal voting power and could possibly increase its stake or even attempt a takeover.

Political power, which was discussed in Chapter 1, also influences environmental uncertainty. Stakeholders with political power have the ability to influence events and outcomes that have an impact on the organization, whether or not they have a financial stake in the organization. On the other hand, if they have no economic stake of any type, but are simply interested in its activities, they are said to possess a social stake in the organization. Activists are most often thought of as having political power; however, political power is available to all stakeholders under certain circumstances. For instance, an angry customer, competitor, or supplier can release information to the media that results in altered behavior from other stakeholders. In one example, some of Wal-Mart's angry competitors have succeeded in convincing local communities and governments in several locations in the Northeastern United States that Wal-Mart harms the community more than it helps by causing small businesses to suffer. The result has been adverse legislation, causing Wal-Mart to lose several new locations for its stores.[5] In another example of stakeholder action, Disney was thwarted in its efforts to build a theme park in northern Virginia because of arguments that the park would trivialize American history.

Economic power is also important to understanding the nature and level of environmental uncertainty. Michael Porter, an economist at Harvard University, assimilated years of economic research into a simple model that helps determine

Figure 3.2 *Sources of Environmental Uncertainty Stemming from External Stakeholders and the Broad Environment*

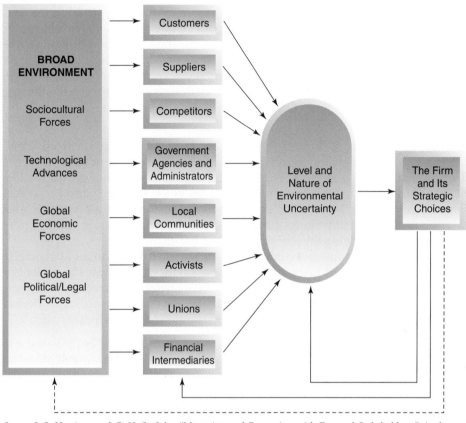

Source: J. S. Harrison and C. H. St. John "Managing and Partnering with External Stakeholders," *Academy of Management Executive* (May 1996), p. 50. Used with permission.

Note: The dashed line means that organizational influence on the broad environment is minimal.

the bargaining power of groups that have an economic stake in an organization, especially suppliers and customers.[6] This model is presented in the next section.

Competitive Forces

Michael Porter, a strategy professor at Harvard University, integrated the theory of industrial organization economics into a "user-friendly" model of the forces that drive industry competition. **Industries** are often difficult to define, but in general they refer to a group of organizations that compete directly with each other to win orders or sales in the marketplace. Porter's model includes suppliers, customers, and industry competitors, three important stakeholder groups that are a part of the operating environment. Competitors are further divided into three types: existing competitors, potential competitors, and indirect competitors. The influence of potential competitors on industry competition is determined by the strength of entry barriers, in other words, the forces that discourage new firms from entering the industry. Indirect competitors sell products that can be substi-

Industries
Groups of organizations who compete directly with each other for market share.

tuted for existing products, such as contact lenses as a substitute for glasses. According to Porter, the five forces largely determine the type and level of competition in an industry and, ultimately, the industry's profit potential.[7] These forces are illustrated in Figure 3.3.

An entire industry (as opposed to a single organization) is placed in the center of the model. One of the most common errors made by new students of strategic management occurs when they place an organization in the middle of the model instead of an industry group. When this happens, substitutes are treated as competing products, which is inconsistent with Porter's ideas concerning the power of substitutes in influencing competition in an industry. We now discuss the five forces of competition in more detail.

Customers. Many business executives and researchers in strategic management have concluded that customers are the most important external stakeholder.[8] Customers provide demand for products and/or services, without which an organization would cease to exist. For instance, the Holland-based global retailer Koninklijke Ahold nv (i.e., Bi-Lo, GFS, and FNS in the United States) has determined that to remain successful, "A large body of customers must regard Ahold as committed, competitive, responsive to their ever-changing needs, and progressive on issues concerning the environment and health."[9]

Although all customers are important, some are more important than others. For instance, when retail giant Home Depot announced that it would no longer buy carpet from Shaw Industries (because Shaw, a carpet manufacturer, was moving into retail), Shaw's stock dropped by 11% in one day.[10] According to Porter, customers tend to exhibit a powerful force on competition in an industry if:

1. *The number of customers that buy the products or services provided by the industry is small.* This creates a situation in which an industry competitor cannot afford to lose a customer. If they do lose a customer, they may have to cut back production substantially or even shut down.
2. *They make high-volume purchases. High-volume purchasers can often dictate contract terms, force price concessions, or even tell the companies they buy from what to produce.* For example, Toys 'R' Us has substantial influence over the toys produced by toy manufacturers. If Toys 'R' Us decides not to stock a toy, there is a high likelihood that the manufacturer will cease production of it. In fact, the FTC recently charged Toys 'R' Us with unfair trade practices based on antitrust grounds for influencing toy makers to shun discount stores.[11]
3. *The purchases they make from the industry represent a large percentage of their total costs.* Here customers will expend considerable effort to shop for the best price. For example, automobile manufacturers drive a *very* hard bargain when negotiating steel prices because so much of the cost of a car or truck is tied up in the steel from which it is made.
4. *The sellers' products are undifferentiated (also known as standard or generic) and plentiful.* This means that customers are sure they can find alternative suppliers. It also means that switching costs are low. For instance, food processing companies can purchase raw materials such as salt, yeast, and sugar from a multitude of sellers, which gives them great power in negotiating favorable prices and contract terms.
5. *They earn low profits.* If customers earn low profits, they are under constant pressure to keep the costs of their purchases down. For example, grocery store retailing and the textile industry are traditionally low profit industries. Consequently, companies selling to those industries are under constant pressure to offer attractive pricing to avoid hurting their own customers.

Figure 3.3 *Porter's Five-Forces Model of Industry Competition*

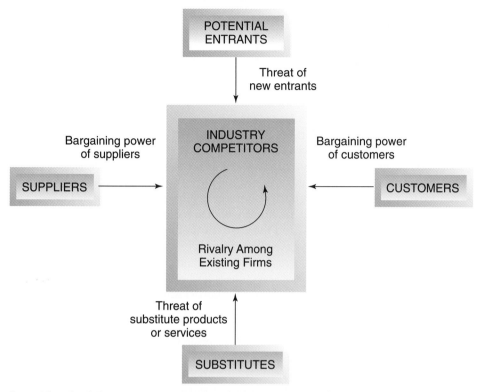

Source: Adapted with the permission of The Free Press, a Division of Simon & Schuster, Inc. from *Competitive Strategy: Techniques for Analyzing Industries and Competitors* by Michael E. Porter. Copyright © 1980 by The Free Press, p. 4.

6. *They can easily integrate backward and become their own suppliers.* Both Sears and General Motors have been known to buy supplier capability when they are unhappy with pricing.

7. *Sellers' products or services do not have much influence on the quality of their customer's products or services.* If quality is not greatly affected, customers will be primarily interested in obtaining the lowest possible price. For example, many of the components that are assembled into products have to be there, but do not affect quality in the eyes of the ultimate consumers. Fire wall insulation in automobiles is one example.

8. *Information on sellers' costs and demand is readily available to buyers.* For instance, *Consumer Reports* publishes information concerning how much dealers are paying for various makes and models of automobiles and the costs associated with stocking, financing, and adding extras. Consequently, an astute customer can negotiate away almost all of the profit when purchasing an automobile.

In combination, these forces determine the bargaining power of customers, that is, the degree to which customers exercise active influence over pricing and the direction of product development efforts. Powerful customers must be given high priority in strategic management activities.

Suppliers. Powerful suppliers can raise their prices and therefore reduce profitability levels in the buying industry. They can also exert influence and increase environmental uncertainty by *threatening* to raise prices, reducing the quality of goods or services provided, or not delivering supplies when needed. In general, supplier power is greater if:

1. *There are only a few suppliers of the raw material, product, or service.* This limits the ability of buying organizations to negotiate better prices, delivery arrangements, or quality. Makers of patented products frequently exercise great power.

2. *There are few or no substitutes for the product or service that is supplied.* If there are no substitutes, the buying industry must buy from suppliers and is, in essence, forced to pay whatever price is asked.

3. *Suppliers do not sell a large percentage of their products or services to the buying industry.* Since the buying industry is not an important customer, suppliers can reduce shipments during capacity shortages, ship partial orders or late orders, or refuse to accept orders at all, all of which can create turbulence for the buying industry, reduce profits, and increase competition.

4. *The buying industry must have the product or service that suppliers provide to manufacture its own products or services.* For example, companies that manufacture diet soft drinks must have artificial sweeteners and microcomputer manufacturers need microprocessing chips. In these situations, suppliers can take advantage of buyers, in essence playing them off one another to gain attractive contract terms.

5. *Suppliers have differentiated their products or made it costly to switch suppliers.* For example, American Hospital Supply installs computer systems in hospitals to make ordering of supplies easy for its customers. However, if a hospital chooses to purchase from a different supplier, it must remove American Hospital's system, purchase a new system, and retrain employees to use it.

6. *Suppliers can easily integrate forward and thus compete directly with their former buyers.* For example, a supplier of electronic equipment to retail chains that is dissatisfied with prices or contract terms can open its own retail outlets to handle sales of its products.

These forces combine to determine the strength of suppliers and the degree to which they can exert influence over the profits earned by the firms in the industry. The notebook computer industry is one that is particularly susceptible to the power of suppliers. Most of the industry competitors purchase microprocessors, batteries, operating system software, and flat-panel displays from suppliers. Consequently, the manufacturing costs, performance characteristics, and innovativeness of the notebook computer are largely in the hands of suppliers.

Existing Competitors. In most industries, competitive moves by one firm affect other firms in the industry, which may incite retaliation or countermoves. In other words, competing firms have an economic stake in each other. Examples of competitive moves and countermoves include advertising programs, sales force expansion, new product introductions, capacity expansion, and long-term contracts with customers. In many industries, competition is so intense that profitability suffers, as has been the case in the airline, computer, and fast food industries.

Some of the major forces that lead to high levels of competition include slow industry growth, high fixed costs, lack of product differentiation (which means that products are standard or "generic"), a large number of competitors, and high exit barriers (i.e., factors that make it expensive to discontinue operations in an industry.) Slow industry growth leads to high levels of competition since the only way to grow is through taking sales or market share from competitors. High fixed costs mean that firms are under pressure to increase sales to cover their costs and earn profits. Lack of product differentiation puts a lot of pressure on prices and often leads to price cutting strategies that appeal to customers, but that reduce the profitability of industry participants. Large numbers of competitors can lead to high levels of competition because the total market must be divided in more ways. Finally, when exit barriers are high, firms may lose all or most of their investments in the industry when they withdraw from it. Therefore, they are more likely to remain in the industry even if profits are low or nonexistent.

Industry rivals apply a variety of competitive tactics in order to win market share, increase revenues, and increase profits at the expense of rivals. Competitive tactics include advertising, new product launches, cost reduction efforts, new distribution methods, and quality improvements. Typically a particular industry can be characterized by the dominance of one or more of these tools. For example, the soft drinks industry is dominated by high levels of advertising as a competitive weapon. In addition, the presence of foreign competition in the automobile industry has placed an increasing emphasis on product differentiation through high levels of quality. Other common competitive tactics include providing high levels of customer service and achieving economies of scale through manufacturing a high volume of products in a large plant (which can lead to lower costs, thus allowing customers to enjoy lower prices).

In recent years, Richard D'Aveni has identified some industries that experience **hypercompetition**.[12] According to D'Aveni, hypercompetition is a condition of rapidly escalating competition based on price, quality, first-mover actions, defensive moves to protect markets, formation of strategic alliances, and reliance on wealthy parent companies. Short product life cycles, international competitors, global market opportunities, and deep pockets are causing some industries to stay in turmoil. Firms take great risks as they jockey for position, but the results are not sustainable because their competitors match them move for move. Cutthroat competitive practices are forcing profits to lower and lower levels. The airlines, with their expensive advertising and promotion programs, ruthless price cutting, and expensive acquisition of failing competitors, are just one example of a hypercompetitive industry.

Even in more typical industries, firms should pay critical attention to the products, services, and resource conversion processes of their competitors to avoid being left behind. One technique for keeping up with competitors that has gained wide acceptance is competitive benchmarking. **Competitive benchmarking** is a tool for assessing the best practices of direct competitors and firms in similar industries, then using the resulting "stretch" objectives as design criteria for attempting to change organizational performance.[13] For example, Federal Express is often cited as a model for customer satisfaction, Motorola in flexible manufacturing and quality, Procter & Gamble in marketing, 3M in new product development, and Disney in worker training.[14] Xerox pioneered competitive benchmarking in the United States after discovering that competitors were selling products at prices that were equal to Xerox's costs of producing them. They responded by establishing benchmarks as a fundamental part of their business planning.[15]

One way to keep track of the strategies of competing firms is with a strategic group map such as the one shown in Figure 3.4. A **strategic group map** categorizes existing industry competitors into groups that follow similar strategies. To construct a strategic group map, first identify strategic dimensions that are important

Hypercompetition
A condition of rapidly escalating competition based on price, quality, first-mover actions, defensive moves to protect markets, formation of strategic alliances, and reliance on wealthy parent companies.

Competitive Benchmarking
A tool in which management uses the best practices of competitors in setting objectives to encourage improvement in organizational performance.

Strategic Group Map
Tracking of strategies of competing firms by plotting two or more important strategic dimensions of the industry.

Figure 3.4 *Strategic Group Map of Department Store and Specialty Retailing*

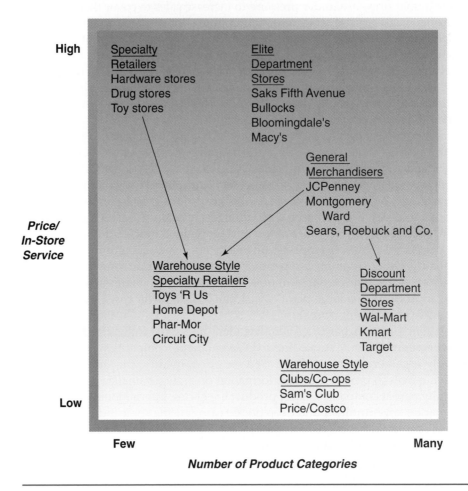

in the industry, such as breadth of product line, quality level, or national versus regional distribution. The axes of a strategic group map should describe strategy and not performance. Therefore, variables such as pricing strategy, customer service approach, level of advertising and product mix are appropriate, whereas return on assets and earnings per share are not. Furthermore, to reveal more about the industry, the dimensions should not be highly correlated with one another. Once the variables are selected, a grid may be constructed by plotting industry rivals on the relevant dimensions.

Organizations that end up in the same general location on a map are called strategic groups. Consequently, they have similar strategies based on the dimensions found in the map. Companies in one strategic group experience the external forces differently from companies in other strategic groups. For instance, in the retail industry, the recession of the early 1990s hurt traditional department stores but actually helped discounters.

Strategic group maps can help an organization understand the strategies of competitors. For example, competitors within the same strategic group, such as Marriott and Hilton, are in direct competition for customers, whereas competitors in different strategic groups, such as Days Inn and Hilton, often do not compete intensely. Strategic group maps may also highlight an area in the industry in which no firms are presently competing (an opportunity). For example, ValuJet and other short-haul, no-frill airlines occupy a competitive arena that was completely empty before airline deregulation. Another helpful use is in tracking the evolution of an industry over time. In the last twenty years, general merchandisers such as Sears, JCPenney, and Montgomery Ward have come under siege from discounters. Some of the discounters have chosen to follow the lead of the old "dime store" chains by offering a full line of discount priced products. Others, like Toys 'R Us, Home Depot, and Phar-Mor, have taken one product category and offered extreme inventory depth and discount pricing in a warehouse-like environment. Consequently, traditional department stores are seeing entire segments of their industry closed out by these "category killers" that are pursuing their own unique strategies. For example, JCPenney and other regional department stores that once carried large selections of toys no longer do. Montgomery Ward and Sears, who were once clearly general merchandisers, have responded by moving in the direction of the discounters. However, recent strategic shifts indicate that Sears may have dropped its discounting strategy. It is currently difficult to predict where the company will land.

On the other hand, one of the weaknesses associated with strategic group maps is that organizations can belong to several different strategic groups, depending on the dimensions used to form the groups. Since the choice of dimensions is somewhat subjective and dependent entirely on the industry under study, strategic group maps do not provide answers, they just help raise relevant questions about the current state and direction of competitive rivalry.

Potential Competitors and Entry Barriers. Several forces determine how easy it is to enter the industry and, therefore, how many new entrants can be expected. New entrants increase competition in an industry, which may drive down prices and profits. They may add capacity, introduce new products or processes, and bring a fresh perspective and new ideas—all of which can work to drive down prices, increase costs, or both. Forces that keep them out, providing a level of protection for existing competitors, are called **entry barriers**.

Examples of entry barriers that are found in many industries include the following:

1. *Economies of scale.* Economies of scale occur when it is more efficient to produce a product in a larger facility at higher volume. For example, the big oil companies enjoy substantial cost savings through economies of scale in petroleum refinement. These economies make it hard for a small firm to compete. A similar principle applies to service organizations such as banks, who set up centralized loan processing and credit card departments that process large amounts of transactions somewhat more efficiently than small-volume local banks, or large hospitals that can support and utilize expensive laboratory and x-ray equipment more efficiently than a small hospital. If a new entrant will be at a substantial cost disadvantage because of size, few firms will enter.

2. *Capital requirements.* Also known as start-up costs, high capital requirements can prevent a small competitor from entering an industry. High capital requirements are sometimes associated with economies of scale, since new entrants need to invest in a large facility to be cost competitive. However, they also result from research and development costs, start-up losses, or expenses associated with building inventories or extending credit to customers.

Entry Barriers
Forces such as economies of scale, capital requirements, product differentiation, governmental policy or regulation, access to distribution channels, and other factors that keep potential competitors out of the market.

3. *Product differentiation.* In some industries, established firms enjoy a loyal customer base, which comes from many years of past advertising, customer service, product differences, word of mouth, or simply being one of the first competitors in the industry. These factors make it very hard for a new entrant to compete. Consider, for example, how hard it would be to enter the automobile industry and compete with well-established advertising giants such as GM, Ford, and Toyota.

4. *Switching costs.* Switching costs were mentioned earlier in our discussions of supplier and buyer power, but they can also serve as an entry barrier protecting competing firms. For example, for many years IBM mainframe computer products were intentionally designed so that they would only be compatible with other IBM products. To make sales, a new entrant would have to convince an IBM user to drop the entire IBM system. IBM combined high switching costs with product differentiation based on outstanding service to gain the highest market share in mainframe computers.

5. *Access to distribution channels.* In industries where supply networks are strong and competition is intense, access to distribution channels may effectively thwart new entry. Significant distribution channel barriers exist in processed foods. Large companies such as Procter & Gamble can introduce new products into their markets with relative ease, due to their existing distribution networks. However, a new competitor would find it almost impossible to introduce a product on a large scale. Snapple, for example, was able to enter grocery retailing only after creating a strong name brand in delis and convenience outlets, which created a form of pull-through demand.

6. *Other cost advantages.* Firms may have a variety of cost advantages that have nothing to do with size. These advantages can include patents, favorable locations, proprietary product technology, government subsidies, or access to scarce raw materials. Since these types of advantages are difficult or impossible to duplicate in the short term, they often form the base for a sustainable competitive advantage that will discourage new entrants. For example, the formula for the automotive additive Slick 50 was a carefully guarded secret. Only those who needed to know had the combination to a fireproof vault with eight-inch-thick walls in which the sole printed copy of the formula was housed.[16] Unfortunately, the formula was recently revealed.

7. *Government policy.* Sometimes governments limit entry into an industry, effectively preventing new competition. For example, airline companies for many years enjoyed a protected status, with their routes and prices protected from competitive pressures. However, when the airline industry became deregulated, many new competitors entered and existing competitors greatly expanded their routes. These forces resulted in fare wars and lower profitability for all of the firms in the industry. Currently, airline companies are consolidating to build competitive strength.[17]

Taken together, these forces can result in high, medium, or low barriers. Examples of industries that are traditionally associated with high barriers to entry are aircraft manufacturing (technology, capital costs, reputation) and automobile manufacturing (capital costs, distribution, brand names). Medium barriers are associated with industries such as household appliances, cosmetics, and books. Low entry barriers are found in industries such as apparel manufacturing and most forms of retailing.[18]

An understanding of entry barriers is important from two perspectives. For firms inside an industry, erection of entry barriers can keep out other firms, which can preserve or stabilize industry profitability. For firms outside of the industry, particularly small businesses, an understanding of entry barriers can help a firm determine an entry wedge, or strategy for hurdling entry barriers. For example, if the industry is capital intensive and experiences production economies of scale that would deter entrants, a prospective entrant could arrange for subcontracted production rather than be deterred by demands for large-scale production.

Indirect Competitors and Substitutes. If organizations provide goods or services that are readily substitutable for the goods and services provided by an industry, these organizations can become indirect competitors. Close substitutes serve the same function for customers, and can place a ceiling on the price that can be charged for a good or service.[19] For example, if the price of artificial sweeteners becomes too high, many consumers who typically prefer artificial sweeteners would probably switch back to sugar. Also, aspirin, ibuprofen, and acetaminophen are all substitute pain relievers. In the service sector, credit unions are substitutes for banks and bus travel is a substitute for airline travel. Close substitutes also set new performance standards. The availability of the smaller, direct satellites with pay-per-view options puts pressures on cable providers and video rental stores to offer a broader selection of offerings at lower prices.

Whether a product or service qualifies as a substitute depends on how the boundaries of the industry are drawn. For example, health care providers such as hospitals, private physicians, and health maintenance organizations (HMOs) would be considered substitutes for one another if each type of provider were classified in a separate industry. However, if all of the providers were classified in the same industry called, for example, the health industry, then hospitals, private physicians, and HMOs would be treated as direct competitors that exist in separate strategic groups. It is important to maintain consistency between whatever definition of industry is being used and the way substitutes are identified. Regardless of how they are defined, organizations should pay close attention to the actions of producers of close substitutes when formulating and implementing strategies.

Combining the Five Forces. An analysis of the five forces is useful from several perspectives. First, by understanding how the five forces influence competition and profitability in an industry, a firm can better understand how to position itself relative to the forces, determine any sources of competitive advantage now and in the future, and estimate the profits that can be expected. For small and start-up businesses, a five-forces analysis can reveal opportunities for market entry that will not attract the attention of the larger competitors. Firm managers may also decide to alter the five forces by actions such as erecting higher entry barriers through large-scale economies or greater product differentiation, or by creating switching costs to encourage customer loyalty.

An organization can also conduct a five-forces analysis of an industry prior to entry or as a basis for deciding to leave an industry. On the basis of such an analysis, a firm may conclude that an industry is not attractive because of low entry barriers, powerful suppliers or buyers, close substitutes, or the number and strength of current competitors. An abbreviated example of Porter's five forces at work in the brewing industry is provided in Strategic Application 3.1.

Although Porter's model was developed primarily for industry analysis, examination of the five forces is also relevant at the firm level. For example, when Monsanto bought the Nutrasweet Company from G. D. Searle in 1985, it acquired the patent to the aspartame artificial sweetener by the same name. Purchase of

STRATEGIC APPLICATION 3.1

ABBREVIATED EXAMPLE OF THE FIVE FORCES IN THE BREWING INDUSTRY

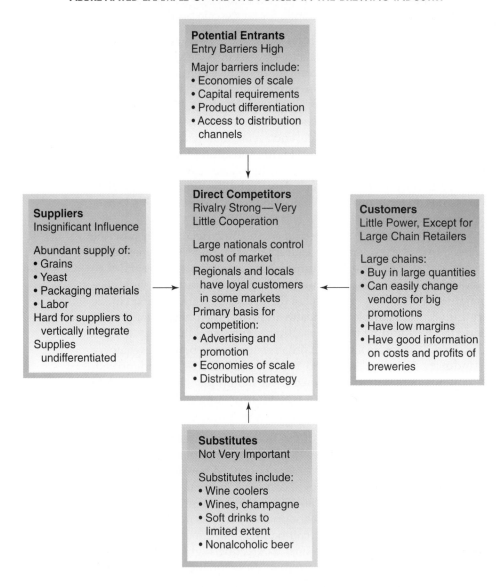

this patent created an entry barrier which put Monsanto in a strong position relative to its customers. Even though Monsanto was the sole producer of aspartame and could, in theory, charge high prices, the amount charged to customers was somewhat limited because of substitutes such as sugar, corn sweeteners, and saccharin. Furthermore, large customers such as soft drink companies also had power because of their large purchases. The end result of this analysis was that Monsanto was in a fairly strong position to enjoy unusually large profits because of the absence of competition, but this position was tempered somewhat by substitutes and large customers.[20] Then, in 1992, the patent ran out, which changed everything.

It is interesting to note the change in attitude in the Nutrasweet division now that they no longer hold a monopoly position. According to M. L. Lowenkron, CEO of A&W Brands, "They behaved with all the arrogance of a classic monopolist. But they've done a complete turnabout."[21] Now the Nutrasweet division is much more focused on satisfying the customer.

This completes our discussion of Porter's model, which included a consideration of the power of several important stakeholder groups. The greater the power of a stakeholder, the more impact that stakeholder will have on the environmental uncertainty facing a firm. Consequently, powerful stakeholders should be given higher priority in the strategic management process. The next section provides suggestions for how to manage important stakeholders.

MANAGING AND PARTNERING WITH EXTERNAL STAKEHOLDERS

Establishment of the priority of stakeholders provides direction as to the amount of attention they should be given during the development of a corporate direction, strategies, and implementation plans. However, prioritizing stakeholders also provides clues concerning the types of strategies that may be appropriate in managing them. The previous section argued that high-priority stakeholders have larger stakes in the organization and greater economic and political power. These stakeholders should be given high priority because they have a large impact on the environmental uncertainty the firm is facing—in other words, the ability of the firm to chart a successful course through the environment. For example, Intel, the microprocessing chip manufacturer, should give high priority to IBM, Dell, and other large customers. Nucor, the steel maker, would want to give government regulators and construction companies high priority. A not-for-profit organization such as the United Way should pay close attention to each local community in which it is involved because funds are raised and services are provided at the community level. A small business would likely emphasize customers and creditors because of the cash flow problems that tend to plague new businesses.

Priority is also a matter of strategic choice, as indicated in Figure 3.5. For example, a particular special interest group such as a church or environmental group may be given high priority because of the values of the CEO. For instance, Ben and Jerry's, the ice cream maker, gives high priority to environmental concerns. Also, Harris Corporation gives high corporate priority to the local communities in which it does business. Some companies, like Harris, build these values into their corporate mission statement or publicly stated goals. Chapter 5 discusses this sort of leadership in greater detail.

Traditional Stakeholder Management Techniques

Organizations use two basic postures when managing relationships with external stakeholders.[22] One posture involves *buffering* the organization from environmental uncertainty through techniques designed to stabilize and predict environmental influences and, in essence, raise the boundaries higher. They soften the jolts that might otherwise be felt as the organization interacts with members of its external environment. These are traditional stakeholder management techniques such as marketing research, creation of special departments to handle specific areas of the external environment (e.g., legal, recruiting, purchasing), efforts to ensure regulatory compliance, and advertising and public relations efforts. **Buffering** tech-

Buffering
Stakeholder management techniques of planning for and adapting to the environment so that the needs and demands of critical stakeholders are met.

Figure 3.5 *Factors Influencing the Strategic Importance of External Stakeholders and the Basic Approach to Managing Them*

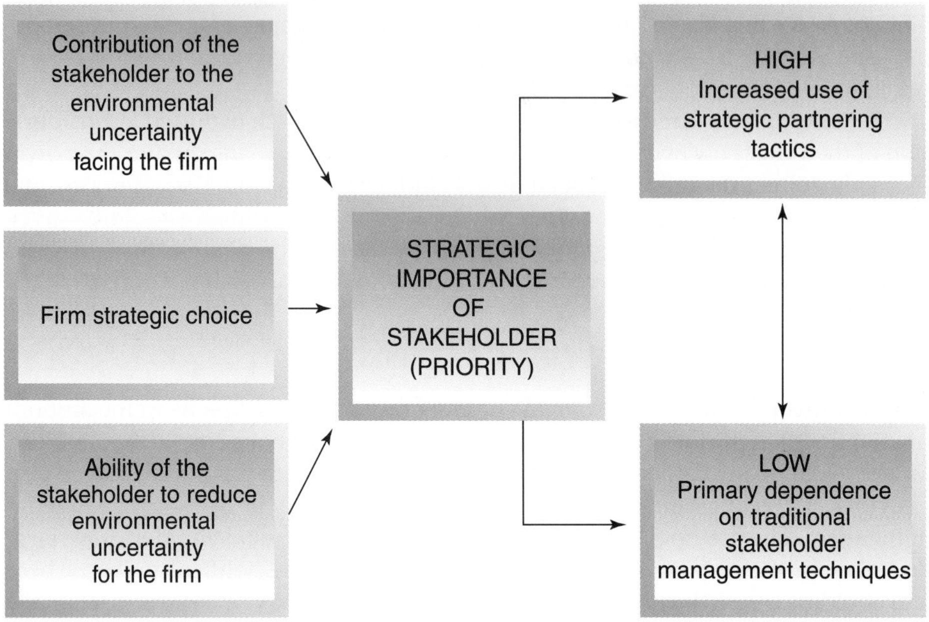

Source: J. S. Harrison and C. H. St. John, "Managing and Partnering with External Stakeholders," *Academy of Management Executive* (May 1996). Used with permission.

niques focus on planning for and adapting to the environment so that the needs and demands of critical stakeholders are met.

Table 3.1 provides a list of examples of traditional stakeholder management techniques, grouped by type of external stakeholder. These techniques are both common and essential, and should be used where appropriate. However, recently the emphasis in stakeholder management has been shifting away from buffering the organization from external stakeholders in the direction of treating them almost as if they are part of the internal organization. Partnering tactics are not new. What is new is that they are being used with ever increasing frequency.

Strategic Partnering

Bridging
Stakeholder management techniques that build on interdependencies rather than buffer them.

When environments are more complex and uncertain, webs of interdependencies are created among stakeholders.[23] In these environments, **bridging** (also called boundary-spanning) techniques are needed that build on interdependencies rather than buffer them. According to Pfeffer and Salancik, two famous organizational researchers, "The typical solution to problems of interdependence and uncertainty involves increasing the mutual control over each other's activities."[24] Joint ventures with competitors, cooperative product development efforts involving suppliers and customers, and industry-level lobbying efforts are examples of partnering techniques that bring the firm into closer alliance with its critical stakeholders. Recent research suggests that strategic alliances are a device for reducing both the uncertainties that arise from unpredictable demand and the pressures that come from high levels of interdependence among organizations.[25]

Table 3.1 *Examples of Tactics for Managing and Partnering with External Stakeholders*

Stakeholder	Traditional Management Tactics	Partnering Tactics
Customers	Customer service departments Marketing research Advertising On-site visits 800 Numbers Long-term contracts Product/service development Market development	Customer involvement on design teams Customer involvement in product testing Joint planning sessions Enhanced communication linkages Joint training/service programs Sharing of facilities Financial investments in customer Appointments to board of directors
Suppliers	Purchasing departments Encourage competition among suppliers Sponsor new suppliers Threat of vertical integration Long-term contracts	Supplier involvement on design teams Integration of ordering system with manufacturing (i.e., just-in-time inventory) Shared information systems Joint development of new products Coordinated quality control (i.e., TQM) Simultaneous production Appointments to board of directors
Competitors	Competing on the basis of product and service differentiation, technological advances, innovation, speed, price cutting, market segmentation Intelligence systems Corporate spying and espionage*	Keiretsu* Joint ventures for R&D or market development Collective lobbying efforts Informal price leadership or collusion* Industry panels to deal with labor or other problems Mergers (horizontal integration)
Government agencies/ administrators	Legal departments Tax departments Government relations departments Lobbying/political action committees Campaign contributions Self-regulation Personal gifts to politicians*	Consortia on international trade and competitiveness Jointly or government-sponsored research Joint ventures to work on social problems Joint foreign development projects Panels on product safety Appointment of retired government officials to the board of directors

(continued)

Partnering activities allow firms to build bridges with their stakeholders in the pursuit of common goals, whereas traditional stakeholder management techniques (buffering) simply reduce shocks and facilitate the satisfaction of stakeholder needs and/or demands. Partnering can lead to more timely and complete information about stakeholders, to trust-building and enhanced reputations, and to influence over beliefs and actions.

Table 3.1 *(continued)*

Stakeholder	Traditional Management Tactics	Partnering Tactics
Local communities/ governments	Community relations offices Public relations advertising Involvement in community service/politics Local purchases of supplies/ local employment Donations to local government organizations Donations to local charities Gifts to local government officials*	Task forces to solve skilled-labor shortages Joint urban renewal programs Cooperative training programs Development committees/boards Employment programs for workers with special needs such as the handicapped Joint education programs
Activist groups	Internal programs to satisfy demands Public/political relations efforts to offset or protect from negative publicity Financial donations	Consultation with members on sensitive issues Joint ventures for research/ research consortia Appointment of group representatives to board Jointly sponsored public relations efforts
Unions	Avoid unions through high levels of employee satisfaction Avoid unions by thwarting attempts to organize* Hiring of professional negotiators Public relations advertising Chapter XI protection	Mutually satisfactory (win–win) labor contracts Contract clauses that link pay to performance (i.e., profit sharing) Joint committees on safety and other issues Joint employee development programs Joint industry/labor panels Labor leaders appointed to board of directors and included in major decisions
Financial intermediaries	Financial reports Close correspondence Finance and accounting departments High-level financial officer Audits	Inclusion in decisions requiring financial backing Contracts and linkages with other clients of the financial intermediary Appointments to the board of directors Shared ownership of new projects

* These tactics are of questionable ethical acceptability to some internal and external stakeholders in the United States and elsewhere.

Source: Adapted from J. S. Harrison and C. H. St. John, "Managing and Partnering with External Stakeholders," *Academy of Management Executive* (May 1996), p. 53. Used with permission.

The potential benefits of proactive stakeholder management can be illustrated using relationships with customers as an example. Firms with a traditional buffering posture toward customers focus on arms-length information gathering about new product needs and expected demand, and compliance with current quality and service expectations, all in an effort to buffer the organization from uncertainty and customer complaints. Under a more proactive stakeholder management approach, a firm might choose to create stronger linkages with customers by involving them directly in the firm's product development programs, continuous improvement programs, and production planning and scheduling (via computer networks).

The proactive stakeholder management approach builds on the interdependency rather than buffering it. By working closely with customers, the firm is likely to have earlier, more complete information about the direction of the marketplace, will anticipate ahead of time the types of improvements and new products that the customer will need from the firm, will improve the likelihood of success and speed of new product introductions, and will create trust and respect between the two groups, possibly leading to an enduring relationship. The thrust of the proactive, bridging approach is to create common goals, rather than just adapt to stakeholder initiatives.

It would be naive, and possibly deceptive, to suggest that strategic partnerships only result in benefits. There are disadvantages as well. For example, company culture clashes can erode cooperation between firms and prevent true partnering from taking place. Strong ties with one stakeholder may force a firm to sever or restrict ties with another stakeholder to avoid conflicts of interest, the appearance of impropriety, or the loss of confidential information. Furthermore, joint decision making can be slow and result in too many compromises. Small businesses often find that partnering tactics are essential for entering some industries, such as when supplying a much larger firm, but they run the risk of being dominated completely by their partner. Overall, however, the benefits seem to outweigh the disadvantages if the partnering tactics are used appropriately.

The following sections discuss some of the types of tactics that are used to partner with external stakeholders and the recent experiences of several firms. The third column of Table 3.1 contains a list of these tactics.

Customers. Proactive tactics for managing important customers include joint planning sessions to identify driving forces for industry change, joint product and market development efforts, enhanced communication linkages, sharing of facilities, and joint training and service programs (other examples are found in Table 3.1). Efforts to strengthen linkages with customers often provide significant benefits. For example, sales representatives at U.S. Surgical don gowns and coach surgeons during surgery in the use of their company's instruments. Experiences with surgeons led to the development of laparoscopic instruments, which are used to perform procedures through tiny incisions. U.S. Surgical has about an 85% share of the laparoscopic instruments market, which is an estimated $3 billion market.[26]

Caterpillar, the heavy equipment manufacturer, intends to create a jointly shared information system that will link its thirty manufacturing facilities with customers and suppliers. Through shared communications, Caterpillar will be able to better serve the needs of customers and also pass essential information and orders on to suppliers. Customers will have their needs satisfied quicker, Caterpillar will benefit from improved ordering efficiency, and suppliers will have better information on which to base production.[27] Shared information systems are increasing in their importance as a form of corporate alliance.

In a final example, IBM joined forces with an unlikely customer of its PC hardware and software, Sears, to form the Prodigy service network. Sears brought to the table its market research and a desire to develop electronic retailing capacity. IBM contributed its considerable expertise with home computers.[28]

Suppliers. Many firms are involving strategically important suppliers in product and process design, in quality training sessions, and in on-line production scheduling. Most firms that rely on just-in-time delivery have involved suppliers in their internal processes. For example, Digital Equipment Corporation (DEC) and Hewlett-Packard include suppliers on their product planning teams. DEC also asks managers to evaluate their suppliers as if they were part of the internal organization.[29] Bailey Controls, a $300-million-a-year manufacturer of control systems, does likewise, but they go a step further by providing Arrow Electronics, a major supplier, with a warehouse in a Bailey factory.[30] G&F Industries, a plastic components manufacturer, has dedicated an employee to Bose, one of their major customers. The employee works full time inside the Bose facility.[31]

A recent cover story in *The Wall Street Journal* stated that the "next manufacturing revolution is under way, and U.S. companies are bringing airplanes, cars, even kitchen stoves to market faster and cheaper by leaning on their suppliers to help engineer and bankroll new projects."[32] These types of relationships are providing tremendous cost savings and other benefits. For instance, Whirlpool contracted with a supplier, Eaton Corp., to develop the burner system for its new gas range. Also, McDonnell Douglas is saving $300 million by having suppliers pay upfront tooling and development costs and by subcontracting assembly of its new 100-seat jetliner.

Competitors. Competitors pose a difficult stakeholder management problem because it is often in the best interests of one competitor to cause another competitor to falter. However, to combat collapsing product and process life cycles and to get a jump on new emerging technologies, competitors are joining forces in increasing numbers. Rival organizations are forming alliances to enhance technological advancement and new product development, to enter new or foreign markets, and to pursue a wide variety of other opportunities.[33] Strategic Insight 3.1 provides several examples of strategic alliances among international rivals. The underlying motive sometimes seems to be to put the remaining firms that are not included in an alliance at a competitive disadvantage. For example, Oster has provided evidence that "regulatory barriers created by firm conduct may be used by groups in the industry as a competitive weapon against other groups."[34]

In oligopolies, where a few major rivals dominate an industry, the major firms may cooperate with each other in setting prices. Formal price-setting cooperation is called **collusion**. In the United States and many other countries, collusion is illegal. However, firms may still cooperate informally by being careful not to drop prices enough to start a price war. Price wars can damage the profits of all firms in the industry, as demonstrated several times in the airline industry since it was deregulated. Alternatively, some industries have an established price leader, usually one of the largest firms in the industry, who establishes a pricing pattern that other firms follow.

In some countries and regions, collusion is not illegal or is widely practiced in spite of its illegality. For example, the OPEC cartel established the price charged for crude oil produced by Middle Eastern countries for many years. Ultimately, the cartel lost power when countries participating in OPEC discovered that great financial rewards were available for individual firms that were willing to violate OPEC agreements.

In Japan and elsewhere, organizations may participate in powerful cooperative alliances called **keiretsu**. These alliances are composed of manufacturers, suppliers, and finance companies who often own stock in each other. Although keiretsu are often accused of collusion and other competition reducing actions, they also

Collusion
Formal price-setting cooperation within an industry.

Keiretsu
Cooperative alliances of manufacturers, suppliers, and finance companies in Japan that often own stock in each other and lead to greater efficiency for their members.

STRATEGIC INSIGHT 3.1

International Rivals Join Forces in Major Alliances

Very few international rivalries are as intense as the rivalry between film makers Kodak and Fuji. After World War II, Kodak held almost a monopoly position in the photographic film industry in the United States. No other competitor had sufficient technology to be a threat. However, Fuji of Japan gradually developed great skill in film production and used profits generated in Japan, the largest per-capita film market in the world, to subsidize operations in the United States, thus eroding Kodak's market share. Kodak eventually responded by marketing low-cost photographic paper in Japan.

Because of their intense rivalry, some analysts were surprised when Kodak and Fuji began a joint research and development project with three Japanese camera makers to establish a new standard for photographic film. Eugene Glazer, an analyst at Dean Witter Reynolds, explained, "Fuji has to be granted the same technology. If they don't include Fuji, Fuji would fight very hard against the introduction of a new system." The venture has already produced the new Advanced Photo System (APS), which incorporates a new type of "smart" film that allows correction of photographer errors.

In the computer chip industry, IBM formed a joint venture with rivals Toshiba Corp. of Japan and Siemens AG of Germany to develop an advanced line of memory chips that will be suitable for computers in the next century. This is a particularly surprising move for IBM, previously a strong advocate of an independent U.S. semiconductor industry. Also, Advanced Micro Devices Inc. formed an alliance with Fujitsu Ltd. of Japan to develop a new kind of memory chip. The alliance includes the purchase of each other's common stock.

In the airline industry, rivals are teaming up to provide coordinated service on international routes. United has allied with Lufthansa, Delta with Swissair, Austrian Airlines with Sabena, Northwest with KLM, and American with British Airways. CEO of American Airlines, Robert Crandall, in justifying his own company's venture, said, "The government changed the rules. I don't have to like it, but we understand the rules and we will play by them."

Sources: M. Maremont, "Will A New Film Click?" *Business Week* (February 5, 1996), p. 46; D. Rosato, "American Alliance Signals Something New in the Air," *USA Today* (June 13, 1996), p. 2B; J.. Schneidawind, "Kodak Joins Fuji, Others for Project," *USA Today* (March 26, 1992), p. B1; L. Hooper, "Pragmatism Wins as Rivals Start to Cooperate on Memory Chips," *The Wall Street Journal* (July 14, 1992), p. B1.

lead to greater efficiency for keiretsu members. Historically, U.S. firms have had a hard time breaking into Japanese keiretsu. However, times have changed. For example, Toshiba just completed a new $1 billion chip-making facility that uses state-of-the art ultraviolet technology. The plant was completed, in part, through a joint venture between Toshiba, Siemens of Germany, and IBM. Also, Mitsubishi, a leader in one of the biggest keiretsu in the world, is involved in a long-term joint venture with Caterpillar. The venture has already produced an excavator line manufactured in Japan, the United States, Indonesia, and China.[35]

To remain competitive, U.S. firms are beginning to adopt keiretsu-like cooperative practices in research, design, financing, production, and marketing. For instance, some competing manufacturers are selling and servicing each other's products. One example is IBM, which now sells Novell's network software. In another example, Ford has formed an extensive keiretsu through equity holdings, acquisitions, international alliances, and research consortia. Ford has large equity stakes in five foreign vehicle assembly companies, including Mazda, as well as stakes in three U.S. and foreign auto parts producers. On the marketing side, Ford owns 49% of Hertz car rental company, which is also one of its biggest customers. Ford is also involved in eight research consortia with other automobile industry participants and owns seven subsidiaries that offer financial services, among them dealer purchases and automobile loans.[36] Keiretsu may be one of the most powerful tools for dealing with competition in an increasingly competitive global marketplace.

Alliances may also form among rivals in an effort to influence common stakeholders such as government agencies, activist groups, unions, or local communities. These alliances then become a part of the organization's **political strategy**, which includes all organizational activities that have as one of their objectives the creation of a friendlier political climate for the organization. Lobbying is part of a political strategy, but it is only a small part of the bigger political picture. In the rest of this section on competitors and also in the sections on managing government agencies, administrators, and local communities we continue our discussion of political strategy.

Political Strategy
All of an organization's strategies that have as an objective the creation of a friendlier political climate for the organization.

Collective activity may include membership in trade associations, chambers of commerce, and industry and labor panels. Firms join associations to gain access to information and to obtain legitimacy, acceptance, and influence.[37] Trade associations, although not as powerful in the United States as in Japan and Europe, often serve an information management and monitoring purpose for member firms. They provide information and interpretation of legislative and regulatory trends, may collect market research, and sometimes provide an informal mechanism for exchanging information about competitors. Firms may also join industry and labor panels to manage negotiations with activist groups and unions.

Some scholars have suggested that individual firm lobbying efforts are ineffective. Fragmented involvement, in which each firm represents its own interests, has resulted in a free-for-all and the collective interests of business have been the real loser.[38] The suggestion for fixing this problem is to increase efforts to strengthen collective institutions such as the Business Roundtable and the Committee on Economic Development. On a smaller scale, the seven Baby Bells had to join political forces to win the ability to compete with AT&T in long-distance services and equipment.[39] Some trade associations, such as the U.S. League of Savings Institutions, have had success influencing and sometimes even "rewriting" regulations before they are made law.[40]

Automobile manufacturers in the United States, because of their size and limited number, might be expected to have almost overwhelming economic power in comparison to automobile dealers, who are numerous (more than 25,000) and widely dispersed. However, dealers have been effective in counteracting the power of manufacturers through unified political activity. An average of 57 auto dealers sit in every congressional district, and an average of 250 dealers reside in each senator's state. In contrast, auto manufacturing is concentrated primarily in six states. When conflict emerges between manufacturers and dealers, "grassroots" efforts are organized by the dealers' two powerful trade groups, the National Automobile Dealers Association and the American International Auto Dealers Association. Dealers usually prevail in political conflicts with manufacturers.

Consequently, the threat of legislation is a valuable bargaining tool for dealers when negotiating contract terms with manufacturers.[41]

Government Agencies and Administrators. Business organizations and governments share a number of common goals, among them creating a favorable environment for international trade, stable market conditions, a healthy economy, and production of desirable goods and services. Consequently, many organizations form alliances with government agencies and officials to pursue a wide variety of objectives, including basic research, finding answers to social problems, and establishing trade policies.

Government/business partnerships are even more widely used outside of the United States, where governments often play a more active role in economic development. One such effort resulted in the formation of the major aerospace company, Airbus Industrie, jointly owned by aerospace companies from Britain, France, Germany, and Spain. The Japanese Ministry of International Trade and Industry (MITI) examines segments of Japanese industry and provides support for those that are determined to be most closely linked to the growth of the Japanese economy.

In one of the most interesting government/industry alliances to date, the U.S. Justice Department actually helped aluminum manufacturers form a cartel to regulate the production and, ultimately, the price of aluminum. The accord resulted from fear of Russian influence in the world aluminum market. The former Soviet Union, rich in natural resources such as aluminum and starved for foreign cash, began flooding the world market with aluminum. In response, major U.S. and European producers decided to offer $2 billion to close one huge smelter for two years to modernize it. President Bush squashed the deal. The dumping situation continued and became so extreme that eventually U.S. aluminum makers begged the government for intervention. The administration changed and Bowman Cutter, President Clinton's deputy of the National Economic Council, eventually took the aluminum manufacturers' situation to heart. The council brought together a broad group of government agencies, but they could not agree on how to attack the problem. Finally, a group consisting of industry and government representatives from seventeen nations, including three antitrust lawyers from the U.S. Justice Department, met in Brussels to decide who would produce how much aluminum.[42]

In another interesting alliance, Loral Chairman Bernard Schwartz, due to his ties with the late Ron Brown, secretary of the Department of Commerce, got a boost to his business that most managers just dream about. Schwartz was invited to accompany Brown to China with the objective of helping the fast growing nation develop their telecommunications capability. The trip is expected to bring Loral as much as $1 billion in Chinese contracts during the next ten years. To keep this unusual alliance strong, Mr. Schwartz has donated nearly $200,000 to Democratic interests favored by Mr. Brown since 1991. Although the relationship is advantageous in some respects to both the United States and Loral, the ethics of the situation have been questioned.[43]

Local Communities. Organizations take a proactive role in their local communities for a variety of reasons. Good relationships with local communities and governments can result in favorable local regulation or tax breaks. In the case of the Kiamichi Railroad Company of Oklahoma and Texas, good relationships with the community were instrumental in turning around a failing business. Burlington-Northern sold the unprofitable railroad in 1987. Workers, afraid of losing their high-paying union jobs, resisted the sale and stirred up animosity among local communities. New management turned the community situation around through such efforts as establishing a service club, buying from local suppliers, sponsoring a rodeo, and taking an active role in the United Way. These efforts were part of a turnaround plan that eliminated the need for a union and put the company in a strong financial condition. The company is now growing and profitable.[44]

Other organizations find opportunities to achieve financial or operating objectives while satisfying a need in the local community. For instance, Creative Apparel of Waldo County, Maine, helped a depressed local economy by establishing a partnership with a local tribe of Indians. A training program was put in place and a grant was obtained from the Department of Commerce to assist with the construction of a new manufacturing building. In 1990, the Department of Defense awarded Creative Apparel a $2.95 million contract for flame-retardant flyer jackets.[45]

Social partnerships are a good way to achieve common goals. For example, a task force was formed among business leaders, educational institutions, and local government representatives to address skilled labor shortages in the upstate South Carolina region. It was comprised of 21 members, including local employers, a county school board executive, faculty members from a local university, and representatives from a literary society and a job service. Efforts of the task force resulted in specific recommendations to find more job applicants, improve the qualifications of applicants, and upgrade the skills of current employees. In addition, the task force developed a Human Resources Workforce Information and Preparedness Program (the WIPP) to address human resource needs on a longer term basis. Not only did companies participating in the upstate task force have an opportunity to promote goodwill with several stakeholder groups, but they could also work on filling unmet human resource needs and potentially begin to develop a distinctive competence through the creation of a labor pool composed of better skilled workers.[46]

Quasi-public alliances between local governments and business leaders are flourishing across many sections of the United States. For example, the Economic Development Commission of Mid-Florida Inc. represents four central Florida counties. The commission works with government and business leaders to create economic plans and initiatives. Recent activities include the development of an economic action plan for Osceola County, promotion of an industrial park, the matching of companies that sell goods with foreign companies that buy them, and finding ways to make use of the Orlando Naval Training Center, one of several military facilities the Navy has decided to abandon. The commission is flush with cash, including $425,000 in state and local government grants.[47]

Martin Marietta, which has merged with Lockheed (another corporation with a strong presence in Central Florida), is among the companies that has formed a partnership with the commission to preserve employment, reduce operating costs, and bring new business to the Central Florida economy. Rick Tesch, who heads the commission, describes their successes this way: "We've proven that partnerships like this work. By streamlining permitting, helping reduce operating costs and assisting them in obtaining state training and incentive dollars, we were able to solidify Martin's presence in metro Orlando and bring an additional 1,500 jobs into our community."[48]

Activist Groups. Activist groups such as the Sierra Club, Greenpeace International, the National Association for the Advancement of Colored People (NAACP), the National Organization for Women (NOW), and Mothers Against Drunk Driving (MADD) represent a variety of social and environmental perspectives. Public interest groups (e.g., MADD) represent the position of a broad cross-section of society, whereas special interest groups (e.g., NAACP) focus on the needs of smaller subgroups. Although these groups are most often seen in an adversarial role relative to the desires of other organizational stakeholders, this does not have to be the case. However, it is difficult for executives to break out of the old mind-set and adopt an attitude of common goal achievement. To adopt a win–win attitude with activist groups, executives should consider potential benefits from partnering activities, especially in situations in which an activist group is strategically important.

One of the best ways to reduce unfavorable regulation in an industry is to operate in a manner that is consistent with the values of society. Organizations that respond to the widely held positions of **public interest groups** on issues such as pollution, fair hiring practices, safety, and waste management do not need to be regulated. They find themselves in the enviable position of solving their own problems, instead of having a regulatory body of individuals with less experience in the industry dictating how problems will be solved. Public interest groups are particularly important in helping organizations avoid conflicts with social values, which can result in unfavorable media and a damaged reputation. They are experts in the causes they represent. As a result, many companies invite public interest group members that may have an interest in what they are doing to participate in strategic planning processes either as advisors or board members.

Organizations should also consider the needs of **special interest groups,** which represent the views of smaller social groups. However, buffering techniques may be more applicable because these groups, by virtue of their smaller social scope, are likely to be less strategically important than public interest groups.

Both types of activists can also provide an alternative perspective on issues that affect the environment, consumers, minorities, or other interests. This alternative perspective can lead to new ways to solve organizational problems. For example, the Conservation Law Foundation, a New England based environmental organization, formed a partnership with the New England Electric System, a medium-sized utility, that was concerned with conservation, load management, and regulatory and rate adjustments. As a result of this collaboration, it is estimated that one-third of the planned power plants in the region will not have to be built out to the year 2010, releasing this capital for other uses. New England Electric saved capital and the Conservation Law Foundation helped reduce, among other things, air pollution and respiratory problems in the affected areas. It was a win–win situation.[49]

Another benefit to allowing participation by important public interest or special interest groups during planning processes is that there may be fewer obstacles during strategy implementation. The groups involved would be less likely to protest or seek government intervention. This may also result in good public relations and publicity. For example, Sun Company (oil) worked directly with the Coalition for Environmentally Responsible Economies (CERES) in developing a new policy for health, safety, and the environment. Sun has recently been cited by Friends of the Earth as a model company that other companies should emulate.[50]

Alliances with activist groups can also help companies develop new products. The increasing social emphasis on environmental protection has left companies rushing to introduce products that are environmentally acceptable.[51] Examples include McDonald's conversion back to paper packaging and Rubbermaid's environmentally friendly "Sidekick" lunch box. Also, organizations in the mature PC industry may find new growth opportunities in developing products for the phys-

Public Interest Groups
Activist groups that represent the position of a broad cross-section of society on such issues as pollution, fair hiring practices, safety, and waste management.

Special Interest Groups
Activist groups that represent the views of smaller subgroups in society.

ically and mentally challenged by partnering with the Institute of Applied Technology, a Boston-based nonprofit organization that does research and training on computer applications for these individuals.[52]

Unions. Unions are formed to protect and advance the welfare of their members. The strength of unions varies from state to state and country to country. In the United States, union strength has declined recently; however, unions are far from dead. For example, the Service Employees International Union (SEII) employs shock tactics and harassment to influence janitorial contractors to pressure their employees to unionize.[53] As a result, the SEII is growing steadily. Also, a very visible strike at a GM brake plant shut down the entire organization.[54]

The values of unions were reflected well in a statement by Owen Bieber, president of the United Auto Workers:

> *I'm struck by the widespread confusion between means and ends that is hampering public understanding of the competitiveness issue. Competitiveness should be viewed as a means, useful only if it moves us toward such ends as full employment at decent wages, rising living standards, and fairness in the distribution of income and wealth. If competitiveness simply implies reducing costs, it can work against the goal of improving our quality of life. For example, the same company could improve its competitiveness by investing in training for its workers, forcing them to take wage cuts, or moving its production overseas. While all three strategies may improve competitiveness, they have very different consequences for employment, living standards, and quality of life.[55]*

Unions are making great strides in pursuing common goals with managers. The AFL-CIO recently urged the eighty-six unions it represents to "become partners with management in boosting efficiency."[56] This is an unprecedented move for the AFL-CIO.

Unions are being treated as partners instead of adversaries in some of the companies that have had the greatest success with programs such as self-managed work teams. For example, Xerox has implemented three teamwork programs since 1982 with its 6,200 copier assemblers, represented by the Amalgamated Clothing and Textile Workers Union (ACTWU). The efforts have worked so well that Xerox is now bringing 300 jobs home from abroad to a new plant in Utica, where it expects to save $2 million a year. Xerox shares internal financial documents with union leaders and provides executive development for them with their own managers. CEO Paul Allair commented on the success of these programs, "I don't want to say we need unions if that means the old, adversarial kind. But if we have a cooperative model, the union movement will be sustained and the industries it's in will be more competitive."[57]

Organizations that are successful in labor/management relationships are starting to include representatives from labor unions on their boards of directors and/or involving them in strategic planning decisions. For example, in 1993 LTV Corp. signed a pact with the United Steel Workers (USW) that allows them to nominate a board member in return for union support of teams and other efficiency measures. In another example, five years ago Scott Paper Co. formed a committee combining ten of its top executives with ten top officials from the union. They pledged to "work together to meet the needs of employees, customers, shareholders, the union and the community."[58] The results were so successful in terms of cutting costs and boosting quality that now other paper companies are doing the same thing.

Financial Intermediaries. Financial intermediaries consist of a wide variety of institutions, including banks, stock exchanges, brokerage houses, investment advisors, mutual fund companies, pension fund companies, and other organizations or individuals that may have an interest in investing in the firm. This list is not exhaustive and many financial service firms play more than one role.

Trust is especially important in dealing with creditors. Disclosure of financial records helps establish trust, as do timely payments. Many organizations, in an effort to manage their relationships with creditors and develop trust, have invited their representatives onto the board of directors. In some cases this is a loan requirement. This type of involvement allows creditors to determine first hand the financial condition of the company and to have a say in major financial decisions such as acquisitions, restructuring, and new offerings of stock and debt. Another type of linkage occurs when an organization does business with a company that is represented by the same financial institution. This type of cooperation, which can facilitate contracting and financial transactions, is common among the keiretsu in Japan. Banks and other lenders may also participate as part owners of business ventures of client firms.

Financial intermediaries are the last of the external stakeholders that will be discussed in this book; however, note that other external stakeholders, of varying importance, exist on a firm-by-firm basis. For example, donors are a key stakeholder in nonprofit organizations. Donors should probably be treated more like customers than anything else. In fact, individuals who donate to charities or religious organizations are forgoing other purchases. Nonprofit organizations should communicate with donors, involve them in the processes of the organization, and create a high-quality service that donors will want to support. In the case of charities, the recipients of goods and services should also be treated as customers.

This concludes the segment on analysis and management of stakeholders in the operating environment. Information collected from the operating and broad environments can be used by managers to identify opportunities and threats. Some of the partnering tactics described in this chapter provide vehicles for organizations to take advantage of opportunities and diminish or eliminate threats. The next chapter delves into the internal environment and the identification of organizational strengths and weaknesses.

Summary

This chapter dealt with influences in the operating environment. The operating environment includes stakeholders such as customers, suppliers, competitors, government agencies and administrators, local communities, activist groups, unions, and financial intermediaries. The first three of these stakeholders—customers, suppliers, and competitors—are the primary forces that drive competition in an industry.

One important distinction between the operating and broad environments is that the operating environment is subject to a high level of organizational influence, while the broad environment is not. Important tactics for influencing stakeholders in the operating environment include joint ventures and other forms of strategic alliances, contracting, various forms of stakeholder involvement in organizational processes and decisions, and exercising political influence to promote favorable regulations. Analysis of external stakeholders and the broad environment can result in the identification of opportunities and threats, which are then considered by managers as they establish a strategic direction and develop and implement strategies.

At this point, you should begin to appreciate the enormity and importance of the stakeholder analysis and management task faced by strategic managers. The themes, tools, and ideas contained in this chapter are applied with regularity throughout the remaining chapters, because stakeholder analysis and management is central to all of the activities of strategic management.

Discussion Questions

1. What is the difference between the operating and broad environments? Describe the stakeholders and elements that are contained within these environments.
2. Which stakeholder in the operating environment do you think is most important to the economic well-being of most for-profit business organizations in the United States? Justify your answer.
3. What are the primary factors that make some stakeholders more important than others? How should high-priority stakeholders be managed? How do management techniques for high-priority stakeholders differ from those for low-priority stakeholders? Give examples.
4. What are the five forces of competition? Describe their potential influence on competition in an industry with which you are familiar.
5. What role can political strategy play in influencing favorable regulations? How can firms use political influence to balance power with strong competitors, suppliers, or customers?
6. How can organizational managers effectively manage relations with local communities, activists, unions, and financial intermediaries?
7. Who are the key stakeholders in a typical nonprofit organization? How would your list compare with a list regarding typical for-profit firms?

References

1. C. S. Sankar, W. R. Boulton, N. W. Davidson, C. A. Snyder, and R. W. Ussery, "Building a World-Class Alliance: The Universal Card—TSYS Case," *Academy of Management Executive* (May 1995), pp. 20–21. Used with permission.
2. W. Weitzel and E. Jonsson, "Reversing the Downward Spiral: Lessons from W.T. Grant and Sears Roebuck," *Academy of Management Executive* (August 1991), pp. 7–22.
3. Some of what follows is found in J. S. Harrison and C. H. St. John, "Managing and Partnering with External Stakeholders," *Academy of Management Executive* (May 1996), pp. 46–50.
4. J. D. Thompson, *Organizations in Action* (New York: McGraw-Hill Book Company, 1967); J. R. Lang and D. E. Lockhart, "Increased Environmental Uncertainty and Changes in Board Linkage Patterns," *Academy of Management Journal* 33(1) (1990), pp. 106–128; A. D. Meyer and G. R. Brooks, "Environmental Jolts and Industry Revolutions: Organizational Responses to Discontinuous Change," *Strategic Management Journal* 11 (1990, Special Issue), pp. 93–110.
5. J. Perreira and B. Ortega, "Once Easily Turned Away by Local Foes, Wal-Mart Gets Tough in New England," *The Wall Street Journal* (September 7, 1994), pp. B1, B4.
6. M. E. Porter, *Competitive Strategy: Techniques for Analyzing Industries and Companies* (New York: The Free Press, 1980); see also D. F. Jennings and J. R. Lumpkin, "Insights Between Environmental Scanning Activities and Porter's Generic Strategies: An Empirical Analysis," *Journal of Management* 18 (1982), pp. 791–803.
7. This section on competitive forces draws heavily on the pioneering work of Michael Porter. See M.E. Porter, *Competitive Strategy: Techniques for Analyzing Industries and Competitors* (New York: The Free Press, 1980), pp. 1–33.
8. For example, T. Peters and R.H. Waterman, Jr., *In Search of Excellence* (New York: Harper and Row, 1982), p. 14.
9. *Annual Report*, Koninklijke Ahold nv, 1990, p. 2.
10. "Retail," *Orlando Sentinel* (February 1, 1996), p. C1.
11. B. Grueley, "FTC says Toys 'R' Us Competes Unfairly," *The Wall Street Journal* (May 23, 1996), pp. A3-A4.
12. R. D'Aveni, "Coping with Hypercompetition: Utilizing the 7S's Framework," *Academy of Management Executive* (August 1995), pp. 45–57.
13. K. Jennings and F. Westfall, "Benchmarking for Strategic Action," *Journal of Business Strategy* (May/June 1992), p. 22.
14. O. Port, "Beg, Borrow and Benchmark," *Business Week* (November 30, 1992), pp. 74–75.
15. R. C. Camp, "Learning from the Best Leads to Superior Performance," *Journal of Business Strategy* (May/June 1992), p. 3.
16. A. Reifenberg, "How Secret Formula for Coveted Slick 50 Fell into Bad Hands," *The Wall Street Journal* (October 25, 1995), pp. A1, A9.
17. Barriers to entry form a major portion of the literature in industrial organization economics. See J. S. Bain, *Barriers to New Competition* (Cambridge, Mass.: Harvard University Press, 1956); J. S. Bain, *Industrial Organization*, rev. ed. (New York: John Wiley, 1967); B. Gold, "Changing Perspectives on Size, Scale and Returns: An Integrative Survey," *Journal of Economic Literature*, 19 (1981), pp. 5–33; Porter, *Competitive Strategy*, pp. 7–17; W. G. Shepherd, *The Economics of Industrial Organization* (Englewood Cliffs, N.J.: Prentice-Hall, 1979). For applications of barriers to entry to competitive strategy, see K.R. Harrigan, "Barriers to Entry and Competitive Strategies," *Strategic Management Journal* 2 (1981), pp. 395–412.
18. Bain, *Barriers to New Competition*; H.M. Mann, "Seller Concentration, Barriers to Entry and Rates of Return in Thirty Industries, 1950–1960," *Review of Economics and Statistics* 48 (1966), pp. 296–307.
19. Porter, *Competitive Strategy*, p. 23.

20. J.E. McCann, *Sweet Success: How Nutrasweet Created a Billion Dollar Business* (Homewood, Ill.: Irwin, 1990).

21. R. Henkoff, "Learning from Its Mistakes?" *Fortune* (January 27, 1992), p. 81.

22. This is the view of many organization theorists. For example, see R. L. Daft, *Organization Theory and Design*, 4th ed. (St. Paul, Minn.: West Publishing Company, 1992), Chap. 3.

23. Thompson, *Organizations in Action*; Lang and Lockhart, "Increased Environmental Uncertainty."

24. J. Pfeffer and G. R. Salancik, *The External Control of Organizations* (New York: Harper & Row, 1978), p. 43.

25. W. P. Burgers, C. W. L. Hill, and W. C. Kim, "A Theory of Global Strategic Alliances: The Case of the Global Auto Industry," *Strategic Management Journal* 14 (1993), pp. 419–432.

26. J. Reese, "Getting Hot Ideas from Customers," *Fortune* (May 18, 1992), p. 86.

27. F. K. Sonnenberg, "Relationship Management Is More Than Wining and Dining," *Journal of Business Strategy* (May/June 1988), pp. 60–63; B. Bremner, "Can Caterpillar Inch Its Way Back to Heftier Profits?" *Business Week* (September 27, 1989), pp. 75–78.

28. R. Stutzman, "Budget Constraints and a New Global Attitude Is Creating Some Unusual Corporate Partnerships," *The Orlando Sentinel* (April 10, 1994), p. D-2.

29. R. M. Kantar, "The New Managerial Work," *Harvard Business Review* (November/December 1989), pp. 85–92.

30. E. Schonfeld, "The New Golden Rule of Business," *Fortune* (February 21, 1994), pp. 60–64.

31. F. R. Bleakley, "Some Companies Let Suppliers Work on Site and Even Place Orders," *The Wall Street Journal* (January 13, 1995), pp. A1, A6.

32. N. Templin and J. Cole, "Manufacturers Use Suppliers to Help Them Develop New Products," *The Wall Street Journal* (December 19, 1994), p. A1.

33. A good review of this literature is found in J. Hagedoorn, "Understanding the Rationale of Strategic Technology Partnering: Interorganizational Modes of Cooperation and Sectoral Differences," *Strategic Management Journal* 14 (1993), pp. 371- 385. See also E. R. Auster, "International Corporate Linkages: Dynamic Forms in Changing Environments," *Columbia Journal of World Business* 22 (1987), pp. 3–13; K.R. Harrigan, "Joint Ventures and Competitive Strategy," *Strategic Management Journal* 9 (1988), pp. 141–158.

34. S. Oster, "The Strategic Use of Regulatory Investment by Industry Sub-groups," *Economic Inquiry* 20 (1982), p. 604.

35. B. Bremner, Z. Schiller, T. Smart, and W. J. Holstein, "Keiretsu Connections," *Business Week* (July 22, 1996), pp. 52–54.

36. K. Kelly, "Learning from Japan," *Business Week* (January 27, 1992), pp. 52–60.

37. W. R. Scott, *Organizations: Rational, Natural, and Open Systems*, 3rd ed. (Englewood Cliffs, N.J.: Prentice-Hall, 1992).

38. Empirical support of this phenomenon is found in K. B. Grier, M. C. Munger, and B. E. Roberts, "The Determinants of Industry Political Activity, 1978–1986," *American Political Science Review* 88 (1994), pp. 911–925; a descriptive review of this problem is found in I. Maitland, "Self-Defeating Lobbying: How More Is Buying Less in Washington," *Journal of Business Strategy* 7(2) (1986), pp. 67–78.

39. L. Cauley, J. J. Keller, and D. Kneale, "Battle Lines Harden as Baby Bells Fight to Kill Restrictions," *The Wall Street Journal* (July 22, 1994), pp. A1-A2.

40. M. Langley, "Thrift's Trade Group and Their Regulators Get Along Just Fine," *The Wall Street Journal* (July 16, 1986), pp. A1, A14; Maitland, "Self-Defeating Lobbying."

41. B. Shaffer, *Regulation, Competition and Strategy: Evidence from the Automobile Industry*, Unpublished Doctoral Dissertation, University of California, 1992; F. M. Smith, "Franchise Regulation: An Economic Analysis of State Restrictions on Automobile Distribution," *Journal of Law and Economics* 25 (1982), pp. 125–157.

42. E. Norton and M. DuBois, "Don't Call It a Cartel, But World Aluminum Has Forged New Order," *The Wall Street Journal* (June 9, 1994), pp. A1, A5.

43. H. Cooper and R. Wartzman, "How Ron Brown Picks Who Joins His Trips Abroad Raises Doubts," *The Wall Street Journal* (September 9, 1994), pp. A1, A4.

44. "Kiamichi Railroad Company, Inc.," *Strengthening America's Competitiveness: The Blue Chip Enterprise Initiative* (Warner Books on behalf of Connecticut Life Insurance Company and the U.S. Chamber of Commerce, 1991), p. 132.

45. "Creative Apparel, Inc.," *Strengthening America's Competitiveness: The Blue Chip Enterprise Initiative* (Warner Books on behalf of Connecticut Mutual Life Insurance Company and the U.S. Chamber of Commerce, 1991), pp. 9–10.

46. T. P. Summers and J. S. Harrison, "Alliance for Success," *Training and Development* (March 1992), pp. 69–75.

47. B. Kuhn, "Business Growth on the Rise. Central Florida Faces Good News, Bad News Scenario," *The Orlando Sentinel* (January 10, 1994), p. 24; J. DeSimone, "A Boost for Business," *The Orlando Sentinel* (October 31, 1994), p. 8; A. Millican, "Want New Industry? House It," *The Orlando Sentinel* (October 7, 1994), p. 1.

48. "How Can Central Florida Position Itself to Benefit from the Merger of Martin Marietta and Lockheed?" *The Orlando Sentinel* (September 5, 1994), p. 4.

49. T. A. Hemphill, "Strange Bedfellows Cozy Up for a Clean Environment," *Business and Society Review* (Summer 1990), pp. 38– 45.

50. A. VanBuren, "Shareholders Seek to Color the Corporate World Green," *Business and Society Review* (Summer 1994), pp. 45–47.

51. J. J. Davis, "A Blueprint for Green Marketing," *The Journal of Business Strategy* (July/August 1991), pp. 14–17; J. S. Scerbinski, "Consumers and the Environment: A Focus on Five Products," *The Journal of Business Strategy* (September/October 1991), pp. 44–47; Z. Schiller, "At Rubbermaid, Little Things Mean a Lot," *Business Week* (November 11, 1991), p. 126.

52. T. L. O'Brien, "Aided by Computers, Many of the Disabled Form Own Businesses," *The Wall Street Journal* (October 8, 1993), pp. A1, A9.

53. M. J. Ybarra, "Janitors' Union Uses Pressure and Theatrics to Expand Its Ranks," *The Wall Street Journal* (March 21, 1994), pp. A1–A8.

54. "Business and Finance," *The Wall Street Journal* (March 9, 1996), p. A1.

55. "Competitiveness: 23 Leaders Speak Out," *Harvard Business Review* (July/August 1987), pp. 116–117.

56. A. Bernstein, "Why America Needs Unions But Not the Kind It Has Now," *Business Week* (May 23, 1994), pp. 70–82.

57. Bernstein, "Why America Needs Unions," p. 71.

58. Bernstein, "Why America Needs Unions," p. 82.

2

Organizational Analysis and Strategic Direction

4

The Internal Environment and Competitive Advantage

High Pay *and* High Profits Achieved Simultaneously at Lincoln Electric

Lincoln Electric Company is the largest manufacturer of arc-welding products in the world. In the United States alone, market share is estimated at 40%. In addition, Lincoln employees are, by the company's own report, twice as productive as employees in similar manufacturing operations.

They are also paid twice as much, due to a year-end bonus that is approximately equal to base salary.

How does Lincoln do it? Most experts agree that the key to Lincoln's success is the way employees are managed. According to George Willis, CEO, "Employees are our most valuable asset. They must feel secure, important, challenged, in control of their destiny, confident in their leadership, be responsive to common goals, believe they are being treated fairly, have easy access to authority and open lines of communication in all possible directions."

Lincoln is known for innovative personnel policies. Early in this century, James F. Lincoln, brother of the founder, asked employees to elect representatives to an "Advisory Board" to advise the CEO on company operations. An employee's association was formed in 1919 to provide health benefits and social activities. Other early innovations included a reduction in working hours from 55 to 50, a stock purchase plan, and paid vacations. A suggestion system was begun in 1929. Employee suggestions for process improvements have contributed to steadily increasing pro-

ductivity levels at Lincoln ever since that time. Also, Lincoln guarantees its employees continuous employment. Worker turnover is almost nonexistent.

Employees are not, however, provided with lush working conditions. One of Lincoln's plants was described as a "cavernous, dimly lit factory" that looks a lot like a big-city YMCA. Most employees are not provided with base salaries either. To the extent possible, Lincoln has translated all of its work processes into piece rates. The piece rate system, combined with year-end bonuses based on quality, dependability, output, and ideas and cooperation, provide substantial motivation to work hard and improve the manufacturing process.[1]

The humans that comprise an organization are its lifeblood—its most unique and valuable asset. Most of the other factors of production, such as properties, machinery, and even special knowledge, can be duplicated over the long term, but every human being is totally unique. Lincoln has been able to tap the capacity of its human resources in ways that its competitors have not been able to duplicate. This ability has led to a sustainable competitive advantage.

This chapter is about the organization: the internal stakeholders, the resources, and how management of internal stakeholders and resources can result in higher performance. The first section describes key stakeholders inside the organization, their roles in organizations, and how their values influence strategic thinking and leadership. The second section provides guidance in identifying, creating, and managing internal resources to develop competitive advantages leading to high performance.

INTERNAL STAKEHOLDERS AS COMPETITIVE RESOURCES

Internal stakeholders include managers, employees, and owners, including the boards of directors that usually represent them. One of the most significant internal stakeholders is the chief executive officer (CEO). Most of the research evidence indicates that CEOs have a significant impact on the strategies and performance of their organizations.[2] Certainly, a CEO like Michael D. Eisner at Disney or Andy Grove at Intel can leave little doubt that much of the success of an organization is dependent on the person at the top.

The Chief Executive and Organization Managers

Chief Executive Officer
Highest ranking officer in an organization with primary responsibility for setting the firm's strategic direction.

Top Management Team
A group of high-ranking officers within an organization who make the important strategic and operating decisions.

The highest ranking officer in a large organization can be called by a number of titles, but the most common is **chief executive officer**, or CEO. The CEO has primary responsibility for setting the strategic direction of the firm; however, other executives and managers are expected to show leadership qualities and participate in strategic management activities. While the smallest organizations may have a single owner/manager who makes all important strategic and operating decisions, larger organizations are typically led by several high-ranking officers who form the **top management team**. Furthermore, as organizations grow they tend to have more managers and more levels of management. The variety and number of these other managers are as varied as the organizations themselves. Strategic Insight 4.1 provides insights into the personality and role of a highly successful CEO, Linda Wachner of Warnaco.

Organizational executives and managers play a variety of roles both inside and outside of their organizations. Based on in-depth observations of managers at work, Henry Mintzberg concluded that these roles include figurehead, spokesperson, leader, resource allocator, monitor, liaison, disseminator, disturbance handler, entrepreneur, and negotiator.[3] Most of these roles deal specifically with managing stakeholders. Indeed, the CEO is the primary stakeholder manager in most organizations. The ten roles identified by Mintzberg can be further grouped as interpersonal, informational, and decisional (see Table 4.1).

Individual Ethics and Decision Making. One important way in which executives and managers influence an organization is through the values that they bring to their work activities and organizational roles. Ethics were described in Chapter 1 as values that influence decisions. One way ethics guide decisions is by helping decision makers decide which stimuli are important. For example, ethics may

STRATEGIC INSIGHT 4.1

BUSINESS

STRATEGY

America's Most Successful Businesswomen

"Good morning. What do we have for me to look at today?" Linda Joy Wachner, the chief executive of Warnaco, breezes through the small "stitch room" on the twelfth floor of her headquarters at 90 Park Avenue in Manhattan. Her question is directed at the eight seamstresses who are bent over their sewing machines, busily turning out samples of the bras, panties, and other lingerie that Warnaco will eventually manufacture in its factories and sell to department and specialty stores.

Even though she strides through the room nearly every day snatching up pieces of whatever fabric, lace, or trim the women happen to have on their tables, some of the seamstresses seem awed at the presence of their boss. One, enjoying a homemade lunch, nearly drops a chicken leg into her lap as Wachner sails by with her gaze riveted on a leopard-print bra and panties across the room. "These are to die for," Wachner declares as she holds up the garments with a supremely satisfied smile. "Beautiful, just beautiful."

Linda Wachner is among America's most successful businesswomen. At fifty, she is at the forefront of a new generation of women in the upper echelons of American management. Part mogul and part Jewish mother, Wachner has injected a once sleepy apparel maker with energy, focus, financial discipline, and fashion flair. Since she took over Warnaco in a hostile leveraged buyout in 1986, Wachner has cut debt by 40%, pumped up operating cash, and brought the company public.

Wachner has worked her magic in a brutal economic climate that has seen growth in white-collar employment evaporate, pinched consumer spending on apparel to virtually nothing, and bankruptcies for many of her department store customers. Like other managers who prosper in difficult times, Wachner has learned to run her company with a near-fanatical devotion to three guiding principles: Stay close to the customer, keep on top of the business, and watch the till.

Other women are joining Wachner in the top ranks of American corporations. Marion Sandler shares the top job with her husband at Golden West Financial, a *Fortune 500* company. Jill Barad is expected to become the next CEO of Mattel, Brenda Barnes is president and CEO of Pepsi-Cola North America, Bridget Macaskill is president and CEO of Oppenheimer Funds, and Sherry Lansing is chairman of Paramount's Motion Pictures Group.

Sources: Adapted from S. Caminiti, "America's Most Successful Businesswoman," *Fortune* (June 15, 1992), p. 102; P. Sellers, "Women, Sex and Power," *Fortune* (August 5, 1996), pp. 42–61. Used with permission.

influence whether a manager perceives the need to make a decision. What one manager considers a problem worthy of attention, because of moral implications or the potential effect on stakeholders, may not be very important to other managers. For instance, McDonnell Douglas recently tested to see if 410 passengers could safely evacuate from its MD-11 jetliner in ninety seconds. In a morning test, 28 people were injured, 18 of whom were hospitalized. Many managers would have perceived the need to step in with decisive action at this point. However, during the afternoon of the same day, the test was repeated with new volunteers, none

Table 4.1 Ten Roles of the CEO

Interpersonal

Figurehead—legal and symbolic leader
Leader—motivates and directs subordinates
Liaison—sits at the center of a network of contacts

Informational

Monitor—collects strategically relevant information
Spokesperson—communicates with external stakeholders
Disseminator—communicates with internal stakeholders

Decisional

Entrepreneuer—makes decisions concerning innovations
Disturbance handler—resolves crises
Resource allocator—provides adequate resources to key areas
Negotiator—forms agreements with stakeholders

Source: Based on H. Mintzberg, *The Nature of Managerial Work* (New York: Harper and Row, 1973).

of whom were informed of the earlier injuries. This evacuation resulted in 22 injured, with 14 sent to the hospital. One sixty-year-old woman was paralyzed from the neck down as a result of her injury.[4]

The McDonnell Douglas example also illustrates another important point: A decision to ignore stimuli or not change a previous decision when new stimuli emerge is still a decision. A value system can also influence the way a problem is defined. In the preceding example, a manager could consider the problem to be primarily financial and therefore define the problem as one of creating legal liabilities. This definition could result in use of a cost–benefit financial analysis before future tests are conducted. On the other hand, another manager may see the problem as a breach of the organization's responsibility to one of its stakeholder groups, the people who volunteer for tests. As in the need step, ethics can also provide a filter for stimuli flowing from various stakeholders, helping a manager determine which items of information are worth considering.

In addition, ethics provide a basis for determining which alternatives to select and how they are to be selected, which alternative is ultimately selected, and how the decision will be communicated and to whom. The personal values of a manager have a significant impact on the decisions that are made. However, if a manager is also responsive to the values of key stakeholders when making and communicating decisions, the decisions are more likely to be perceived as ethical by those stakeholders.

Strategic Leadership. Although most managers are effective at their various tasks and roles, the most difficult responsibility of executives, particularly the CEO, is to exercise strategic leadership. The traditional view of leaders in organizations is that they set direction, make the important decisions, and rally the followers (usually employees). According to Peter Senge, this traditional view is particularly common in the West where leaders are often equated with heroes.[5] Our great leaders, our heroes, are the extraordinary men and women who take charge during times of crisis. There are many examples of visionary decision makers throughout political and business history. Lee Iaccoca of Chrysler, Steven Jobs, the founding CEO of Apple Computer, and Ross Perot of Electronic Data Systems are just a few

STRATEGIC INSIGHT 4.2

BUSINESS

STRATEGY

Sam Walton: A Visionary Leader

Many CEOs have been described as visionaries. They have a vision of what the organization should become and they communicate that vision to other managers and employees. They *make* their vision a reality. Often described as charismatic and dynamic, their enthusiasm (or lack of it) can be contagious. Sam Walton, founder of Wal-Mart, was such an individual.

Right up until his death, Sam Walton would fly his plane across the country visiting existing Wal-Mart stores, attending store openings, and instilling in employees the value of customer service. There were only a handful of his hundreds of stores that he never had the time to visit. His visits included greeting customers and asking them, "Ladies, are they treatin' you right? Do they look you in the eye and ask if they can help?" Actions like this communicate a sense of vision of what Wal-Mart is all about. And what a vision! Thirty years ago Sam Walton desired to make his retail chain the biggest and best in the country. Even when Sam discovered he was losing a battle with bone cancer, he did not slow down. He was not about to "kick back, congratulate himself, and let some sly devil like that Dayton Hudson discount chain, Target, sneak up behind him." Sam Walton's vision will live forever in the hearts of the associates who knew him.

Visionary leadership can be divided into three stages: (1) envisioning what the organization should be like in the future, (2) communicating this vision to followers, and (3) empowering these followers to enact the vision. Sam Walton developed a vision of making Wal-Mart the biggest and best retailer in the country, then he tirelessly communicated this vision in word and deed to managers and associates. He also gave them the power to fulfill the vision by providing them with detailed computer analyses on a store-by-store and department-by-department basis and developing the most efficient distribution system in the industry. In short, Sam Walton was a model visionary leader.

Sources: J. Huey, "America's Most Successful Merchant," *Fortune* (September 23, 1991), pp. 46–59; F. Westley and H. Mintzberg, "Visionary Leadership and Strategic Management," *Strategic Management Journal* 10 (1989), pp. 17–18.

of the CEOs who are widely viewed as charismatic and visionary leaders. Strategic Insight 4.2 describes the visionary leadership style of Sam Walton, founder of Wal-Mart. It is common for organizations to incorporate stories about their great leaders in the myths and rituals that form the organizational culture.[6]

Bill Gates of Microsoft, the largest software company in the world, is described as a charismatic leader. Gates is the chairman of Microsoft and the richest man in America. As a hands-on manager who is involved in every detail of the business, Gates inspires fear and respect among employees, competitors, and customers.

> *Employees speak knowingly of "Bill meetings," which sound only slightly better than the Spanish Inquisition. He challenges, he makes judgments, he finds flaws. Employees have been known to crib for weeks, even holding practice, for one 60-minute session with Gates. "These meetings work," says software developer Neil Konzo. "He focuses in on the negative. He beats the living hell out of you. At the end he says: 'Hey, you're doing good.' "*[7]

Table 4.2 *Four Responsibilities of Leadership*

1. Design organizational purpose, vision, and core values.
2. Develop policies, strategies, and structure.
3. Create an environment for organizational learning.
4. Serve as a steward for the organization.

Sources: P. Senge, "The Leader's New Work: Building Learning Organizations," *Sloan Management Review* 32(1) (Fall 1990), pp. 7–24; L. J. Bourgeois, "Strategic Implementation: Five Approaches to an Elusive Phenomenon," *Strategic Management Journal* 4 (1984), pp. 241–264.

In the traditional model of leadership, the CEO decides where to go and then, through a combination of persuasion and edict, directs others in the process of implementation.[8] For many organizational scholars, the traditional view of the CEO and upper management as brilliant, charismatic leaders with employees who are "good soldiers" is no longer valid in many organization settings. Turbulent global competitive environments and multibusiness organizations are far too complex for one person to stay on top of all the important issues.

Many organizational scholars believe that the true role of a leader is to harness the creative energy of the individual, so that the organization as a whole learns over time.[9] In this capacity, the leader has four primary responsibilities, which are summarized in Table 4.2. First, the leader must create or design the organization's purpose, vision, and core values. Second, the leader must oversee the creation of policies, strategies, and structure that translate purpose, vision, and core values into business decisions. These first two responsibilities are consistent with what we expect of all of our managers: They establish direction and purpose, and then install the management systems that coordinate decisions and actions.

It is with the third responsibility of leadership that a new role begins to emerge, one that distinguishes it from good management. Rather than directing, the leader should create an environment for organizational learning by serving as a coach, teacher, and facilitator.[10] A learning environment is created by helping organizational members question their assumptions about the business and its environment: what customers want, what competitors are likely to do, which technology choices work best, and how to solve a problem. If learning is to take place, members must understand that the organization is an interdependent network of people and activities. Furthermore, learning requires that members keep their work focused on creating patterns of behavior that are consistent with strategy rather than reacting haphazardly to problems. Leaders play the essential role in creating an environment where employees question assumptions, understand interdependency, see the strategic significance of their actions, and are empowered to lead themselves.[11]

Finally, leaders must serve as stewards for their organizations: They must care about the organization and the society in which it operates. Leaders must feel and convey a passion for the organization, its contribution to society, and its purpose. They should feel that "they are part of changing the way businesses operate, not from a vague philanthropic urge, but from a conviction that their efforts will produce more productive organizations, capable of achieving higher levels of organization success and personal satisfaction than more traditional organizations."[12] This concept is best exemplified with a quote from Stanley Gault, former CEO of Rubbermaid, shortly after he left retirement to take over struggling Goodyear Tire and Rubber Company:

People would say, "Why would you undertake this challenge?" Well, frankly, the decision was 98% emotional because Goodyear is the last major American-owned tire company. . . . Therefore, I decided that I was willing to change my life for three years if there was any way I could lead the charge to rebuild Goodyear." [13]

There are many different ways to lead, depending on the circumstances and the personality of the individual. Bourgeois and Brodwin identified five distinct leadership approaches or styles.[14] The styles differ in the degree to which CEOs involve other managers and lower level employees in the strategy formulation and implementation process. The first two styles correspond to the traditional model of a leader as the director and decision maker; the latter three styles represent more participative styles of leadership.

1. *Commander.* The CEO formulates strategy and then directs top managers to implement it.
2. *Change.* The CEO formulates strategy and then plans the changes in structure, personnel, information systems, and administration required to implement it.
3. *Collaborative.* The CEO initiates a planning session with executive and division managers. After each participant presents ideas, the group discusses and agrees to a strategy. Participants are then responsible for implementing strategy in their areas.
4. *Cultural.* After formulating a vision and strategy for the company, the CEO and other top-level managers mold the organization's culture so that all organizational members make decisions that are consistent with the vision. In this approach, the culture inculcates organizational members into unity of purpose and action.
5. *Crescive.* Under this leadership model, lower level managers are encouraged to formulate and implement their own strategic plans. The CEO's role is to encourage innovation while still filtering out inappropriate programs. Unlike the other models, the Crescive model of leadership makes use of the creative energies of all members of the organization, which is consistent with the philosophy of total quality management that is influencing American industry.

Not only do different executives have different leadership styles; they also have varying capabilities and experiences that prepare them for different strategic environments. While managers are capable of adapting to changing environments and strategies, it is not likely that they are equally effective in all situations. A manager who is part of the turbulent growth years of a start-up company may have serious difficulty adjusting to the inevitable slowdown in growth. Steven Jobs, one of the highly successful founders of Apple Computer, had difficulty adjusting to the increasingly large and complex Apple Computer company that his success had created. He hired John Sculley, a former PepsiCo executive, to bring professional management techniques to Apple. Jobs' management style was incompatible with that of Sculley, and eventually Jobs was forced out of the organization he had created. On the other hand, the young founder of Microsoft, Bill Gates, has successfully managed Microsoft through its early start-up years to its current position as the largest computer software company in the world.

The debate continues regarding whether it is appropriate to match the manager to the strategy.[15] Some research suggests that low-cost strategies are best implemented by managers with production/operations backgrounds because of the internal focus on efficiency and engineering. The research also suggests that differentiation strategies need to be managed by marketing and R&D-trained executives because of the innovation and market awareness that are needed.[16] There is also some tentative evidence that strategic change or innovation in organizations is more likely to occur with managers that are younger (both in age and in time in the organization) but well educated.[17] Growth strategies may be best implemented by managers with greater sales and marketing experience, willingness to take risks, and tolerance for ambiguity. However, those same characteristics may be undesirable in an executive managing the activities of a retrenchment strategy.[18]

When radical restructuring is required, an outsider may be needed:

> *Obviously, the person who helped create the mess won't easily take to the idea of selling off cherished assets, shuttering plants, or throwing thousands of people out into the streets. "In many cases, the emotional ties of the career CEO are just too strong," says Ferdinand Nadherny, vice-chairman of Russell Reynolds Associates, the nation's largest executive-recruiting firm. "The guy would be firing close friends."*[19]

Owners

Sole Proprietorship
Business run by a single owner/manager who is personally responsible for its activities, debts, liabilities, taxes, and profits.

Partnership
Two or more owners share management and responsibility for the activities and liabilities of an organization.

The simplest owner structure is that of the owner/manager. In this form, the owner is the top manager and the business is run as a **sole proprietorship**. This means that the owner/manager is personally responsible for any taxes, debts, or other liabilities incurred by the organization and also has total control over its actions. **Partnerships** are similar to sole proprietorships, except that liabilities and sometimes operating responsibilities are shared among several parties, which may include individuals or other organizations. Organizations or individuals may form partnerships exclusively to develop new technologies or enter new markets.

Most larger companies, and smaller companies that need funds for growth, issue stock. Therefore, their owners are the shareholders. If all of the stock is owned by a few individuals, often within the same family, the company is referred to as closely held or private. The financial liability of stockholders is limited to their investments in the company; however, their control over the actions of the company is also limited. Subchapter-S corporations and limited partnerships provide a middle ground between publicly owned corporations and sole proprietorships in both liability and control.

Shareholders are primarily interested in receiving a steady and increasing stream of financial returns. Shares of stock have value because shareholders expect that, at some future point in time, they will receive dividends. However, many fast growing or highly profitable organizations decide to reinvest most of their cash flow instead of paying dividends. Consequently, the value of many stocks is dependent more on expectations of future dividends than current payments. If a company does not pay high dividends but the stock increases in value, shareholders can receive the increase in value by selling their stock. Managers have a fiduciary duty to direct the organization in such a way that shareholders' financial returns are as high as they can be, given other constraints such as laws, regulations, and formal and informal contracts.

Many organizations have developed policies concerning the way they should manage shareholder interests. For example, the Bristol-Myers Squibb pledge contains the statement: "We pledge a companywide dedication to continued profitable growth, sustained by strong finances, a high level of research and development, and facilities second to none."[20]

The interests of shareholders are protected by a board of directors, which is elected by the voting shareholders. In most corporations, each share of common stock has one vote in these elections. The board of directors is responsible for hiring, firing, supervising, advising, and compensating top managers within the firm.

Boards typically also reserve the right to reject major strategic decisions such as the development of a new line of business, mergers, acquisitions, or entrance into foreign markets.

We discuss now the two major and interrelated issues of strategic importance concerning ownership in a publicly held corporation. The first deals with the conflicts of interest that sometimes emerge between owners and managers of the firm. The second major issue deals with the relationship between the composition and behavior of the board of directors and organizational performance.

Conflicts of Interest and Agency Problems. In sole proprietorships, the owner and top manager are the same individual. Therefore, no owner/manager conflicts of interest exist. This is also the case in privately held companies in which the owners have direct control over their firms. However, as soon as ownership and management are separated, the potential for conflicts of interest exists. In this case, top managers become **agents** for the owners of the firm—they have a fiduciary duty to act in the owners' best interests.

> **Agents**
> Individuals with a fiduciary duty to act in the best interests of other groups or individuals; for example, managers are agents when ownership and management responsibilities are separated.

Theoretically, in the publicly held corporation, both shareholders and managers have an interest in maximizing organizational profits. Shareholders want maximum organizational profits so that they can receive high returns from dividends and stock appreciation. Managers should also be interested in high profits to the extent that their own rewards, such as salary and bonuses, are dependent on profitability. However, top managers, as human beings, may attempt to maximize their own self-interests at the expense of shareholders. This is called an **agency problem**. Entrenchment occurs when "managers gain so much power that they are able to use the firm to further their own interests rather than the interests of shareholders."[21] Agency problems often arise because of the way executives are compensated. For example, an executive who is compensated according to year-end profitability may use his or her power to maximize year-end profits at the expense of long-range investments in research and development or of capital improvements. An in-depth discussion of agency problems, their consequences, and ways to avoid them is offered at the end of this chapter in the Appendix.

> **Agency Problem**
> Occurs when managers maximize their own self-interests at the expense of shareholders.

The fiduciary responsibility for preventing agency problems lies with boards of directors. Some business experts believe that many boards of directors have not lived up to their fiduciary duties. Boards often are reluctant to reprimand or replaced top managers who were acting against the best interests of shareholders. However, the incidence of shareholder suits against boards of directors has increased.[22] In addition, big investors are putting lots of pressure on board members and directly on CEOs to initiate sweeping organizational changes that will lead to more accountability and higher performance.[23] Many boards have responded to these and other forces by taking a more active role in corporate governance, as the following example demonstrates:

> *Lloyd E. Reuss was replaced by John F. "Jack" Smith as president of General Motors. The replacement was orchestrated by John G. Smale, past CEO of Procter and Gamble and a 10 year veteran of GM's board of directors. Smale, who was dissatisfied with GM's lackluster performance, convinced other board members to elect him to the position of chairman of the executive committee, which is a miniboard comprised of the chairmen of all board committees. This action effectively put him in control of GM. He then named Smith, who was the former chief of GM's successful international operations, as the new president.[24]*

The GM board coup was followed by a wave of similar actions in several large companies, including IBM, Time Warner, American Express, and Westinghouse.[25]

Even Greenpeace, the nonprofit environmental group based in Amsterdam, ousted its chairman, probably as a result of the reduction in contributions and political clout the group has been experiencing (although some Greenpeace officials didn't like his background of not having participated in any "direct action" protests).[26]

The inclusion of several nonemployee individuals (outsiders) on the board can help ensure that shareholder interests are well served. Outsiders were an important factor in the board revolt at GM. In fact, research indicates that the percentage of outsiders on the board of directors is increasing.[27] However, inclusion of outsiders may not be a potent force in reducing agency problems if external board members are personal friends of the CEO or other top managers. These types of relationships limit the objectivity of outsiders.

Board Membership and Organizational Performance. The previous discussion demonstrated the importance of boards of directors in governing the behavior of top managers. However, boards can also play other important strategic roles. For example, **interlocking directorates** can lead to important strategic alliances. Interlocking directorates occur when the CEO of one company sits on the board of another company. As mentioned previously, this is a common practice in many countries, especially Japan (e.g., keiretsu). It is typically illegal in America to have the CEO of a direct competitor on the board (e.g., Coke and Pepsi), but firms do often include suppliers or customers. Linkages such as these can facilitate contract negotiations and the transfer of information and technology, although they may also lead to some of the conflicts of interest discussed previously in this chapter. In some cases, strategic alliances can even create barriers that make it hard for new firms to compete.

Boards can also provide guidance to top managers and participate in decisions. Two recent studies discovered higher performance in companies with boards that participated more actively in organizational decisions, compared to companies with "caretaker" boards.[28] Boards need sufficient power to both monitor and discipline CEOs. Vigilant boards are the best defense against executive entrenchment.[29]

To gain maximum benefits from board participation, it is important to include both internal and external stakeholders on the board.[30] Internal stakeholders provide stability and enhanced understanding of internal operations. External stakeholders bring a breadth of knowledge and a fresh point of view to the challenges that face an organization. For example, inclusion of labor union representatives on boards can help firms avoid decisions that are likely to be blocked by the union. By including environmentalists, firms can enhance their social image and decrease the likelihood that something that is proposed will be resisted due to potential damage to the environment. Some corporations appoint retired government officials, such as generals or presidential cabinet members, to their boards. The knowledge and contacts of these retirees can facilitate government contracting.

Of course, outside directors can be expensive. Furthermore, the increasing incidence of legal suits against directors has led many companies to provide liability insurance to members of their boards. Salaries, insurance, perks, and other expenses associated with boards of directors are some of the **agency costs** corporations pay to ensure that managers act in the best interests of shareholders.

Nonprofit organizations are typically directed by a board of trustees and/or a board of directors that performs many of the same functions performed by the board of directors in a for-profit corporation. The principal difference in responsibility between the director of a for-profit and nonprofit organization is that the director of a nonprofit organization must ensure that the firm uses revenues from

---

Interlocking Directorates
Occur when the CEO of one company sits on the board of another company.

Agency Costs
Costs such as salaries, insurance, perks, and other expenses associated with boards of directors that corporations pay to ensure that managers act in the best interests of shareholders.

both internal operations and external donations in such a manner that the tax-exempt status granted by the Internal Revenue Service is maintained. Part of this role means that directors must make sure that the organization is pursuing its philanthropic mission.

There are no owners, stocks, or shareholders of a nonprofit organization. However, agency problems do exist. For example, the CEO of the national organization of the United Way recently came under attack for his luxurious lifestyle, which was made possible by a high salary and perquisites or "perks." Scandals like this happen in both the for-profit and nonprofit sector; however, in the nonprofit sector they seem particularly offensive because donors give freely of their funds to support causes they think are worthy of support. A strong, active, and probing board of a nonprofit organization can have the same effect as the board of a for-profit organization in reducing agency problems.

In summary, boards of both for-profit and nonprofit organizations play a critical role in supervising managerial actions and decisions and in looking out for the interests of the owners and other stakeholders. Another important internal stakeholder is employees.

Employees and Human Resource Management

The strategic importance of employees became evident when the United States lost its competitive edge in several global markets, including consumer electronics and steel. Shortages of qualified workers, especially in the technical areas, are contributing to competitiveness problems.[31] Furthermore, these shortages are expected to intensify. The Council on Competitiveness determined that well-trained employees will be a key to the future competitiveness of U.S. companies, but discovered that training programs in the United States are inadequate.[32] These trends make the effective management of employees critical to strategic success.

Employees and the way they are managed can be important sources of competitive advantage. Because of their importance to competitiveness, employees are being given increasing amounts of managerial attention in the organizational planning of a lot of large organizations. Research has shown that more sophisticated human resource planning, recruitment, and selection strategies are associated with higher labor productivity, especially in capital-intensive organizations.[33] Also, a large-sample study of nearly 1,000 firms indicated that "high-performance work practices" are associated with lower turnover, higher productivity, and higher long- and short-term financial performance.[34] According to a famous management scholar, Jeffrey Pfeffer:

> *Achieving competitive success through people involves fundamentally altering how we think about the work force and the employment relationship. It means achieving success by working with people, not by replacing them or limiting the scope of their activities. It entails seeing the work force as a source of strategic advantage, not just as a cost to be minimized or avoided. Firms that take this different perspective are often able to successfully outmaneuver and outperform their rivals.[35]*

Strategic Insight 4.3 shows how two firms have used human resource management to develop competitive advantages.

Many organizations have established policies that govern the way they manage employees as stakeholders. For example, Johnson & Johnson's credo includes the following passage:

> *We are responsible to our employees, the men and women who work with us throughout the world. Everyone must be considered as an individual. We must*

STRATEGIC INSIGHT 4.3

BUSINESS

STRATEGY

Effective Human Resource Management Leading to Competitive Advantage

At Advanced Micro Devices' submicron development facility, some 70% of the technicians come from older facilities at ADM. In keeping with ADM's emphasis on employment stability, as old facilities were closed, people were evaluated with respect to their basic skills. If accepted, they were put through a seven-month program at Mission College—and then went to work in the new facility. This training not only demonstrated the firm's commitment to its employees, which was then reciprocated, but also ensured that the facility would be staffed with highly qualified people who had been specifically trained for their new jobs.

At a Collins and Aikman carpet plant in Georgia, more than a third of the employees were high school dropouts, and some could neither read nor write. When the firm introduced computers to increase productive efficiency, however, it chose not to replace its existing workforce but to upgrade its skills. After spending about $1,200 per employee on training, including lost job time, the company found that the amount of carpet stitched increased 10%. Moreover, quality problems declined by half. The employees, with more skills and better morale, submitted some 1,230 suggestions, and absenteeism fell by almost half.

The Japanese are well known for their lifetime employment practices, a system that is still very strong. However, the Dutch oil giant, Shell, has a similar practice. According to Ernest Van Mourik Broekman, coordinator of Human Resources and Organization at Shell, "In the first place, our company recruits and develops with the purpose of a full career. We recruit extensively in Europe at universities, and bring people to training programmes and job development programmes until they can be considered to be full professionals in their particular disciplines. The general characteristic is that a strong identification with the company is being pursued, so that people feel that there is a common interest building up between the objectives of the company and their personal aims. And on the whole, people feel that a full career in our company is worthwhile, rather than using it just as a stepping stone towards something else."

Sources: R. Calori and B. Dufour, "Management European Style," *Academy of Management Executive* (August 1995), p. 68; J. Pfeffer, "Producing Sustainable Competitive Advantage Through the Effective Management of People," *Academy of Management Executive* (February 1995), p. 62; used with permission. Information on Japan from E. Fingleton, "Jobs For Life: Why Japan Won't Give Them Up," *Fortune* (March 30, 1995), pp. 120–125.

respect their dignity and recognize their merit. They must have a sense of security in their jobs. Compensation must be fair and adequate, and working conditions clean, orderly and safe. Employees must feel free to make suggestions and complaints. There must be equal opportunity for employment, development and advancement for those qualified. We must provide competent management, and their actions must be just and ethical.[36]

Effective stakeholder management of employees virtually always includes getting them involved in organizational improvements. For example, Dow Chemical Company discovered that employee suggestions and involvement were the key to high quality in one of their large aspirin facilities.[37] Employee empowerment, which is often associated with total quality management (TQM), is also an important trend. The following excerpts came from a recent annual report of Union Pacific Corporation:

> *The people in our empowerment programs are deliberately encouraged to take their work in their own hands—to become their own bosses—and they are taking to the process with terrific enthusiasm. Under empowerment, managers manage the people—but people manage the work. It's the only way that American industry and Union Pacific are going to stay ahead of the mounting competition of the Nineties.*
>
> *Empowerment, of course, is not an end in itself. It is a means to achieve the highest quality work and the greatest customer satisfaction.*[38]

Employee stock ownership plans (ESOPs) are also becoming increasingly popular.[39] ESOPs merge the interests of employees with the interests of other shareholders. Because employees become owners, they are motivated to enhance shareholder welfare. Performance-based compensation schemes can accomplish some of the same results.[40]

Human resource management becomes difficult and complex when an organization operates in more than one country. Figure 4.1 is an illustration of the wide differences that exist from country to country regarding assumptions about manager/subordinate relationships. In countries such as the United States, Sweden, the Netherlands, and Denmark, managers are typically not expected to have precise answers to subordinates' questions. In France, Italy, Indonesia, and Japan, most employees expect managers to be able to deal with most of their questions in a precise manner. Other global differences among employees are described in Strategic Insight 4.4.

Organizational Culture. An organization's culture, the system of shared values of its members, is another important component of the organization and may be thought of as an intangible resource. Organization culture often reflects the values and leadership styles of the executives and managers, and is, to a great degree, a result of the past human resource management practices, such as recruitment, training, and rewards.

An organization's culture can be its greatest strength or its greatest weakness. Some organizations have succeeded in creating cultures that are completely consistent with what the organization is trying to accomplish—high-performance cultures. At Nucor, the mini-mill steel company, the stated commitment to a low-cost strategy is supported by a culture that expects efficiency and tight fiscal policy. At Johnson & Johnson, the company's commitment to customers as its primary stakeholder is reflected in policy statements and adopted by employees. Strategic Application 4.1 provides direction in how to identify the essential elements of an organization's culture.

Many organizations are realizing the benefits of a shared set of values as a potential source of competitive advantage. Stakeholders look for an intangible quality when making decisions about the products and services that they purchase or when selecting alliance partners. They want to be able to *rely* on the company. They want promises and commitments to be fulfilled. There are many pragmatic benefits to a high-profile organizational culture, which can help an organization in its recruiting, employee development, and relationships with customers.[41] To achieve the benefits, shown in Table 4.3, an organization must take proactive steps to create and sustain a culture that meets the needs of the organization's strategies and creates commitment to organizational goals and values.

Figure 4.1 *Cross-Cultural Human Resource Differences*

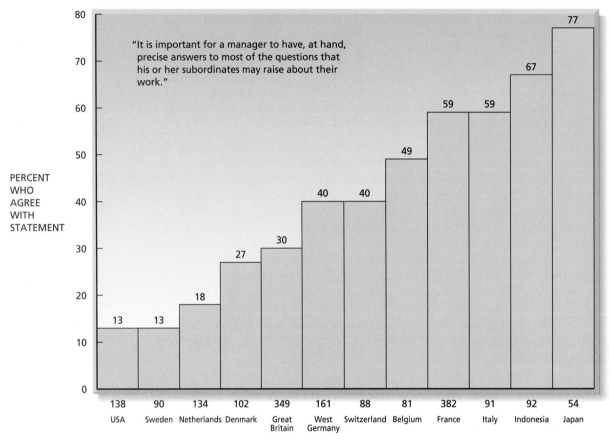

"It is important for a manager to have, at hand, precise answers to most of the questions that his or her subordinates may raise about their work."

PERCENT WHO AGREE WITH STATEMENT

138	90	134	102	349	161	88	81	382	91	92	54
USA	Sweden	Netherlands	Denmark	Great Britain	West Germany	Switzerland	Belgium	France	Italy	Indonesia	Japan

NUMBER OF RESPONDENTS AND COUNTRY

Source: A. Laurent, "The Cross-Cultural Puzzle of International Human Resource Management," *Human Resource Management* 25 (1986), p. 94, Copyright © 1986 by John Wiley & Sons, Inc. Reprinted by permission of John Wiley & Sons, Inc.

Nevertheless, a strong culture can be a two-edged sword. Sometimes very successful corporations so firmly attach themselves to their successful business practices that they exaggerate the features of the successful culture and strategy and fail to adapt them to changing industry conditions. Four very common organization orientations associated with excellent performance can lead to four extreme orientations that can lead to poor performance:

1. *Craftsmen*. In craftsmen organizations, employees are passionate about quality. Quality is the primary driver of the corporate culture and a source of organizational pride. However, a culture that is focused on quality and detail can evolve to an extreme where craftsmen become *tinkerers*. Obscure technical details and obsessive engineering perfection result in products that are overengineered and overpriced. Another version of the obsessive concern for quality is the passion for low costs that can paralyze an organization's ability to make timely, necessary investments.

STRATEGIC INSIGHT 4.4

Analyzing Geographically Diverse Employees

It is a mistake to lump all European countries together, all Asian countries in another block, and all African or Middle Eastern countries in their respective groups. In fact, the difference between Indonesia and Korea is greater than that between Japan and the United States.

The Danish culture is closer to the Indonesian culture than to the Swedish culture in terms of the mindscape characteristics. Let us take one aspect of the Danish culture as an example. In the Danish culture, the main purpose of interpersonal communication is to maintain a familiar atmosphere and convey affection. A small group of friends will often sit together in the same cafe, eating the same pastry week after week, telling the same or similar gossip. Subtle variations are considered interesting. For example, everyone knows that Mr. X ties his left shoe first, then his right shoe. One day he reverses the sequential order. This becomes big news. Less subtle information is avoided because it may disturb the familiar atmosphere. It is impolite to explain things, because such an act assumes that someone is ignorant. It is also impolite to ask questions on anything beyond immediate personal concern, because the respondent may not know the answer. It is often considered aggressive to introduce new ideas. A foreign businessperson eager to discuss anything outside the immediate business needs is likely to be met with a strong silent resistance.

In contrast, in Sweden, the purpose of daily interpersonal communication is transmission of new information or frank feelings. One prefers to be silent unless he or she can convey an important message, while in Denmark one must keep talking. While Danes are affect oriented, Swedes are performance oriented.

As this example demonstrates, your friendly behavior of asking questions or explaining things may have a negative effect in some cultures, and you may not know why it does not work. Unfortunately, Americans are seldom trained regarding foreign cultures and languages, though there are exceptions such as Teradyne of Boston.

Some Korean firms have very thorough training programs. An example is the use of "culture houses." An employee who will be sent to Germany, for example, is put in a "German house" where he is confined until he is able to eat, live, and sleep like a German.

Source: Excerpted and adapted from M. Maruyama, "Changing Dimensions in International Business," *Academy of Management Executive* (August 1992), pp. 88–96. Used with permission.

2. *Builders*. In builder organizations, growth is the primary goal. Managers are rewarded for taking risks that result in growth, new acquisitions, and new market niches. When efforts to grow and expand become careless, builders become *imperialists* with high debt, too many unrelated businesses, and neglected core businesses.

3. *Pioneers*. Pioneers build their businesses through leadership positions in new product and new technology development. The strengths of these organizations lie in their design teams and flexible structures which promote idea shar-

STRATEGIC APPLICATION 4.1

CONDUCTING A CULTURAL AUDIT

An organization's culture may be profiled using the dimensions listed in the following table. When auditing an organization's culture as part of the strategy implementation process, ask the following questions:

1. Which characteristics of the culture support the planned strategy and should be sustained in the future?
2. Which characteristics of the culture do not support the planned strategy and should be modified?
3. What efforts will be required to make the changes happen?

Dimensions	Description
Attitude toward customers	Respect vs. indifference
Attitude toward competitors	Compliance vs. cooperation vs. competitiveness
Achievement orientation	Industry leader or follower
Risk tolerance	Degree to which individuals are encouraged to take risks
Conflict tolerance	Degree to which individuals are encouraged to express differences
Individual autonomy	The independence and responsibility allowed individuals in decision making

Dimensions	Description
Employee relations	Cooperative vs. adversarial relationships among employees
Management relations	Cooperative vs. adversarial relationships between managers and employees
Goal identification	Identification with goals and concerns of organization as a whole vs. identification with work group or department
Management support	Cooperative vs. adversarial relationships between managers and employees
Peer identification	Identification with goals and concerns of organization as a whole vs. identification with work group or department
Perceived equity	Perceived relationship between performance and rewards
Decision-making style	Rational, structured vs. creative, intuitive
Work ethic	Diligent, high performance vs. compromising, average performance
Moral integrity	Degree to which employees are expected to be truthful in all dealings

Sources: Adapted from P. McDonald and J. Gandz, "Getting Value from Shared Values," *Organization Dynamics* (Winter 1992), p. 68; E. H. Schein, *Organization Culture and Leadership* (San Francisco: Jossey-Bass, 1985).

ing. Pioneers begin to decline when they evolve into *escapists* who invent impractical products and pursue technologies with limited customer value.

4. *Salesmen.* Salesmen are excellent marketers who create successful brand names and distribution channels, and pursue aggressive advertising and innovative packaging. They become so confident in their marketing abilities that they ignore product capability and quality, and begin to market imitative, low-quality products that customers do not value. They evolve into *drifters.*[42]

In all of the orientations described here, the organization becomes too focused on its own capabilities and loses sight of its customers and evolving industry conditions. One stakeholder group becomes too dominant at the expense of others and is resistant to change. Several contributing factors can drive a successful organization to an unsuccessful extreme. First, leadership may become overconfident as a

Table 4.3 *Benefits of Effective Values Management*

Consistent values will attract the kind of people who genuinely want to work for the company, and mutually held values create the trust necessary for flexibility and effectiveness.

Trust, created by common values, allows efficient delegation. People will work independently toward commonly held goals.

People work harder to fulfill values they believe in, thus enhancing personal motivation and enterprise productivity.

People who share common values will help each other, generating teamwork and adding value through shared solutions.

Creative people can work efficiently on their own toward commonly held goals and can share the long time horizons needed for innovative success.

Common values create group identity, improve morale, and eliminate the need for more detailed controls.

High-morale organizations will band together, work intensively for short spurts to solve critical problems, and protect group secrets.

People at distant points in the organization can be trusted to use their intuition to solve unique problems in ways consistent with organization purposes.

Value-activated people will consciously seek new opportunities to fulfill these values and will not waste time on those that do not.

Commonly held values tend to minimize squabbles, decrease internal frictions, and reduce time needed to manage them.

Source: Used by permission of The Free Press, a Division of Simon & Schuster, Inc. From *Intelligent Enterprise: A Knowledge and Service Based Paradigm for Industry* by James Brian Quinn. Copyright © 1992, James Brian Quinn, p. 318.

result of past successes and think that what has worked in the past will continue to work in the future. Second, one department may become overly dominant, attracting the best managerial talent and exercising unbalanced influence over the decisions made within other departments. Third, the dominant managers and departments may keep the organization focused on strategies and policies that may no longer be relevant. An acknowledgment that change is needed would erode their base of power and influence. Finally, the successful strategies of the past may have become embedded in the routine policies and procedures of the organization. Those policies and procedures create an air of continuity that is very resistant to change.[43]

This concludes our introduction to internal stakeholders and their roles and responsibilities. Strengths and weaknesses can arise from any of the internal stakeholders or in the way they are managed. Strategic Application 4.2 contains questions about internal stakeholders that can assist managers (or students) in identifying organizational strengths and weaknesses. The next section explores other organizational resources that likewise can be a source of strength or weakness.

INTERNAL RESOURCES AND COMPETITIVE ADVANTAGE

The resources and capabilities that lead to a competitive advantage are different in each industry and can also change over time. For example, researchers discovered that high-performing film studios during the period from 1936 to 1950 possessed superior property-based resources such as exclusive long-term contracts with stars and theaters. However, during the period from 1951 to 1965 knowledge-based

COMPETITIVE RESOURCES ASSOCIATED WITH INTERNAL STAKEHOLDERS

Answers to the following questions can help an organization assess strengths and weaknesses resulting from key internal stakeholders.

The CEO as a Competitive Resource

Is the background and training of the CEO strong for this type of firm and industry? Does the CEO have global experience?

Is the CEO a visionary? Is he/she able to lead and inspire?

Is the CEO well connected with other important stakeholders or potential stakeholders?

Is his/her style of management the commander, change, collaborative, cultural, or crescive type? How well does this style fit the competitive situation?

Is he/she willing to take risks?

What is the reputation of the CEO among internal and external stakeholders?

Does the CEO have a good track record for making strategic decisions? If there have been mistakes, can you tell why?

Do the CEO's personal values prevent him/her from making decisions that would be beneficial to other stakeholders? Does the CEO ignore any important stakeholders?

What is the CEO's ownership stake in the organization? Is there any evidence of agency problems related to the decisions of the CEO? Is salary tied to performance through stock payments and options? Is salary excessively high?

Other Managers as Competitive Resources

Is the background and training of other managers strong for this type of firm and industry? Do they have global experience?

Do they have good track records for making decisions?

Are they team players?

What is their level of ownership?

Does the organization run efficiently? Are there any functional areas that require attention or are problematic?

Do women and minorities advance to higher level management positions?

Is there a well-qualified successor for the CEO?

Ownership Structure as a Competitive Resource

What is the ownership structure of the organization (i.e., private, publicly held, subsidiary)? Who owns most of the organization or is it widely owned? Does the ownership structure present any problems in the way the firm is managed?

Does the organization have an active or passive board of directors?

Does the CEO chair the board? If so, is this a strength or weakness in the current situation?

Does the board have a broad global scope?

Does the board represent a wealth of experience?

Are there insiders and outsiders on the board?

Are there any representatives from suppliers, creditors, customers, government, labor, competitors (if legal), or special interest groups?

Employees

Are human resource management practices different from those of rival firms? Are the differences, if any, a source of strength or weakness?

Are employees happy with their situations and roles in the organization? How high is turnover?

Are employees well trained? Do they have special skills? Are they cross-trained in various jobs?

Are they socially, racially, and globally diverse? Is diversity important in this company and industry?

Do women and minorities have an opportunity to advance professionally?

Are employees productive? Are they creative? Do they make suggestions for improvements?

resources in the form of production and coordinative talent and budgets were associated with high performance. They attributed these findings to the capabilities needed to deal with increasing uncertainty in the film industry.[44] Their study also demonstrates that organizational resources only result in a competitive advantage if they are uniquely valuable in the external environment. Chapter 1 introduced this concept, and we now continue the discussion.

Uniquely Valuable Resources

Chapter 1 described internal resources and capabilities as falling into four general categories: financial, physical, human, and organizational. In general, capabilities and resources become strengths leading to a competitive advantage if three conditions are met:

1. *Valuable.* They allow the firm to exploit opportunities and/or neutralize threats. For example, Sony has developed the capability to design, manufacture, and sell miniaturized electronics. This capability has value to external stakeholders—namely, customers. Sony has applied this capability to numerous market opportunities such as stereos, tape players, disc players, televisions, and video cameras.
2. *Unique.* If an organization is the only one with a particular capability, then that capability may be the source of competitive advantage. If numerous organizations possess a particular resource or capability, then the situation is described as competitive parity—no company has the advantage. Note that uniqueness does not imply that only one organization possesses a capability or resource— only that few firms do.
3. *Hard to imitate.* Competing firms face a cost disadvantage in imitating a resource or capability. The more difficult or costly a resource or capability is, the more valuable it is in producing a sustainable competitive advantage. In the case of a patent or a trademark, competing firms face an absolute cost disadvantage.[45]

Figure 4.2 demonstrates how resources and capabilities become potential sources of sustainable competitive advantage. For that potential to be realized, the firm must also be organized to take advantage of it. For example, Xerox formed a research laboratory called PARC, which, in the late 1960s and 1970s, developed an amazing assortment of technological innovations, including the personal computer, the "mouse," the laser printer, and Windows-type software. However, the company did not take advantage of many of PARC's innovations because it did not have an organization in place to do so. For instance, poor communications prevented most Xerox managers from knowing what PARC was doing and a highly bureaucratic system mired a lot of the innovations in red tape. On the other hand, companies like Wal-Mart and Disney are masters at exploiting their sources of competitive advantage.[46]

If a resource or capability is valuable, unique, hard to imitate, *and* it can also be applied to more than one business area, it is called a **core competency** or **capability**. For example, General Electric has been able to apply its skill in managing financial assets across a broad range of industries. In addition, Motorola has applied its skills in producing high quality across its diverse product portfolio. Procter & Gamble is known for its excellent marketing.[47] Finally, Circuit City is applying its "value-priced" high-volume retailing capability to used cars through its CarMax outlets.[48] The most successful companies pay critical attention to developing and applying their core competencies.

Core Competency (or Core Capability)
A resource or capability that is valuable, unique, hard to imitate, and can be applied to more than one business area.

Figure 4.2 *Organizational Resources and Capabilities Leading to Compeitive Advantage*

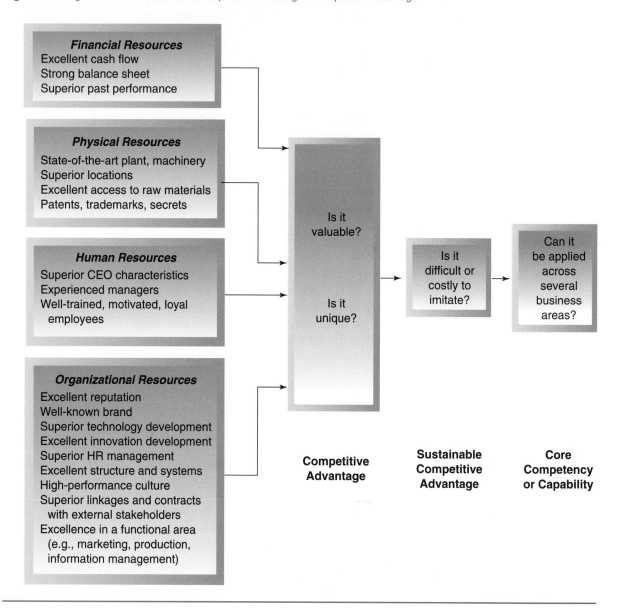

Most of the resources and capabilities that have been described are tangible. They can be seen, touched, and/or quantified.[49] However, some of the most important resources are hard to quantify. These include good relationships with external stakeholders, organizational reputation, a high-performance learning culture, and a well-known corporate brand. Often intangible resources and capabilities are the most difficult for competitors to imitate because it is difficult to determine exactly how the source of capability was created. Whereas a new product can be imitated, the processes used over time to hire, develop, retain, and build loyalty and shared values within the workforce are difficult to observe, and even more difficult to imitate. Consequently, intangible resources and capabilities are often the ones most likely to lead to competitive advantage.

John Reed, CEO of Citicorp, would like to turn "Citibank" into "a worldwide consumer brand, establishing it in effect as the Coca-Cola or McDonald's of financial services." What goes with the brand equity that those companies have, and he covets, is the ability to set themselves above the competition, either in the prices they can obtain or quantities sold or both.[50] Disney also takes full advantage of its brand, which is one of its core competencies. According to Michael Eisner, CEO:

> *We are fundamentally an operating company, operating the Disney Brand all over the world, maintaining it, improving it, promoting and advertising it with taste. Our time must be spent insuring that the Brand never slides, that we innovate the Brand, nurture the Brand, experiment and play with it, but never diminish it. Others will try to change it, from outside and from within. We must resist. We are not a fad! The Disney name and products survive fads!*[51]

Financial Resources

Financial resources can also be a source of advantage, although they rarely qualify as "unique" or "difficult to imitate." Nevertheless, strong cash flow, low levels of debt, a strong credit rating, access to low interest capital, and a reputation for creditworthiness are powerful strengths that can serve as a source of strategic flexibility. Firms that are in a strong financial position can be more responsive to new opportunities and new threats, and are under less pressure from stakeholders than competitors that suffer from financial constraints. Financial ratios, such as the ones found in Table 4.4, may be used to determine the financial strength of an organization and its ability to finance new growth strategies.

Financial resources are becoming particularly important in hypercompetitive environments, as described in Chapter 3. Deep financial resources are needed to wage battles in those markets where other forms of advantage are not sustainable for long. Also, the ability to invest in unique, valuable, difficult-to-imitate capabilities is often tied completely to the available financial resources. For example, the ability to build a brand name, to create a new, innovative process, or to compensate fairly and retain a highly creative workforce is dependent on financial resources. Although financial resources may not be unique or difficult to imitate, they provide the leverage for developing those resources elsewhere.

Value-Creating Activities

As described, valuable, unique, and difficult-to-imitate resources and capabilities may provide an organization with a competitive advantage. Another way of thinking about organizational capabilities is to visualize the activities and processes of an organization and determine how they add value to the products and services that the organization provides in the marketplace.

Michael Porter developed a framework, called the value chain, that is a useful in identifying potential sources of competitive advantage.[52] The **value chain** divides organizational processes into distinct activities that create value for the customer. The value-adding activities are a source of strength or competitive advantage if they meet the requirements identified earlier: (1) valuable (or value adding), (2) unique or different, and (3) difficult to imitate.

The primary activities include inbound logistics, operations, outbound logistics, marketing and sales, and service (see Figure 4.3). **Inbound logistics** includes activities associated with acquiring inputs that are used in the product, such as warehousing, materials handling, and inventory control. **Operations** refers to transforming inputs into the final product through activities such as machining,

Value Chain
Distinct organizational processes that create value for the customer.

Inbound Logistics
Activities associated with acquiring inputs used in the product.

Operations
Activities that transform inputs into the final product.

Table 4.4 *Commonly Used Financial Ratios*

Ratio	Calculation	What it Measures
Profitability Ratios		
Gross profit margin	$\dfrac{\text{Sales} - \text{COGS}}{\text{Sales}} \times 100$	Efficiency of operations and product pricing
Net profit margin	$\dfrac{\text{Net profit after tax}}{\text{Sales}} \times 100$	Efficiency after all expenses are considered
Return on assets (ROA)	$\dfrac{\text{Net profit after tax}}{\text{Total assets}} \times 100$	Productivity of assets
Return on equity (ROE)	$\dfrac{\text{Net profit after tax}}{\text{Stockholders' equity}} \times 100$	Earnings power of equity
Liquidity Ratios		
Current ratio	$\dfrac{\text{Current assets}}{\text{Current liabilities}}$	Short-run debt paying ability
Quick ratio	$\dfrac{\text{Current assets} - \text{inventories}}{\text{Current liabilities}}$	Short-term liquidity
Leverage Ratios		
Debt to equity	$\dfrac{\text{Total liabilities}}{\text{Stockholders' equity}}$	Extent to which stockholders' investments are leveraged (common measure of financial risk)
Total debt to total assets (debt ratio)	$\dfrac{\text{Total liabilities}}{\text{Total assets}}$	Percent of assets financed through borrowing (also financial risk measure)
Activity Ratios		
Asset turnover	$\dfrac{\text{Sales}}{\text{Total assets}}$	Efficiency of asset utilization
Inventory turnover	$\dfrac{\text{COGS}}{\text{Average inventory}}$	Management's ability to control investment in inventory
Average collection period	$\dfrac{\text{Receivables} \times 365 \text{ days}}{\text{Annual credit sales}}$	Effectiveness of collection and credit policies
Accounts receivable turnover	$\dfrac{\text{Annual credit sales}}{\text{Receivables}}$	Effectiveness of collection and credit policies

Outbound Logistics
Activities related to storing and physically distributing the product to customers.

Marketing and Sales
Processes through which the customer is induced to and is able to purchase the product.

Service
Activities that enhance or maintain the product's value to the customer.

assembly, molding, testing, and printing. **Outbound logistics** are activities related to storing and physically distributing the final product to customers, such as finished goods warehousing, order processing, and transportation. **Marketing and sales** include processes through which customers can purchase the product and through which they are induced to do so, such as advertising, distribution of catalogs, direct sales, distribution channeling, promotion, and pricing. Finally, **service** refers to providing service to enhance or maintain product value, such as repairing, supplying parts, or installation.

Figure 4.3 *The Value Chain, Including Support Activities*

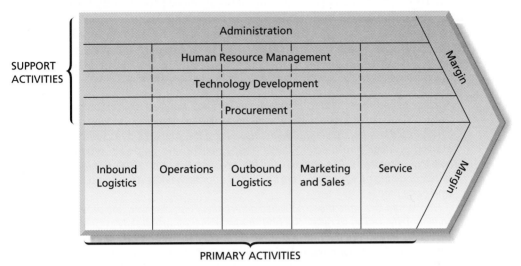

Source: Adapted with permission of The Free Press, a Division of Simon & Schuster, Inc., from *Competitive Advantage: Creating and Sustaining Superior Performance* by Michael E. Porter. Copyright © 1985 by Michael E. Porter, p. 37.

Organizations also engage in activities that support these primary functions. These activities are placed above the primary activities in Figure 4.3 **Procurement** refers to the actual purchase of inputs and not to the inputs themselves or to the way they are handled once they are delivered. All of the primary processes need purchased inputs, many of which are not raw materials. Examples of these inputs include typewriters, accounting firm services, and computers. **Technology development** refers to learning processes, which result in improvements in the way organizational functions are performed.

Human resource management includes human-based activities such as recruiting, hiring, training, and compensation. Finally, **administration** consists of general management activities such as planning and accounting. The dashed lines connecting most of the support activities with the primary activities demonstrate that they can be associated with each of the primary activities and also support the complete chain. Administration is the only exception, because it applies to the complete chain instead of to any one unit. Margin, which is on the right-hand side of Figure 4.3, indicates that firms can achieve higher profit margins through the development of competencies and superior resources based on their value chain activities.

An organization can develop a competitive advantage (1) in any of the primary or support activities *or* (2) in the way they are combined *or* (3) in the way internal activities are linked to the external environment. The cumulative effect of value chain activities and the way they are linked inside the firm and with the external environment determine organizational performance relative to competitors. Each of the three means of creating a value chain-based competitive advantage are discussed next.

An organization can develop a competitive advantage in any of the primary or support activities. For each area, the relevant question is "How much value is produced by this area versus our cost of producing that value?" This analysis of value and costs is then compared with competing firms. For example, one firm

Procurement
The actual purchase of inputs at any stage of the value chain.

Technology Development
Learning processes that result in improvements in the way organizational functions are performed.

Human Resource Management
Human-based activities of the organization such as recruiting, hiring, training, and compensation.

Administration
General management activities of the firm, such as planning and accounting.

may have superior customer service, accompanied by higher service costs, while another firm may have superior manufacturing quality accompanied by higher operations costs. These two firms may actually have products that are similarly valued in the market (as indicated by price and demand).

Competitive advantages can also occur through the manner in which activities are combined inside the firm. According to one expert, the success of Honda in moving from motorcycles into many other businesses is at least partially attributable to superior combinations of value chain activities:

> *Another capability central to Honda's success has been its skill at "product realization." Traditional product development separates planning, proving, and executing into three sequential activities: assessing the market's needs and whether existing products are meeting those needs; testing the proposed product; then building a prototype. The end result of this process is a new factory or organization to introduce the new product. This traditional approach takes a long time—and with time goes money.*
>
> *Honda has arranged these activities differently. First, planning and proving go on continuously and in parallel. Second, these activities are clearly separated from execution. At Honda, the highly disciplined execution cycle schedules major product revisions every four years and minor revisions every two years...when a new product is ready, it is released to existing factories and organizations, which dramatically shortens the amount of time needed to launch it.[53]*

Finally, competitive advantages can be created through superior linkages with stakeholders in the external environment. For example, a firm may develop exclusive relationships with its suppliers or customers, which can lead to a cost advantage. For instance, Caterpillar's global electronic network with its suppliers and customers allows information to be passed from customers back to suppliers more quickly than its competitors.[54]

Systematic analysis of the value chain activities is a useful tool for understanding how a business creates value for its customers. Value chain analysis may be combined with stakeholder analysis to identify strengths and weaknesses and to uncover opportunities for cost savings or ways to add value for customers. For instance, the intersection between activist groups and technology development could result in low-cost solutions to problems with pollution and other externalities. Also, customers may be able to help a firm increase the effectiveness of its marketing, sales, or service activities. The combination of stakeholder analysis with value chain analysis holds great potential for developing strategies that are both efficient and effective.

As we will describe in the following chapters, strategy should be based on what the organization does well relative to competitors *or* on the capabilities or resources the firm *wants to develop* that will create a competitive advantage in the future. Organizational constraints should be considered but should not place absolute limits on strategy. Instead, long-term organizational success often depends on developing new competencies.

In conclusion, this chapter has explored a multitude of internal stakeholders, resources, capabilities, and organizational activities and processes, any of which are potential sources of competitive advantage. For each potentially valuable resource, capability, or process, these questions should be asked: "Is it valuable?," "Is it unique?," "Is it difficult or expensive for competitors to imitate?" Answers to these questions can form the basis for establishment and execution of successful strategies.

Summary

This chapter described internal stakeholders and the important roles they play in strategic management processes. Three primary groups were identified for discussion—managers, owners, and employees. Any of these stakeholders or the way they are managed can result in resources and capabilities that lead to a competitive advantage.

The CEO is the primary orchestrator of organizational vision and strategies. CEOs play interpersonal, informational, and decisional roles in organizations, and influence the organization through their personal values and style of strategic leadership.

Owners in a for-profit, publicly held corporation, the shareholders, are typically represented by a board of directors, which acts as their agent. Directors have the responsibility to oversee the activities of organizational managers and ensure that shareholder interests are protected. They are obligated to hold CEOs and other organizational officials accountable for their actions. Agency problems can exist when boards of directors are weak in carrying out these responsibilities, when CEOs also serve as chairs of their own boards (i.e., CEO duality), or any time CEOs or other managers act in their own personal interests at the expense of shareholders. Recently, boards of directors in the United States have been playing a more significant role in supervising top managers, participating in managerial decisions, and even replacing marginally successful CEOs.

Organizations need highly qualified employees if they are going to succeed in the global economy. Unfortunately, the skill and knowledge levels of job applicants in the United States are deteriorating. These trends make training and other human resource management activities crucial to long-term competitiveness. Innovative human resource management techniques such as employee empowerment are increasing employee effectiveness for some successful companies.

An organization's culture is the shared values of its members. Culture often reflects the values of management, the human resource management practices that create the working conditions, and the past experiences of employees. Culture can be a tremendous source of advantage for a firm, or a millstone.

Other tangible resources include superior financial resources, excellent physical resources, and organizational resources such as excellent management systems and structures. Intangibles such as brands, business relationships, and reputation are harder to quantify but are some of the most important sources of competitive advantage. For each potential resource or capability, the following questions should be asked: "Is it valuable?," "Is it unique?," "Is it difficult or expensive for competitors to imitate?" Finally, for potential sources of competitive advantage to become real, firms should be organized in such a manner that the full potential is realized.

Another way of thinking about organizational capabilities is to visualize the various activities and determine the degree to which those activities and processes create value. As with resources, organizational processes and activities can serve as sources of competitive advantage if they are (1) valuable (value adding), (2) unique, different, or unusual, and (3) difficult for competitors to imitate.

Discussion Questions

1. Describe the three broad roles of the CEO. What types of activities fall within each of these roles?
2. Describe the five distinct leadership approaches or styles CEOs use. Which of these styles is more authoritarian? Which is more participative? Is any one style the best? Why?
3. What is the nature of the relationships that exist among shareholders, boards of directors, and CEOs? What is an agency problem? How can agency problems be avoided?

4. Why is human resource management becoming an even more important part of strategic management in many organizations?

5. When do an organization's resources and capabilities lead to a sustainable competitive advantage? A core competency or capability?

6. Use Figure 4.2 to identify the financial, physical, human, and organizational resources of an organization with which you are familiar. Apply the four questions to determine which of these resources and capabilities may lead to a sustainable competitive advantage or core capability. If a financial statement is available, use some of the ratios contained in Table 4.4 to assess the financial strength of the company.

7. Explain the value chain and how it can be used to identify organizational strengths, weaknesses, and sources of competitive advantage.

References

1. E. I. Porteus and S. Whang, "On Manufacturing/Marketing Incentives," *Management Science* 37 (1991), pp. 1166–1182; A. D. Sharplin, "Lincoln Electric Company, 1989," in M. J. Stahl and D. W. Grigsby, eds., *Strategic Management for Decision Making* (Boston: PWS-Kent, 1992), pp. 788–812; P.T. Taplin, "Profit-Sharing Plans as an Employee Motivator," *Employee Benefit Plan Review* (January 1989), pp. 10–11.

2. S. Finkelstein and D. C. Hambrick, *Strategic Leadership: Top Executives and Their Effects on Organizations* (St. Paul, Minn.: West Publishing Company, 1996), Chap. 2.

3. H. Mintzberg, *The Nature of Managerial Work* (New York: Harper and Row, 1973).

4. A. Farnham, "Biggest Business Goofs of 1991," *Fortune* (January 13, 1992), pp. 80–82.

5. P. M. Senge, "The Leader's New Work: Building Learning Organizations," *Sloan Management Review* 32(1) (Fall 1990), pp. 7–24.

6. E. H. Schein, *Organization Culture and Leadership* (San Francisco: Jossey-Bass, 1985).

7. K. Rebello and E.I. Schwartz, "Microsoft," *Business Week* (February 24, 1992), pp. 60–64.

8. P. Nutt, "Selecting Tactics to Implement Strategic Plans," *Strategic Management Journal* 10 (1989), pp. 145–161.

9. Senge, "The Leader's New Work"; C. C. Manz and H. P. Sims, "SuperLeadership," *Organization Dynamics* 17(4) (1991), pp. 8–36.

10. Senge, "The Leader's New Work."

11. Senge, "The Leader's New Work"; Manz and Sims, "SuperLeadership."

12. Senge, "The Leader's New Work," p. 13.

13. Graves, "Leaders of Corporate Change," p.106.

14. L. J. Bourgeois and D. R. Brodwin, "Strategic Implementation: Five Approaches to an Elusive Phenomenon," *Strategic Management Journal* 5 (1984), pp. 241–264.

15. J. G. Michel and D. C. Hambrick, "Diversification Posture and Top Management Team Characteristics," *Academy of Management Journal* 35 (1992), pp. 9–37; S. F. Slater, "The Influence of Style on Business Unit Performance," *Journal of Management* 15 (1989), pp. 441–455; A. S. Thomas, R. J. Litschert, and K. Ramaswamy, "The Performance Impact of Strategy-Manager Coalignment: An Empirical Examination," *Strategic Management Journal* 12 (1991), pp. 509–522.

16. V. Govindarajan, "Implementing Competitive Strategies at the Business Unit Level: Implications of Matching Managers to Strategies," *Strategic Management Journal* 10 (1989), pp. 251–269.

17. K. A. Bantel and S. E. Jackson, "Top Management and Innovations in Banking: Does the Composition of the Top Team Make a Difference?" *Strategic Management Journal* 10 (1989), pp. 107–124; C. M. Grimm and K. G. Smith, "Management and Organizational Change: A Note on the Railroad Industry," *Strategic Management Journal* 12 (1991), pp. 557–562; M. F. Wiersema and K. A. Bantel, "Top Management Team Demography and Corporate Strategic Change," *Academy of Management Journal* 35 (1992), pp. 91–121.

18. A. K. Gupta and V. Govindarajan, "Business Unit Strategy, Managerial Characteristics, and Business Unit Effectiveness at Strategy Implementation," *Academy of Management Journal* 27 (1984), pp. 25–41.

19. B. Brenner, "Tough Times, Tough Bosses: Corporate America Calls in a New, Cold-eyed Breed of CEO," *Business Week* (November 25, 1991), pp. 174–180.

20. "The Bristol-Myers Squibb Pledge," *Annual Report*, Bristol-Myers Squibb, 1989.

21. S. Weisbach, "Outside Directors and CEO Turnover," *Journal of Financial Economics* 20 (1988), pp. 431–460.

22. I. F. Kesner and R. B. Johnson, "Crisis in the Boardroom: Fact and Fiction," *Academy of Management Executive* (February 1990), pp. 23–35.

23. M. Magnet, "Directors, Wake Up!" *Fortune* (June 15, 1992), pp. 86–92.

24. A. Taylor, III, "The Road Ahead at General Motors," *Fortune* (May 4, 1992), pp. 94–95; J.B. Treece, "The Board Revolt," *Business Week* (April 20, 1992), pp. 31–36.

25. J. A. Byrne, "Requiem for Yesterday's CEO," *Business Week* (February 15, 1993), pp. 32–33; C. J. Loomis and D. Kirkpatrick, "The Hunt for Mr. X: Who Can Run IBM?" *Fortune* (February 22, 1993), pp. 68–72; A. A. Morrison, "After the Coup at Time Warner," *Fortune* (March 23, 1992), pp. 82–90.

26. T. M. Burton, "Greenpeace Is Battling Slide in Contributions and in Political Clout," *The Wall Street Journal* (March 3, 1993), p. A1.

27. I. F. Kesner, B. Victor, and B. T. Lamont, "Board Composition and the Commission of Illegal Acts: An

Investigation of Fortune 500 Companies," *Academy of Management Journal* 29 (1986), pp. 789–799; I.B. Kesner and R.B. Johnson, "An Investigation of the Relationship Between Board Composition and Shareholder Suits," *Strategic Management Journal* 11 (1990), pp. 327–336.

28. W. Q. Judge, Jr., and C. P. Zeithaml, "Institutional and Strategic Choice Perspectives on Board Involvement in the Strategic Decision Process," *Academy of Management Journal* 35 (1992), pp. 766–794; J. A. Pearce II and Shaker A. Zahra, "The Relative Power of CEOs and Boards of Directors: Associations with Corporate Performance," *Strategic Management Journal* 12 (1991), pp. 135–153.

29. E. F. Fama and M. C. Jensen, "Separation of Ownership and Control," *Journal of Law and Economics* 26 (1983), pp. 301–325.

30. M. J. Stahl and D. W. Grigsby, *Strategic Management for Decision Making* (Boston: PWS-Kent, 1992), pp. 12–13.

31. T. P. Summers and J.S. Harrison, "Alliances for Success," *Training and Development* (March 1992), pp. 69–76.

32. "Analysis of U.S. Competitiveness Problems," in *America's Competitive Crisis: Confronting a New Reality*, a report by the Council on Competitiveness (April 1987), pp. 121–126.

33. M. J. Koch and R. G. McGrath, "Improving Labor Productivity: Human Resource Management Policies Do Matter," *Strategic Management Journal* 17 (1996), pp. 335–354.

34. M. A. Huselid, "The Impact of Human Resource Management Practices on Turnover, Productivity and Corporate Financial Performance," *Academy of Management Journal* 38 (1995), pp. 635–672.

35. J. Pfeffer, "Producing Sustainable Competitive Advantage Through the Effective Management of People," *Academy of Management Executive* (February 1995), pp. 55–72.

36. "Our Credo," Johnson & Johnson company documents, used by permission of Johnson & Johnson.

37. K. Bemowski, "People: The Only Thing That Will Make Quality Work," *Quality Progress* (September 1988).

38. *Annual Report*, Union Pacific Corporation, 1991, p. 1.

39. J. W. Henry, "ESOPs with Productivity Payoffs," *Journal of Business Strategy* (July/August 1989), pp. 32–36; C. Rosen, "The Growing Appeal of the Leveraged ESOP," *Journal of Business Strategy* (January/February 1989), pp. 16–20.

40. A. Sharplin, "The Lincoln Electric Company, 1989," in J. R. Montanari, C. P. Morgan, and J. S. Bracker, *Strategic Management: A Choice Approach* (Chicago: Dryden, 1990), pp. 807–826.

41. J. B. Quinn, *Intelligent Enterprise: A Knowledge and Service Based Paradigm for Industry* (New York: The Free Press, 1992).

42. Based on information from D. Miller, *The Icarus Paradox*, (New York: Harper Business, 1990).

43. Based on information from Miller, *The Icarus Paradox*.

44. D. Miller and J. Shamsie, "The Resource-Based View of the Firm in Two Environments: The Hollywood Film Studios from 1936 to 1965," *Academy of Management Journal* 39 (1996), pp. 519–543.

45. J. B. Barney, "Looking Inside for Competitive Advantage," *Academy of Management Executive* (November 1995), pp. 49–61.

46. Barney, "Looking Inside for Competitive Advantage."

47. Some of these companies were cited in O. Port, "Beg, Borrow—and Benchmark," *Business Week* (November 30, 1992), p. 75.

48. L. Backman, "Circuit City to Add CarMax in Tampa Area," *The Tampa Tribune* (June 10, 1995), p. 1B.

49. M. A. Hitt, R. D. Ireland, and R. E. Hoskisson, *Strategic Management: Competitiveness and Globalization* (St. Paul, Minn.: West Publishing Company, 1995), p. 73.

50. C. L. Loomis, "Citicorp: John Reed's Second Act," *Fortune* (April 29, 1996), p. 90.

51. *Annual Report*, Walt Disney Company, 1995, pp. 6–7.

52. M. E. Porter, *Competitive Advantage: Creating and Sustaining Superior Performance* (New York: The Free Press, 1985), Chap. 2.

53. G. Stalk, P. Evans, and L. E. Shulman, "Competing on Capabilities: The New Rules of Corporate Strategy," *Harvard Business Review* (March/April 1992), pp. 57–69.

54. B. Bremner, "Can Caterpillar Inch Its Way Back to Heftier Profits?" *Business Week* (September 27, 1989), pp. 75–78.

Agency Problems: Consequences and Preventions

As defined in the chapter, an agency problem arises when an executive has an incentive to make decisions that are in his or her own best interest, rather than in the interests of owners. In the following sections, we discuss agency problems as they relate to executive compensation, short-run versus long-run decision making, growth plans, and participation on boards of directors.

Executive Compensation

Some business writers argue that the extremely high salaries of some CEOs are evidence that agency problems exist. The average CEO of a *Fortune 500* company receives around $4 million in total compensation each year.[1] Because shareholders are numerous and often not very well organized, their influence on decisions such as CEO compensation is nominal. Consequently, self-serving forces within the organization can sometimes prevail. For example, Roberto Goizueta of Coke once received an $81 million restricted stock award. The award was initiated by an old associate whose firm received $24 million in fees from Coke over the previous six years.[2] Unfortunately, conflicts of interest of this type are common. *Business Week* published a list of similar conflicts at Merck, Pennzoil, Philip Morris, RJR Nabisco, and many other corporations.[3] The embattled Apple Computer is currently fighting a class-action suit that was filed due to CEO Gil Amelio's pay package of more than $10 million, which the lawyer representing shareholders calls "wildly excessive."[4]

The real issue concerning salary is whether CEOs are worth what they receive. For example, in *Business Week*'s annual report on executive pay, compensation is compared to the performance of the organizations for which they work. This analysis is revealing, and often demonstrates that some CEOs are a real bargain. Also, recent research has provided evidence that CEOs that have more demanding jobs, as indicated by the amount of information they have to process and the firm's strategy, tend to be more highly paid.[5] Because of all of the ramifications associated with executive pay, it is a decision that is as much ethical as it is financial.

To help overcome problems with excessive compensation of some CEOs, top management compensation should probably be linked to corporate performance. For example, one study found higher performance in firms whose CEOs *perceive* greater connections between their personal wealth and the wealth of the organization.[6] Unfortunately, another study found no link between shareholder returns and management compensation.[7] The conclusion of this last study was that boards of directors are hesitant to cut top managers' pay when they are performing poorly, thus biasing the results.

One risk in relating compensation to performance is that a lot of these schemes tie annual compensation to annual, as opposed to long-term, performance. Whenever possible, compensation packages should be developed that encourage, instead of discourage, actions that will lead to high long-term performance. For example, if CEO bonuses are dependent on profit, board members in charge of compensation should add back R&D expenditures before calculating profits for the year. This helps ensure that CEOs will not be hesitant to allocate resources to potentially profitable long-term R&D projects. Another trend in compensation is rewarding CEOs with stock instead of cash. When managers receive stock and stock options they become owners and their interests should converge with those of other shareholders.[8]

Short-Run versus Long-Run Decision Making

Another frequently cited agency problem occurs as a result of the difference between short-term and long-term benefits that accrue to the firm. For example, R&D activities are typically beneficial to the firm because they provide new products and new technologies. However, the financial benefits from R&D activities often take many years to appear, even though the expenses are incurred immediately. Therefore, it may be in the best interests of top managers to reduce R&D expenditures to enhance short-term profits (and associated bonuses), thus jeopardizing long-term competitiveness.

Some top managers have been accused of maximizing short-term profits by cutting programs like R&D or capital expenditures, taking large bonuses, and leaving before their companies experience performance problems. Johnson & Johnson, the large and highly diversified consumer drugs company, has adopted a corporate-wide policy to counteract these tendencies:

> *Our final responsibility is to our stockholders. Business must make a sound profit. We must experiment with new ideas. Research must be carried on, innovative programs developed and mistakes paid for. New equipment must be purchased, new facilities provided and new products launched. Reserves must be created to provide for adverse times. When we operate according to these principles, the stockholders should realize a fair return.[9]*

Agency and Growth

Another agency problem is associated with growth. Some power-hungry or status-conscious top managers may expand the size of their empires at the expense of organizational shareholders. For example, a few years ago Harding Lawrence led Braniff Airways to financial ruin through overzealous growth.[10] Also, the highly unsuccessful unrelated acquisitions of the 1960s may have resulted, in part, from the actions of managers who were more interested in short-term growth than in long-term performance. This agency problem can be precipitated by compensation systems that link organizational size to pay.

Agency and Boards of Directors

Perhaps the greatest agency problems occur when top managers serve on the board of directors, which is often the case in U.S. corporations. In fact, it is not

CEO Duality
Occurs when the same person fills roles of both chief executive officer and chairman of the board.

uncommon to find the CEO in the position of chairman of the board. This condition is known as **CEO duality**. As chairman of the board of directors, the CEO is in a strong position to ensure that personal interests are served even if the other stakeholders' interests are not. For example, a CEO/chairman may influence other board members to provide a generous compensation package. Also, a CEO/chairman is instrumental in nominating future board members and therefore has the opportunity to nominate friends and colleagues who are likely to "rubber stamp" future actions and decisions.

In spite of these theoretical arguments against CEO duality, research findings are inconclusive.[11] However, when a relationship between CEO duality and performance is found, it is typically negative. For example, one study examined the financial performance of 141 corporations over a six-year period and discovered that firms opting for independent leadership consistently outperformed those relying on CEO duality.[12]

References

1. J. A. Byrne, "How High Can CEO Pay Go?" *Fortune* (April 22, 1996), pp. 100–122.
2. Byrne, "What, Me Overpaid? CEOs Fight Back," *Business Week* (May 4, 1992), pp. 142–148.
3. Byrne, "What, Me Overpaid?" p. 147.
4. P. Burrows, "The Sweet and Sour at Apple," *Business Week* (March 11, 1996), p. 6.
5. A. D. Henderson and J. W. Fredrickson, "Information Processing Demands as a Determinant of CEO Compensation," *Academy of Management Journal* 39 (1996), pp. 575–606.
6. E. J. Zajac, "CEO Selection, Succession, Compensation and Firm Performance: A Theoretical Integration and Empirical Analysis," *Strategic Management Journal* 11 (1990), pp. 217–230.
7. J. Kerr and R. A. Bettis, "Boards of Directors, Top Management Compensation, and Shareholder Returns," *Academy of Management Journal* 30 (1987), pp. 645–664.

8. C. W. L. Hill, "Effects of Ownership Structure and Control on Corporate Productivity," *Academy of Management Journal* 32 (1989), pp. 25–46.
9. "Our Credo," Johnson & Johnson company documents, used by permission of Johnson & Johnson.
10. J. A. Pearce II and S. J. Teel, "Braniff International Corporation (A) and (B)," in *Strategic Management: Strategy Formulation and Implementation*, 2nd ed. (Homewood, Ill.: Richard D. Irwin, 1985), pp. 820–838.
11. P. L. Rechner and D. R. Dalton, "The Impact of CEO as Board Chairperson on Corporate Performance: Evidence vs. Rhetoric," *Academy of Management Executive* (May 1989), pp. 141–143; Rechner and D. R. Dalton, "CEO Duality and Organizational Performance: A Longitudinal Analysis," *Strategic Management Journal* 12 (1991), pp. 155–160.
12. Rechner and Dalton, "CEO Duality and Organizational Performance."

5

Strategic Direction

Aggressive Vision Leads Compaq to the Head of the Pack

Most weekday mornings, around 7 A.M., a black Porsche convertible darts from an exclusive high-rise in Houston's ritzy Tanglewood section. Behind the wheel is a handsome, gray-haired 54-year-old German in expensive sunglasses, face impassive, foot on the pedal. Darting deftly in and out of traffic, as if Beltway 8 had suddenly become the Autobahn, he heads 25 miles north to a sprawling complex of anonymous eight-story glass-and-steel buildings hidden in a scrubby South Texas pine forest. The guy doesn't drive; he flies—sometimes at close to 100 mph.

Inside those buildings toil men and women who aim to dominate the world of computing; the speeder in the Porsche, Compaq Computer CEO Eckhard Pfeiffer, has convinced them they can do it. Under the leadership of this perfectionist, Compaq has proved itself a master of what may be the most critical task of business in the Nineties: doing everything fast. Since 1991, when the board ousted co-founder Rod Canion and put Pfeiffer in the driver's seat, annual revenues have nearly quadrupled, from $3.3 billion to $14.8 billion. Pfeiffer sets outsized goals and meets them. In late 1993 he said he wanted Compaq to be the leading PC maker in the world by 1996 (at the time it was third). Compaq got there in 1994.

Now Pfeiffer is giving his charges even more audacious targets. He wants Compaq to own at least twice as much share as its nearest competitor in every market it enters. He wants Compaq to become one of the top three computer companies in the world. In 1996 it was fifth, behind IBM, Fujitsu, Hewlett-Packard, and NEC.[1]

Strategic managers are charged with the responsibility of providing long-term direction for their organizations, while at the same time balancing the competing interests of key stakeholders. One of the critical errors that some organizations make is that they do not know who they are, how they got to where they are, and where they are going. They suffer an "identity crisis." For example, Josten's, the Minnesota-based manufacturer of class rings, yearbooks, and other products for schools, had a thirty-four-year record of sales and earnings increases. Then, in the late 1980s, they diversified into computer systems and started losing money. A New York stock analyst who has followed the company for years believes that "Nobody was taking a hard look at what was going on—nobody seemed to be asking the right questions."[2]

Strategic direction is established and communicated through tools such as visions, missions, business definitions, enterprise strategies, and long-term goals, all of which are discussed in this chapter. There are no widely accepted guidelines managers use to provide strategic direction. In some companies, very little is written down. Other companies have adopted formal statements for each of these areas. However, regardless of the medium of communication, high-performing companies tend to have an organizational identity that is understood by both internal and external stakeholders. On the inside, a well-established organizational identity can provide guidance to managers at all levels as they make strategic decisions.[3] In addition, communicating strategic direction to external stakeholders can increase their understanding of the motives of the organization and may also facilitate the creation of alliances, since potential alliance partners have a greater ability to judge the existence of common goals. One corporate president recently stated that "his company's mission statement has helped create a 'partnering attitude' instead of an adversarial relationship" between his company and its customers.[4]

ESTABLISHMENT OF STRATEGIC DIRECTION

As Figure 5.1 illustrates, stakeholder interests are paramount in the creation of a strategic direction. The remote environment is also very influential. In addition, feedback resulting from strategy formulation and implementation processes is integrated into the direction a firm should take. An organization can also learn from feedback concerning the way its outputs and processes are received by stakeholders. This feedback becomes a part of the organization's history.

The history of an organization can potentially assist strategic planning processes, since organizations can learn from past successes and failures. Unfortunately, history can also be a weakness that stands in the way of forward progress. Past successes can create strong **structural inertia**, the term for forces at work to maintain the status quo.[5] These forces can include systems, structures, processes, culture, sunk costs, internal politics, and barriers to entry and exit. Anything that favors the "status quo" has the potential to cause inertia.

Structural inertia is also related to human nature. Most humans desire a certain amount of predictability in their work. In other words, they have learned to cope with their organizational environment—they are comfortable. They may also fear that changes will reduce their own power or position in the organization or that they will no longer be considered competent. If the forces favoring inertia are strong and if the organization has been successful in the past, people will be highly resistant to any major shift in missions or strategies. Inertia based on past successes was one of the main reasons for the decline of the railroads as a form of pas-

Structural Inertia
Forces within the organization that work to maintain the status quo.

Figure 5.1 *Primary Influences on Strategic Direction*

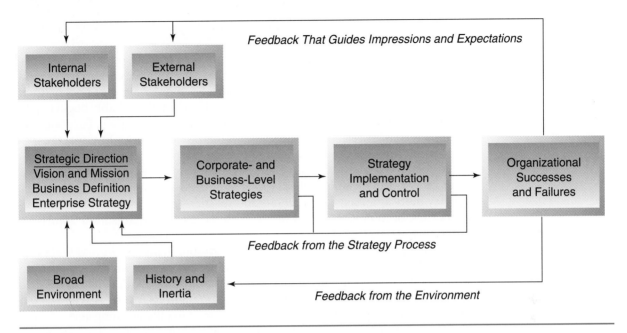

senger transportation. They continued to pursue the same strategies until it was simply too late.[6] Structural inertia, then, is another potential threat to the survival and prosperity of an organization.

One of the most commons means to communicate strategic direction is a written mission statement. In the following sections, we discuss the development of organizational mission, use of business definition concepts to develop a strong sense of mission, creation of a vision for the future, development of enterprise strategies that link ethics to mission, and then creation of more specific organizational goals.

Organizational Mission

An organization's mission, whether written down or just apparent from the organization's pattern of decisions and actions over time, provides an important vehicle for communicating ideals and a sense of direction and purpose to internal and external stakeholders. It can also help guide organizational managers when making resource allocation decisions. Sometimes students of strategic management confuse the terms *mission* and *vision*. In general, organizational mission is what the organization is and its reason for existing, whereas vision is a forward-looking view of what the organization wants to become. However, when mission statements are written down, a vision statement is often included or embedded in the formal mission statement. In fact, a formal written mission statement often includes many or all of the elements of strategic direction: vision, business definition, enterprise strategy, and goals. Consequently, a mission is a "catch-all" statement of organizational purpose.

As organizations are established, their mission may be as simple as "Provide software services to the local business community while generating a profit for the owner." The mission is often informal and is seldom written down. But notice that even in its simplest form, this mission encompasses a purpose, a brief definition of the business and two important stakeholders, the owner and the customer. Most businesses begin with a mission that is just as simple as the example given. The mission is an extension of the entrepreneur or entrepreneurs who form the organization.

As organizations succeed in their business environments, opportunities arise that allow the organization to grow in revenues and number of employees, and encourage it to expand into new product and market areas. The original mission may seem too restrictive. At this point, the organization will probably begin to pay more attention to previously overlooked or neglected stakeholders. For example, the company may increase employee benefits (employees), hire additional tax specialists (government), designate a public relations officer (society), attempt to negotiate better discounts with suppliers (suppliers), or increase borrowing to help sustain growth (financial intermediaries). In addition, the organization will certainly pay more attention to the actions and reactions of competitors. These stakeholders then become forces that are considered as the organization adjusts or enlarges its mission.

At some point in the growth of an organization, planning processes are formalized. At this point, the mission statement may be put into words. Articulating a specific mission forces top managers to come to terms with some key issues regarding the current direction of the organization and its future. A well-written mission statement can be an excellent tool for conveying the meaning and intent of an organization to its internal and external stakeholders. Clearly not all "opportunities" that organizations face will be compatible with their missions. If used properly, an organization's mission should provide a screen for evaluating opportunities and proposals.

Organizations often prepare written mission statements as a way of communicating with the public. For example, mission statements are frequently included in annual financial reports to shareholders. Table 5.1 contains the mission statement of Rhone-Poulenc Rorer, a global pharmaceutical organization that resulted

Table 5.1 *Sample Mission Statement of Rhone-Poulenc Rorer*

Our Mission is to become the BEST pharmaceutical company in the world by dedicating our resources, our talents and our energies to help improve human health and the quality of life of people throughout the world.

Being the best means:

- Being the BEST at satisfying the needs of everyone we serve: Patients, health care professionals, employees, communities, governments and shareholders;
- Being BETTER AND FASTER than our competitors at discovering and bringing to market important new medications in selected therapeutic areas;
- Operating with the HIGHEST professional and ethical standards in all our activities, building on the Rhone-Poulenc and Rorer heritage of integrity;
- Being seen as the BEST place to work, attracting and retaining talented people at all levels by creating an environment that encourages them to develop their potential to the fullest;
- Generating consistently BETTER results than our competitors, through innovation and a total commitment to quality in everything we do.

Source: Annual Report.

from the 1990 merger of Rhone-Poulenc and Rorer. On the other hand, some missions are never written down, even in the most successful companies. Nevertheless, the purpose of the organization is made clear through its actions or through other, less formal statements, often by the CEO. For example, Walt Disney does not have a formal mission statement. However, the organization's actions over time as well as the statements by Michael Eisner from a recent annual report (reproduced in Table 5.2), make Disney's mission very clear.

Unfortunately, in many organizations, the process of developing a written mission statement has deteriorated into an exercise in slogan writing. Managers often worry more about writing a catchy, short phrase that can be printed on a business card than about managing with purpose. For an organization's mission to be a management tool, it must be grounded in the realities of the business. One of the first steps in creating a clear sense of mission is to fully understand the nature of the business in which the organization participates. This first step, business definition, is discussed in the next section.

Business Definition

Derek Abell has argued that clear business definition is the starting point of all strategic planning and management.[7] A clear business definition provides a framework for evaluating the effects of planned change, and for planning the steps needed to move the organization forward.

Table 5.2 *Disney's "Unwritten" Mission*

Although Walt Disney Company does not have a formal written mission statement, these statements from Michael Eisner, CEO, make Disney's purpose very clear. They are found at the beginning of one of Disney Company's recent annual reports.

Our goal is to increase wealth for our shareholders. We must do this while never forgetting the value of our Brand, never forgetting our responsibility to our cast members, never forgetting the communities in which we serve and never forgetting the high quality standards of our work. We must always operate in an ethical way and never take the expedient or slippery path.

Our goal is to increase creative productivity through superior work. We will build upon our conviction that doing it better pays off, that short cuts lead to short earnings and that setting the highest standards derives the highest results. The rush to mediocrity, the rush to short-term results, and the acceptance of the lowest common entertainment denominator do not work for us. We believe in always striving for excellence. We believe we have an obligation to carry on the Disney tradition.

We must concentrate on continuing to lead creatively. We must throw out mediocrity. Our only criteria for our products should be excellence and fiscal viability. We must not commit to anything that is cheap and average or expensive and average. *Average is awful.* We must, however, not commit to any venture, no matter how great, unless the project can promise a good fiscal return.

Our strategic direction is quality and innovation. We know our audience, and predominantly it is a family audience. We should not lament that others appeal more strongly to the disenfranchised teenage audience. They always come back when they become re-enfranchised adults with children.

Source: Annual Report, Walt Disney Company, 1995, pp. 6–7.

Markets
Consumer groups that an organization attempts to satisfy through its products or services.

Functions
The specific needs of consumers that are being satisfied by an organization's products or services.

Resource Conversion Processes and Capabilities
The manufacturing or service processes and capabilities an organization uses to satisy consumers' needs.

Products or Services
The actual output an organization provides in an attempt to satisfy consumers' needs.

Scope
The breadth of an organization's activities across markets, functions, resource conversion processes, and products or services.

When defining the business, the question "What is our business?" should be answered from three perspectives: (1) Who is being satisfied? (2) What is being satisfied? (3) How are customer needs satisfied?[8] The first question refers to the **markets** served by the organization, the second question deals with the specific **functions** provided to the customers identified in question 1, and the third question refers to the **resource conversion processes and capabilities** used by the firm to provide the functions identified in question 2. In actuality, most mission statements also identify specific **products or services** provided by the organization. In this regard, a fourth question, which is an extension of the third question, can be stated as "What are our products and services?" This approach is, admittedly, marketing oriented. Its greatest strength is that it focuses on the customer, a very important external stakeholder for most firms.

Organizational Scope. The **scope** of an organization is the breadth of its activities across markets, functions, resource conversion processes, and products. Some large organizations, such as PepsiCo and Nestlé, have a very broad scope. Other firms, including L. L. Bean and Nucor, have a narrower scope. Also, there are firms, such as McDonald's, that are very broad in one dimension (markets served), but narrow in all the rest.

Table 5.3 contains three examples of firms and their business definitions, organized around the four areas of a business definition—products and services, markets, functions served, and resource conversion processes. (Church & Dwight is the 150-year-old manufacturer of Arm & Hammer baking soda.) Notice that the concepts that have been discussed thus far apply equally well to both product and service firms. For illustration purposes, the firms described in Table 5.3 represent both product and service orientations, with Church & Dwight providing a tangible product, Toys 'R' Us combining service with tangible products, and Delta Airlines focusing exclusively on services.

Many organizations begin with a very narrow business definition and then expand in various directions. For instance, Church & Dwight, traditionally a narrowly defined company, began a market development program several years ago to find new applications for its basic product, baking soda. Initially, baking soda was advertised as an odor absorbent for the refrigerator and shoes. This move increased sales by increasing the number of functions served, but had no effect on the product (baking soda), the market (grocery store consumers), or the resource conversion processes and capabilities of the company. Later, the company began marketing products containing baking soda such as rug and room deodorizers and oven cleaner. Notice that these later moves were still aimed at grocery stores (building on brand name recognition), but greatly increased the number of products and functions. The resource conversion process was altered only slightly to include new packaging (e.g., aerosol cans). However, Church & Dwight is still predominantly involved in chemical processing and packaging.

When Toys 'R' Us entered the children's apparel market through its Kids 'R' Us retail outlets, the products and functions increased some, the markets and resource conversion processes remained the same.[9] Like Toys 'R' Us, the Kids 'R' Us chain requires buying, inventory management, distributing, limited service, promotion, and advertising. Toys 'R' Us mastered these skills before the Kids 'R' Us chain was even envisioned. In addition, Toys 'R' Us could draw on its rich experience in marketing to children, grandparents, and parents.

Delta Airlines has adhered to a very narrow business definition. Instead of venturing into new areas, in 1986 Delta acquired Western Airlines. This move allowed Delta to greatly increase its western U.S. route coverage and establish an

Table 5.3 *Business Definitions of Well-Known Companies*

	Church & Dwight	Toys 'R' Us	Delta Airlines
Products and services	Baking soda and related consumer products	Toys and clothing for children	Air transportation
Markets	Grocery stores and bakeries	Children, grandparents, and parents	Business travelers, vacationers, and infrequent travelers
Functions served	Odor absorbent, baking, cleaning	Availability, entertainment, clothing	Fast, long-distance transportation
Resource conversion processes	Chemical processing/ packaging, promotion, and advertising	Buying, inventory mgt., distributing, limited service, promotion, and advertising	Flying, logistics, fleet management, baggage handling, reservations, promotion, and advertising

international presence, thus expanding the geographic size of its markets.[10] However, the type of customer served, function, service, and resource conversion process remained intact.

Studying changes in business definitions can help determine the nature of the distinctive competencies a firm is trying to or has developed. For instance, Church & Dwight continues to focus on the same basic resource conversion process. Although Toys 'R' Us is in a completely different business from Church & Dwight, the basic approach to business, expanding into areas that draw on the same resource conversion processes, is the same. Both of these companies have expanded into areas in which they could excel, due to their own areas of expertise. Delta, on the other hand, has concentrated on only one line of business, while expanding geographic territory and thus market size.

Industry Supply Chain Positioning. An organization may expand its business definition to include markets, functions, resource conversion processes, and/or products across a broad segment of the global economy, or it may decide to move forward or backward in the industry supply chains in which it is currently participating. An **industry supply chain**, which is also sometimes referred to as a value-added chain, represents the flow of goods in an industry from their crudest forms to their final forms, where they are ultimately consumed.

A typical industry supply chain, which is illustrated in Figure 5.2, begins with extraction of raw materials such as timber, ore, and crude oil. These raw materials are then manufactured into commodities such as wood pulp and iron. Primary manufacturing sometimes also involves the creation of components that are used to assemble final products. Therefore, the primary manufacturing stage can be short or long, depending on the nature of the final products.

Final product manufacturing involves the creation of a product that is in its final form prior to consumption. At this point branding becomes very important, since consumers associate brand names of final products with particular levels of quality, service, and reliability. Finally, wholesaling entails channeling final prod-

Industry Supply Chain Represents the flow of goods in an industry from their crudest forms to their final, consumable forms.

Figure 5.2 *Industry Supply Chain for Manufacturing Firms*

Source: Adapted from J. R. Galbraith and R. K. Kazanjian, *Strategy Implementation: Structure, Systems and Process*, 2nd ed. (St. Paul, Minn.: West Publishing Company, 1986), p. 51.

ucts to retail outlets, and retailing consists of selling these products to the ultimate consumer. Some products bypass the wholesaling and/or retailing stages due to direct sale by the manufacturer to customers.[11]

Although the model in Figure 5.2 is intuitively appealing, the industry supply chain is actually more complex than it looks. For instance, some products, such as salt, are both final products and products that are used as raw materials in other products. An example of a complete industry supply chain for a simple product is shown in Figure 5.3. Note that many of the outputs in this model are used in many more products than just the ones in this simplified supply chain. For example, both crude oil and cotton end up as part of literally thousands of products.

Vertical Integration
The extent to which a firm is involved in several stages of the industry supply chain.

An organization can be involved in all or a subset of the activities that comprise the industry supply chain, depending on its business definition. **Vertical integration** is the term used to describe the extent to which a firm is involved in several stages of the industry supply chain. Oil companies such as Exxon are totally vertically integrated because they explore for oil, extract it from the earth, refine it into gas and other products, and store, distribute, advertise, and sell the refined products to consumers. On the other hand, some oil companies are not at all vertically integrated. For example, several companies exist that do nothing more than provide engineering services to oil rigs. They are in the same industry, but they have chosen to limit their organizations to one specific activity in the industry supply chain.

Organizational Vision

Peter Drucker suggested that the business definition question should be stated not only as "What is our business?," but also as "What will it be?" and "What should it be?"[12] The second question refers to the direction in which the organization is heading at the current time. In other words, where will the organization end up if it continues on its current course? The third question, "What should it be?," allows for modifications to the existing strategy to move the organization in an appropriate direction.

Organizations that struggle to come to grips with those questions are forced to look forward in time and to think about a vision for the future. If the railroads had asked these questions soon enough, they might have realized that they should enlarge their business definitions to include transportation instead of just "railroads." Narrowness of definition may have been one of the leading causes of their decline in American industry.[13] In other words, they needed to develop a *vision* of the future industry and their role in it.

In contrast, many years ago, IBM (International Business Machines) and NCR (National Cash Register) understood the basic changes their typewriter and cash

Figure 5.3 *Simplified Industry Supply Chain for a Bed Sheet Purchased at a Department Store*

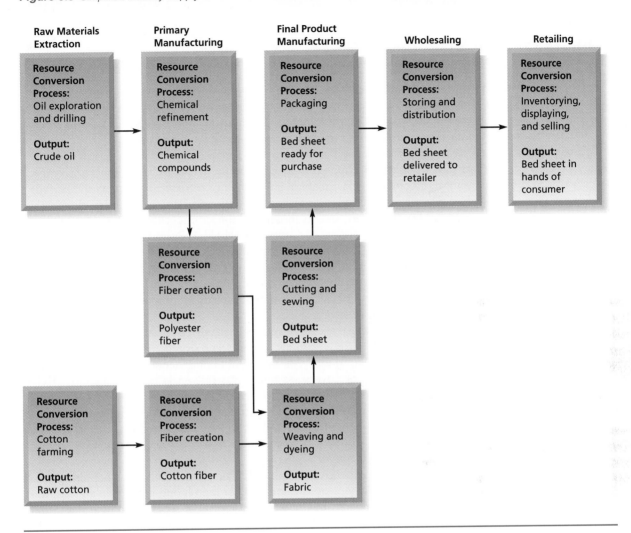

register industries were undergoing. They developed a vision of what the future industry would look like and the role they wanted to play in it. To participate in the new industry, they had to make fundamental, but well-planned, changes in their business definitions. To pursue the new opportunities, IBM developed a vision that altered their business definition to include office computing, then implemented the strategies necessary to make the changes. Strategic Insight 5.1 demonstrates how broadening a business definition can lead to significant opportunities and high levels of organizational success.

Unlike mission, which addresses an organization's purpose at the present time, an organization's vision is very future oriented. An organization with a vision has a definite sense of what it wants to be in the future. For example, Bill Gates has a clear vision of how he expects his industry to evolve and the role he wants to play in it. He wants Microsoft to dominate the software systems that link all digital transactions and communications, in business, entertainment, and leisure. That vision, which involves a very different "business definition" for the

STRATEGIC INSIGHT 5.1

BUSINESS

STRATEGY

TLC Group Uses Tragedy As an Opportunity for Redefining Its Business

The Total Logistic Control Group (TLC) of Zeeland, Michigan, was established in 1904 as a wholesale produce company. By the early 1950s, the company had become a small, regional refrigerated warehousing and distribution company. In the late 1970s, TLC added dry warehousing to its service offerings.

Recently, the company's resourcefulness enabled it to overcome a series of disasters that would have crippled most companies. TLC's 215,000-square-foot dry warehousing complex was caught in the middle of a freak rainstorm that dumped 13.5 inches of rain during a three-hour period and caused extensive damage. Business as usual ceased, and a massive cleanup operation was implemented. Within months, TLC's president and major stockholder, Robert B. Hall, died from a heart attack. Three days later, as the company was still reeling from the death of its CEO and trying to recover from the storm's devastation, a major fire swept through TLC's refrigerated warehouse and corporate offices. The fire completely destroyed almost one million cubic feet of refrigerated warehouse space along with the main shipping and receiving docks.

TLC responded to these events by redefining their business. According to Keith Klingenberg, president of TLC, "Usually it takes some significant event to knock you out of your comfort zone, to take you out of that complacent, ho-hum mode. And we have had our share of adversities and it has proven to be our blessing." TLC implemented a multilevel, company-wide mission to become a transparent extension of its customers. Craig Hall, CEO, explains, "We found out that we were not in the warehousing business at all, but in fact, in the field of logistics, providing the warehousing function." TLC was promoted as a one-stop source for storage, transportation, and inventory control.

To support its customer-driven mission, TLC employs a philosophy of hiring talented people when they become available rather than hiring only when there is an opening. TLC also pioneered computer-aided logistical support with the development of TINMAN (total information manager). This development, along with an expanded product offering, helps customers eliminate capital-intensive overhead, lower total costs, and improve profitability.

This combination of marketing focus, human resource excellence, and technological innovation enabled the firm to realize a 400% sales growth over a three-year period. Today, TLC warehouses distribute all Slim-Fast products in the United States. TLC is in the process of extending its concept of total logistic control from the national to the international marketplace by applying to become a Foreign Trade Zone.

Source: Adapted from "The TLC Group," *Strengthening America's Competitiveness: The Blue Chip Enterprise Initiative* (Warner Books on behalf of Connecticut Mutual Life Insurance Company and the U.S. Chamber of Commerce, 1991), pp. 156–157.

future, provides the framework for creating new businesses and forming new partnerships.

For many years, Wal-Mart's vision was to become the largest discount retailer in the United States, a vision that was achieved shortly before Sam Walton's death. In the case of Wal-Mart, the organizational vision did not require a departure from the existing business definition, although it did require continued growth along the "markets served" dimension as new regions were entered. More importantly, Sam Walton and Wal-Mart illustrate how a well-articulated vision of what the company wants to be in the future can be a strong motivational tool. Once it is stated, it may be used to focus the efforts of the entire organization.[14] For example, plans, policies, or programs that are inconsistent with the corporate vision may need to be altered or replaced. A well-understood vision can help managers and employees believe that their actions have meaning.

Enterprise Strategy and Ethics

Some economists argue that the only legitimate purpose of for-profit corporations is to produce profits. While it is true that profits are desirable, they are only one outcome of successful corporations. If profits are the only legitimate goal, then any firm could argue for just investing in the stock of other corporations rather than being in business itself. However, for-profit corporations are also in business to create products and/or provide services. A corporation that becomes too focused on profits is likely to lose the support and cooperation of key stakeholders such as suppliers, activist groups, competitors, society, and the government. In the long run, this sort of strategy may result in problems such as legal suits, loss of goodwill, and, ultimately, a loss of profits.

One fundamental question an organization should ask in determining its purpose is "What do we stand for?" This question is the critical link between ethics and strategy. **Enterprise strategy** is the term used to denote the joining of ethical and strategic thinking about the organization.[15] It is the organization's best possible reason (assuming there is a reason) for the actions it takes. An enterprise strategy can contain statements concerning a desire to maximize stockholder value, satisfy the interests of all or a subset of other stakeholders, or increase social harmony or the common good of society.[16] For example, in the mission statement of Rhone-Poulenc Rorer (Table 5.1), the enterprise strategy is to "help improve human health and the quality of life of people throughout the world."

The development of an enterprise strategy is a legal requirement in not-for-profit organizations. To gain tax-exempt status, not-for-profits have to be organized around a societal mission, whether it is educational, religious, charitable, or otherwise. The mission statement of the American Red Cross contains a clear statement of enterprise strategy: "The mission of the American Red Cross is to improve the quality of human life; to enhance self-reliance and concern for others; and to help people avoid, prepare for, and cope with emergencies."[17]

Some for-profit organizations also get very specific about how they will deal with stakeholder interests. For example, Harris Corporation, a maker of electronics, created broad goals concerning how the organization endeavors to satisfy its customers, shareholders, suppliers, employees, and communities. Table 5.4 contains these stakeholder goals. Johnson & Johnson, whose corporate credo was cited twice in earlier chapters, is another good example of an organization that integrates stakeholder concerns with its corporate purpose. Both of these organizations are highly diversified in their activities, yet a common corporate

Enterprise Strategy
The organization's best possible reason for the actions it takes; it represents the joining of ethical and strategic thinking about the organization.

Table 5.4 *Harris Corporation's Broad Stakeholder Goals*

Customers—For customers, our goal is to achieve ever-increasing levels of satisfaction by providing quality products and services with distinctive benefits on a timely and continuing basis worldwide. Our relationships with customers will be forthright and ethical and will be conducted in a manner to build trust and confidence.

Shareholders—For shareholders, the owners of our company, our goal is to achieve sustained growth in earnings-per-share. The resulting stock-price appreciation combined with dividends should provide our shareholders with a total return on investment that is competitive with similar investment opportunities.

Employees—The people of Harris are our company's most valuable asset, and our goal is for every employee to be personally involved in and share the success of the business. The company is committed to providing an environment that encourages all employees to make full use of their creativity and unique talents, and to providing equitable compensation, good working conditions, and the opportunity for personal development and growth that is limited only by individual ability and desire.

Suppliers—Suppliers are a vital part of our resources. Our goal is to develop and maintain mutually beneficial partnerships with suppliers who share our commitment to achieving increasing levels of customer satisfaction through continuing improvements in quality, service, timeliness, and cost. Our relationships with suppliers will be sincere, ethical, and will embrace the highest principles of purchasing practice.

Communities—Our goal is to be a responsible corporate citizen. This includes support of appropriate civic, educational and business activities, respect for the environment, and the encouragement of Harris employees to practice good citizenship and support community programs. Our greatest contribution to our communities is to be successful so that we can maintain stable employment and create new jobs.

Source: Annual Report.

philosophy toward stakeholders helps create a unity of purpose among the diversified business units.

Some researchers have found that organizational mission statements containing the elements of an enterprise strategy are more likely to be found in high-performing than low-performing corporations. The mission statements of sixty-one *Fortune 500* companies were analyzed, and researchers looked for key components that were believed to be associated with good mission statements. Only three components were found more frequently in high-performing than low-performing companies. These components were an organizational philosophy, an organizational self-concept, and the identification of the firm's desired public image.[18] These are all concepts associated with an enterprise strategy.

Enterprise strategy is a natural extension of the ethics of the organization, which are an extension of the values of key managers within the organization (as was discussed in Chapter 4). The ethics of an organization are not just a matter of public statements. Ethical decision making is a way of doing business. An organization that specifically works to build ethics into its business practice and to develop and implement an enterprise strategy will have a frame of reference for handling potential ethical problems. In the following sections, we discuss organizational ethics, codes of ethics, and the problems of ethical decision making in a global business environment.

Organizational Ethics. The pattern of decisions made by organizational managers establishes strategy and creates expectations among other organizational members and external stakeholders. For example, a firm that has specialized in the highest quality products and services creates an expectation among customers that all products will be high quality. If the firm chooses to change its strategy to include lower quality products, it runs the risk that customers will perceive the change as a breach of faith. Similarly, if an organization has an established relationship with a customer as its sole source of supply of a particular product, then the customer comes to depend on the organization. If the organization then chooses to drop that product from its product line, what might seem to be a clear-cut business decision takes on an ethical dimension: Can the customer's business survive if the product is dropped? Should other alternatives be considered? What obligation does the company have to that customer?

These types of decisions carry an ethical dimension because they go against what some important stakeholders think is right. An ethical dilemma exists when the values of different stakeholders of the organization are in conflict. Although there is no real legal dimension, there is an issue of trust or good faith that is very apparent. The values that organizational members bring to their work—the shared values that make up the organizational culture—determine whether the issues of trust, good faith, and obligation are raised when decisions are being deliberated and the degree to which they influence the final outcome.

In addition to decisions that violate stakeholder expectations, ethical dilemmas also relate to the gray area surrounding legal behavior: the definitions of what society views as right and wrong. In some cases, they are part of an obvious organizational crisis such as a plant closing, product recall, or environmental or safety accident. However, employees face decisions all day that have ethical implications: whether to tell a customer the truth that their order will be shipped late, whether to exaggerate a travel expense claim for a particularly inconvenient business trip, whether to ship a marginal product as first quality in order to meet the daily output quota. Although some of these decisions concern personal honesty more than business practice, the organization's culture—its system of shared values—determines in large part how employees deal with them.

In making decisions that deal with ethical issues, it is important to have a frame of reference. Very few ethical dilemmas have simple right or wrong answers. Instead, they are complex and require balancing the economic and social interests of the organization.[19] Five theoretical models that often influence organizational decisions follow[20]:

1. *Economic theory.* Under economic theory, the purpose of a business organization is to maximize profits. Profit maximization will lead to the greatest benefit for the most people. Other than profit maximization, there are no ethical issues in business.
   Limitations. Assumptions of profits being evenly distributed is naive. Not all business decisions relate to profit making and some ways of increasing profits hurt society.
2. *Legal theory.* Laws are a reflection of what society has determined is right and wrong. Compliance with the law ensures ethical behavior.
   Limitations. The social and political processes used to formulate laws are complex and time consuming. Because the processes are subject to manipulation, the laws may not truly reflect the interests of society.

3. *Religion*. Everyone should act in accordance with religious teachings.
   Limitations. As a model for business decision making, religious values are difficult to apply. There are many different religious beliefs and no consensus on the behaviors that are consistent with the beliefs.
4. *Utilitarian theory*. Utilitarian theory says to focus on the outcome of a decision. Everyone should act in a way that generates the greatest benefits for the largest number of people.
   Limitations. Under this model, immoral acts that hurt society or a minority group can be justified if they benefit the majority.
5. *Universalist theory*. Universalist theory says to focus on the intent of the decision. Every person is subject to the same standards. Weigh each decision against the screen: Would I be willing for everyone else in the world to make the same decision?
   Limitations. This model provides no absolutes. What one person believes is acceptable for all in society may be offensive to others.

As you can see, the five models do not provide absolute guidance on how to handle an ethical dilemma. Instead, they provide a departure point for discussing the implications of decisions. In some cases, actions are patently illegal, in which case they would be judged unethical by legal theory. However, some ethical dilemmas do not have a legal dimension. Strategic Application 5.1 shows how the five theories can be used to evaluate a strategic decision.

Codes of Ethics. As we mentioned in Chapter 4, high-level managers, especially the CEO, have a great deal of influence on the ethics of the organization. When a new top manager takes charge, his or her personal values help shape the ethics of the entire organization. Managers who work with the CEO quickly identify his or her value system and communicate it to lower level managers and employees. The CEO may also discuss organizational values in speeches, news releases, and memos. To the extent that the CEO controls the rewards systems subjectively, managers who make decisions that are consistent with the values of the CEO are likely to be rewarded, thus reinforcing what is expected. Many of the people who strongly disagree with the new values will leave the organization voluntarily. Or, if their own behavior pattern is inconsistent with the new rules of the game, they will be "forced out" through poor performance evaluations, missed promotions, and/or low salary increases. Thus, over a period of time, the example and actions of the CEO are reflected in most of the major decisions that are made by the organization.[21]

In spite of the power of the CEO, he or she is not the only determinant of organizational ethics. The ethics of an organization are also a reflection of the social groups from which managers and other employees are drawn (which makes global management even more challenging). These individuals bring a personal value system with them when they are hired. Also, if ethical change in society is not incorporated into the organization voluntarily, an employee or manager may "blow a whistle," which is an attempt to force the organization to cease a behavior that society currently finds unacceptable or to incorporate a practice that is in keeping with the new social value.

For example, antidiscrimination legal suits have prompted many organizations to adopt more stringent equal employment opportunity policies and even affirmative action programs. The ethics of various social groups are constantly changing. Therefore, strategic managers need to keep abreast of these changes in order to position their firms successfully. This task is especially difficult in global organizations.

STRATEGIC APPLICATION 5.1

APPLYING THE ETHICAL THEORIES TO AN ETHICAL DILEMMA

Suppose an organization produces a small amount of a toxic pollutant as part of its manufacturing process. Although the law requires that the material be disposed of in a special, costly manner, the company is sure that the small amount of pollutant it produces is not enough to damage local water supplies. Furthermore, the disposal method costs more than the original cost of some raw materials. If the company releases the small quantities of toxin into the sewer system, it is unlikely that it will be caught or fined.

Economic theory. Since there is a cost attached to disposal and it is unlikely that the firm will have to pay fines, the profit maximizing option is to release the toxin into the sewer system.

Legal theory. It is illegal to release the toxin.

Religion. In most religions, deceit of any kind is considered to be wrong.

Utilitarian theory. The costs of complying with the law are material and paid by the company and its shareholders. The costs of not complying are borne by society in the form of cleanups. In this case of a very small amount of toxin that is immediately diluted, there are no material costs to society.

Universalist theory. If every person in the world made the decision to allow a small amount

of toxin into the sewer system, the problem would be overwhelming.

* * *

Suppose an organization is having a tough year and chooses to lay off some employees at the end of the year to quickly improve the financials. The layoffs are not part of a permanent down-sizing strategy, just a temporary means for improving end-of-year performance.

Economic theory. Profit maximization is the goal. If the layoffs will improve profits, then they are the proper alternative, assuming the costs of hiring back employees later will not outweigh the benefits.

Legal theory. As long as all labor laws are followed in the process, there is no law against layoffs.

Religion. More than one interpretation possible.

Utilitarian theory. Lower costs of smaller workforce benefit shareholders and other employees whose jobs are presumably more secure as a result. Another alternative may be to reduce a few executive salaries or release a few high-paid consultants in order to keep the greater number of workers employed.

Universalist theory. If every employer used layoffs to improve end-of-year financial performance, the economy would be disrupted and large numbers of workers would suffer emotional and financial stress.

Many organizations create a code of ethics to communicate the values of the corporation to employees and other stakeholders. Codes of ethics are also a part of strategic direction, an extension of the organization's enterprise strategy.

The code of ethics of United Technologies states:

Our code of ethics, comprised of corporate principles and standards of conduct, governs our business decisions and actions. The integrity, reputation, and profitability of United Technologies ultimately depend upon the individual actions of our employees, representatives, agents and consultants all over the world. Each employee is personally responsible and accountable for compliance with our code.[22]

The United Technologies code of ethics addresses specific standards of conduct the organization will exhibit in its dealings with customers, suppliers, employees, shareholders, competitors, and worldwide communities, as shown in

Table 5.5 *Topics Covered by United Technologies' Code of Ethics*

Customers and Suppliers

Conflicts of interest	Marketing and selling
Antitrust compliance	Consultants and agents
U.S. government procurements	Proprietary information
Product quality and safety	Suppliers, vendors, and subcontractors

Employees

Equal employment opportunity	Open communication
Workplace environment	Employee development
Drug and alcohol abuse	Compensation and benefits
Employee privacy	

Shareholders

Return on investment	Accuracy of company records
Protection of assets	Shareholder communications

Worldwide Communities

Political contributions	International boycotts and restrictive trade practices
Employee involvement in the political process	Local laws and customs
Export control	Environmental issues
Foreign Corrupt Practices Act	Community support

Competitors

Antitrust laws	Marketing, selling, and advertising
Competitive information	

Employee Responsibilities

Compliance	Reporting of violations

Source: Code of Ethics, United Technologies, 1991.

Table 5.5. Employees are encouraged to report violations to their supervisors or the vice president for business practices. One of the statements in the code of ethics specifies that corporate policy prohibits retribution against employees for making reports of violations. Some codes of ethics set a minimum standard of behavior by stating that employees are expected to obey all laws. Other organizations, like Johnson & Johnson, make specific statements about values, duties, and obligations to customers, employees, and societies. Clearly, in those cases, the organization expects members to maintain standards of ethical behavior that transcend minimum legal standards.

To ensure that employees abide by the corporate code of ethics, some companies establish an ethics system, including an audit process to monitor compliance. However, Strategic Insight 5.2 demonstrates that sometimes formal systems are not enough to ensure ethical behavior.

In an award-winning article titled "The Parable of the Sadhu," Bowen McCoy, an investment banker with Morgan Stanley, discussed what he thought was the core, underlying problem when an organization handles ethical dilemmas poorly.[23] In his view, people who are part of an organization often do not personalize

STRATEGIC INSIGHT 5.2

BUSINESS

STRATEGY

Dow Corning's Ethics Audit Process

Dow Corning established a system in the 1970s that was widely regarded as a model of extraordinary organizational commitment to ethics. The system involved company training sessions on ethics, an ethics section on the company's semiannual employee opinion survey, and audits of each business operation every three years. The ethics system provided for six managers to serve three-year terms on a Business Conduct Committee. Every three years, each location was audited by two members of the Business Conduct Committee. The audits involved a three-hour review session with employees at that location. The results of the audit were reported to the Audit and Social Responsibility Committee of the board of directors.

Although it was an ambitious and well-intentioned attempt to create an ethical culture, the formal system was not enough. The same year the ethics system was implemented, an engineer warned Dow Corning of the health hazards of silicone breast implants and, when no action was taken, resigned from the company in protest. A series of internal documents from Dow Corning suggest that the company was aware of potential health problems and tried to keep the information from the public. When the health problems were revealed in the 1990s, the ethics system came under close scrutiny. It is possible that smaller groups and auditors from outside the company would have helped surface the problems. It is also possible that the system was not enough to change the fundamental culture.

Source: J. A. Byrne, "The Best-Laid Ethics Programs," *Business Week* (March 9, 1992), pp. 67–69.

ethical issues. It is as if the "organization" is responsible, and the individuals are not. Even individuals who see themselves as very ethical will tend to pass through an ethical dilemma without recognizing it as one, or will view the dilemma as ultimately someone else's problem. For many ethical dilemmas, one person is not physically capable of correcting the problem alone.

When faced with a major crisis, such as finding out that a key product is dangerous to the customers who buy it, many organizations do not know what to do. There is no guiding precept, no system of shared values, to unite the organization behind a clear understanding of correct behavior. Although some organization members may feel discomfort with the course of action being pursued by the organization, a change in action requires a structured, systematic effort by the entire organization. According to McCoy:

> *Some organizations do have a value system that transcends the personal values of the managers. Such values, which go beyond profitability, are usually revealed when the organization is under stress. . . .Members need to share a preconceived notion of what is correct behavior, a "business ethic," and think of it as a positive force, not a constraint.*[24]

The individual has a critical role in the development of the shared values. McCoy writes, "What is the nature of our responsibility if we consider ourselves to be ethical persons? Perhaps it is to change the values of the group so that it can, with all its resources, take the other road."[25]

STRATEGIC INSIGHT 5.3

Is the Japanese Market Open to Foreign Companies?

If Japan's policies and business culture really do deny foreign companies a fighting chance, governments around the world may feel pressured to enact greater protectionist legislation. Overall, is the playing field level? "The Japanese market is not as closed as Americans think," says Akio Morita, former chairman of Sony, "but not as open as the Japanese think."

Japan has greatly changed since the mid-1980s. In many markets today's tilt is less steep than it was, and an official, orchestrated policy of thwarting the *gaijin* (foreigner) is mostly gone. In fact, Japan has cut average tariffs on manufactured goods below America's (2.1% versus 5%). Japan even subsidizes some imports. For the last three years, Japan has offered tax credits to Japanese companies that substantially boost imports of a wide array of manufactured goods. The real problems American and other foreign companies have in Japan stem from the way the Japanese do business. Japanese values concerning what is considered fair business practice, combined with cartels that would be largely illegal in the United States, make it difficult for outsiders to compete.

The word *keiretsu* is usually associated with giant industrial groups linked by cross-ownership, such as Mitsubishi or Sumitomo. But the term can also apply to long-standing business relationships among smaller companies. Members of a Japanese keiretsu give preferential treatment to other members and are reluctant to offer business to new entrants, regardless of the economic advantages. They sometimes set price and volume limits on imports. They may also divvy up market share among themselves. Actions such as these provide enormous barriers against foreign competitors.

Nevertheless, the situation is improving. Japan's Fair Trade Commission has intervened on several occasions to help level the playing field. The commission even issued a "cease and desist" order against the Japanese flat glass oligopoly. Also, a new report by the Keidanren, Japan's prestigious organization of top industrial leaders, calls for *kyosei* (symbiosis) with the United States. One way to achieve it, the report says, is "for keiretsu members to provide ample opportunities for newcomers, particularly those from foreign countries." Kazuo Nukazawas, the Keidanren's managing director, says he hopes for a future in which critics like Edith Cresson, France's former prime minister, will no longer describe his country as an anthill.

Source: Adapted from E. Faltermayer, "Does Japan Play Fair?" *Fortune* (September 7, 1992), pp. 38–52. Used with permission.

Ethics in Global Organizations. Dealing with the ethics of employees, customers, and other stakeholders and the society from which they are drawn is a difficult task even in organizations that compete within a single domestic economy. However, the difficulty level increases for global organizations because value systems are highly divergent across international boundaries. For example, a recent survey of 3,783 female seniors attending 561 universities and colleges in Tokyo revealed that they not only expected sexism in the work place, but did not seem to mind it. "More than 91% said they would not mind being treated as 'office flowers.' Nearly 25% considered that to be a woman's role. Over 66% said acting like an office flower would make the atmosphere more pleasant."[26] This attitude concerning the role of women, which is widely held in Japan, is inconsistent with the values of most Americans.

In fact, Japanese companies are responding to pressure to conform to the values of the countries in which they compete. For instance, Akio Morita, former chairman of Sony, once argued that Japanese corporations must adapt the way they do business, in response to resentment from U.S. and European rivals. His formula was to "seek profits ahead of market share, increase dividends to shareholders, treat employees more humanely, (and) contribute more to the community and environmental protection."[27] This represents a major departure from the way some Japanese managers think. U.S and other foreign competitors in Japan also have a difficult time dealing with Japanese values, as Strategic Insight 5.3 illustrates. As Akio Morita suggests, American managers need to find ways to adapt to the countries in which they operate.

This concludes our discussion of strategic direction, including missions, visions, business definition, and, finally, ethics and enterprise strategy. A few questions that can help you determine the strategic direction of an organization are contained in Strategic Application 5.2. You may want to apply this application to some of the cases you analyze. The next section discusses an organization's orientation toward growth, which is another essential element of strategic direction.

STRATEGIC APPLICATION 5.2

IDENTIFICATION OF STRATEGIC DIRECTION

Answers to the following questions can help an organization identify its strategic direction. These elements are often a part of the organization's mission statement.

Organizational Vision

> What do top managers (especially the CEO) believe the organization can become?
>
> Is the organization headed in that direction?
>
> Is the vision widely shared among employees and managers?
>
> What are the organization's long-term goals?

Business Definition

> Who is being satisfied (i.e., markets)?
>
> What is being satisfied (i.e., functions)?

How are customer needs being satisfied (i.e., resource conversion processes)?

What are the products of the organization?

To what extent is the organization vertically integrated?

What should the business definition be?

Enterprise Strategy

> What does the organization stand for?
>
> What is its purpose?
>
> What are the basic values and ethics of the organization?
>
> What is the basic attitude of the organization toward each of its stakeholder groups?
>
> Does the organization have a stated code of ethics?

ATTITUDE TOWARD GROWTH

Prospectors
Organizations that aggressively seek new market opportunities and are willing to take risks.

Defenders
Organizations with a strategy that protects their current position and which engage in little or no new product/market development.

Analyzers
Organizations that attempt to maintain existing market positions while still locating conservative growth opportunities.

Reactors
Organizations with no distinct strategy except to respond to environmental situations.

The scope of a business depends, among other things, on the attitude of its managers toward growth. The findings of Raymond Miles and Charles Snow are illustrative of this point. Based on field studies in four industries, they classified firms into one of four categories based on the rate at which they changed their products and markets. They were able to identify four general categories.[28] **Prospectors** pursue what could be termed an offensive strategy. They aggressively seek new market opportunities and are willing to take risks. **Defenders**, on the other hand, are turf protectors that engage in little or no new product/market development. Their strategic actions are intended to preserve market share through reducing the impact of offensive moves by competitors. **Analyzers** occupy a position in between prospectors and defenders. They attempt to maintain positions in existing markets, while locating growth opportunities on the fringes. **Reactors** do not have a distinct strategy. They simply react to environmental situations.

The Miles and Snow classifications illustrate two fundamentally different positions with respect to, among other things, growth. Prospectors aggressively pursue growth, while defenders tend to pursue stability. Firms in the other two classifications are somewhere in between these two extremes. Attitude toward growth is critical to guiding the effective allocation of resources, which is one of the purposes of a mission statement. Depending on how managers pursue growth, an organization's mission may change over time. Strategic Insight 5.4 shows how a small firm increased the scope of its business activities to pursue a higher growth strategy.

Growth Strategies

Market Penetration
Investing in advertising, expanding capacity, and/or increasing sales force in order to increase market share in the current business.

Market Development
Broadening an organization's definition of its markets by seeking new market segments or new applications of its products.

Product/Service Development
Modifying existing products or developing new products/services for the purpose of selling more to existing customers or creating new market segments.

Businesses can accomplish growth through internal or external means. By investing its resources (i.e., time, money, people) internally, the firm can pursue market penetration, market development, or product/service development. External growth options involve investing organizational resources in another company or business and include horizontal integration, joint ventures, vertical integration, and related or unrelated acquisitions. All of these approaches are outlined in Table 5.6.

Market penetration entails investing in advertising, capacity expansion, and/or the sales force with the intent of increasing market share in the current business. This strategy requires no changes in the scope of the organization. On the other hand, **market development**, in which the organization seeks new market segments or new applications of its products, requires a broadened definition of the markets or functions served. To support market development, firms may need to invest in market research, new market development, a new sales force, or applications development and testing. For example, a nylon fabric manufacturer who sells fabric to windsuit manufacturers would likely have to invest in market and applications development in order to sell nylon fabric to tent or sleeping bag manufacturers.

Firms pursuing **product/service development** seek to *modify* existing products or *develop* new products/services for the purpose of selling more to existing customers or creating new market segments. In addition to changes in the scope of products/services, this type of development may require expanded definitions in markets, functions served, or the resource conversion process. Resource allocations focus on product/service development, applications development, basic research and development, and perhaps process development or market development, depending on the nature of new or modified products/services. For exam-

STRATEGIC INSIGHT 5.4

BUSINESS

STRATEGY

Culligan Water Conditioning Expands Its Scope

Culligan Water Conditioning has not only survived but has grown in an economically depressed region by increasing the scope of its operations. The company, a water-conditioning equipment dealer and bottled water business, is based in Havre, Montana, a small community in the heart of an agricultural region. Its main challenge was to maintain cash flow and grow the business in an economically depressed region.

After hitting the saturation point in water-conditioning equipment, Culligan used its own water conditioners to enter the water bottling market. As demand grew, the company had to open two bottling facilities to create an effective distribution system. The company also discovered that coffee, tea, and snack foods were natural extensions of its product lines, since bottled water is often delivered to lobbies and business areas.

In addition to increasing the scope of its business, Culligan practices good stakeholder management. Culligan constantly keeps its name in front of the public through advertising on television and radio, in newspapers, and through coupons and specials. The company also stresses prompt, professional service and encourages employees to develop greater expertise in their fields by attending conventions and seminars. Culligan supports its community by buying locally and contributing to schools, churches, and civic organizations, including donations of free services and products.

All of these efforts paid off. The company experienced 33% sales growth and 50% employee growth over a period of three years. It is in the process of building its third water bottling plant.

Source: Adapted from "Culligan Water Conditioning of Havre," *Strengthening America's Competitiveness: The Blue Chip Enterprise Initiative* (Warner Books on behalf of Connecticut Mutual Life Insurance Company and the U.S. Chamber of Commerce, 1991), pp. 40–41.

ple, pharmaceutical companies continuously make investments in new and improved products. Johnson & Johnson manufactures an effective drug for the treatment of colon cancer which started out as a sheep wormer sold through veterinarians! Through product and applications development, the drug now serves a very different function and a completely different customer group. Consequently, the types of customers served and the functions served by a particular company's product/service line may change over time.

Horizontal integration, an external growth strategy, involves the purchase of an organization in the same line of business. Typically, horizontal integration is accomplished for the purpose of gaining market share in a particular market, expanding a market geographically, or augmenting product or service lines. This was the motivation behind Delta Airlines' acquisition of Western Airlines. However, the products or services of the firm that is purchased may be different enough to require a broader definition of products/services, functions served, or the resource conversion process.

The second external tactic for achieving growth is through joint ventures, which, as defined earlier, are strategic alliances formed with other organizations to

Table 5.6 *Attitude Toward Growth and the Scope of the Business*

Internal Options

1. Market Penetration
   Tactic: Increase market share in current business through advertising, promotions, stepped-up sales effort.
   Change in scope: None.
2. Market Development
   Tactic: Identify new market segments or new applications for products/services.
   Change in scope: Broaden definition of markets or functions served by products/services.
3. Product/Services Development
   Tactic: Modify existing products/services or develop new products/services for existing or potential customers.
   Change in scope: Definite change in products/services. Possible changes in markets, functions served, and/or resource conversion processes.

External Options

1. Horizontal Integration
   Tactic: Purchase company in same line of business.
   Change in scope: Extend market base. May also include other changes, depending on the company acquired.
2. Joint Ventures
   Tactic: Create alliances with other organizations to achieve market position, product development, or process development.
   Change in scope: Extend products/services, markets, functions served, and/or alter resource conversion process.
3. Vertical Integration
   Tactic: Purchase company or internally develop capacity forward or backward in the industry supply chain.
   Change in scope: Substantial change in products/services, markets, functions served, and resource conversion process.
4. Related or Unrelated Acquisitions
   Tactic: Purchase other company for a wide variety of strategic reasons.
   Change in scope: Depends entirely on the nature of the company acquired.

penetrate new domestic or foreign markets, develop new products and services, or improve existing processes for producing products and services. For example, a joint venture between General Motors and Toyota led to the Geo. Also, Corningware cookware was developed through a joint venture between Corning Glass Works and Dow Chemical called Dow-Corning.

Ventures that penetrate new markets require a broadening of the market definition, while ventures to develop new products/services require changes to the products/services and perhaps functions also. Finally, ventures that seek to improve processes probably require changes in the resource conversion process.

Vertical integration is classified as an external growth option because it is often accomplished through purchase of a supplier or a customer. However, vertical integration can also be accomplished "in house" by enlarging the firm's scope to include more resource conversion processes. Vertically integrated businesses may appear, on the surface, to be highly related to existing businesses. However, vertical integration typically involves a change in *every* dimension of scope—products/services, markets (unless all goods and services of the new company are kept in house), functions served, and certainly resource conversion processes. Consequently, vertical integration provides substantial diversification, or movement into "new" businesses, and a firm that can master one stage of the industry supply chain will not necessarily excel at other stages. For instance, Southland's (7-Eleven Stores) venture into petroleum refining (Citgo) proved to be unsuccessful.

The final option for external growth includes all types of acquisitions that do not fall into the categories of horizontal integration or vertical integration. Organizations use acquisitions for a variety of strategic purposes. Their influence on the scope of the organization depends entirely on the nature of the business acquired. Acquisitions are discussed in depth in Chapter 7.

Whereas the seven options of market penetration, market development, product development, horizontal integration, joint ventures, vertical integration, and related or unrelated acquisitions are all intended to produce growth, not all organizational missions stress growth. The next subsection deals with organizations that desire a stable investment strategy to maintain what they have.

Stability Strategies

While most for-profit organizations actively seek growth, some organizations do not. They may be family-owned businesses, nonprofit organizations that are satisfied with the current level of operations, or simply business organizations that are content with their share of a mature market. In these situations, no overt actions are taken to achieve growth. The prevalent theme of operations is "business as usual." These types of organizations maintain fairly level investments in marketing, operations, and services and only engage in enough R&D to maintain their share of the market. As mentioned previously, they are best described as defenders.

Some executives are bothered by the concept of limited or no growth. However, the stakeholder framework developed in this text provides a vehicle for understanding why and when a no-growth philosophy may be appropriate. The appropriateness of any strategic position depends on the attitudes of the stakeholders that the organization intends to serve. Some organizations are composed of people who enjoy stability and security. These firms may stress lifetime employment, a family atmosphere, and slow but certain promotion as managers age and retire. They may also take pride in excellent craftsmanship or superior service to long-standing clients. Lincoln Electric Company fits this description fairly well.

Nevertheless, a limited or no-growth position is hard to defend for organizations that are publicly held because managers, as agents for the owners, are responsible for actions that will enhance shareholder wealth. Lincoln gets around this agency problem because its stock is owned almost entirely by managers and employees. However, there are also situations in which investing for the objective of growth is ineffective.

For instance, a firm may find itself in a mature, declining, or rigidly segmented market in which efforts to increase sales would cost more than they are worth. This situation is typical of industries with low profits, no growth, and high **exit barriers**. Exit barriers exist when the capital equipment and skills an organization possesses are not applicable to other businesses.[29] For example, equipment used in brewing has almost no potential for other uses. Consequently, many smaller breweries are barely able to survive against large organizations such as Anheuser-Busch, but they do not close down because their entire investment would be lost.

Organizations may also pursue a temporary no-growth strategy during periods of restructuring. **Restructuring** often involves streamlining and reorienting

Exit Barriers
Occur when the capital equipment and skills of an organization are not applicable to other businesses or when there are other significant costs associated with exiting a business area or market.

Restructuring
Streamlining and reorienting an organization's current format of operations to place it in a position in which it is better able to compete; often involves reducing the scope of the business at the corporate level combined with refocusing efforts on the things the organization does well.

the organization. Product lines are trimmed, unnecessary workers are laid off, and investment priorities are altered to bring the organization more in line with the external environment. The intent is usually to place the organization on a sound footing, followed by more effective growth in the future. Restructuring is discussed in depth in Chapter 10.

This concludes our discussion of the scope of the business as it relates to organizational purpose and attitude toward growth. The next section discusses how strategic direction and growth strategy are affected as an organization moves into the global arena.

INTERNATIONAL EXPANSION AND STRATEGIC DIRECTION

Domestic Stage
The organization focuses its efforts on domestic operations but begins to export its products and services.

International Stage
Export becomes an important part of the organization's strategy.

Multinational Stage
The organization has marketing and production facilities throughout the world, with over one-third of sales from overseas operations.

Global Stage
The organization is no longer associated primarily with any one country.

As the examples in this chapter have clearly demonstrated, some organizations are more globally oriented than others. An organization's attitude toward international expansion is also a part of its strategic direction. Organizations seem to evolve through four stages of international development.[30] In the first stage, the **domestic stage,** organizations focus their efforts on domestic operations, but begin to export their products and services, sometimes through an export department or a foreign joint venture. Toys 'R' Us, a fairly recent entrant into foreign markets, is currently in this stage. In the **international stage**, exports become an important part of organizational strategy. The organization typically forms international divisions to handle sales, service, and warehousing in the foreign markets. Marketing programs are tailored to suit the needs of each country. Hasbro, the toy maker, is in this stage.[31]

In the third stage, the **multinational stage,** the organization has marketing and production facilities throughout the world. More than a third of firm sales originate overseas, and the organization has worldwide access to capital markets. Nike, the shoe distributor, just entered the multinational stage, passing the point at which one-third of revenues come from non-U.S. sales.[32] Finally, in the **global stage,** the organization is no longer associated primarily with any one country. Global firms, such as Phillips N.V., Unilever, and Matsushita Electric, operate in as many as forty countries or more.

Unfortunately, not all U.S. companies are ready for global expansion. According to Sheth and Eshghi, experts on international strategy:

Many companies become multinational reluctantly. They start off as export houses, and as international business grows and becomes a significant part of corporate revenues, they become more involved in foreign operations. However, the corporate culture still remains domestic, and the international division is treated as a stepchild. The situation becomes one of them vs. us...what is lacking is a true worldwide orientation in product design, manufacturing, and marketing functions.[33]

Structural inertia within U.S. companies has been a major impediment to their transformation into true global competitors. Historically, North American companies have been able to prosper by selling goods to the largest and richest market in the world. In the past, some managers considered overseas operations nuisances or simply organizational appendages that generated a few extra dollars in sales revenue.[34] Now, the world has changed. Since global competitors have invaded U.S. markets, U.S. companies must also learn to compete overseas.

Global expansion requires an adjustment in the business definition of the organization. The answer to "Who is being satisfied" is enlarged to include worldwide customers. However, this is not the only stakeholder group that is affected. Depending on the nature of the venture, any of the stakeholder groups may be enlarged. At a minimum, all global ventures rely on cooperation from a foreign government; however, most foreign ventures involve many other stakeholder groups as well. These new stakeholders add a new dimension to stakeholder analysis and management. They also increase the need for a state-of-the-art business intelligence system.

International activities should also be accompanied by a new mind-set for all members of an organization, from top managers to the lowest level employees. Where will this new global mind-set come from? It has to start at the top of the organization. CEOs who want to create global organizations can start by expanding their organizational visions to include overseas operations. However, they should also assign specific individuals to monitor global stakeholder groups, economic trends, and markets and integrate this information into ongoing strategic management processes through the business intelligence system.

CEOs can create a sense of urgency in the organization by constantly discussing global customers, operations, strategies, and successes and failures with subordinates, the board of directors, employees, and the media. They will also want to make visits to global operations a part of their regular routines. Finally, CEOs can communicate the value of employees from countries that are outside of the home country by making sure that they are both hired and promoted as often as Americans.

Organizations are also sending some of their managers to special training programs to help increase their global awareness and vision. The University of Michigan provided an intensive, in-depth five-week program for twenty-one executives from Japan, the United States, Brazil, Great Britain, and India to help them become global thinkers. They first made the participants more aware of the differences that existed among them. Then they helped them to work out these differences. The training program was so successful that organizers are planning to make it an annual event.[35]

Summary

Strategic direction should be based, in part, on an analysis of the internal and external environments and the history of success or failure of the organization. Strategic managers are charged with the responsibility of providing long-term direction for their organizations, while at the same time balancing the competing interests of key stakeholders. The development of a mission can help managers with this responsibility.

A mission often contains statements concerning the basic purposes and broad goals of an organization, as reflected in its enterprise strategy, a vision of what it can become, and a definition of its business or businesses. Some missions are not written, but this does not necessarily reduce their effectiveness as long as they are clearly communicated through other means. Attitude toward growth, whether stated or implied, was found to be a key factor in determining the scope of an organization's businesses.

An organization's enterprise strategy is determined by the ethics of the organization, which in turn are determined by the ethics of the key strategic decision makers. Five basic ethical systems underlying ethics are economic, legal, religious, utilitarian, and universalist.

An organization's attitude toward international expansion was the final area of strategic direction discussed in this chapter. The four stages of international development, in order of greater global involvement, are the domestic stage, the international stage, the multinational stage, and the global stage. Increased global participation requires a new mind-set in organizations, which can be encouraged through training and the specific actions of the CEO.

Discussion Questions

1. What, really, is an organizational mission? What is the difference between a mission and a vision? What can a mission include? Does a mission have to be formally written down to be effective?

2. What is an enterprise strategy? Why is an enterprise strategy important to an organization?

3. Describe the four elements that are critical in defining the business or businesses of an organization. Define the business of a large, diversified organization with which you are familiar. Do not use a company that was described in this chapter.

4. Describe the basic internal and external options for pursuing growth.

5. In what situations might a no-growth philosophy be warranted?

6. Using the questions contained in Strategic Application 5.2 as a guide, create a mission statement for the university or college you are attending. Make any logical assumptions that are necessary to complete the task.

7. Describe the four stages of global development. What can top managers do to make their organizations more globally oriented?

References

1. D. Kirkpatrick, "At Compaq," *Fortune* (April 1, 1996), pp. 121–122. © 1996 Time Inc. All Rights Reserved.

2. K. Labich, "Why Companies Fail," *Fortune* (November 14, 1994), p. 53.

3. L. J. Bourgeois, "Performance and Consensus," *Strategic Management Journal*, 1 (1980), pp. 227–248; G. G. Dess, "Consensus on Strategy Formulation and Organizational Performance: Competitors in a Fragmented Industry," *Strategic Management Journal* 8 (1987), pp. 259–277; L. G. Hrebiniak and C.C. Snow, "Top Management Agreement and Organizational Performance," *Human Relations* 35 (1982), pp. 1139–1158; Labich, "Why Companies Fail."

4. S. Nelton, "Put Your Purpose in Writing," *Nation's Business* (February 1994), p. 63.

5. J. Betton and G. G. Dess, "The Application of Population Ecology Models to the Study of Organizations," *Academy of Management Review* 10 (1985), pp. 750–757.

6. T. Levitt, "Marketing Myopia," *Harvard Business Review* (July/August 1960), pp. 45–60.

7. D. F. Abell, *Defining the Business: The Starting Point of Strategic Planning* (Englewood Cliffs, N.J.: Prentice-Hall, 1980), p. 169.

8. Abell, *Defining the Business.*

9. C. H. St. John, "Toys 'R' Us," in M. J. Stahl and D. W. Grigsby, *Strategic Management for Decision Making* (Boston: PWS-Kent, 1992), pp. 648–660.

10. J. S. Bracker, "Delta Airlines," in J. R. Montanari, C. P. Morgan, and J. S. Bracker, *Strategic Management: A Choice Approach* (Chicago: Dryden Press, 1990), pp. 657–670.

11. J. R. Galbraith and R. K. Kazanjian, *Strategy Implementation: Structure, Systems and Process*, 2nd ed. (St. Paul, Minn.: West Publishing Company, 1986), Chap. 4.

12. P. F. Drucker, *Management—Tasks, Responsibilities, Practices* (New York: Harper and Row, 1974), pp. 74–94.

13. Levitt, "Marketing Myopia."

14. D. J. Isenberg, "The Tactics of Strategic Opportunism," *Harvard Business Review* (March/April 1987), pp. 92–97.

15. L. T. Hosmer, "Strategic Planning as if Ethics Mattered," *Strategic Management Journal* 15 (1994), pp. 17–34; D. Schendel and C. Hofer, *Strategic Management: A New View of Business Policy and Planning* (Boston: Little, Brown, and Company, 1979).

16. R. E. Freeman and D. R. Gilbert, Jr., *Corporate Strategy and the Search for Ethics* (Englewood Cliffs, N.J.: 1988).

17. *Annual Report*, American Red Cross, 1989.

18. J. A. Pearce II and F. David, "Corporate Mission Statements: The Bottom Line," *Academy of Management Executive* (May 1987), pp. 109–115.

19. L. T. Hosmer, *The Ethics of Management*, 2nd ed., (Homewood, Ill.: Irwin, 1991).

20. Based on information in Hosmer, *The Ethics of Management.*

21. E. H. Schein, *Organizational Culture and Leadership* (San Francisco: Jossey-Bass, 1985); E. H. Schein, "The Role of the Founder in Creating Organizational Culture," *Organizational Dynamics* (Summer 1983), p. 14; P. Selznik, *Leadership in Administration* (Evanston, Ill.: Row, Peterson, 1957).

22. *Code of Ethics*, United Technologies, 1991.

23. B. McCoy, "The Parable of the Sadhu," *Harvard Business Review*, (September–October 1983), pp. 103–108.

24. McCoy, "The Parable of the Sadhu," p. 107.

25. McCoy, "The Parable of the Sadhu," p. 108.

26. E. Thronton, "Japan: Sexism OK with Most Coeds," *Business Week* (August 24, 1992), p. 13.

27. "Why Japan Must Change," *Fortune* (March 9, 1992), p. 66.

28. R. E. Miles and C. C. Snow, *Organization Strategy, Structure and Process* (New York: McGraw-Hill, 1978); R. E. Miles, C. C. Snow, A. D. Meyer, and H. J. Coleman, Jr.," Organizational Strategy, Structure and Process," *Academy of Management Review* 3 (1978), pp. 546–562.

29. K. R. Harrigan, "Deterrents to Divestiture," *Academy of Management Journal* 24 (1981), pp. 306–323.

30. N. J. Adler, *International Dimensions of Organizational Behavior*, 2nd ed. (Boston: PWS-Kent, 1991); R.L. Daft, *Organization Theory and Design*, 4th ed. (St. Paul, Minn.: West

Publishing Company, 1992), pp. 228–229; T. T. Herbert, "Strategy and Multinational Organizational Structure: An Interorganizational Relationships Perspective," *Academy of Management Review* 9 (1984), pp. 259–271.

31. D. W. Grigsby, "Hasbro, Inc.," in M. J. Stahl and D. W. Grigsby, *Strategic Management for Decision Making* (Boston: PWS-Kent, 1992), pp. 725–738.

32. "Nike Net Surged 21% In Quarter to Record; Stock Rises by $6.375," *The Wall Street Journal* (July 9, 1992), p. B4.

33. J. Sheth and G. Eshghi, *Global Strategic Management Perspectives* (Cincinnati: South-Western Publishing, 1989), p. 13.

34. C. A. Bartlett and S. Ghoshal, "Global Strategic Management: Impact on the New Frontiers of Strategy Research," *Strategic Management Journal* 12 (1991), pp. 5–16.

35. S. Tully, "The Hunt for the Global Manager," *Fortune* (May 21, 1990), pp. 140–144; J. Main, "How 21 Men Got Global in 35 Days," *Fortune* (November 6, 1989), p. 71.

3

Strategy Formulation

chapter

6

Business-Level Strategy

Pep Boys at War

Mitchell Leibovitz, CEO of Pep Boys—Manny, Moe and Jack—wants to annihilate other auto parts retailers. When intense competition from Pep Boys forces chains like Auto Zone, Western Auto, or Genuine Parts to abandon a location, he adds a snapshot of the closed-down store to his collection. He burns and buries baseball caps bearing their corporate logos and videotapes the ritual to show his 14,500 employees. "I don't believe in friendly competition," he says. "I want to put them out of business."

An accountant who got his MBA at Temple University at night, Leibovitz, 47, treats retailing like war. He says consolidation is under way in the $125-billion-a-year aftermarket for parts and servicing, so Pep Boys must be "a killer." That means offering superior selection, price, and service. For instance, Pep Boys stocks fan belts not just for current car models but for 98% of all cars on the road.

Alone among its major competitors, Pep Boys can install what it sells. Nearly all its stores have ten or so service bays that keep long hours. They stay open thirteen hours a day Monday through Sunday, no appointment needed. To curb the overcharging and superfluous repairs that are endemic in auto service, Leibovitz mixes sticks with carrots. Mechanics get a percentage of their labor charge, but—contrary to common practice—no share of the price of the parts they install. If work has to be done over, they may forfeit their cut. Customers can register complaints and compliments through an 800 "squeal" number and postage-paid feedback cards that Leibovitz reads himself. Says Leibovitz: "The service business is hard to manage. But if it were easy, everyone would do it."[1]

Business-level strategy defines an organization's approach to competing in its chosen markets. Pep Boys' strategy can be described as a combination of low-cost leadership and differentiation, a combination called "best cost," which is increasing in popularity. Pep Boys achieves low cost through high volume and a massive distribution network. However, Pep Boys also differentiates its service in the eyes of the consumer through an innovative pricing policy, a huge supply of even hard-to-get parts, convenient hours, and an 800 number.

Some of the major strategic management responsibilities of business-level managers are listed in Table 6.1. They include establishing the overall direction of the business unit, ongoing analysis of the changing business situation, selecting a generic strategy and the specific strategies needed to carry it out (strategic posture), and managing resources to produce a sustainable competitive advantage. These responsibilities and the methods for carrying them out are similar in for-profit and nonprofit organizations.[2] They also apply well to organizations that are oriented toward services, as the Pep Boys example illustrates. This chapter focuses on selecting specific business-level strategies and developing distinctive competencies that lead to competitive advantages.

GENERIC BUSINESS STRATEGIES

Business strategies are as different as the organizations that create them. That is, no two business strategies are exactly alike. However, classifying strategies into generic types helps firms identify common strategic characteristics. For example, a firm that is trying to achieve a competitive advantage by producing at lowest cost should emphasize production efficiency, low levels of administrative overhead, and high volume. Also, since generic strategies are widely understood, they provide a means of meaningful communication. Instead of having to explain the strategy each time, managers can simply use the generic label. The generic strat-

---

Table 6.1 *Major Business-Level Strategic Management Responsibilities*

Major Responsibilities	Key Issues
Direction setting	Establishment and communication of mission, vision, ethics, and long-term goals of a single business unit
	Creation and communication of shorter term goals and objectives
Analysis of business situation	Compilation and assessment of information from stakeholders and other sources
	Identification of strengths, weaknesses, opportunities, threats, sources of sustainable competitive advantage
Selection of strategy	Selection of a generic approach to competition—cost leadership, differentiation, focus, or best cost
	Selection of a strategic posture—specific strategies needed to carry out the generic strategy
Management of resources	Acquisition of resources and/or development of competencies leading to a sustainable competitive advantage
	Development of functional strategies and an appropriate management structure to support business strategy

Figure 6.1 *Three Generic Business Strategies*

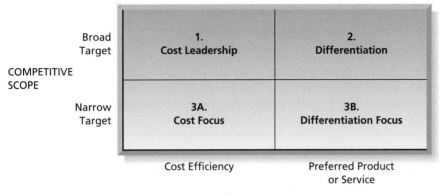

Source: Adapted with the permission of The Free Press, a Division of Simon & Schuster, from *Competitive Advantage: Creating and Sustaining Superior Performance* by Michael E. Porter. Copyright © 1985 by Michael E. Porter, p. 12.

egy types proposed by Michael Porter are perhaps the most widely used and understood.

Porter advanced the idea that a sustainable competitive advantage is related to the amount of value a firm creates for its most important stakeholder, the customer.[3] According to Porter, firms create superior value for customers by either offering them a basic product or service that was produced at the lowest possible cost or by offering them a preferred product or service at a somewhat higher price, for which the additional value received exceeds the additional cost of obtaining it. The first option necessitates efficient cost production, while the second requires the ability to differentiate the product or service on the basis of higher quality, more innovative features, greater selection, better service after sale, more advertising, or some other attribute. Porter combined these two bases for competitive advantage with the scope of the market in which a firm competes to form the generic strategies of cost leadership, differentiation, and focus. Focus is further divided into cost focus and differentiation focus, since a firm can focus on a particular segment of the market through either low-cost leadership or differentiation. These divisions are illustrated in Figure 6.1.

Since Porter originally described the generic strategies, increasing global competition has made a hybrid strategy increasingly popular. In this book, we refer to it as "best cost," which means that an organization pursues both strategies simultaneously. These generic strategies are now described in detail.

Cost Leadership

Firms pursuing cost leadership set out to become the lowest cost providers of a good or service. The broad scope of cost leaders means that they attempt to serve a large percentage of the total market. Firms pursuing cost leadership include McDonald's and Panasonic. Strategic Insight 6.1 contains a detailed description of Chaparral Steel, the low-cost leader in the steel industry.

To fully appreciate the significance of the low-cost producer strategy, it is important to understand the factors that underlie cost structures in firms. Firms pursuing a low-cost producer strategy will typically employ one or more of the fol-

STRATEGIC INSIGHT 6.1

BUSINESS

STRATEGY

Chaparral Steel Unleashes Worker to Cut Costs

A car full of executives from U.S. Steel rolled down Highway 67 not long ago, past a billboard advertising Deer Processing, and into Midlothian, Texas, home of Dee Tee's coffee house and Dizzy Daisey's floristry. What brought this entourage so far out of its way was a desire to learn how little Chaparral Steel has achieved a big distinction: becoming the world's low-cost steel producer.

Chaparral is remarkable because, like a sculling crew that pulls in flawless synchronism, it has all the basic elements of good management—customer service, empowerment, quality training, and more—working in concert. As a result, it produces steel with a record low 1.6 hours of labor per ton, versus 2.4 hours for other mini-mills and 4.9 hours for integrated producers. Making such products as skyscraper beams and concrete reinforcing rods, Chaparral is in a down and dirty commodity business. But by sticking to its low-cost philosophy, it has shown that any company can make money in a mature industry, even when times are tough.

Behind Chaparral's success is mild-mannered CEO Gordon Forward, a native of British Columbia with a Ph.D. in metallurgy. Texas Industries, a cement company that owns 81% of Chaparral, asked Forward in 1975 to leave his job at a Canadian steel company to help found a mini-mill. To become the world's low-cost producer, he focused on three ideas: the classless corporation, universal education, and freedom to act.

In return for extraordinary freedom and trust (e.g., employees don't punch a clock), workers are expected to take the initiative, use their heads, and get the job done. To help them use their noggins, Chaparral makes sure that at least 85% of its 950 employees are enrolled in courses, cross-training in such varied disciplines as electronics, metallurgy, and credit history.

How does this lower costs? In scores of ways: When Chaparral was designing its new mill for making wide-flange steel beams used in bridges and buildings, the employees developed a patent-pending technology that manufactures a final product with just 12 passes through the system, versus traditional methods that require up to 50 passes. In another part of the mill, two maintenance workers invented a machine for strapping bundles of steel rods together that cost only $60,000, versus $250,000 for the old machines, and it did the job faster and more flexibly.

Source: B. Dumaine, "Unleash Workers and Cut Costs," *Fortune* (May 18, 1992), p. 88. Used with permission.

lowing factors to create their low cost positions: (1) accurate demand forecasting combined with high-capacity utilization, (2) economies of scale, (3) technological advances, or (4) learning/experience effects.[4] We explain these factors next.

High-Capacity Utilization. When demand is high and production capacity is fully utilized, a firm's fixed costs are spread over more units, which lowers unit costs. However, when demand falls off, the fixed costs are spread over fewer units so that unit costs increase. This basic concept suggests that a firm which is able to maintain higher levels of **capacity utilization**, either through better demand forecasting, conservative capacity expansion policies, or aggressive

Capacity Utilization
Higher levels of capacity utilization spread fixed expenses, leading to lower unit costs.

pricing, will be able to maintain a lower cost structure than a competitor of equal size and capability.

High-capacity utilization is particularly important in industries in which fixed costs represent a large percentage of total costs (a highly capital-intensive industry). In these situations, entry barriers exist that make industry participants extremely sensitive to even small fluctuations in customer demand. For example, in the pulp and paper industry and in the chemical processing industries, fixed costs are high and small variations in demand can cause wide fluctuations in profitability. It is typical in these types of industries, where capacity utilization is so important, to see massive price cutting when demand falls off in order to stimulate sales.

Economies of Scale. The second major factor with the potential to lead to cost advantages is **economies of scale.** Economies of scale are often confused with increases in the "throughput" of a manufacturing plant or other facility. As described earlier, increases in capacity utilization that spread fixed expenses can lead to lower unit costs. However, true economies of scale are associated with *size* rather than capacity utilization. The central principle of economies of scale is that in some industries production costs per unit are less in a large facility than in a small facility. For example, the cost of constructing a 200,000-unit facility will not necessarily be twice the cost of building a 100,000-unit facility, so the initial fixed cost per unit of capacity will be lower.

Economies of Scale Per-unit cost reductions associated with a larger production facility.	

Other scale economies are also evident in many industries. Continuing with the previous example, the manager of the larger facility will not generally receive double the salary of the manager of the smaller facility. Also, activities such as quality control, purchasing, and warehousing typically do not require twice as much time or twice as many laborers. In addition, the purchasing manager of the larger facility may be able to negotiate better volume discounts on orders. In summary, the larger firm may be able to achieve per-unit savings in fixed costs, indirect labor costs, and materials costs. If per-unit costs are not lower in the larger plant, then the company has *not* achieved economies of scale. In fact, **diseconomies of scale** occur when a firm builds facilities that are so large that the sheer administrative costs and confusion associated with the added bureaucracy overwhelm any potential cost savings.

Diseconomies of Scale Per-unit cost savings are overwhelmed by administrative and other costs associated with a larger production facility.

Technological Advances. Companies that make investments in cost-saving technologies are often trading an increase in fixed costs for a reduction in variable costs. If technological improvements result in lower total unit costs, then firms have achieved a cost advantage from their investments that is referred to as **economies of technology.**[5] Although investments of this type are typically associated with the factory floor, it is just as common for investments to be made in office and service automation. For example, the automated distribution system at Wal-Mart, the automated ordering and warehouse system at Lands' End, and the reservation systems maintained by the major airlines all represent investments in technology that serve to lower overall costs and provide a degree of information and product control that was previously impossible.

Economies of Technology Technological improvements that result in lower total unit costs.

Learning/Experience Effects. A final factor that influences cost structures is **learning effects.** You probably spent a long time the first time you registered for classes as a freshman. Now, as a veteran of several registrations, you know how to get through the process much faster. When an employee learns to do a job more efficiently as a result of repetition, then learning is taking place. The learning curve effect says that the time required to complete a task will decrease as a predictable

Learning Effects Time required to complete a production task decreases as a predictable function of the number of times the task is repeated.

function of the number of times the task is repeated. In theory, the time required to complete the task will fall by the same percentage each time cumulative production doubles. For example, a firm might see a 10% reduction in the time required to manufacture its products between the first and second unit of product, another 10% reduction between the second and fourth units, and another 10% reduction between the fourth and eighth unit.

Clearly, dramatic time savings are achieved early in the life of a company. However, as the company matures, tangible cost savings from labor learning are harder to achieve because it takes longer to see a true doubling of cumulative volume and because most of the opportunities for learning have already been exploited. Also, learning effects do not just happen. They require a relatively labor-intensive process since people learn but machines do not. Also, learning effects only occur when management creates an environment that is favorable to both learning and change, and then rewards employees for their productivity improvements.

Many factors can interfere with the achievement of learning effects. Products and processes that change frequently create an environment where employees do not gain sufficient experience with a particular activity and cannot improve on it. Also, the technological innovations of competitors can wipe out a company's cost advantages from learning.

Experience Effects
Time required to complete indirect labor tasks decreases as a predictable function of the number of times the tasks are repeated.

Experience effects are the same thing as learning effects but they relate to indirect labor as well as direct production labor. For example, with experience a salesperson becomes more efficient at identifying prospective clients and preparing sales presentations, and a purchasing manager becomes more efficient at negotiating supply agreements. In modern organizations, experience effects are even more important than direct labor learning effects because direct labor often represents less than 15% of total product costs. Much of the downsizing of middle management that we are seeing in industry today is an attempt to combine experience effects with economies of technology (networked computer systems) to achieve a higher level of organization efficiency and effectiveness with fewer people.

Learning and experience effects can be described by a learning/experience curve such as the one found in Figure 6.2.[6] Following from the logic of these two curves, the market share leader should enjoy a cost advantage relative to competitors because of the extra learning and experience that has occurred by producing the additional output. This concept has led many firms to fight aggressively on price in order to obtain the highest market share and thus move to the right on the curve as far as possible. As the curve flattens, it becomes increasingly difficult to gain cost advantages from learning and experience effects. The same sort of phenomenon exists with respect to economies of scale.

Companies that are able to achieve high-capacity utilization, economies of scale, economies of technology, and/or learning/experience effects may have lowest cost, but do not have to charge the lowest price. In other words, a *cost* leader does not have to be a *price* leader. If an organization is able to achieve the lowest cost, but charge a price that is the same as competitors, then it will still enjoy higher profits. However, if the low-cost producer's price is the same as or higher than the price others charge, then customers may switch to competing products, which can undermine the low-cost producer's efforts to benefit from capacity utilization, learning effects, and scale effects. Consequently, many low-cost producers try to underprice competitors slightly in order to give customers an incentive to buy from them, and to keep their volumes high enough to support their low-cost strategy.

Some risks are associated with the low-cost producer strategy. Firms pursuing cost leadership may not detect required product or marketing changes because

Figure 6.2 *A Typical Learning/Experience Curve*

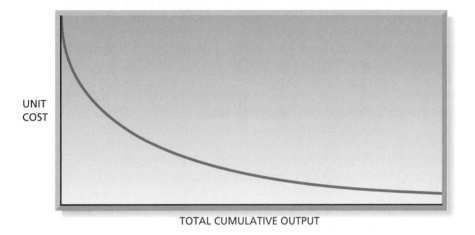

of a preoccupation with cost. Finally, these firms run the risk of making large investments in plants or equipment only to see them become obsolete because of technological breakthroughs. Their large investments make them reluctant to keep up with changes that are not compatible with their technologies.

Another risk associated with a low-cost strategy is that the company will go too far and perhaps even endanger customers or employees in the process. ValuJet's "penny-pinching" allowed it to achieve a very low cost position in the airline industry. ValuJet passed the savings on to consumers and experienced unprecedented growth. However, their stinginess came under close scrutiny after the crash of ValuJet Flight 592 into the Florida Everglades. Federal investigators found some of ValuJet's procedures, especially maintenance procedures, to be unsafe and ultimately shut down the airline until safety concerns could be worked out.[7]

Differentiation

In differentiation strategies, the emphasis is on creating value through uniqueness, as opposed to lowest cost. Uniqueness can be achieved through product innovations, superior quality, superior service, creative advertising, better supplier relationships, or in an almost unlimited number of other ways. However, for a differentiation strategy to succeed, customers must be willing to pay more for the uniqueness of a product or service than the firm paid to create it. Competitive scope is still broad, which means that the differentiated product or service should be designed so that it has wide appeal to many market sectors. Examples of organizations that are pursuing differentiation strategies include Maytag through its highly reliable appliances, L. L. Bean through its reliable, high-quality mail order services, and Coca-Cola through promoting its well-known brand name.

Firms pursuing differentiation strategies cannot ignore their cost positions. When costs are too high relative to competitors, a firm may not be able to recover enough of these additional costs through higher prices. Therefore, differentiators have to attempt to reduce costs in the areas that are not directly related to the sources of differentiation. The only way a differentiation strategy will work is if buyers value the attributes that make a product unique enough to pay a higher price for it or choose to buy from that firm preferentially. A firm may charge the same price as competitors, but achieve a much larger share of the market, resulting in higher profits. The difference in value may be one of buyer perception rather than actual product or service attributes. Consequently, the major risks associated with a differentiation strategy center on the difference between added costs and incremental price. One risk is that customers will sacrifice some of the features, services, or image possessed by a unique product or service because it costs too much. Another risk is that customers will no longer perceive an attribute as differentiating. For example, customers may come to a point at which they are so familiar with a product that brand image is no longer important.

Finally, imitation by competitors can eliminate perceived differentiation among products or services. This is what happened when a VCR manufacturer introduced the "HQ" (high-quality) feature into VCRs. Within a few months, all VCRs had "HQ," thus eliminating any basis for higher prices based on the "HQ" feature. Rivalry in an industry can make it very difficult to sustain a competitive advantage from innovation for very long. For example, competitors are able to obtain detailed information on 70% of all new products within one year after development.[8] Consequently, staying ahead of the competition in product development requires *constant* innovation. As one business writer put it, "For outstanding performance, a company has to beat the competition. The trouble is the competition has heard the same message."[9]

Some of the more popular differentiation strategies organizations are pursuing are described next.

Quality. Much has been written and said recently about the inferior quality of American products relative to some of their foreign counterparts. The American Assembly, which consisted of sixty-five leaders of business, labor, government, and academia, met in 1987 to discuss how to get the United States back on track in global competition. In their final report, they emphasized the importance of quality: "This does not mean quality merely to specifications but that improves constantly, quality that is characterized by constant innovations that create a loyal customer. It means achieving this attitude from top to bottom, from the board room to the factory floor."[10]

Many organizations are pursuing total quality management (TQM) programs in an effort to improve quality. The principles of TQM are presented in Table 6.2. TQM is so comprehensive in its scope that virtually all parts of an organization are affected. Consequently, although TQM is described in this section on quality, it also applies to other sections because TQM can lead to the development of many other bases for competitive advantage, including lower costs.

Although quality is extremely important, it does not guarantee success. More and more, high quality is becoming a necessary but not sufficient criterion for product success. Consumers are coming to expect a combination of high quality and low price, as described in our earlier discussion of hypercompetitive industries. In the words of Harold Poling, CEO of Ford Motor Company, "In the nineties, quality's got to be a given."[11] The ability of quality to differentiate a product depends on how long it takes for rivals to imitate the quality difference. For example, in the personal computer industry, in which product components are easily interchangeable, quality is easy to imitate. It is also difficult for firms competing in this segment to differentiate their products because many of the components of PCs are manufactured by a core group of suppliers who sell to all competitors. As described in Chapter 3, if a resource or capability is easy to imitate, then it cannot provide a basis for a sustainable competitive advantage.

Table 6.2 *Principles of Total Quality Management*

General

1. Get to know the next and final customer.
2. Get to know the direct competition, and the world-class leaders (whether competitors or not).
3. Be dedicated to continual, rapid improvement in quality, response time, flexibility, and cost.
4. Achieve unified purpose via extensive sharing of information and involvement in planning and implementation of change.

Design and Organization

5. Cut the number of components or operations and number of suppliers to a few good ones.
6. Organize resources into chains of customers, each chain mostly self-contained and focused on a product or customer "family."

Operations

7. Cut flow time, distance, inventory, and space along the chain of customers.
8. Cut setup, changeover, get-ready, and start-up time.
9. Operate at the customer's rate of use (or a smoothed representation of it).

Human Resource Development

10. Continually invest in human resources through cross-training (for mastery), education, job switching, and multiyear cross-career reassignments; and improved health, safety, and security.
11. Develop operator-owners of products, processes, and outcomes via broadened owner-like reward and recognition.

Quality and Process Improvement

12. Make it easier to produce or provide the product without mishap or process variation.
13. Record and own quality, process, and mishap data at the workplace.
14. Ensure that front-line associates get first chance at process improvement—before staff experts.

Accounting and Control

15. Cut transactions and reporting; control causes and measure performance at the source, not via periodic cost reports.

Capacity

16. Maintain/improve present resources and human work before thinking about new equipment and automation.
17. Automate incrementally when process variability cannot otherwise be reduced.
18. Seek to have multiple workstations, machines, flow lines, cells for each product or customer family.

Marketing and Sales

19. Market and sell your firm's increasing customer-oriented capabilities and competencies.

Source: R. J. Schonberger, "Is Strategy Strategic? Impact of Total Quality Management on Strategy," *Academy of Management Executive* (August 1992), p. 83. Used with permission.

Therefore, the ability of quality to create a sustainable competitive advantage is dependent, in part, on the industry. Where quality is more difficult to imitate in the short run, firms can achieve success by constantly staying one step ahead of competitors in quality.

Innovation and Research. Some firms seek to achieve differentiation through innovations, which usually requires aggressive investment in research and development (R&D). Product innovation, process innovations, and quality advantages often go hand in hand. The amount of R&D investment required to be competitive tends to vary by industry. Some industries, such as the pharmaceutical and electronics industries, require large investments in R&D to keep up with changing customer expectations, and to stay ahead of competitor product and process innovations. In other industries, such as textile and building products, investments in R&D are minimal.

All industries require some investment in improvements, however. Inadequate R&D expenditures for improvements in innovation and quality relative to foreign rivals led, in part, to the decline of American firms in several global industries in the 1980s.[12] American firms often devote a much smaller percentage of their revenues to R&D than many foreign competitors. The differences are sometimes significant. However, some global competitors also use their R&D expenditures more efficiently, which increases the problem for American firms.

> *Sony, perhaps Japan's best known company, is a multibillion dollar global consumer electronics firm. It is one of the most consistently inventive consumer electronics enterprises on the planet. Throughout its 45-year history, Sony has pumped out hit after high-tech hit. Often it has sculptured billion-dollar markets out of thin air with ingenious, attractively designed devices that have altered people's work and leisure. Sony popularized the pocket-sized transistor radio, the battery-powered TV set, the VCR, the camcorder, and the Walkman. Each year the company unleashes 1,000 new products—an average of four every business day.*
>
> *All these products are the progeny of Sony's 9,000 engineers and scientists, most of whom work ten- or 12-hour days in laboratories and workshops scattered around Tokyo. Sony spends over $1 billion annually in supporting their research and development efforts—over 5% of revenues. That's not unusual in the electronics industry, but few companies get so many results for their investments in R&D.[13]*

Of course, not all U.S. companies have neglected R&D, and many U.S. companies are increasing their investments in this critical area. For example, Intel, the market leader in microprocessor chips for PCs, pours millions of dollars into R&D each year.[14] Also, Bellcore is a $1-billion-a-year research venture owned by the Baby Bells.[15] Innovation can be important not only to product differentiation, but to technological advances leading to low-cost leadership as well.[16] Consequently, R&D is critical to the future competitiveness of U.S. firms.

Speed and Flexibility. In this fast-paced world, where innovations are widely understood by competitors within a year, speed and flexibility are becoming a key part of the strategies of many successful companies.[17] According to Michael Porter, "It's gone from a game of resources to a game of rate-of-progress. Competition today is a race to improve."[18] Speed allows organizations to satisfy customer needs before the competition does, providing yet another way to differentiate.

> *Here's the good news: American business's campaign to improve quality is paying off so well that in many areas the Japanese no longer enjoy a clear lead. Now the bad news: While the quality gap narrows, the world's best competitors are suiting*

up for an even more challenging contest. It's called flexibility, and its watchwords are change fast, keep costs low, and respond quickly to customers. In the race between the U.S. and Japan, guess who's ahead? Says Aleda Roth, a manufacturing expert at Duke University's business school: "Most American companies are a generation behind—as far behind as they were on quality."

The theory behind flexibility is simple. If you and I are competing and I can read the market quicker, manufacture many new products on the same line, switch from one to another instantly and at low cost, make as much profit on short runs as on long ones, and bring out new offerings faster than you—or do most of these things—then I win.[19]

Speed is often the result of rethinking processes and procedures, and building on the strengths of a well-trained, capable workforce. Speed is sometimes accompanied by a flexible manufacturing system (FMS), a battery of sophisticated machine tools that allows for the manufacture of immense varieties of products in the same plant. A good illustration is Benetton. This clothing company has orders electronically relayed to manufacturing sites where computer-automated design systems, which contain all of the specifications for various clothing items, control the machinery that make the clothes. Not only is the system fast, but Benetton only employs eight people in its warehouse, which ships 230,000 items of clothing daily.[20] In another example, Michelin, the French tire manufacturer, unveiled its "C3M" manufacturing process, which is a simultaneous manufacturing system designed to increase flexibility in manufacturing while cutting the required number of workers and factory size.[21]

While small entrepreneurial organizations may be at a disadvantage relative to larger organizations in developing some of the other competitive weapons, they actually have an advantage when it comes to speed and flexibility.[22] Smaller firms are typically less constrained by large investments in capital equipment. Consequently, they may be more willing to fluctuate their output or produce in small batches to satisfy customer demands. In addition, less bureaucracy often means that changes that are required due to new technology can be made in a shorter period of time. This also means that managers are typically closer to their customers and have fewer customers, thus allowing them to really get to know customers and understand their needs.

Big companies are trying to emulate the flexibility of small firms by altering their organizational structures and management systems. For example, some firms are attempting to become worldwide "modular corporations." A modular corporation nurtures a few core activities that it does best and then lets outside specialists do the rest. "The new breed avoid becoming monoliths with plants and bureaucracy. Instead, they are exciting hubs surrounded by networks of the world's best suppliers. Those manufacturing or service units are modular: They can be added or taken away with the flexibility of switching parts in a child's Lego set."[23] Dell Computer and Chrysler are examples of companies that are pursuing flexibility in this way.

Another way large organizations are trying to improve flexibility is by decentralizing responsibility and rewarding employees for innovations and flexibility. 3M maintains a highly innovative, responsive organization by setting goals and establishing reward systems for encouraging flexible, creative behavior.

Organizational Reputation and Brand Name. A good reputation can be linked to any of the other sources of differentiation. For example, a good reputation may be associated with excellent quality or highly innovative products or services, excellent human resource management, or speed and flexibility, or a combination of these factors. Merck was once rated first for quality products, first in human resource management, and second in innovativeness in a *Fortune* poll of 8,000 corporate executives.[24]

Much has been said in this book about how to develop a good reputation through socially responsible actions and stakeholder satisfaction. Some of the potential benefits of a good reputation include the ability to attract talented workers, charge premium prices, keep loyal customers, raise capital with less difficulty by attracting investors, avoid constant scrutiny by regulators and activists, or enter international markets with less difficulty.[25] Some business writers have argued that a corporate reputation may be the only truly sustainable competitive advantage.[26] It is the only component of competitive advantage that cannot ever be duplicated in its entirety. Therefore, organizations should devote considerable time and effort to building and safeguarding a good reputation. Organizations with the best reputations in the *Fortune* survey had strong financial performance, but it was combined with strong performance in nonfinancial areas as well.[27]

Of course, an organization's reputation is often linked to a well-known brand name. Earlier cited examples provided evidence that companies such Disney, Citicorp, and Coke understand and foster the strength of their brands.

In summary, business-level strategies that incorporate elements of quality, innovation, speed and flexibility, and reputation are likely to contribute to competitiveness in the 1990s and beyond. All of these important sources of differentiation have one organizational element in common: a well-trained workforce that is capable of learning new methods and ways of doing business as the environment changes. Consequently, in the future, successful companies will have to devote even more attention to human resource development activities such as recruiting and training and development. For example, companies may have to form strategic alliances with educational institutions and local governments to help prepare qualified applicants for tomorrow's jobs.[28] In summary, management of human resources will be the key to the implementation of many differentiation strategies, and will increase in importance as a basis for sustained competitive advantage.

Best Cost

Porter referred to firms that are not pursuing a distinct generic strategy as "stuck-in-the- middle."[29] According to Porter, these uncommitted firms should have lower performance than committed firms because they have no consistent basis for creating superior value. On the other hand, he argued that firms that pursue one of the generic strategies exclusively can center all of their resources on becoming good at that strategy.

In spite of Porter's arguments that firms generally cannot successfully pursue more than one generic strategy at the same time, many firms have been successful at pursuing cost leadership and differentiation simultaneously. Profits generated from the successful pursuit of one element of strategy (e.g., low cost) allow investment in other elements such as differentiating features. Also, it is well established that high product quality and low cost are complementary rather than conflicting strategies.[30] For example, Wal-Mart was successful at providing high-quality customer service in its industry at lowest cost. A key part of Wal-Mart's strategy is a technologically advanced distribution system that allows fast and efficient delivery of products.[31] Porter concedes that such advances can sometimes allow a firm to successfully pursue both strategies simultaneously.[32] However, in today's highly competitive global marketplace, this may be the rule more than the exception.

Some strategy scholars are now arguing that a combination of differentiation and low cost may be necessary to create a sustainable competitive advantage: "The immediate effect of differentiation will be to increase unit costs. However, if costs fall with increasing volume, the long-run effect may be to reduce unit costs."[33] Volume would be expected to increase because differentiation would make the product more attractive to the market. Then, as volume increases, costs will decrease. Edwards Deming, a world famous expert on quality, argues that producing higher quality products though superior designs also reduces manufacturing costs. Research supports Deming's assertion.[34] Also, consumers now expect both high quality and low price. Jack Welch, CEO of General Electric, puts it this way:

> *We're playing in a game where we'll show up and we'll be selling an engine against another engine competitor. Now, to get the deal,* you've got to have performance and all the other things, *but you'd better have low cost. And as you go around the world, and you want to sell turbines to developing countries, you'd better have a low cost base. Because in the end, you could have performance, you can have quality, but you'd better have cost (italics added).*[35]

For example, Anheuser-Busch has been very successful in creating brewing products that have a good image and high quality, yet A-B is a cost leader due to efficiencies created by high-volume production and sales. Kellogg, best known for breakfast cereals, enjoys a similar situation of low-cost production due to economies of scale combined with higher prices made possible due to differentiation through advertising and new product development. Pep Boys, cited at the beginning of this chapter, is also pursuing a best cost strategy.

The key to a best cost strategy is simple supply and demand economics. For example, assume that three organizations manufacture hunting knives. The first firm pursues a low-cost strategy. It is able to produce a knife for $10 and sell 100,000 a year at $16, for a total profit of $600,000. On the other hand, the second firm uses a differentiation strategy. It produces a premium product with features that the market finds attractive. The premium product costs $40 to make. The firm can sell 50,000 at $60. The total profit is $1 million. Both companies seem to be successful; however, they are each achieving success using a different generic strategy.

However, assume that a third company can create a very good product, through a variety of product and process technological advances, for $20. This product is almost as appealing as the product of the second firm. The firm can sell 75,000 at $50. The total profit is over $2 million and consumers believe they are getting a great deal (saving $10). This is the essence of a best cost strategy—finding a level of differentiation that will bring a premium price while doing so at a reasonable cost. Unlike a differentiation strategy in which the emphasis is on creating extra value or a low-cost strategy that stresses cutting costs, the best cost strategy gives equal weight to both factors. Wal-Mart and Pep Boys have been successful with it. General Electric is pursuing it across a wide range of markets. It just may be the premiere strategy of the future.

Focus

Focus strategies can be based on differentiation or lowest cost. The key to a focus strategy is providing a product or service that caters to a particular segment in the market. Firms pursuing focus strategies have to be able to identify their target market segment and both assess and meet the needs and desires of buyers in that seg-

STRATEGIC INSIGHT 6.2

BUSINESS

STRATEGY

Norton Manufacturing Focuses on Precision Crankshafts

Norton Company of Fostoria, Ohio, was founded in 1950 as a small tool and die shop. In the early 1980s, Norton began to see the market for its products erode. Small machine shops with lower overhead were underpricing the firm. Norton needed to look beyond what it had been to what it might become.

When its bread-and-butter business dried up, the company searched out industries that would fully utilize the talents of its workforce. Norton found an untapped opportunity to supply high-performance crankshafts to the auto racing industry. Norton decided to develop the high-performance racing crankshaft operations as a separate company. Norton used the new organization and also employee training and supplier communication to send a clear message to the public about its high standards of excellence.

Norton's success with its new direction is demonstrated in the 208% growth in sales it achieved during the last three years. The company recognized the value and motivation of its own employees, redirected its business, and refused to become a victim of economic circumstances. By modifying its product to meet the needs of a new industry, Norton created a new market for its work. The firm now employs a staff of ninety-six.

Source: Adapted from "Norton Manufacturing Company, Inc.," *Strengthening America's Competitiveness: The Blue Chip Enterprise Initiative* (Warner Books on behalf of Connecticut Mutual Life Insurance Company and the U.S. Chamber of Commerce, 1991), pp. 94–95.

ment better than any other competitor. For example, the manufacturing company in Strategic Insight 6.2 created a new market for its work by focusing on one segment of its industry.

Cooper Tire and Rubber is an example of a company that pursues a cost focus strategy. Cooper is the only major tire company that does not sell tires to automobile manufacturers in the original equipment market (OEM). Instead, the company focuses on replacement tires. Cooper is very efficiency oriented: "Its low-rise corporate headquarters could pass for a 1950s suburban elementary school, right down to the linoleum floors and the flagpole out front. The annual report is printed in living black and white."[36] Cooper saves on R&D costs by copying the designs of OEM manufacturers instead of designing its own products. The cost focus strategy is so successful that Cooper provides the highest returns to its investors of any firm in the tire industry.

On the other hand, Porsche pursues a differentiation focus strategy. The focus is on elite consumers. One time a group of students was taking a plant tour at Porsche headquarters in Germany. One of the students, looking at a particularly stylish sports car, asked the tour guide, who was a high official in the company, how Porsche had managed to create a bumper that was so elegant and yet conformed to U.S. safety regulations. This top company official told the student that Porsche had simply poured enough money into the bumper to make it work. This example demonstrates that Porsche spares no expense in meeting the precise needs and desires of its target customer.

In another example, Japan Airlines is catering to wealthy passengers by investing $95,000 each in luxury bathrooms for its first-class cabins on its routes between Tokyo and New York. According to a JAL spokesperson, "Especially on long-distance flights, the toilet is something that leaves a deep impression." The larger bathrooms will feature piped-in music, soft lighting, a three-sided mirror, a window, and faucets that stay on so that passengers can wash both hands at once. A first-class round-trip ticket from Tokyo to New York costs $9,300. New York–Tokyo costs $12,200.[37]

The risks of pursuing a focus strategy depend on whether the strategy is cost focus or differentiation focus. The risks of each of these strategies are similar to the risks faced by adopters of the pure strategies themselves. However, the focus strategy has two risks that are not associated with the emphasis on low cost or differentiation. First, the desires of the narrow target market may become similar to the desires of the market as a whole, thus eliminating the advantage associated with focusing. Second, a competitor may be able to focus on an even more narrowly defined target and essentially "outfocus the focuser."

Best cost focus is another generic strategy that firms can pursue. However, this strategy is more difficult than a basic best cost strategy because the narrow market focus means lower volume. At lower volume, it is hard to achieve low cost while still providing meaningful differentiation.

This completes our discussion of generic strategies. We have also devoted considerable attention to how to implement those strategies successfully. Low-cost leadership may be achieved through high-capacity utilization, scale economies, technological advances, and learning or experience effects. Differentiation is often pursued on the basis of satisfying customers through higher quality, state-of-the-art research and development, superior human resources, speed, flexibility, or establishing a strong reputation and/or brand. Best cost strategies combine elements from both differentiation and low-cost leadership. Focus strategies apply one of the generic orientations to a specific market niche. Strategic Application 6.1 provides an opportunity to apply these concepts to an industry with which you are familiar.

World markets also provide outstanding opportunities with regard to business-level strategy. Some of the special circumstances surrounding the formulation of global business strategies are addressed in the next section.

GLOBAL BUSINESS STRATEGY

Throughout this book, we have developed strong arguments for the global expansion of U.S. firms. Furthermore, we have applied the theory of strategic management to many non-U.S.-based firms in an effort to demonstrate that strategic management principles apply to all firms, regardless of origin. Nevertheless, significant differences exist between U.S. and other markets. This section demonstrates how firms can take advantage of the differences associated with participating in global markets and industries.

Michael Porter, whose name should now be familiar to you, expanded his analysis of competition to include the global arena. Strategic Insight 6.3 contains a description of why, according to Porter, some countries seem to produce a disproportionate share of highly successful firms in particular global industries. Due to differences that exist between the United States and foreign countries, many strategic opportunities are available to global firms that are not available to domestic firms.

STRATEGIC APPLICATION 6.1

ANALYSIS OF BUSINESS-LEVEL STRATEGIES

This application provides an opportunity to compare and contrast business-level strategies of companies in a familiar industry. First select an industry with which you feel comfortable. A few industries that will facilitate this analysis include airlines, hospitality, and grocery stores. Now identify the five or six major competitors in the industry. When you get to this point, create a

chart like the one below and fill in the blanks. This analysis is a good starting point for determining which strategies seem to work in particular industries. If most or all of the competitors seem to be pursuing the same generic strategy, success may be determined more by the way the strategy is pursued (strategic posture) rather than a particular strategy itself.

Industry Selected:

	Firm A	Firm B	Firm C	Firm D
Name of Firm				
Generic strategy (cost leadership, differentiation, best cost, focus, or combination)				
Strategic posture (specific tactics used to execute the strategy— see chapter for specifics)				
How successful has the strategy been in the past?				
If the firm continues in the same strategic direction, how likely is success?				

Multidomestic Product/Market Strategy Handling product design, assembly, and marketing on a country-by-country basis determined by individual market needs.

As Porter points out, organizations should take advantage of the unique resources that exist in their home countries. Also, although difficult, it may be possible to tap special resources in countries in which an organization is involved. One of the most important issues with regard to global strategy is the general approach the firm will take in its international products and markets.

Global Product/Market Approach

One of the key issues facing top managers as their organizations pursue international development is selection of a product/market approach. A **multidomestic product/market strategy** entails handling product design, assembly, and marketing on a country-by-country basis by custom tailoring products and services around individual market needs. On the other hand, organizations pursuing a

Porter's Competitive Advantage of Nations

Michael Porter expanded his analyses of competitive environments to include the global economy. In his book *The Competitive Advantage of Nations,* he developed arguments concerning why some nations produce so many stellar companies in particular industries. For example, Germany is the home base for several top luxury car manufacturers and Switzerland has many leading companies in pharmaceuticals and chocolate. He explains that four characteristics of countries actually create an environment that is conducive to creating globally competitive firms in certain business areas. The four characteristics are:

1. *Factor conditions.* Is the nation endowed with any special factors of production, such as uncommon raw materials or laborers with specific skills, that can lead to an advantage in a particular industry? Does the nation have superior factor-producing mechanisms such as excellent schools or universities?

2. *Demand conditions.* Are the nation's buyers of a particular product or service the most discriminating and demanding in the world? Does the nation's market typically foreshadow global trends?

3. *Related and supporting industries.* Are the suppliers to an industry the very best in the world? Are there firms in related industries that are also global leaders?

4. *Firm strategy, structure, and rivalry.* Are the management techniques that are customary in the nation's businesses conducive to success in a particular industry? Does the industry attract the most talented managers in the nation? Are competitors in the same industry strong?

Positive answers to most of these questions concerning a particular industry or industry niche indicate the potential for developing a nucleus of companies that are globally competitive.

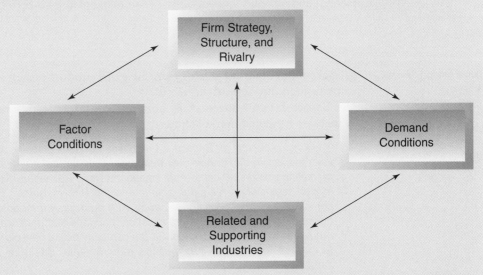

Source: Adapted with the permission of the Free Press, a Division of Simon & Schuster, from *The Competitive Advantage of Nations* by Michael E. Porter. Copyright © 1990 by Michael E. Porter, p. 72.

(continued)

Basically, the reason companies can develop a highly competitive nucleus is that tough market environments can create world-class competitors only if the competitors are also endowed with the resources they need to compete. If home markets are uncompetitive, firms will not be sufficiently motivated to produce a superior product. On the other hand, if home markets are highly competitive but the factors of production, support industries, and human talent are not available, firms will likewise be incapable of producing globally competitive products. When these two conditions are met, however, an environment is created that both motivates and rewards excellence.

The logical conclusion from Porter's analysis would seem to be to locate subsidiaries in the nations with the strongest home bases in particular industries. However, he argues that this rarely happens. First, it is difficult in some cases for an "outsider," a foreign firm, to become an "insider." In other words, it may be difficult for a foreign firm to tap into the sources of supply or obtain the highly valued resources that make home base competitors so successful. Second, Porter suggests that it is unlikely that the foreign subsidiary in the nation with the natural advantages will be able to influence the parent company "long distance." For example, if Hershey locates a subsidiary in Switzerland to take advantage of the natural advantages that are found there, it is unlikely that the Swiss subsidiary would have much of an impact on Hershey's operations in the United States.

Porter does, however, suggest that firms should take advantage of their own nation's natural advantages. He also recommends that some of the principles that apply to the competitive advantages of nations can be applied in any company that wants to become more competitive in the world economy. Specifically, organizations can seek out the toughest, most discriminating buyers, choose from the best suppliers in the world, seek to excel against the most outstanding global competitors, form alliances with outstanding foreign competitors, and stay abreast of all research findings and innovations that are relevant to their core businesses.

Global Product/Market Strategy
Organizations produce one product design and market it in the same fashion throughout the world.

global product/market strategy produce one product design and market it in the same fashion throughout the world.[38]

Bausch & Lomb successfully adopted a multidomestic strategy to significantly increase its global market share:

The key to success for Bausch & Lomb was to "Think globally, act locally," letting local managers make their own decisions. Until the big change, production and marketing policies all came from headquarters in Rochester, New York, treating foreign subsidiaries "as sales adjuncts to the U.S. divisions." For example, the company was unsuccessful in Japan with rigid gas-permeable contact lenses because ophthalmologists there insist on a surface that goes well beyond clinical requirements to near perfection. So the company built a new plant in South Korea to manufacture lenses that met the requirements. B&L now has 11% of the Japanese market for those lenses.

This strategy also extended to Bausch & Lomb's Ray Ban division. More than half of Ray-Ban's new sunglasses are developed specifically for international sale. In Europe, Ray Bans tend to be flashier, more avant-garde, and costlier than in the

U.S. In Asia the company redesigned them to better suit the Asian face—with its flatter bridge and higher cheekbones—and sales took off. Ray Ban commands an awesome 40% of the world market for premium-priced ($40 to $250) sunglasses. Operating margins have jumped from the low teens in 1984 to just under 25%.[39]

Multidomestic strategies are intuitively appealing from a stakeholder point of view, since they emphasize the satisfaction of segmented customer needs. One of the reasons that Japanese firms are so successful in the U.S. market may be that they tailor their products to meet the needs of U.S. consumers. This is quite different from the attitude sometimes found in U.S. firms that foreign consumers should naturally want to buy U.S. products as they are.

However, customization may add more costs to the products or services than can be successfully recaptured through higher prices. A well-known marketing scholar, Theodore Levitt asserts that:

> *. . . well managed companies have moved from emphasis on customizing items to offering globally standardized products that are advanced, functional, reliable— and low priced. Multinational companies that concentrated on idiosyncratic consumer preferences have become befuddled and unable to take in the forest because of the trees. Only global companies will achieve long-term success by concentrating on what everyone wants rather than worrying about the details of what everyone thinks they might like.*[40]

As a counterargument, some researchers explain that a global product/market strategy is only appropriate if (1) there is a global market segment for a product or service, (2) there are economic efficiencies associated with a global strategy, (3) there are no external constraints such as government regulations that will prevent a global strategy from being implemented, and (4) there are no absolute internal constraints.[41]

Some organizations are now pursuing a hybrid **transnational product/market strategy**. An international counterpart to the best cost strategy discussed previously, a transnational strategy entails seeking both global efficiency and local responsiveness. This difficult task is accomplished through establishing an integrated network that fosters shared vision and resources while allowing individual decisions to be made to adapt to local needs.[42]

Transnational Product/Market Strategy Organizations seek both global efficiency and local responsiveness by establishing an integrated network with shared vision and resources but individual decision making to adapt to local needs.

Global Expansion Tactics

Firms can apply a variety of expansion tactics as they pursue global opportunities. The following are among the most common:

1. *Exporting.* Transferring goods to other countries for sale through wholesalers or a foreign company.
2. *Contractual arrangements,* such as:
   Licensing. Selling the right to produce and/or sell a brand name product in a foreign market.
   Franchising. This is the services counterpart to a licensing strategy. A foreign firm buys the legal right to use the name and operating methods of a U.S. firm in its home country.
3. *Foreign direct investment,* such as:
   Joint venture. Cooperative agreement among two or more companies to pursue common business objectives.
   Greenfield venture. Creation of a wholly owned foreign subsidiary.[43]

Some organizations combine these tactics in interesting ways. For example, Molson Breweries, a joint venture between Toronto's Molson Companies and

Australia's Foster's Brewing Group, brews Miller Genuine Draft under license from Miller Brewing Company.[44] If that isn't confusing enough, Miller Brewing Company is actually a subsidiary of Philip Morris.

Among the most important criteria when deciding on an option for international growth are cost, financial risk, profit potential, and control. In general, moving down the list of alternatives entails greater cost and greater financial risk but also greater profit potential and greater control. Consequently, these alternatives represent a trade-off between cost and financial risk on the one hand, and profit and control on the other. Of course, this is a gross generalization. Some of the options, such as joint ventures, are hard to judge on the basis of these four criteria because the exact nature of the agreement can vary so widely from venture to venture.

Recent research demonstrates some of the major differences between Western and Japanese firms in the way they enter foreign markets. U.S. firms tend to favor big overseas investments, often through acquisitions. On the other hand, Japanese firms favor sequential investment. They make frequent, smaller investments in foreign operations over a long period of time, "Typically, Japanese companies make a small initial investment in their core businesses and expand their operations if this investment performs well. The companies might later make big investments . . . ."[45] For example, Fuji began small, but continually increased its business investments in the United States during the past several decades. Recently, Fuji built a $100 million film-packaging plant in the United States.[46] Sequential entry can help an organization reduce the risks associated with foreign investments, regardless of which method of entry is used.

Enhancing Global Business-Level Strategy

Organizations that are involved in multiple global markets have advantages available to them for pursuing their business-level strategies. Examples of the many options available for improving competitive position vis-a-vis cost leadership through a global strategy include the following:

1. *Cost reductions through foreign assembly or manufacturing.* Many firms are currently shipping components to foreign countries for assembly by low-cost laborers. The maquiladora industry in Mexico consists of hundreds of these assembly operations just south of the U.S.–Mexico border. The opening up of East Germany will provide similar opportunities for European firms. Some companies are also having some of their manufacturing done in foreign countries.

2. *Branding of finished products that are subcontracted to low-cost foreign manufacturers.* Nike designs shoes but does not manufacture them. They are manufactured in Third World countries according to Nike specifications. Likewise, Liz Claiborne products are entirely produced overseas.

3. *Global sourcing.* Purchase of low-cost foreign components or raw materials. Many U.S. firms buy Japanese semiconductors or Japanese steel for use in their products.

4. *Expanding markets leading to economies of scale.* Some companies could not grow large enough to enjoy the lowest possible production costs on the basis of domestic demand alone. However, expansion into foreign markets can lead to significant increases in demand.

5. *Transfer of technological know-how through joint ventures (learning from competi-*

tors). Some foreign firms are more efficient than U.S. firms in producing similar products. Joint ventures with these firms may provide opportunities to learn new technologies that can lead to significant cost reductions.[47]

Global strategies can also lead to competitive advantages through differentiation. Some strategies for doing this include:

1. *Distribution of foreign products in the United States.* American firms can purchase elite products from foreign manufacturers for sale in the United States. This strategy is easy to imitate unless the companies sign a contract that provides the American firm exclusive rights to market the product in the United States.
2. *Sale of U.S. products in foreign countries.* In some countries, American products command a premium price because of the image they convey. For example, Coca Cola Co. enjoys higher operating profits in Japan than in the United States.
3. *Superior quality through joint ventures.* Just as U.S. companies can learn cost-saving technologies through joint ventures, they can also learn how to better differentiate their products, through higher quality or some other unique feature.
4. *Licensing of product technology from abroad.* A joint venture is not the only way to learn new technologies. U.S. firms sometimes have the option of licensing product technologies to differentiate their present products.[48]
5. *Forcing an open, learning mind-set.* U.S. companies that attempt to differentiate themselves on speed and flexibility in the international marketplace must develop an innovative mind-set, or culture, and must be willing to learn from and adapt to a variety of conflicting circumstances. They can then bring what they learn back to the United States and apply it to local businesses.

Although world markets provide many opportunities, a decision to pursue these opportunities creates additional costs and risks. Managing businesses in foreign countries can result in additional costs associated with such things as travel, communications (including translation costs), export and import duties and tariffs, transportation of products, advertising, taxes, and fees. In addition, managers may find themselves unable to understand or effectively manage businesses in countries that are unfamiliar to them. We mentioned earlier that this might make hiring a local manager desirable.

Many risks are also associated with global expansion. Organizations face the risk that citizens in some countries may not be receptive to some foreign products because of prejudices they hold against the countries in which they were produced. The same sort of risk applies to service firms. Also, the risks associated with managing international joint ventures and currency translations were discussed previously. These are only a few of many potential risks. Wise selection of countries in which to pursue opportunities can reduce costs and risks associated with global expansion.

In conclusion, organizations can use global strategies to strengthen their cost positions or increase differentiation. However, they must be careful to choose foreign environments that are conducive to the type of enterprise they are considering. Several regions in the world economy offer significant opportunities for growth and development, for organizations that are willing and able to take the risks. Globalization of both operations and management thinking will be required for U.S. firms to regain strategic competitiveness.

POSITIONING COMPETITIVE STRATEGIES IN A DYNAMIC ENVIRONMENT

Our previous discussion of business-level strategies focused on the types of growth and competitive strategies that are available to organizations. Unfortunately, many organizations find that the strategy that they performed so well one year is no longer viable in subsequent years. As we have described in earlier chapters, the expectations of customers and the abilities of competitors change constantly, which creates a dynamic environment for planning strategy. A strategy that is appropriate at one point in the life of an industry, may be inappropriate at another point. Although there are certainly exceptions, industries tend to evolve along similar paths, creating somewhat predictable conditions, or stages, for strategy development. Although the stages of an industry life cycle do not dictate which business strategies should be chosen, they can help a strategist understand the context within which the chosen strategy will be implemented and the likely strategies of competitors. As an industry moves through the stages of the life cycle, different strategies and organizational resources are needed to compete effectively.

Industry Life Cycle
How sales volume for a product-market area changes over its lifetime.

Introduction Stage
Initial offering and gradual building of sales for a product as consumers come to understand the product and its uses.

Growth Stage
Product experiences a large increase in demand; often attracts new competitors.

Maturity Stage
Sales growth of a product levels off.

Commodity (or Decline) Stage
Demand for product either declines as it is outdated or is replaced, or it becomes a basic part of consumers' lives.

The **industry life cycle** portrays how sales volume for a product-market area changes over its lifetime. As Figure 6.3 illustrates, demand for a product gradually builds during the **introduction stage,** as customers come to understand the product and its uses. During the **growth stage,** demand greatly increases as product variations proliferate, new customer groups are developed, and as new product applications are identified. The growth opportunities tend to attract new competitors, which intensifies the jockeying to achieve forms of differentiation. Sales growth eventually begins to level off during the **maturity stage** of the life cycle, because markets are fully penetrated and opportunities for additional market and applications development are limited. This slowing of growth can lead to a competitive "shake out" of weaker producers, resulting in fewer competitors. During the **commodity** or **decline stage,** the demand patterns can take on many shapes. The traditional curve representing decline of the industry's products is labeled C in Figure 6.3. However, if the product group becomes a commodity, which means that it is used in many other products or becomes a basic part of life for some consumers, demand may just level off, as in B, or may gradually increase over an extended time period, represented by A.[49]

Understanding the product life cycle not only helps an organization understand demand, but can also help the organization formulate strategies.[50] During the introduction stage, as demand for a product gradually builds, organizations are primarily concerned with survival—producing the product at low enough cost and selling it at a high enough price so that they will be able to sustain operations and enter the next stage of the life cycle. The competitive environment at this stage is often turbulent and fragmented. Often customer needs for the new product are not that well understood and new firms enter with different product versions and new methods. Those firms that identify, through their product and market development, those characteristics that matter most to customers are likely to be the most successful. Since businesses often lose money during this stage, this is a difficult challenge.

In the introduction stage, firms also attempt to produce a product that is of sufficiently high quality that they will be able to establish a good reputation in the market. The emphasis is often on research and development, and on market penetration strategies. Early producers sometimes enjoy a "first-mover advantage," because of the experience they are gaining, the image they have the opportunity to build, and the opportunity they may have to create barriers to entry such as

Figure 6.3 *The Product Life Cycle*

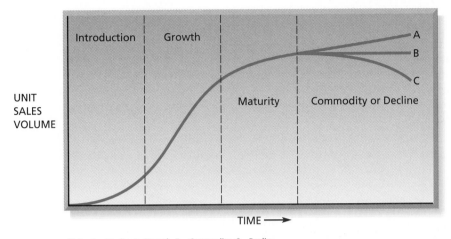

Note: A = Moderate Growth, B = Commodity, C = Decline

patents or exclusive distribution channels.[51] There is some evidence to support these ideas.[52] In fact, products sometimes come to be associated with early innovators, as in the case of Scott towels, Scotch tape, Linoleum floor coverings, and Xerox machines.

During the growth stage, sales volume increases as the number of competitors increases and those competitors all pursue various market penetration, market development, applications development, and product development strategies. Industry competitors also attempt to differentiate themselves to customers through advertising or through new features and services. It is during the growth stage that some competitors will begin to gain the benefits of size. They will build plants that are large enough to enjoy economies of scale, locking in contracts for supplies or distribution of products, or differentiating products through advertising and new features or service. During the latter part of the growth stage, customer expectations will become more standardized, and competitors will begin to offer similar products of similar quality. Since products of the industry are increasingly similar, price will become more of a factor in the purchase decision. As growth begins to level off toward the end of the growth stage, price competition heats up, and some firms fail to develop product characteristics that customers value or try to grow faster than their resources allow, a **competitive shakeout** usually occurs. Since the market is no longer growing at an increasing rate, the weaker competitors discover that they can no longer generate enough sales or profits to sustain themselves. They sell off their assets, declare bankruptcy, or are acquired by stronger competitors.

During the maturity stage, as demand continues to level off, efficient, high-volume production tends to dominate manufacturing strategy. Since price is now one of the most important factors in the purchase decision, competitors must pursue cost reductions as a way to stay profitable. A dominant design for the product has probably emerged at this point, so consumers typically focus on price and service. When an organization discovers a successful innovation, it is quickly incorporated into other firms' products. Consequently, product differentiation becomes increasingly difficult. Often firms will shift their focus from market penetration

Competitive Shakeout
When market growth slows, weaker competitors can no longer generate enough sales or profits and drop out of the market.

Figure 6.4 *Breaking Out of the Product Life Cycle*

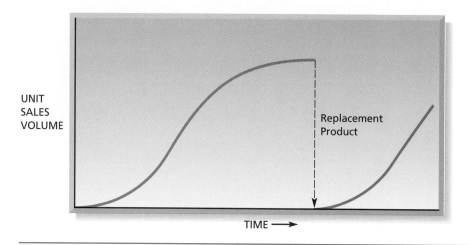

and product development to process development that will reduce costs and international market development to support large-volume operations. Marketing, distribution efficiency, and low-cost operations gain increasing importance during this stage.

Finally, during the commodity or decline stage, tight cost controls leading to efficiency are essential to success. Since the product has become highly standardized at this point, price is still a very important basis for competition. Competition is intense, and firms may begin to drop out again, especially if demand takes the shape of curve C in Figure 6.3 and if exit barriers are low. Examples of exit barriers that might motivate organizations not to drop out include owning a lot of assets that cannot be used for anything else, high costs of terminating contracts or tearing down buildings, or social costs such as laying off workers.[53]

To avoid the full effects of decline, firms may focus on a particular niche in the market that is still growing. Or, as demonstrated in Figure 6.4, innovative firms may be able to introduce a product that totally replaces the old product and makes it obsolete. For example, microcomputers are replacing typewriters and CDS have replaced records. Finally, some organizations may just "hang on" until other firms have dropped out, at which time reduced competition can result in improved profitability and market share.[54] This is happening right now in the tobacco industry.

One of the lessons that we learn from the product life cycle is that organizations must adapt as their products move through the stages of evolution. Whereas product innovation and attempts to differentiate products may have value in the early stages, once a dominant design emerges, the focus of strategy must shift toward low costs and service, even if efforts to develop new products continue. For example, Tandem Computer was once a *very* loosely structured firm in a growing industry segment. However, as the computer industry matured, Tandem had to adapt to increasing competition by tightening up cost controls.[55]

Most industries in the U.S. have already matured and are represented by one of the three demand curves on the right side of Figure 6.3. This means that competition is fierce in most industries and that a careful analysis based on concepts found in this chapter is essential to success. However, even mature industries can experience growth in some product segments due to product innovations or other forms of differentiation that make older products undesirable or obsolete. Consequently, we come back to the notion that for the majority of firms, value creation through cost leadership or differentiation with controlled costs (or a focus strategy that emphasizes cost leadership or differentiation) is essential to higher than normal performance.

In summary, identifying the stage of the product/industry life cycle can provide strategic direction as firms develop their business-level strategies. As organizations fine-tune their strategies, they need to specify the distinctive competencies they will try to develop in order to achieve a competitive advantage.

Summary

The responsibilities of business-level managers include establishing the overall direction of the business unit, ongoing analysis of the changing business situation, selecting strategy, and choosing a business-unit strategic posture. These responsibilities and the way they are carried out are similar in for-profit, nonprofit, and service organizations.

The generic business-level strategies described in this chapter are cost leadership, differentiation, best cost, and focus. Firms that are cost leaders actively pursue ways to produce products and services at the lowest possible cost. Organizations that pursue differentiation attempt to differentiate their products or services in such a way that they have greater value to their consumers. Best cost strategies entail a combination of differentiation and low cost. Focus strategies can be pursued through cost leadership or differentiation (or even best cost, although this may be difficult due to the smaller market targeted). The distinguishing feature of a focus strategy is that firms focus their energies on a narrow, as opposed to a broad, segment of the market.

World markets provide many outstanding business opportunities; however, they are sometimes associated with higher costs and additional risks. Firms may have a multidomestic or globalization approach to their international product/markets. Methods for pursuing business opportunities in global markets include licensing, franchising, exporting, joint ventures, and wholly owned foreign operations. Global strategies can be used to enhance an organization's cost position or further differentiate its products and services. The additional costs and risks can be minimized and the potential benefits enhanced through careful selection of host countries for international operations.

An understanding of the industry life cycle is useful in determining the distinct characteristics of a business-level strategy. Business strategies that address growth, competitive positioning, and international expansion must be adapted to fit the circumstances of the industry as it evolves through the introduction, growth, and maturity stages and then settles into commodity or decline stage.

Discussion Questions

1. What are the strategic management responsibilities of a business unit manager?
2. Describe the generic business-level strategies found in this chapter.
3. How can an organization pursue each of the business-level strategies? Be specific with regard to factors on which these strategies can be based.
4. What are some of the major sources of competitive advantage? How can TQM contribute to the development of more than one of these advantages?
5. What are some of the potential opportunities and risks associated with global expansion? Describe several methods for expansion into international markets. Which of these methods is associated with more organizational control? More risk?
6. What is the industry life cycle? What are some of the important factors to consider at each stage of the life cycle? How do those factors affect choice of business strategies?

References

1. A. Taylor, III, "How to Murder the Competition," *Fortune* (February 22, 1993), p. 87, © 1993 Time Inc. All Rights Reserved.

2. H. J. Bryce, *Financial and Strategic Management for Nonprofit Organizations* (Englewood Cliffs, N.J.: Prentice-Hall, 1987).

3. This discussion of generic strategies draws heavily from concepts found in M. E. Porter, *Competitive Strategy: Techniques for Analyzing Industries and Competitors* (New York: The Free Press, 1980), Chap. 2.

4. This discussion of factors leading to cost savings is based, in part, on Porter, *Competitive Strategy; M. E. Porter, Competitive Advantage: Creating and Sustaining Superior Performance* (New York: The Free Press, 1985); and R. W. Schmenner, "Before You Build a Big Factory," *Harvard Business Review* 54 (July–August 1976), pp. 100–104.

5. As defined by Schmenner, "Before You Build a Big Factory."

6. W. J. Abernathy and K. Wayne, "Limits of the Learning Curve," *Harvard Business Review* (September–October 1974), pp. 109–119; Boston Consulting Group, *Perspectives on Experience* (Boston: Boston Consulting Group, 1972); W. B. Hirschman, "Profit from the Learning Curve," *Harvard Business Review* (January–February 1964), pp. 125–139.

7. A. Paszton, M. Branningan, and S. McCartney, "ValuJet's Penny-Pinching Comes Under Scrutiny," *Wall Street Journal* (May 14, 1996), pp. A2, A4.

8. E. Mansfield, "How Rapidly Does New Industrial Technology Leak Out?" *Journal of Industrial Economics* (December 1985), p. 217.

9. P. Ghemawat, "Sustainable Advantage," *Harvard Business Review* (September–October 1986), p. 53.

10. M. K. Starr, ed., *Global Competitiveness: Getting the U.S. Back on Track* (New York: W. W. Norton and Company, 1988), p. 307.

11. H. Kahalas and K. Suchon, "Interview with Harold A. Poling, Chairman, CEO, Ford Motor Company," *Academy of Management Executive* (May 1992), p. 74.

12. L. G. Franko, "Global Corporate Competition: Who's Winning, Who's Losing, and the R&D Factor as One Reason Why," *Strategic Management Journal* 10 (1989), pp. 449–474.

13. Adapted from B. R. Schlender, "How Sony Keeps the Magic Going," *Fortune* (February 4, 1992), p. 77.

14. A. Grove, "How Intel Makes Spending Pay Off," *Fortune* (February 22, 1993), p. 57.

15. E. Faltermayer, "Invest or Die," *Fortune* (February 22, 1993), pp. 42–52.

16. V. Scarpello, W. R. Boulton, and C. W. Hofer, "Reintegrating R&D into Business Strategy," *Journal of Business Strategy* (Spring 1986), pp. 49–56.

17. W. M. Bulkeley, "The Latest Thing at Many Companies Is Speed, Speed, Speed," *Wall Street Journal* (December 23, 1994); J. T. Vesey, "The New Competitors: They Think in Terms of 'Speed-to-Market,'" *Academy of Management Executive* (May 1991), pp. 23–33.

18. Bulkeley, "The Latest Thing at Many Companies," p. A1.

19. T. A. Stewart, "Brace for Japan's Hot New Strategy," *Fortune* (September 21, 1992), p. 63.

20. J. B. Barney and R. W. Griffin, *The Management of Organizations: Strategy, Structure, Behavior* (Boston: Houghton Mifflin,

1992). p. 505; B. Dumaine, "How Managers Can Succeed Through Speed," *Fortune* (February 13, 1989), pp. 54–59.

21. B. Davis, "Automation Is Key to Efficiency," *European Rubber Journal* (Special Issue, 1992/1993), p. 32.

22. A. Fiegenbaum and A. Karnani, "Output Flexibility—A Competitive Advantage for Small Firms," *Strategic Management Journal* 12 (1991), pp. 101–114.

23. S. Tully, "The Modular Corporation," *Fortune* (February 8, 1993), pp. 106–115.

24. J. Reese, "America's Most Admired Corporations," *Fortune* (February 8, 1993), p. 46.

25. R. P. Beatty and J. R. Ritter, "Investment Banking, Reputation, and Underpricing of Initial Public Offerings," *Journal of Financial Economics* 15 (1986), pp. 213–232; C. Fombrun and M. Shanley, "What's in a Name? Reputation Building and Corporate Strategy," *Academy of Management Journal* 33 (1990), pp. 233–258; B. Klein and K. Leffler, "The Role of Market Forces in Assuring Contractual Performance," *Journal of Political Economy* 89 (1981), pp. 615–641; P. Milgrom and J. Roberts, "Price and Advertising Signals of Product Quality," *Journal of Political Economy* 94 (1986), pp. 796–821; P. Milgrom and J. Roberts, "Relying on the Information of Interested Parties," *Rand Journal of Economics* 17 (1986), pp. 18–32; G. J. Stigler, "Information in the Labor Market," *Journal of Political Economy* 70 (1962), pp. 49-73.

26. S. Caminiti, "The Payoff from a Good Reputation," *Fortune* (February 10, 1992), pp. 74–77.

27. J. Reese, "America's Most Admired Corporations," *Fortune* (February 8, 1993), p. 46.

28. T. P. Summers and J. S. Harrison, "Alliance for Success," *Training and Development* (March 1992), pp. 69–76.

29. Porter, *Competitive Strategy.*

30. M. Walton, *Deming Management at Work* (New York: G. P. Putnam's Sons, 1990).

31. T. C. Hayes, "Behind Wal-Mart's Surge, a Web of Suppliers," *The New York Times* (July 1, 1991), pp. D1–D2.

32. M. E. Porter, *Competitive Advantage*, p. 20.

33. C. W. L. Hill, "Differentiation Versus Low Cost or Differentiation and Low Cost: A Contingency Framework," *Academy of Management Review* 13 (1988), p. 403. See also A. I. Murray, "A Contingency View of Porter's 'Generic Strategies,'" *Academy of Management Review* 13 (1988), pp. 390–400.

34. W. E. Demming, *Out of the Crisis* (Cambridge, Mass.: MIT Press, 1982); L. W. Phillips, D. Chang, and R. D. Buzzell, "Product Quality, Cost Position, and Business Performance," *Journal of Marketing* 47 (1983), pp. 26–43.

35. "A Conversation with Roberto Goizueta and Jack Welch," *Fortune* (December 11, 1995), pp. 98–99.

36. A. Taylor, III, "Now Hear This, Jack Welch!" *Fortune* (April 6, 1992), p. 94.

37. Associated Press, "Japan Airlines Puts Money in Toilet to Lure 1st-Class Travellers," *Orlando Sentinel* (May 8, 1996).

38. K. Ohmae, "Managing in a Borderless World," *Harvard Business Review* (May–June 1989), pp. 152–161.

39. Adapted from R. Jacob, "Trust the Locals, Win Worldwide," *Fortune* (May 4, 1992), p. 76. Used with permission.

40. T. Levitt, "The Globalization of Markets," *Harvard Business Review* (May–June 1983), p. 92.

41. S. P. Douglas and Y. Wind, "The Myth of Globalization," *Columbia Journal of World Business* (Winter 1987), pp. 19–29.

42. M. A. Hitt, R. D. Ireland, and R. E. Hoskisson, *Strategic Management: Competitiveness and Globalization* (St. Paul, Minn.: West Publishing Company, 1995).

43. This discussion of tactics for global expansion was based, in part, on C. W. L. Hill, P. Hwang, and W. C. Kim, "An Eclectic Theory of the Choice of International Entry Mode," *Strategic Management Journal* 11 (1990), pp. 117–128; C. W. L. Hill and G. R. Jones, *Strategic Management: An Integrated Approach* (Boston: Houghton Mifflin, 1992), pp. 254–259.

44. "Court Dismisses Rivals' Bid to Stop Sale of Beer Brand," *Wall Street Journal* (July 14, 1992), p. B9.

45. S. J. Chang, "International Expansion Strategy of Japanese Firms: Capability Building Through Sequential Entry," *Academy of Management Journal* 38 (1995), p. 383.

46. "Business and Finance," *Wall Street Journal* (February 21, 1996), p. A1.

47. Some of the options contained in this list were based on information found in M.L. Fagan, "A Guide to Global Sourcing," *Journal of Business Strategy* (March–April, 1991), pp. 21–25; J. Sheth and G. Eshghi, *Global Strategic Management Perspectives* (Cincinnati: South-Western Publishing Co., 1989) and M. J. Stahl and D. W. Grigsby, *Strategic Management for Decision Making* (Boston: PWS-Kent, 1992), pp. 205–206.

48. Some of the options contained in this list were based on information found in Sheth and Eshghi, *Global Strategic Management Perspectives*, and Stahl and Grigsby, *Strategic Management for Decision Making*.

49. Use of the term *commodity* to describe curves A and B was borrowed from R. H. Hayes and S. C. Wheelwright, *Restoring Our Competitive Edge: Competing Through Manufacturing* (New York: John Wiley and Sons, 1984), p. 203.

50. This discussion of strategy during the stages of product market evolution is based on C. R. Anderson and C. P. Zeithaml, "Stage of the Product Life Cycle, Business Strategy and Business Performance," *Academy of Management Journal* 27 (1984), pp. 5–24; Barney and Griffin, *The Management of Organizations*, pp. 229–230; Hayes and Wheelright, *Restoring Our Competitive Edge*, Chap. 7; C. W. Hofer and D. Schendel, *Strategy Formulation: Analytical Concepts* (St. Paul, Minn.: West Publishing Company, 1978), Chap. 5.

51. M. B. Lieberman and D. B. Montgomery, "First-Mover Advantages," *Strategic Management Journal* 9 (1988), pp. 41–58.

52. M. Lambkin, "Order of Entry and Performance in New Markets," *Strategic Management Journal* 9 (1988), pp. 127–140.

53. K. R. Harrigan and M. E. Porter, "End-Game Strategies for Declining Industries," *Harvard Business Review* (July–August 1983), pp. 111–120.

54. Harrigan and Porter, "End-Game Strategies for Declining Industries."

55. J. B. Levine, "How Jim Treybig Whipped Tandem Back Into Shape," *Business Week* (February 23, 1987), pp. 102–104.

7

Corporate-Level Strategy

Percy Barnevik Makes the Monster Dance

If lean and mean could be personified, Percy Barnevik would walk through the door. A thin, bearded Swede, Barnevik is Europe's leading hatchet man. He is also the creator of what is fast becoming the most successful cross-border merger since Royal Dutch Petroleum linked up with Britain's Shell in 1907.

In four years, Barnevik, 51, has welded ASEA, a Swedish engineering group, to Brown Boveri, a Swiss competitor, bolted on 70 more companies in Europe and the U.S., and created ABB, a global electrical equipment giant that is bigger than Westinghouse and can go head to head with GE. It is a world leader in high-speed trains, robotics, and environmental control.

To make the monster dance, Barnevik cut more than one in five jobs, closed dozens of factories, and decimated headquarters staffs around Europe and the U.S. Whole businesses were shifted from one country to another. He created a corps of just 250 global managers to lead 210,000 employees. IBM has talked with Barnevik and his team about how to pare down its own overstaffed bureaucracy. Du

Pont recently put Barnevik on its board. Says a senior executive at Mitsubishi Heavy Industries: "They're as aggressive as we are. I mean this as a compliment. They are sort of super-Japanese."

ABB isn't Japanese, nor is it Swiss or Swedish. It is a multinational without a national identity, though its mailing address is in Zurich. The company's 13 top managers hold frequent meetings in different countries. Since they share no common first language, they speak only English, a foreign tongue to all but one.[1]

This chapter and the next deal with the functions top executives perform as they formulate corporate-level strategy, some of the tools they use, and theory concerning how corporate-level actions enhance the value of organizations. We discuss the way business units can be related to each other and provide a rationale for building distinctive competencies based on similarities among them. Then we describe specific tactics firms use to diversify.

At the corporate level, primary strategy formulation responsibilities include setting the direction of the entire organization, formulation of a corporate strategy, selection of businesses in which to compete, selection of tactics for diversification and growth, and management of corporate resources and capabilities. These responsibilities and the key issues associated with each responsibility are listed in Table 7.1.

The three broad approaches to corporate-level strategy are concentration, vertical integration, and diversification. These options, and the way they unfold in many organizations, are discussed next.

DEVELOPMENT OF CORPORATE-LEVEL STRATEGY

Concentration
Corporate-level strategy in which the organization produces a single or small group of products or services.

Most organizations begin with a single or small group of products and services and a single market. This type of corporate-level strategy is called **concentration.** When firms are involved in a single business, they are primarily concerned with the growth and competitive strategies that we described in Chapter 6. Some organizations never stop concentrating, in spite of their size. For instance, McDonald's is only engaged in one line of business, with limited backward integration to ensure a high level of quality for some of its raw materials (e.g., potatoes). The only real diversity pursued by McDonald's is geographic, since McDonald's operates worldwide. However, the same basic growth and competitive strategies are pursued at every McDonald's location in the world (although some of the food ingredients may change).

Table 7.1 *Major Corporate-Level Strategic Management Responsibilities*

Major Responsibilities	Key Issues
Direction setting	Establishment and communication of organizational mission, vision, enterprise strategy, and long-term goals
Development of corporate-level strategy	Selection of a broad approach to corporate-level strategy—concentration, vertical integration, diversification, international expansion
	Selection of resources and capabilities in which to build corporate-wide distinctive competencies
Selection of businesses and portfolio management	Management of the corporate portfolio
	Emphasis given to each business unit—allocation of resources for capital equipment, R&D, etc.
Selection of tactics for diversification and growth	Choice among methods of diversification—internal venturing, acquisitions, joint ventures
Management of resources	Acquisition of resources and/or development of competencies leading to a sustainable competitive advantage
	Ensure development of business-level strategies and an appropriate management structure for the corporation
	Foster development of an appropriate corporate structure

Figure 7.1 *The Development of Corporate-Level Strategy*

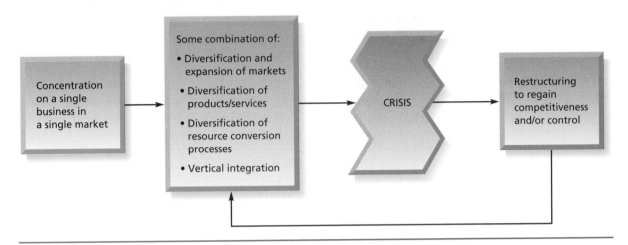

Most successful organizations abandon their concentration strategies at some point due to market saturation, excess resources that they need to find a use for, or some other reason. Corporate strategy typically evolves from concentration to some form of vertical integration or diversification of products, markets, or resource conversion processes (see Figure 7.1).[2] Organizations may continue to pursue vertical integration and/or diversification successfully for many years, creating business units where necessary. However, many organizations eventually come to a point at which slow growth, declining profits, or some other crisis forces corporate-level managers to "rethink" their entire organizations. Disgruntled stakeholders, including stockholders, employees, and managers, often drive this process. The result of this process is usually some form of restructuring.

Restructuring often involves reducing the scope of the business at the corporate level combined with refocusing efforts on the things the organization does well. Most successful restructuring efforts result in a leaner (i.e., fewer employees, less capital equipment), less-diversified organization. As depicted in Figure 7.1, the organization may then cycle back and begin a cautious, better educated, and more focused program of diversification or vertical integration.

This evolutionary process is typical of corporate-level development, but does not apply to all firms. Furthermore, the corporate-level strategy may take shape as a result of systematic analysis and planning or simply through taking advantage of opportunities as they present themselves. The broad corporate-level strategies of concentration, vertical integration, and diversification, along with their major strengths and weaknesses, are now discussed in greater detail.

Restructuring
Streamlining and reorienting an organization's current format of operations to place it in a position in which it is better able to compete; often involves reducing the scope of the business at the corporate level combined with refocusing efforts on the things the organization does well.

Concentration

Concentration is the simplest corporate-level strategy. It is pursued by many large and successful companies such as Federal Express, Domino's Pizza, McDonald's, and Delta Airlines. Many other companies, such as Eastman Kodak, Polaroid, and Xerox, built their reputations while pursuing concentration strategies, but have since diversified into other businesses.

The strengths of a concentration strategy are readily apparent. First, concentration allows an organization to master one business. This specialization allows top executives to obtain in-depth knowledge of the business, which should reduce strategic mistakes. Also, since all resources are directed at doing one thing well, the organization may be in a better position to develop the resources and capabilities necessary to establish a sustainable competitive advantage. Furthermore, organizational resources are under less strain. Lack of ambiguity concerning strategic direction may also allow consensus to form among top managers. High levels of consensus are sometimes associated with superior organizational performance. In fact, a concentration strategy has sometimes been found to be more profitable than other types of corporate-level strategy.[3] Of course, the profitability of a concentration strategy is largely dependent on the industry in which a firm is involved.

On the other hand, concentration strategies entail several risks, especially when environments are unstable. Since the organization is dependent on one product or business area to sustain itself, change can dramatically reduce organizational performance. The airline industry is a good example of the effects of uncertainty on organizational performance. Prior to deregulation of the airline industry, most of the major carriers were profitable. They had protected routes and fixed prices. However, deregulation and the ensuing increase in competition hurt the profitability of all domestic carriers. Since most of the major carriers were pursuing concentration strategies, they did not have other business areas to offset their losses. Consequently, several airlines were acquired or went bankrupt.

Product obsolescence and industry maturity create additional risks for organizations pursuing a concentration strategy. If the principal product of an organization becomes obsolete or matures, organizational performance can suffer until the organization develops another product that is appealing to the market. Some organizations are never able to duplicate earlier successes. Furthermore, since they have experience in only one line of business, they have limited ability to switch to other areas when times get tough; consequently, many are eventually acquired by another company or go bankrupt.

Concentration strategies are also susceptible to problems when the chosen industry is undergoing significant evolution and converging with other industries. For example, as the telecommunications industry evolves, entire segments are converging. Some local telephone operating companies are now offering cable television services through a modified version of the telephone long lines, which represents a substantial diversification away from local telephone services. Companies that fail to diversify in ways that are consistent with industry evolution and convergence can often find themselves short of the next generation of products and services.

Concentration strategies can also lead to cash flow problems. While the business is growing, the organization may find itself in a "cash poor" situation, since growth often entails additional investments in capital equipment and marketing. On the other hand, once growth levels off, the organization is likely to find itself in a "cash rich" situation, with limited opportunities for profitable investment in the business itself. In fact, this may be one of the most important reasons that organizations in mature markets begin to diversify.[4] Having exhausted all reasonable opportunities to reinvest cash in innovation, renewal, or revitalization, organizational managers may look to other areas for growth. Finally, a concentration strategy may not provide enough challenge or stimulation to managers. In other words, they may get tired of doing the same things year after year. This is less true in organizations that are growing rapidly, since growth typically provides excitement and promotion opportunities.

Some organizations use their dominant business as a base and expand forward or backward in their industry supply chains. This strategy, which was defined earlier as vertical integration, is the topic of the next section.

Vertical Integration

Some industries, such as steel and wood products, contain firms that are predominantly vertically integrated. In other industries, such as apparel, vertical integration is limited and most organizations are only involved in one or a few stages. Research has not generally found vertical integration to be a highly profitable strategy relative to the other corporate-level strategies.[5] However, many of the firms that have been studied are old and large. They may have used vertical integration with success as their industries were forming. As one vertical integration expert explained, vertical integration can "lock firms in" to unprofitable adjacent businesses.[6] However, this does not mean that all vertical integration is unprofitable.

Furthermore, a recent study suggested that vertical integration may be associated with reduced administrative, selling, and R&D costs, but higher production costs. The researchers believe that the higher production costs may be a result of a lack of incentive on the part of internal suppliers to keep their costs down. That is, because the internal suppliers have a guaranteed customer, they do not have to be as competitive.[7]

An important point to remember with regard to all of the strategies is that some companies are pursuing them successfully. **Transaction cost economics,** which is the study of economic transactions and their costs, helps explain when vertical integration is appropriate.[8] From this perspective, firms can either negotiate with organizations or individuals on the open market for the products and services they need or they can produce these products and services themselves. According to Oliver Williamson, an influential transaction cost economist, "whether a set of transactions ought to be executed across markets or within a firm depends on the relative efficiency of each mode."[9] If required resources can be obtained from a competitive open market without allocating an undue amount of time or other resources to the contracting process or contract enforcement, it is probably in the best interests of an organization to buy from the market instead of vertically integrating. However, when transactions costs are high enough to encourage an organization to produce a good or service in house instead of buying it from the open market, a **market failure** is said to exist.

For example, suppose a motorcycle manufacturer needs a new "high-tech" part for its top-of-the-line motorcycle. Unfortunately, the manufacturer does not currently have the capacity or the required skills to build the part in house. For the sake of simplicity, we will assume that the manufacturer can either (1) purchase the required machinery and acquire the knowledge necessary to produce the part in house or (2) contract with another company to produce the part. The easiest solution would be to contract out the part. However, suppose that there is only one company in the world that, due to its "high-tech" nature, currently has the skills and machinery required to produce the part. Obviously, the potential part manufacturer would be in a very strong bargaining position and may try to take advantage of the motorcycle manufacturer. Suppose also that secrecy concerning the new part is critical to competitive advantage. The motorcycle manufacturer may determine that enforcing a contract that includes a covenant of secrecy would be

Transaction Cost Economics
The study of economic transactions and their costs.

Market Failure
Occurs when transaction costs are high enough to encourage an organization to produce a good or service in-house instead of buying it from the open market.

prohibitively expensive. Either one of these conditions can lead to market failure, a situation in which it would be more efficient for the motorcycle manufacturer to develop the manufacturing capability in house than to acquire it from the open market.

The market is likely to fail, which means that transactions costs are prohibitively high, under a variety of conditions.[10] First, if the future is highly uncertain, it may be too costly or impossible to identify all of the possible situations that may occur and incorporate these possibilities into the contract. In other words, humans cannot process enough information to identify all possible contingencies, especially where the future is uncertain. Second, if there is only one or a small number of suppliers of a good or service and these suppliers are opportunistic, which means that they are likely to pursue their own self-interests through a lack of candor or honesty, a market failure may occur. This second condition was illustrated in the example of the motorcycle manufacturer.

The third situation in which transactions costs may be too high is when one party to a transaction has more knowledge about the transaction or a series of transactions than another, once again resulting in opportunism. Finally, if an organization invests in an asset that can only be used for the purpose of producing a specific good or service for the other party to a transaction (called *asset specificity*), the other party can take advantage of the producer after the asset is in place.

If transactions costs are low, an organization would usually be better off contracting for the required goods and services instead of vertically integrating. Remember that transactions costs are assumed to be low only if there are a large number of potential suppliers. Under these circumstances, there is probably no profit incentive to vertically integrate, since competition would eliminate abnormally high profits. Furthermore, vertical integration often requires substantially different skills than those currently possessed by the firm, since it typically involves a change in *every* dimension of scope—products/services, markets (unless all goods and services of the new company are kept in house), functions served, and resource conversion processes. In this regard, vertical integration is similar to unrelated diversification.[11] As mentioned in Chapter 5, a firm that can master one stage of the industry supply chain will not necessarily excel at other stages.

From a strategic perspective, vertical integration contains an element of risk that is similar to concentration. If a firm is vertically integrated and the principal product becomes obsolete, the whole organization can suffer unless its value chain activities are sufficiently flexible to be used for other products and services. Researchers have found that both high levels of technical change and high levels of competition reduce the expected profits from vertical integration.[12] Other advantages and disadvantages of vertical integration are listed in Table 7.2.

Firms may pursue partial vertical integration to overcome some of the disadvantages of full integration.[13] **Taper integration** means that an organization produces part of its requirements in house and buys the rest of what it needs on the open market. **Quasi-integration** involves purchasing most of what is needed of a particular product or service from a firm in which the purchasing organization holds an ownership stake. Also, some firms use long-term contracts to achieve many of the benefits of vertical integration. For example, General Motors signed a long-term contract with Simpson Industries that allowed GM to inspect Simpson's engine parts facilities and books and interview Simpson's employees. In return, Simpson became the sole supplier of a part to GM.[14]

Each of the alternatives to complete integration contains trade-offs. That is, while they each reduce the level of exposure to the ill effects of vertical integration,

Taper Integration
Occurs when an organization produces part of its requirements in-house and buys the rest of what it needs on the open market.

Quasi Integration
Occurs when a firm purchases most of what it needs of a particular product or service from a firm in which it holds an ownership stake.

Table 7.2 *Some Advantages and Disadvantages of Vertical Integration*

Advantages	Disadvantages
Internal Benefits	*Internal Costs*
Integration economies reduce costs by eliminating steps, reducing duplicate overhead, and cutting costs	Need for overhead to coordinate vertical integration
Improved coordination of activities reduces inventorying and other costs	Burden of excess capacity if the organization cannot efficiently use all of the output from one of its vertically linked businesses
Avoids time-consuming tasks, such as price shopping, communicating design details, and negotiating contracts	Poorly organized vertically integrated firms do not enjoy synergies that compensate for the higher costs
Competitive Benefits	*Competitive Dangers*
Avoids getting shut out of the market for hard-to-get inputs (i.e., raw materials, services) by competitors	Obsolete processes may be perpetuated
Improved marketing or technological intelligence since vertical businesses are "in house"	Reduces strategic flexibility due to being "locked in" to one business
Opportunity to create product differentiation through coordinated effort	May link firms to unprofitable adjacent businesses
Superior control of firm's market environment due to direct involvement	Lose access to information from suppliers or distributors
Increased ability to create credibility for new products	There may not be much potential for synergy because vertically integrated businesses are so different
Synergies could be created by coordinating vertical activities carefully	Managers may use the wrong method for vertical integration (i.e., full integration instead of contracting)

Source: Adapted from K. R. Harrigan, "Formulating Vertical Integration Strategies," *Academy of Management Review* 9 (1984), p. 639. Used with permission.

they also reduce the potential for benefits arising from vertical integration. For example, taper integration, quasi-integration, and long-term contracting all yield less control over resources than full integration.

Because of the potential disadvantages of vertical integration and the limited potential for profitability that may exist at other stages in the industry supply chain, some organizations bypass vertical integration and pursue diversification directly. Other organizations may vertically integrate for a while, but eventually pursue diversification. Diversification is the topic of the next section.

Diversification

Diversification, which is one of the most studied topics in all of strategic management, can be divided into two broad categories. **Related diversification** implies organizational involvement in activities that are somehow related to the dominant or "core" business of the organization, often through common markets or similar technologies. **Unrelated diversification** does not depend on any pattern of relatedness. Some of the most common reasons for diversification are listed in Table 7.3.[15] They are divided into strategic reasons, which are frequently cited by executives in the popular business press, and personal motives that CEOs may have for pursuing diversification. In addition to these strategic and personal reasons, some diversification may simply be a result of less familiarity with the diversified busi-

Related Diversification
Organization's involvement in other businesses or activities related to its core business.

Unrelated Diversification
Organization's involvement in businesses or activities not related to its core business.

Table 7.3 *A Few Common Reasons for Diversification*

Strategic Reasons

Risk reduction through investments in dissimilar businesses or less dynamic environments

Stabilization or improvement in earnings

Improvement in growth

Cash generated in slower growing traditional areas exceeds that which is needed for profitable investment in those areas (organizational slack)

Application of resources, capabilities, and core competencies to related areas

Generation of synergy/economies of scope

Use of excess debt capacity (organizational slack)

Ability to learn new technologies

Increase in market power

Motives of the CEO

Desire to increase power and status

Desire to increase salary and bonuses

Desire to increase value of the firm

Craving for a more interesting and challenging management environment

Sources: Information on the strategic arguments can be found in H. I. Ansoff, *Corporate Strategy: An Analytical Approach to Business Policy for Growth and Expansion* (New York: McGraw-Hill Book Company, 1965), pp. 130–132; C. W. L. Hill and G. S. Hansen, "A Longitudinal Study of the Cause and Consequence of Changes in Diversification in the U.S. Pharmaceutical Industry," *Strategic Management Journal* 12 (1991), pp. 187–199; W. G. Lewellen, "A Pure Financial Rationale for the Conglomerate Merger," *Journal of Finance* 26 (1971), pp. 521–537; F. M. McDougall and D. K. Round, "A Comparison of Diversifying and Nondiversifying Australian Industrial Firms," *Academy of Management Journal* 27 (1984), pp. 384–398; and R. Reed and G. A. Luffman, "Diversification: The Growing Confusion," *Strategic Management Journal* 7 (1986), pp. 29–35. The personal arguments are outlined in W. Baumol, *Business Behavior, Value and Growth* (New York: Harcourt, 1967); D. C. Mueller, "A Theory of Conglomerate Mergers," *Quarterly Review of Economics* 83 (1969), pp. 644–660; N. Rajagopalan and J. E. Prescott, "Determinants of Top Management Compensation: Explaining the Impact of Economic, Behavioral, and Strategic Constructs and the Moderating Effects of Industry," *Journal of Management* 16 (1990), pp. 515–538.

ness areas than with the core business areas of the organization. In other words, diversification opportunities may look good because organizational managers do not possess enough information about problems and weaknesses associated with the diversified areas—they "leap before they look."[16]

Unrelated Diversification.[17] Richard Rumelt documented the rise in popularity of unrelated diversification during the 1950s, 1960s, and early 1970s.[18] Large, unrelated diversified firms are often called **conglomerates**, since they are involved in a conglomeration of unrelated businesses. Strategic Insight 7.1 contains an example of one such company, Hitachi of Japan. The increase in conglomerates was precipitated by several forces, including government regulation and the popularity of financial theory and portfolio management.

Rigid antitrust enforcement by the federal government made unrelated diversification attractive.[19] **Antitrust laws** were established to keep organizations from getting large and powerful enough in one industry to engage in monopoly pricing and other forms of noncompetitive or illegal behavior. Many organizational managers pursued unrelated diversification in an effort to use excess cash in ways that would not lead to conflicts with antitrust enforcement agencies.

Another powerful force leading to unrelated diversification was an increase in the popularity of the capital asset pricing model (CAPM), financial portfolio management, and related financial theories. The CAPM was developed in the field of finance as a tool for managing portfolios of financial securities. Its general propo-

Conglomerates
Large, unrelated diversified firms.

Antitrust Laws
Established to prevent an organization from getting large enough to engage in monopoly pricing or other noncompetitive or illegal behavior.

STRATEGIC INSIGHT 7.1

Hitachi's Unrelated Diversification Strategy

Kabushiki Kaisha Hitachi Seisakusho, or Hitachi, Ltd., is a major global organization based in Tokyo, Japan. Founded in 1910, the company has more than one-quarter of a million employees. Operations are divided into the following groups:

Power Systems and Equipment—nuclear, hydroelectric and thermal power plants, water, steam and gas turbines, generators, boilers, transformers, circuit breakers, motors, control equipment, switchboards, and automobile parts.

Consumer Products—VCRs, video cameras, audio equipment, audio- and videotapes, air conditioners, refrigerators, washing machines, microwave ovens, vacuum cleaners, heaters, and dry batteries.

Information and Communications Systems and Electronic Devices—computers, computer terminals and peripherals, workstations, magnetic disks, Japanese word processors, telephone exchanges, facsimile equipment, broadcasting equipment, integrated circuits, semiconductors, picture tubes, test and measurement equipment, and medical electronics equipment.

Industrial Machinery and Plants—compressors, pumps, blowers, rolling mill equipment, chemical plants, construction machinery, cranes, elevators, escalators, refrigeration equipment, air conditioning equipment, environmental control equipment, welding equipment, industrial robots, electric locomotives, electric cars, and monorail cars.

Wire and Cable, Metals, Chemicals, and Other Products—electric wire and cable, rolled copper products, optical fiber cable, special steels, rolls for rolling mills, cast iron products, cast steel products, pipe fittings, synthetic resin products, carbon and graphite products, electric insulating materials, circuit boards, and ceramic materials.

Sources: Annual Report, Hitachi, March 31, 1990; "Hitachi LTD," Moody's International Manual, Vol. 2 (New York: Moody's Investors Service, 1992), pp. 2917–2920.

sition is that financial managers can reduce the risk of a portfolio of securities by investing in securities that have dissimilar return streams. For example, managers should try to invest in companies that prosper under different business conditions so that one or another of the companies will be prospering at any given time. This proposition was also applied, perhaps erroneously, to the business portfolios of individual organizations.[20] In particular, managers believed that by allocating financial resources to business areas that showed the most promise, they would not only be able to reduce risk but also maximize the profitability of a portfolio of businesses.

Related to the CAPM is the theory of **"semistrong" market efficiency,** which advances the idea that information about the value of a financial security is quickly assimilated by the market and absorbed into the price of the security.[21] The theory of "semistrong" market efficiency helps us understand why managers

"Semistrong" Market Efficiency
The idea that information about the value of a financial security is quickly assimilated by the market and absorbed into the price of the security.

responded to the CAPM with increasing amounts of diversification. CEOs, responding to their knowledge about the CAPM, pursued unrelated diversification. The market, which consists of individuals and organizations that are also largely familiar with the CAPM, reacted by bidding up the stock prices of the firms that pursued unrelated diversification. The behavior of the CEOs was reinforced by high stock returns, and so they pursued more unrelated diversification. In one study of acquisition activity during the 1960s and early 1970s, the stock value of the bidding company rose an average of $8 million, after adjusting for market movements, on the announcement of an unrelated acquisition. The stock value fell when a related acquisition was announced.[22] This cycle of behavior and reinforcement was evident in the 1960s, as the stock prices of conglomerates soared.

Nevertheless, Rumelt concluded that unrelated firms had lower profitability than firms pursuing other corporate-level strategies. His findings have been generally, although not unequivocally, supported by other researchers.[23] Perhaps of greater concern, there is some evidence that unrelated diversification is associated with higher levels of risk than other strategies.[24] This is particularly distressing since one of the most frequently cited arguments for unrelated diversification is that it leads to reduced risk.

Unrelated diversification places significant demands on corporate-level executives due to increased complexity and technological changes across industries. In fact, it is very difficult for a manager to understand each of the core technologies and appreciate the special requirements of each of the individual units in an unrelated diversified firm. Consequently, the effectiveness of management may be reduced. By the late 1960s, conglomerates began suffering performance problems. In early 1969, the stock prices of many conglomerates fell by as much as 50% from their highs of the previous year, while the Dow Jones Industrial Average fell less than 10% during the same period.[25]

Now, managers and researchers alike believe that unrelated diversification is not typically a good strategic option to pursue. However, some firms have had great success with it. Ford Motor is making literally billions of dollars each year in profits from its highly successful financial subsidiaries.[26] Also, General Electric, one of the biggest conglomerates in the world, has enjoyed many years of strong financial performance. Jack Welch, CEO of GE, explains his philosophy like this:

> *All our industries don't grow at the same rate. Our plastics business might be more like (a fast growing company) in term's of top line growth. But in our other businesses, it allows us enormous staying power. For example, next year we'll go from A to B. I think I know exactly how I'm going to go from A to B, and I know the company in total will go from A to B. I'm not sure the 30 or so businesses are going to get from A to B exactly as they planned it, but I've got enough muscle that I can get from A to B.*
>
> *If one of the businesses is going to be weak, and it's a great business but it's in a difficult moment, I can support it. If I'm a single-product guy in a weak business like that, in a business that cycles dramatically, I get whacked. So the staying power that our businesses have allows us to stay for the long haul.[27]*

The 1980s were marked by a dramatic decrease in unrelated diversification, accompanied by an increase in related diversification.[28] The Reagan administration's "hands-off" approach to antitrust policy supported the trend toward mergers among related firms, even horizontal mergers among firms in the same industries. Related diversification, accompanied by sell-offs of unrelated businesses, is a continuing trend among U.S. firms.[29]

STRATEGIC INSIGHT 7.2

Grand Metropolitan's Related Diversification Strategy

Grand Metropolitan is an international group that specializes in highly branded consumer businesses, where its marketing and operational skills ensure it is a leading contender in every market in which it operates. These businesses—in food, drinks, and retailing—which are few in number but large in size, have complementary features thus ensuring GrandMet can add value to the parts.

GrandMet's branded foods include Pillsbury, Haagen-Dazs, Green Giant, Hungry Jack, Totino's, and Jenos. Some of GrandMet's most famous drinks are Popov Vodka, J&B Rare Scotch Whiskey, Smirnoff, Malibu, and Jack Daniels Old Time. And, of course, in branded retailing and pubs GrandMet owns Burger King, Pearle Vision, and Chef & Brewer.

According to Sir Allen Sheppard, chairman of GrandMet, "We have focused our business portfolio primarily onto highly branded businesses which offer the opportunity for international development." Grand Met currently operates in dozens of countries, but generates most of its profits in the United Kingdom and the United States.

Sources: Annual Report, Grand Metropolitan, 1992; "Grand Metropolitan PLC," *Moody's International Manual,* Vol. 1 (New York: Moody's Investors Services, 1992), pp. 4739–4742.

Related Diversification. Most of the research on diversification strategies indicates that some form or other of relatedness among diversified businesses leads to higher financial performance.[30] Also, a recent study demonstrated that related diversification is also associated with reduced risk.[31]

Related diversification is based on similarities that exist among the products, services, markets, or resource conversion processes of different parts of the organization. These similarities are supposed to lead to synergy, which means that the whole is supposed to be greater than the sum of its parts. In other words, one organization should be able to produce two related products or services more efficiently than two organizations each producing one of the products or services on its own. The same reasoning applies to similar markets and similar resource conversion processes. For example, Johnson & Johnson is involved in a wide variety of diversified businesses; however, virtually all of them are related to converting chemical substances into drugs and toiletries. Also, Del Monte has diversified into a wide variety of activities, but they center on food production, processing, and distribution. Strategic Insight 7.2 contains a description of the related diversification strategy of Grand Metropolitan, an international organization based in the United Kingdom.

Relatedness comes in two forms, tangible and intangible.[32] **Tangible relatedness** means that the organization has the opportunity to use the same physical resources for multiple purposes. Tangible relatedness can lead to synergy through resource sharing. For example, if two similar products are manufactured in the same plant, operating synergy is said to exist. This phenomenon was referred to earlier as *economies of scope,* which occur any time slack resources that would not have been used otherwise are being put to good use.[33] Sharing of production facil-

Tangible Relatedness
An organization may use the same physical resources for multiple purposes.

ities can also lead to economies of scale through producing products or services in an optimally sized (typically larger) plant.[34]

Other examples of synergy resulting from tangible relatedness include (1) using the same marketing or distribution channels for multiple related products, (2) buying similar raw materials for related products through a centralized purchasing office to gain purchasing economies, (3) providing corporate training programs to employees from different divisions that are all engaged in the same type of work, and (4) advertising multiple products simultaneously, such as advertising Pepsi and Pizza Hut in the same television commercial (PepsiCo owns Pizza Hut).

Intangible Relatedness
Occurs when skills developed in one area of the organization can be applied to another area.

Intangible relatedness occurs any time capabilities developed in one area can be applied to another area. It results in managerial synergy.[35] For example, Toys 'R' Us developed skill in retailing that was directly applicable to Kids 'R' Us. Also, Campbell Soup has applied skills in manufacturing and packaging soup to a variety of other products. Both of these companies make effective use of another intangible resource, image or goodwill. Goodwill means that a company with an established trade name can draw on this name to market new products. For instance, Singer, which has an established reputation in sewing machines, also began marketing small consumer appliances and furniture under the same label. Also, Heinz enjoys a high-quality reputation that is shared by all of its food varieties. Synergy based on intangible resources such as brand name or management skills and knowledge may be more conducive to the creation of a sustainable competitive advantage, since intangible resources are hard to imitate and are never used up.[36]

The potential for synergy based on relatedness in diversified firms is limited only by the imagination. However, some types of relatedness are more imaginary than real. For example, the relatedness between oil and other forms of energy such as solar and coal proved illusive to several of the large oil companies, who experienced performance problems in these "related business ventures." They found much greater synergy with plastics and other petrochemicals, which represented a form of forward vertical integration. In addition, even if relatedness is evident, synergy *has to be created*.[37] The requirements for synergy creation are outlined in Figure 7.2. Some examples of potential sources of synergy from related diversification are shown in Table 7.4.

Strategic Fit
The effective matching of strategic organizational capabilities.

Some managers seem to believe that if business units are somehow related to each other, synergy will occur automatically. Unfortunately, this is not the case. One factor that can block the ability of organizational managers to create synergistic gains from relatedness is a lack of **strategic fit**. Strategic fit refers to the effective matching of strategic organizational capabilities. For example, if two organizations in two related businesses combine their resources, but they are both strong in the same areas and weak in the same areas, then the potential for synergy is diminished. Once combined, they will continue to exhibit the same capabilities. However, if one of the organizations is strong in R&D, but lacks marketing power, while the other organization is weak in R&D, but strong in marketing, then there is real potential for both organizations to be better off—if managed properly. When AT&T purchased NCR as a vehicle for integrating telecommunications and computer technologies, AT&T was dismayed to find that NCR did not possess strong core technical skills. Consequently, the movement into computing did not yield the synergies that were expected, and NCR was divested some years later.

Organizational Fit
Occurs when two organizations or business units have similar management processes, cultures, systems, and structures.

Another factor that can block managers from achieving synergistic gains is a lack of organizational fit. **Organizational fit** occurs when two organizations or business units have similar management processes, cultures, systems, and struc-

Figure 7.2 *Requirements for the Creation of Synergy*

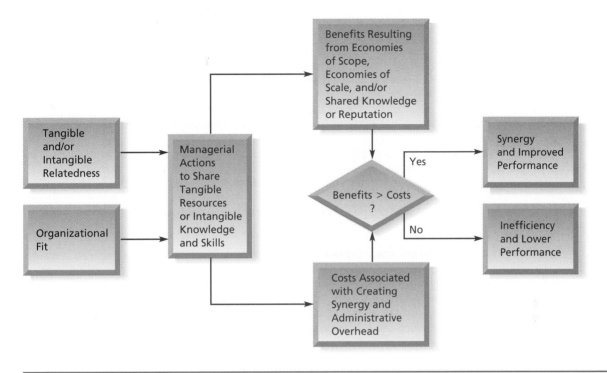

tures.[38] This makes them compatible, which facilitates resource sharing, communication, and transference of knowledge and skills. Unfortunately, relatedness on a dimension such as common markets or similar resource conversion processes does not guarantee that business units within a firm will enjoy an organizational fit. Lack of fit is especially evident in mergers and acquisitions. For instance, two related companies may merge in an effort to create synergy, but find that they are organizationally incompatible. When Federal Express and Flying Tigers joined forces, the intent was to create a total package delivery company. Federal Express specialized in small packages, and Flying Tigers specialized in larger shipments. Unfortunately, the cultures of the two firms were so different that conflicts arose, communications broke down, and synergies never materialized.

The concept of dominant logic provides further insight into why organizations may not fit. The **dominant logic** of an organization consists of the way managers deal with managerial tasks, the things they value, and their general approach to running their businesses: "The characteristics of the core business . . . tend to cause managers to define problems in certain ways and develop familiarity with and facility in the use of those administrative tools that are particularly useful in accomplishing the critical tasks of the core business."[39] Unfortunately, the administrative tools acquired while working in the core or dominant business unit of the organization may not work well in other business environments.[40] This explains, in part, why it is so hard for executives to manage diverse business units. Following this logic, some researchers suggest that organizations should only invest in businesses that would gain from the management style that permeates existing businesses.[41]

Dominant Logic
The way managers deal with managerial tasks, the things they value, and their general approach to running their businesses.

Table 7.4 *Potential Sources of Synergy from Related Diversification*

Synergies are created by linking value activities between two separate businesses.

Potential Operations Synergies

Common parts designs: Larger purchased quantities allows lower cost per unit.
Common processes and equipment: Combined equipment purchases and engineering support allow lower costs.
Common new facilities: Larger facilities may allow economies of scale.
Shared facilities and capacity: Improved capacity utilization allows lower per unit overhead costs.
Combined purchasing activities: Increased influence leading to lower costs and lower cost shipping arrangements.
Shared computer systems: Lower per unit overhead costs and can spread the risk of investing in higher priced systems.
Combined training programs: Lower training costs per employee.

Potential R&D/Technology Synergies

Shared R&D programs: Spread overhead cost and risk of R&D to more than one business.
Technology transfer: Faster, lower cost adoption of technology at the second business.
Development of new core businesses: Access to capabilities and innovation not available in the market.
Multiple use of creative researchers: Opportunities for innovation across business via individual experience and business analogy.

Potential Marketing-Based Synergies

Shared brand names: Build market influence faster and at lower cost through a common name.
Shared advertising and promotion: Lower unit costs and tie-in purchases.
Shared distribution channels: Bargaining power to improve access and lower costs.
Cross-selling and bundling: Lower costs and more integrated view of the marketplace.

Potential Management Synergies

Similar industry experience: Faster response to industry trends.
Transferable core skills: Experience with previously tested, innovative strategies and skills in strategy and program development.

One of the most well-known examples of diversification that was incompatible with dominant logic was when IBM entered the personal computer industry. In the mainframe business, IBM's original computer business, customers expected high levels of technical service support and purchased computers through direct sales groups. The personal computer industry, on the other hand, did not make use of direct sales, and involved very little technical customer service. For IBM, the change in the basic way of doing business was very difficult. Because the dominant logics were so different, IBM was forced to separate the mainframe and personal computer businesses completely, which reduced the opportunities for synergies.

Synergy creation requires a great deal of work on the part of managers at the corporate and business levels. The activities that create synergy include combining similar processes, coordinating business units that share common resources, centralizing support activities that apply to multiple units, and resolving conflicts among business units. Many organizations do not engage in these activities to any degree. Synergy, which is supposed to result in 2 + 2 = 5, often ends up 2 + 2 = 3. Not only are the coordinating and integrating activities expensive, in addition,

Table 7.5 *Forces That Undermine Synergies*

Management Ineffectiveness

Too *little* effort to coordinate between businesses means synergies will not be created.
Too *much* effort to coordinate between businesses can stifle creativity.

Administrative Costs of Coordination

Additional layers of management and staff add costs.
Executives in larger organizations are often paid higher salaries.
Delays occur and expense is created as a result of meetings and planning sessions necessary for coordination.
Extra travel and communications costs are incurred to achieve coordination.

Poor Strategic Fit

Relatedness without strategic fit decreases the opportunity for synergy.
Opportunities for synergies are overstated (or imaginary).
Industry evolution undermines strategic fit.

Poor Organizational Fit

Cultures and management styles are incompatible.
Strategies, priorities, and reward systems are incompatible.
Production processes and technologies are incompatible.
Computer and budgeting systems are incompatible.

corporate-level management creates an administrative overhead burden that must be shared by all of the operating units.[42]

Consequently, organizational performance is increased only if the benefits associated with synergy are greater than the costs related to corporate-level administration, combining activities, or sharing knowledge and resources. When the economic benefits associated with synergy are highest, the administrative costs are highest also because a lot more information and coordination are required to create the synergy.[43] For example, if two business units are unrelated to each other, they do not ever have to communicate or coordinate with one another. On the other hand, if they are related to each other and want to share knowledge or skills, they will have to engage in meetings, joint training programs, and other coordination efforts. If two related businesses are using the same plant for production, they will have to work out production schedules. Coordination is also required when using the same sales force for related products, combining promotional efforts, and transferring products between divisions. Coordination processes can be costly in terms of time and other resources. Consequently, the benefits of synergy may be offset, in part, by higher administrative costs. The various costs and forces that can undermine creation of synergies are shown in Table 7.5.

In summary, organizations may pursue related diversification by acquiring or developing businesses in areas that are related to each other on some basic variable, such as a similar production technology, a common customer, or any number of other dimensions. However, synergy is not instantaneously created if businesses are related. The creation of synergy requires related businesses to fit together common processes. This can be a difficult managerial challenge. The level of difficulty depends on the amount of strategic and organizational fit that exists among related businesses. In addition to the synergy that can be created through related diversification, corporate-level managers sometimes try to add value to their organizations through the development of corporate-level distinctive competencies that may or may not be associated with a relatedness strategy.

Corporate-Level Core Capabilities

The ability to achieve shared competitive advantage in a multibusiness firm—or, distinctive competence—is dependent on the firm's ability to deploy combined resources effectively and efficiently. Many corporations attempt to build core capabilities that can be applied across many businesses in the domestic market or globally. Organizations can develop core capabilities based on skills and resources that "(1) incorporate an integrated set of managerial and technological skills, (2) are hard to acquire other than through experience, (3) contribute significantly to perceived customer benefits, and (4) can be widely applied within the company's business domain."[44] A firm can derive synergistic benefits if it can deploy its pool of experience, knowledge, and systems (core capabilities) from one business to another business so that the costs and time required to create and expand assets and resources are less than that of competitors.[45] For example, AT&T has developed a corporate-level core competence in benchmarking methods, Motorola in flexible manufacturing, and 3M in supplier management.[46]

Strategy researchers identified fifty-five activities that corporations engage in to develop core capabilities and competencies.[47] These activities were based on general administration, production/operations, engineering and R&D, marketing, finance, personnel, and public and governmental relations. A few examples follow:

1. Attracting and retaining well-trained and competent top managers (general administration)
2. Developing a more effective company-wide strategic planning system (general administration)
3. Increased automation of production processes (production/operations)
4. Improvement in research and new product development capabilities (engineering and R&D)
5. Improved marketing research and information systems (marketing)
6. Effective tax management (finance)
7. Effective relations with trade unions (personnel)
8. Better relations with special interest groups such as environmentalists, consumerists, and others (public and governmental relations)[48]

Notice that these activities cover a wide range of activities in the value chain. Any of these activities has the potential to lead to a competitive advantage. Whether the competitive advantage is sustainable depends on the ability of competitors to imitate the resulting competence or capability. However, many of these activities are long term by nature. For example, effective relations with trade unions and special interest groups take many years to develop. Consequently, some competencies are harder to duplicate in the short term and are more likely to lead to a sustainable competitive advantage.

This completes our discussion of the basic corporate-level strategies of concentration, vertical integration, unrelated diversification, and related diversification. In addition, we have argued for the development of corporate-level core capabilities. In the next section, we discuss the methods organizations use to implement their corporate-level strategies.

STRATEGIC INSIGHT 7.3

BUSINESS

STRATEGY

Novell's Corporate-Level Tactics

Novell, incorporated in 1983, is a system software company and developer of services that support network-based computing solutions. Novell's NetWare computing products integrate desktop PCs with each other and with midrange and mainframe computer systems. Novell has a commanding lead in network software, with about half of the world market. About half of Novell's sales are outside of the United States.

The company has developed an infrastructure of related businesses around Novell's core network software business in an attempt to solidify its position in the computer industry. The infrastructure is continuously being created through a wave of acquisitions, joint ventures, and new-product initiatives to "accelerate the momentum of networking."

Some of Novell's joint ventures include a project with Apple Computer and Go Corp. to develop software that ties wireless devices to corporate networks, a venture with AT&T aimed at linking PC networks to corporate phone systems, and a technology project with Kodak to develop a way to send photos and other types of images across networks. Novell has ongoing ventures it calls "systems solution partnerships" with Compaq, Memorex Telex, Olivetti, Digital Equipment, IBM, Hewlett-Packard, and Unisys. Finally, Novell has provided about $25 million in seed money to nine start-ups that are developing new software to use on NetWare, including work group applications software and an object-based services interface.

Novell has been less successful with its acquisitions. Novell acquired Digital Research in 1991. DRI's operating system, DR-DOS, is similar to Microsoft's MS-DOS. In 1993, Novell acquired Unix System Labs and the Unix operating system from AT&T. Then, in a move that would prove to be an enormously costly mistake, Novell bought WordPerfect in 1994. Two years later, the company sold off most of what it acquired with WordPerfect, as well as its Unix software business.

Sources: Annual Report, Novell Inc., 1992; D. Clark, "Novell in Talks to Sell Software Lines It Acquired in WordPerfect Purchase," *The Wall Street Journal* (October 31, 1995), pp. A3–A4; E. I. Schwartz, "The Industry Needs an Alternative—But Will It Be Novell?" *Business Week* (February 1, 1993), pp. 69–70; S. Stahl and C. Gillooly, "Perfect Office Unplugged," *Investor's Weekly* (November 13, 1995), pp. 14–16.

DIVERSIFICATION METHODS

The emphasis in this section is on the techniques available to organizations to pursue diversification once a decision concerning the desired type and level of diversification has been made. These techniques include internal venturing, acquisitions, joint ventures, and various types of restructuring. Companies like Exxon and Johnson & Johnson rely most heavily on internal venturing for diversification. Beatrice Foods and ITT, on the other hand, accomplish virtually all of their diversification through acquisitions. Procter & Gamble and Westinghouse favor a combination of joint ventures and acquisitions over internal venturing.[49] Strategic Insight 7.3 describes how Novell used these tactics to create a related-business network to support its core business.

Internal Venturing

Internal venturing can be viewed as an organizational learning process directed at developing the skills and knowledge necessary to compete in new domains.[50] It is entrepreneurship within an existing organization.[51] Some organizations are very committed to internal venturing. At 3M, a corporate policy that supports internal venturing allows scientists to spend up to 15% of their time on personal research projects. "Post-it" note pads were invented through this program.[52]

The three basic types of internal diversification are (1) product line extension, refinement, and repositioning that draws the organization into a new business opportunity, (2) introduction of new products related to an existing competence of the firm, and (3) development of truly new-to-the-world products not related to the core business of the firm.[53]

The most important strength an internal diversifier brings to a new business venture is its ability to make use of the combined resources and capabilities of its various operations, especially in the technological areas.[54] For example, IBM used its abundant resources in the computer industry to develop and market its very successful line of personal computers in the early 1980s. W. L. Gore and Associates has used its capabilities in Gore-Tex materials to venture into new businesses in health care, industrial applications, and outdoor apparel. Compared to joint venturing, internal venturing provides an organization with complete control over the innovation and marketing processes, as well as the ability to fully exploit new innovations if the venture is a success.[55]

Nevertheless, research suggests that internal venturing is typically associated with slower growth than other diversification options, especially acquisitions. In fact, one researcher discovered that new ventures take, on average, eight years before they become profitable and generate a positive cash flow. Furthermore, it takes ten to twelve years before the return on investment of new ventures equal that of existing products lines.[56] Also, another researcher found that only 12% to 20% of new R&D-based ventures ever become profitable.[57] However, if organizations can quickly learn which new ventures are going to be successful and respond to this knowledge before large amounts of resources have been expended, internal venturing can be a very successful approach to diversification. Also, both acquisitions and joint ventures have low success rates, so an organization is going to have to take risks regardless of tactic.

Many design alternatives are available to organizations for pursuing internal ventures. The selection of an organizational design depends on the strategic importance of the venture and how closely related the venture is to current activities.[58] Strategic importance can be assessed based on factors such as the likelihood that the venture will lead to a competitive advantage relative to competitors and what may be learned during the venture that can move the whole organization forward.

Relatedness of the new venture to current organizational activities can be determined by asking whether the organization currently has the capabilities and resources that will be required to make the venture a success. Many new ventures are actually a result of combining organizational resources in new ways, such as when Toys 'R' Us ventured into children's clothing retailing and when Microsoft, the software company, created the Microsoft Network, a World Wide Web site. Consequently, new capabilities may not be required, but only new combinations of existing capabilities. Managers should also assess what effect the new venture will have on current processes. For example, will the new venture slow down production of other products or services because of the resources it uses?

Figure 7.3 *Internal Venturing Alternatives*

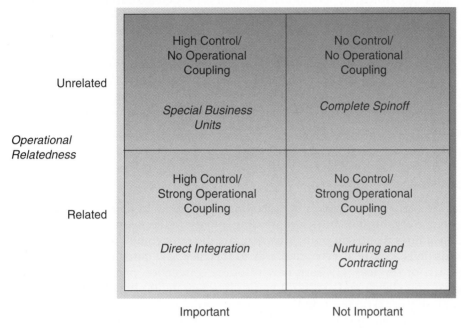

Source: Adapted from R.A. Burgelman, "Designs for Corporate Entrepreneurship in Established Firms," Copyright © 1984 by the Regents of the University of California. Reprinted from the *California Management Review*, Vol. 26, No. 3. By permission of the Regents.

Top management will want to maintain a high level of control over ventures that are strategically important, in that they are closely related to the organization's current or anticipated business activities. For example, managers of new ventures would be expected to report directly to top management, who will stay apprised of the project at every step. High levels of operational relatedness should result in a strong operational coupling between the new and existing businesses. Joint information systems should be established and professionals from new and existing businesses should meet regularly. Depending on the nature of the project, work flows may even need to be coordinated.

Joining operational relatedness with strategic importance results in the model shown in Figure 7.3. The model contains suggested design configurations for each type of internal venture. They are described below:

1. *Strategically important/strongly related.* Top managers will want to maintain a high level of control over these ventures and also create a strong coupling with existing operations. Direct integration can accomplish both of these ends, by integrating the new venture right into the mainstream processes of the organization.

2. *Strategically important/unrelated.* Since these ventures are strategically important but do not draw on existing resources of the organization, special business units should be established. These units are still wholly owned by the organization and their managers still report directly to top management.

3. *Not strategically important/strongly related.* Since the business is not strategically important to the organization, there is no motivation to develop the venture in house. However, operational relatedness may create the opportunity to sell services or excess manufacturing capacity to the new business. Also, the organization may be able to learn from the new business. Consequently, organizations should not create these ventures themselves, but should nurture entrepreneurs as they create their own independent companies.

4. *Not strategically important/unrelated.* A complete spin off of a totally independent company is appropriate in these instances. The organization should not pursue any type of business relationship with the new company.[59]

As an alternative to corporate venturing, some organizations choose to buy diversification in the form of acquisitions.

Acquisitions

Mergers

Occur any time two organizations combine to form one.

Acquisitions

Occur when one organization buys a controlling interest in the stock of another corporation or buys it outright from its owner.

Corporate Raiders

Organizations or individuals who engage in acquisitions, often against the wishes of the managers of the target companies.

Hostile Acquisition

An acquisition that is against the wishes of the management of the target company.

Mergers occur any time two organizations combine into one. **Acquisitions,** in which one organization buys a controlling interest in the stock of another organization or buys it outright from its owners, are the most common types of mergers. Acquisitions are a relatively quick way to (1) enter new markets, (2) acquire new products or services, (3) learn new resource conversion processes, (4) acquire needed knowledge and skills, (5) vertically integrate, (6) broaden markets geographically, or (7) fill needs in the corporate portfolio.[60]

As a portfolio management tool, managers often seek acquisition targets that are faster growing, more profitable, less cyclical, or less dependent on a particular set of environmental variables. For example, Mobil Oil acquired Marcor, which consisted of Montgomery Ward and Container Corporation of America, because Marcor, executives argued, was not as dependent on factors connected to oil.[61]

Corporate raiders are organizations and individuals who engage in acquisitions, often against the wishes of the managers of the target companies. This type of acquisition is called **hostile** and tends to be more expensive than a friendly acquisition.[62] From a social perspective, some corporate raiders have argued that they are doing society a favor, because the threat of takeover motivates managers to act in the best interests of the organization's stockholders.[63] They are keeping managers from becoming "entrenched." Still others believe that assets that are acquired will be under better management than they were previously.

Unfortunately, most of the research evidence seems to indicate that mergers and acquisitions are not, on average, financially beneficial to the shareholders of the acquiring firm.[64] In one study of 191 acquisitions in twenty-nine industries, researchers found that acquisitions were associated with declining profitability, reduced research and development expenditures, fewer patents, and increases in financial leverage.[65]

Table 7.6 provides several explanations for why acquisitions, on average, tend to depress profitability (at least in the short term). High premiums, increased interest costs, high advisory fees and other transaction costs, and poison pills (actions that make a target company less attractive) can cause acquisitions to be prohibitively expensive and thus reduce any potential gains from synergy. In addition, strategic problems such as high turnover among target firm managers, managerial distraction, lower innovation, lack of organizational fit, and increased leverage and risk can reduce any strategic benefits the organization was hoping to achieve. On the other hand, the shareholders of the organization that is acquired typically enjoy an increase in wealth because of increases in the value of the stock

---

Table 7.6 *A Few of Many Potential Problems with Mergers and Acquisitions*

High Financial Costs

1. *High premiums typically paid by acquiring firms.* If a company was worth $50/share in a relatively efficient financial market prior to an acquisition, why should an acquiring firm pay $75 (a typical premium) or more to buy it?
2. *Increased interest costs.* Many acquisitions are financed by borrowing money at high interest rates. Leverage typically increases during an acquisition.
3. *High advisory fees and other transaction costs.* The fees charged by the brokers, lawyers, financiers, consultants, and advisors who orchestrate the deal often range in the millions of dollars. In addition, filing fees, document preparation, and legal fees in the event of contestation can be very high.
4. *Poison pills.* These antitakeover devices make companies very unattractive to a potential buyer. Top managers of target companies have been very creative in designing a variety of poison pills. One example of a poison pill is the "golden parachute," in which target firm executives receive large amounts of severance pay (often millions of dollars) if they lose their jobs due to a hostile takeover.

Strategic Problems

1. *High turnover among the managers of the acquired firm.* The most valuable asset in most organizations is its people, their knowledge, and their skills. If most managers leave, what has the acquiring firm purchased?
2. *Short-term managerial distraction.* "Doing a deal" typically takes managers away from the critical tasks of the core businesses for long durations. During this time period, who is steering the ship?

---

they hold.[66] When organizations pursue diversification through acquisition, they combine the risks outlined in Table 7.5 with a new set of problems associated specifically with mergers. Some of these problems are listed in Table 7.6.

Perhaps the most condemning evidence to date concerning mergers and acquisitions was presented by Michael Porter. He studied the diversification records of thirty-three large, prestigious U.S. companies during the 1950 to 1986 period. He discovered that most of these companies divested many more of their acquisitions than they kept. For example, CBS, in an effort to create an "entertainment company," bought organizations involved in toys, crafts, sports teams, and musical instruments. All of these businesses were sold due to lack of fit with the traditional broadcasting business of CBS. CBS also bought the Ziff-Davis publishers, which they unloaded a few years later for much less than they paid after having run all of its magazines into the ground. Porter's general conclusion was that the corporate-level strategies of most of the companies he studied had reduced, rather than enhanced, shareholder value.[67]

Does this mean that all mergers are doomed to failure? Recently researchers have been able to identify factors that seem to be associated with successful and unsuccessful mergers. Unsuccessful mergers were associated with a large amount of debt, overconfident or incompetent managers, poor ethics, changes in top management or the structure of the acquiring organization, and diversification away from the core area in which the firm is strongest. The successful mergers were related to low to moderate amounts of debt, a high level of relatedness leading to synergy, friendly negotiations (no resistance), a continued focus on the core business, careful selection of and negotiations with the acquired firm, and a strong cash or debt position.[68]

Furthermore, researchers have discovered that the largest shareholder gains from merger occurred when the cultures and the top management styles of the two companies were similar (organizational fit).[69] In addition, sharing resources and activities was found to be important to postmerger success.[70] However, it is fair to say that "there are no rules that will invariably lead to a successful acquisition."[71]

Many of the diversification objectives sought by organizations through acquisitions are also available through joint ventures, which are the topic of the next section.

Strategic Alliances

Strategic Alliances
Formed by two or more organizations to develop new products or services, enter new markets, or improve resource conversion processes.

Joint Venture
An alliance formed by two or more organizations to pursue activities of mutual benefit or interest, which may include entering new markets, developing new products, or improving existing technologies.

Strategic alliances are formed by two or more organizations to develop new products or services, enter new markets, or improve resource conversion processes.[72] A **joint venture,** a special type of strategic alliance, occurs when two firms share an equity position in a new venture. Although joint ventures typically operate independently of the organizations that form them, they are still under their control.

Other types of strategic alliances between firms include contractual relationships for production, marketing, or development work, and "handshake" agreements leading to cooperation. In particular, examples of joint ventures and other strategic alliances between U.S. companies and foreign partners abound. For instance, Hewlett-Packard formed a joint venture with Yokogawa Electric to penetrate the Japanese market.[73] Also, AT&T has joint ventures with Philips, a leading European electronics and communications firm; Olivetti, a giant in European information processing; Lucky Goldstar, a manufacturer of communications equipment in Korea; Compania Telefonica Nacional de Espana, the Spanish telephone company; and three Taiwanese firms engaged in manufacturing switching equipment. Commenting on these alliances, James Olson, chairman of the board at AT&T, stated:

> We can't do everything everywhere—we will need to cooperate and partner with other companies. And we will have to concentrate our resources on activities that contribute to the success of our business and our long-term strategy.
>
> With partners that are established in the information industry overseas, AT&T will concentrate on bringing its evolving data networking capability to countries in the Triad (North America, Western Europe, and the Far East).[74]

Strategic alliances, particularly joint ventures, can help organizations achieve many of the same objectives that are sought through mergers and acquisitions. Joint ventures can lead to improved sales growth, increased earnings, or provide balance to a portfolio of businesses, which are some of the most commonly cited reasons for acquisitions.[75] For example, in 1980 Monsanto and General Electric formed a joint venture called Fisher Control International to make regulators and control valves. Within one year, their joint venture ranked second in sales in the growing process control equipment industry. Also, one of the largest and most profitable robot manufacturers in the world is a joint venture between GM and Fanuc Ltd. called GMF Robotics Corp.[76]

The strongest rationale for forming a joint venture is resource sharing. Because joint ventures involve more than one company, they can draw on a much larger resource base. The resources that are most likely to be transferable through a joint venture are listed here:

1. *Marketing.* Companies can gain marketing information and resources not easily identified by outsiders, such as knowledge of competition, customer behavior, industry condition, and distribution channels.

2. *Technology.* Those participating in a joint venture can use technological skills and specific knowledge that is not generally available.

3. *Raw materials and components.* Some joint ventures are formed to gain access to different elements of the manufacturing process.

4. *Financial.* Companies can obtain external capital, usually in conjunction with other resources.

5. *Managerial.* Joint venture participants can use specific managerial and entrepreneurial capabilities and skills, usually in conjunction with other resources.

6. *Political.* Some joint ventures are obligatory to enter developing countries; others are formed to gain political commitments.[77]

Good examples of resource sharing are easy to find. Disney teamed up with the American Automobile Association (AAA) to provide a "Disney-style" multipurpose rest area for travelers.[78] CBS formed joint ventures with Twentieth Century-Fox to develop videotapes, and with Home Box Office (owned by Time, Inc.) and Columbia Pictures (owned by Coca-Cola) to develop motion pictures.[79] Each of these joint ventures by CBS was similar in that they resulted in related diversification and they drew on the combined strengths of all joint venture partners. In the international sector, the Airbus Industrie venture scored a major victory when United Airlines placed a $3 billion order for jets, bypassing Boeing. The Airbus venture includes Aerospatiale S.A. of France, Daimler-Benz AG of Germany, British Aerospace plc, and Spain's Construcciones Aeronauticas. Airbus is now the number two manufacturer of large jets.[80]

In addition to the advantages associated with resource sharing, joint ventures enhance speed of entry into a new field or market because of the expanded base of resources from which ventures can draw. They also spread the risk of failure among all of the participants. That is, a failure will result in a smaller loss to each partner than it would to an organization that pursues the venture on its own. Consequently, compared to mergers or internal venturing, joint ventures are sometimes considered a less risky diversification option. Joint ventures may also occur as firms try to improve their competitive positions against rivals by locking in exclusive distribution arrangements or depriving competitors of raw materials. These actions can also deter the entry of new competitors.[81] Finally, joint ventures can draw on the specific strengths of countries, such as those described by Porter (see Chapter 6).[82]

In spite of their strategic strengths, joint ventures are limiting, in that one organization only has partial control over the venture and enjoys only a percentage of the growth and profitability it creates. In addition, they create high administrative costs associated with developing the multiparty equity arrangement and managing the venture once it is undertaken.[83] As discussed in previous chapters, joint ventures also entail a risk of opportunism by venture partners. Unfortunately, a stronger venture partner may take advantage of the smaller, or less experienced, partner and structure the deal so that the benefits accrue unfairly to the stronger partner. Good written contracts can help to alleviate but cannot eliminate this risk.

Finally, there is a limited amount of evidence that joint ventures may not be desirable in some environments. For instance, one researcher discovered that joint ventures in the petroleum industry to produce productive oil and gas leases were more expensive and were no more successful than nonjoint ventures.[84] However, the stock market typically responds favorably to announcements of joint ventures.[85]

As in mergers and acquisitions, organizational fit is important to joint ventures. Lack of organizational fit can reduce cooperation and lead to venture failure.

STRATEGIC APPLICATION 7.1

DIVERSIFICATION STRATEGY IMPACT ANALYSIS

The following chart can help you determine the impact on and reaction of key stakeholders to various diversification moves by the firm:

Step 1: Determine the objectives of the diversification (e.g., development of a new area based on existing strengths, profitable use of excess cash, development of new capabilities and/or resources)

Step 2: Create a chart for the organization with the columns and rows labeled as shown. Leave plenty of room between columns and stakeholders. List specific alternatives (e.g., internal development, acquisition of a small company in the area, joint venture with a firm already involved in the area) and describe them in detail.

Also, make sure you list specific, not general stakeholders under each broad heading. If the organization is already involved in multiple environments through its business units, only list the stakeholders that are likely to be affected by this particular decision. Members of the remote environment (e.g., societal groups, the media) can also be listed if they are considered relevant to the analysis.

Step 3: Based on theory and models found in earlier chapters, assign a priority level to each stakeholder. Generally, the levels of high, moderate, and low are adequate for this kind of analysis.

Step 4: Describe the impact of each of the diversification strategies on each of the stakeholders. In particular, which of the strategies is likely to be favored by each stakeholder? Which of the strategies is likely to be resisted by each stakeholder? What will be the nature of the resistance (e.g., legal suits, battle with regulators, unfavorable press releases, strikes, boycott, etc.).

Step 5: Carefully weigh the trade-offs and the priorities and decide.

Desired Outcome from Diversification:

Stakeholder	Priority	Impact Analysis		
		Internal Venture	Acquisition	Joint Venture
Top management				
Other managers				
Employees				
Board of directors				
Owners/shareholders				
Customers				
Suppliers				
Competitors				
Potential competitors				
Government regulators				
Local communities				
Activist groups				
Unions				
Creditors				

Potential differences among partners range from dissimilar ethics to different languages to disparate managerial techniques to incompatible manufacturing methods.[86] For example, a joint venture between Acme-Cleveland and Multi-Arc Vacuum to market a coating technology that was developed by Multi-Arc fell apart because of vastly different management styles between the parent companies.[87]

Successful joint ventures require careful planning and execution. Managers should communicate the expected benefits of the venture to the important external and internal stakeholders so they will understand the role the alliance will play in the organization.[88] They should also develop a strategic plan for the venture that consolidates the views of the partners about market potential, competitive trends, and potential threats. Several additional steps can be used to improve the likelihood of success:

1. Through careful systematic study, identify an alliance partner that can provide the capabilities that are needed. Avoid the tendency to align with another firm just because alliance forming is a trend in the industry.
2. Clearly define the roles of each partner and ensure that every joint project is of value to both.
3. Develop a strategic plan for the venture that outlines specific objectives for each partner.
4. Keep top managers involved so that middle managers will stay committed.
5. Meet often, informally, at all managerial levels.
6. Appoint someone to monitor all aspects of the alliance and use an outside mediator when disputes arise.
7. Maintain enough independence to develop own area of expertise. Avoid becoming a complete "captive" of the alliance partner.
8. Anticipate and plan for cultural differences.[89]

In summary, all of the diversification tactics described in this section suffer from potential weaknesses. Internal venturing is slow, acquisitions are expensive and may stifle innovation, and joint venturing leads to less control and the potential for opportunism. However, any one of these options can be used successfully, as long as basic strategic principles and good management are applied.

It is also important to consider the impact of a diversification tactic on stakeholders. Strategic Application 7.1 contains a chart that is helpful in evaluating the impact of the three basic diversification tactics on stakeholders. Not surprisingly, there is a growing undercurrent in the United States away from mergers and acquisitions, especially those in unrelated industries, and toward internal venturing and joint venturing.

Summary

Corporate-level strategy focuses on the selection of businesses in which the organization will compete and on the tactics used to enter and manage those businesses and other corporate-level resources. The three broad approaches to corporate-level strategy are concentration, vertical integration, and diversification, which is divided into two broad categories, related and unrelated. These strategies and their strengths and weaknesses were discussed in depth.

Concentration strategies allow an organization to focus on doing one business very well; however, a key disadvantage is that the organization is dependent on that one business for survival. Vertical integration allows an organization to become its own supplier or customer. However, according to the theory of transaction cost economics, if required resources can be obtained from a competitive open market without allocating an undue amount of time or other resources to the contracting process or contract enforcement, it is probably in the best interests of an organization to buy from the market instead of vertically integrating.

Unrelated diversification was very popular during the 1950s, 1960s, and the early 1970s. However, research results seemed to indicate that it did not lead to the high performance that many executives had expected. Many organizations are now restructuring to reduce unrelated diversification. Related diversification, on the other hand, is still a very popular strategy. Businesses are related if they share a common market, technology, raw material, or any one of many other factors. However, for a related diversification strategy to have its full positive impact, organizational fit is required. Fit makes combining related businesses feasible. Corporate-level managers can help create value in their organizations not only by combining and managing related operations but by helping their organizations create a corporate-level distinctive competence.

Portfolio management matrices were presented as a method for helping managers allocate resources and anticipate cash flows. Because of their limitations, they should not be relied on as a sole basis for making resource allocation decisions.

Diversification can be accomplished through internal venturing, acquisition of existing businesses, or joint ventures. Each of these tactics has both advantages and disadvantages. Techniques for successfully implementing these tactics were presented.

Discussion Questions

1. Describe the evolution of corporate-level strategy. What are the forces that drive change?
2. What are the strengths and weaknesses of a concentration strategy and a vertical integration strategy? Based on your lists, how are these two strategies similar?
3. Why isn't an unrelated diversification strategy generally a good idea? Why, then, was this strategy so popular during the 1950s, 1960s, and early 1970s?
4. What is required for a related diversification strategy to produce synergy? Please explain.
5. Describe five ways organizations can develop a corporate-level distinctive competence. Give examples.
6. Describe the advantages and disadvantages of the three methods of diversification.
7. What are ten common reasons for mergers and acquisitions? Select three of your reasons and explain how joint ventures could be used to achieve the same results.

References

1. C. Rapoport, "A Tough Swede Invades the U.S.," *Fortune* (June 29, 1992), pp. 76–77. Used with permission.
2. A. D. Chandler, Jr., *Strategy and Structure: Chapters in the History of the Industrial Enterprise* (Cambridge, Mass.: The MIT Press, 1962).
3. R. P. Rumelt, *Strategy, Structure and Economic Performance* (Boston: Harvard Business School, 1974); R. P. Rumelt, "Diversification Strategy and Profitability," *Strategic Management Journal* 3 (1982), pp. 359–369.
4. H. I. Ansoff, *Corporate Strategy: An Analytical Approach to Business Policy for Growth and Expansion* (New York: McGraw-Hill Book Company, 1965), pp. 129–130.
5. Rumelt, *Strategy, Structure and Economic Performance;* Rumelt, "Diversification Strategy and Profitability."
6. K. R. Harrigan, "Formulating Vertical Integration Strategies," *Academy of Management Review* 9 (1984), p. 639.
7. R. A. D'Aveni and D. J. Ravenscraft, "Economies of

Integration Versus Bureaucracy Costs: Does Vertical Integration Improve Performance?" *Academy of Management Journal* 37 (1994), pp. 1167–1206.
8. O. E. Williamson, *Markets and Hierarchies: Analysis and Antitrust Implications* (New York: The Free Press, 1975); O. E. Williamson, *The Economic Institutions of Capitalism* (New York: The Free Press, 1985).
9. Williamson, *Markets and Hierarchies,* p. 8.
10. B. Klein, R. Crawford, and A. A. Alchian, "Vertical Integration, Appropriable Rents and the Competitive Contracting Process," *Journal of Law and Economics* 21 (1978), pp. 297–326; Williamson, *Markets and Hierarchies,* pp. 9–10.
11. R. E. Hoskisson, J. S. Harrison, and D. A. Dubofsky, "Capital Market Implementation of M-Form Implementation and Diversification Strategy," *Strategic Management Journal* 12 (1991), pp. 271–279.
12. S. Balakrishnan and B. Wernerfelt, "Technical Change,

Competition and Vertical Integration," *Strategic Management Journal* 7 (1986), pp. 347–359.

13. K. R. Harrigan, "Exit Barriers and Vertical Integration," *Academy of Management Journal* (September 1985), pp. 686–697.

14. J. B. Treece, "U.S. Parts Makers Just Won't Say 'Uncle,'" *Business Week* (August 10, 1987), pp. 76–77.

15. Citations for the diversification arguments contained in this section are not broken out by author because many of the arguments are repeated by many or most authors. Information on strategic arguments can be found in H. I. Ansoff, *Corporate Strategy: An Analytical Approach to Business Policy for Growth and Expansion* (New York: McGraw-Hill Book Company, 1965), pp. 130–132; J. S. Harrison, "Alternatives to Merger—Joint Ventures and Other Strategies," *Long Range Planning* (December 1987), pp. 78–83; C. W. L. Hill and G. S. Hansen, "A Longitudinal Study of the Cause and Consequence of Changes in Diversification in the U.S. Pharmaceutical Industry," *Strategic Management Journal* 12 (1991), pp. 187–199; W. G. Lewellen, "A Pure Financial Rationale for the Conglomerate Merger," *Journal of Finance* 26 (1971), pp. 521–537; F. M. McDougall and D. K. Round, "A Comparison of Diversifying and Nondiversifying Australian Industrial Firms," *Academy of Management Journal* 27 (1984), pp. 384–398; and R. Reed and G. A. Luffman, "Diversification: The Growing Confusion," *Strategic Management Journal* 7 (1986), pp. 29–35. The personal arguments are outlined in W. Baumol, *Business Behavior, Value and Growth* (New York: Harcourt, 1967); D. C. Mueller, "A Theory of Conglomerate Mergers," *Quarterly Review of Economics* 83 (1969), pp. 644–660; N. Rajagopalan and J. E. Prescott, "Determinants of Top Management Compensation: Explaining the Impact of Economic, Behavioral, and Strategic Constructs and the Moderating Effects of Industry," *Journal of Management* 16 (1990), pp. 515–538.

16. Ansoff, *Corporate Strategy*, pp. 130–131.

17. This section and portions of other sections in this chapter were strongly influenced by M. Goold and K. Luchs, "Why Diversify?: Four Decades of Management Thinking," *Academy of Management Executive* (August 1993), pp. 7–25.

18. Rumelt, "Diversification Strategy and Profitability," p. 361.

19. A. Shleifer and R. W. Vishny, "Takeovers in the '60s and the '80s: Evidence and Implications," *Strategic Management Journal* 12 (Special Issue, 1991), pp. 51–59.

20. T. H. Naylor and F. Tapon, "The Capital Asset Pricing Model: An Evaluation of Its Potential as a Strategic Planning Tool," *Management Science* 10 (1982), pp. 1166–1173.

21. E. F. Fama, "Efficient Capital Markets: A Review of Theory and Empirical Work," *Journal of Finance* 25 (1970), pp. 288–307.

22. J. G. Matsusaka, "Takeover Motives During the Conglomerate Merger Wave," Working Paper (University of Chicago, 1990) as cited in Shleifer and Vishny, "Takeovers in the '60s," p. 52.

23. A few examples of the many studies that demonstrate low performance associated with unrelated diversification are R. Amit and J. Livnat, "Diversification Strategies, Business Cycles, and Economic Performance," *Strategic Management Journal* 9 (1988), pp. 99–110; R. A. Bettis and V. Mahajan, "Risk/Return Performance of Diversified Firms," *Management Science* 31 (1985), pp. 785–799; D. Ravenscraft and F. M.

Scherer, *Mergers, Selloffs, and Economic Efficiency* (Washington, D. C.: Brookings Institution, 1987); P. G. Simmonds, "The Combined Diversification Breadth and Mode Dimensions and the Performance of Large Diversified Firms," *Strategic Management Journal* 11 (1990), pp. 399–410; P. Varadarajan and V. Ramanujam, "Diversification and Performance: A Reexamination Using a New Two-Dimensional Conceptualization of Diversity in Firms," *Academy of Management Journal*, 30 (1982), pp. 380–393. On the other hand, the following studies are among those that support the superiority of unrelated diversification: R. M. Grant and A. P. Jammine, "Performance Differences Between the Wrigley/Rumelt Strategic Categories," *Strategic Management Journal*, 9 (1988), pp. 333–346; A. Michel and I. Shaked, "Does Business Diversification Affect Performance?" *Financial Management* (Winter 1984), pp. 18–25.

24. M. C. Lauenstein, "Diversification—The Hidden Explanation of Success," *Sloan Management Review* (Fall 1985), pp. 49–55; M. Lubatkin and R. C. Rogers, "Diversification, Systematic Risk and Shareholder Return: A Capital Market Extension of Rumelt's 1974 Study," *Academy of Management Journal* 32 (1989), pp. 454–465.; M. Lubatkin and H. G. O'Neill, "Merger Strategies and Capital Market Risk," *Academy of Management Journal* 30 (1987), pp. 665–684; M. Lubatkin, "Value Creating Mergers: Fact or Folklore," *Academy of Management Executive* (November 1988), pp. 295–302; C. A. Montgomery and H. Singh, "Diversification Strategy and Systematic Risk," *Strategic Management Journal* 5 (1984), pp. 181–191.

25. R. S. Attiyeh, "Where Next for Conglomerates?" *Business Horizons* (December 1969), pp. 39–44.

26. A. B. Fisher, "Ford Rolls Out a Money Machine," *Fortune* (April 15, 1996), p. 48.

27. "A Conversation with Roberto Goizueta and Jack Welch," *Fortune* (December 11, 1995), pp. 98–99.

28. R. E. Hoskisson and M. A. Hitt, "Antecedents and Performance Outcomes of Diversification: A Review and Critique of Theoretical Perspectives," *Journal of Management* 16 (1990), pp. 461–509; Shleifer and Vishny, "Takeovers in the '60s and the '80s."

29. Hoskisson and Hitt, "Antecedents and Performance Outcomes," p. 461.

30. A detailed review of this literature is found in Hoskisson and Hitt, "Antecedents and Performance Outcomes," p. 468. More recent evidence is found in P. S. Davis, R. B. Robinson, Jr., J. A. Pearce, and S. H. Park, "Business Unit Relatedness and Performance: A Look at the Pulp and Paper Industry," *Strategic Management Journal* 13 (1992), pp. 349–361; and J. S. Harrison, E. H. Hall, Jr., and R. Nagundkar, "Resource Allocation as an Outcropping of Strategic Consistency: Performance Implications," *Academy of Management Journal* 36 (1993), pp. 1026–1051.

31. M. Lubatkin and S. Chatterjee, "Extending Modern Portfolio Theory Into the Domain of Corporate Diversification: Does It Apply?" *Academy of Management Journal* 37 (1994), pp. 109–136.

32. M. E. Porter, *Competitive Advantage: Creating and Sustaining Superior Performance* (New York: The Free Press, 1985), pp. 317–363.

33. D. J. Teece, "Economies of Scope and the Scope of the Enterprise," *Journal of Economic Behavior and Organization* 1 (1980), pp. 223–247.

34. B. Gold, "Changing Perspectives on Size, Scale and Returns: An Integrative Survey," *Journal of Economic Literature* 19 (1981), pp. 5–33.

35. H. I. Ansoff, *Corporate Strategy* (New York: McGraw-Hill Book Company, 1965).

36. H. Itami, *Mobilizing Invisible Assets* (Cambridge, Mass.: Harvard University Press, 1987).

37. P. R. Nayyar, "On the Measurement of Corporate Diversification Strategy: Evidence from Large U.S. Service Firms," *Strategic Management Journal* 13 (1992), pp. 219–235; R. Reed and G. A. Luffman, "Diversification: The Growing Confusion," *Strategic Management Journal* 7 (1986), pp. 29–36.

38. D. B. Jemison and S. B. Sitkin, "Corporate Acquisitions: A Process Perspective," *Academy of Management Review* 11 (1986), pp. 145–163.

39. C. K. Prahalad and R. A. Bettis, "The Dominant Logic: A New Linkage Between Diversity and Performance," *Strategic Management Journal* 7 (1986), p. 491.

40. R. M. Grant, "On 'Dominant Logic,' Relatedness and the Link Between Diversity and Performance," *Strategic Management Journal* 9 (1988), pp. 639–642.

41. M. Goold and A. Campbell, *Strategies and Styles* (Oxford: Basil Blackwell Ltd., 1987).

42. Lauenstein, "Diversification—The Hidden Explanation."

43. G. R. Jones and C. W. Hill, "Transaction Cost Analysis of Strategy-Structure Choice," *Strategic Management Journal* 9 (1988), pp. 159–172.

44. P. Haspeslagh and D. B. Jemison, *Managing Acquisitions* (New York: Free Press, 1991), p. 23.

45. C. C. Markides and P. J. Williamson. "Corporate Diversification and Organizational Structure: A Resource-Based View," *Academy of Management Journal* 39(2) (1996), pp. 340–367.

46. O. Port, "Beg, Borrow and Benchmark," *Business Week* (November 30, 1993), pp. 74–75.

47. M. A. Hitt and R. D. Ireland, "Corporate Distinctive Competence, Strategy, Industry and Performance," *Strategic Management Journal* 6 (1985), pp. 273–293; M. A. Hitt and R. D. Ireland, "Relationships Among Corporate Level Distinctive Competencies, Diversification Strategy, Corporate Structure and Performance," *Journal of Management Studies* 23 (1986), pp. 401–416.

48. Hitt and Ireland, "Corporate Distinctive Competence," pp. 289–291.

49. M. E. Porter, "From Competitive Advantage to Corporate Strategy," *Harvard Business Review* (May–June 1987), pp. 43–59.

50. R. Normann, "Organizational Innovativeness: Product Variation and Reorientation," *Administrative Science Quarterly* 16 (1971), pp. 203–215.

51. R. A. Burgelman, "Designs for Corporate Entrepreneurship in Established Firms," *California Management Review* (Spring 1984), pp. 154–166.

52. "Lessons from a Successful Entrepreneur," *Journal of Business Strategy* (March–April 1988), pp. 20–24.

53. R. K. Kazanjian and R. Drazin, "Implementing Internal Diversification: Contingency Factors for Organization Design Choices," *Academy of Management Review* 12 (1987), pp. 342–354.

54. R. A. Pitts, "Strategies and Structures for Diversification," *Academy of Management Journal* 20 (1977), pp. 197–208.

55. C. A. Lengnick-Hall, "Innovation and Competitive Advantage: What We Know and What We Need to Learn," *Journal of Management* 18 (1992), pp. 399–429.

56. E. R. Biggadike, "The Risky Business of Diversification," *Harvard Business Review* (May–June 1979), pp. 103–111.

57. E. Mansfield, "How Economists See R&D," *Harvard Business Review* (November–December, 1981), pp. 98–106. See also B. T. Lamont and C. R. Anderson, "Mode of Corporate Diversification and Economic Performance," *Academy of Management Journal* 28 (1985), pp. 926–934.

58. This discussion of corporate entrepreneurship draws heavily from Burgelman, "Designs for Corporate Entrepreneurship."

59. Based on Burgelman, "Designs for Corporate Entrepreneurship," pp. 162–164.

60. M. Lubatkin, "Value Creating Mergers: Fact or Folklore?" *Academy of Management Executive* (May 1988), pp. 295–302; J. Pfeffer, "Merger as a Response to Organizational Interdependence," *Administrative Science Quarterly* 17 (1972), pp. 382–394.; J. H. Song, "Diversifying Acquisitions and Financial Relationships: Testing 1974–1976 Behaviour," *Strategic Management Journal* 4 (1983), pp. 97–108; F. Trautwein, "Merger Motives and Merger Prescriptions," *Strategic Management Journal* 11 (1990), pp. 283–295.

61. A. A. Thompson, Jr., "Mobil Corporation (Revised)," in A.A. Thompson, Jr. and A.J. Strickland, III, *Strategic Management: Concepts and Cases*, 4th ed. (Plano, Tex.: Business Publications, 1987), pp. 671–697.

62. L. L. Fowler and D. R. Schmidt, "Determinants of Tender Offer Post-Acquisition Financial Performance," *Journal of Management* 10 (1989), pp. 339–350.

63. T. B. Pickens, "Professions of a Short-Termer," *Harvard Business Review* (May–June, 1986), pp. 75–79.

64. One of the most active proponents of the view that mergers and acquisitions create value for acquiring-firm shareholders is Michael Lubatkin [see M. Lubatkin, "Value-Creating Mergers: Fact or Folklore?" *Academy of Management Executive* (November 1988), pp. 295–302]. However, he recently reported strong evidence that contradicts his earlier conclusions in S. Chatterjee, M. H. Lubatkin, D. M. Schweiger, and Y. Weber, "Cultural Differences and Shareholder Value in Related Mergers: Linking Equity and Human Capital," *Strategic Management Journal* 13 (1992), pp. 319–334. Other strong summary evidence that mergers and acquisitions do not create value is found in W. B. Carper, "Corporate Acquisitions and Shareholder Wealth," *Journal of Management* 16 (1990), pp. 807–823; D. K. Datta, G. E. Pinches, and V. K. Narayanan, "Factors Influencing Wealth Creation from Mergers and Acquisitions: A Meta-Analysis," *Strategic Management Journal* 13 (1992), pp. 67–84; K. M. Davidson, "Do Megamergers Make Sense," *Journal of Business Strategies* (Winter 1987), pp. 40–48; T. F. Hogarty, "Profits from Merger: The Evidence of Fifty Years," *St. John's Law Review* 44 (Special Edition, 1970), pp. 378–391; S. R. Reid, *Mergers, Managers and the Economy* (New York: McGraw-Hill Book Company, 1968).

65. M. A. Hitt, R. E. Hoskisson, R. D. Ireland, and J. S. Harrison, "Are Acquisitions a Poison Pill for Innovation?" *Academy of Management Executive* (November 1991), pp. 20–35.

66. Lubatkin, "Value-Creating Mergers."

67. Porter, "From Competitive Advantage to Corporate Strategy," p. 59.

68. These findings are based on original research by the authors, soon to be published in a book by Oxford University Press. See also J. B. Kusewitt, Jr. "An Exploratory Study of Strategic Acquisition Factors Relating to Success," *Strategic Management Journal* 6 (1985), pp. 151–169; L. M. Shelton, "Strategic Business Fits and Corporate Acquisition: Empirical Evidence," *Strategic Management Journal* 9 (1988), pp. 279–287.

69. Chatterjee, Lubatkin, Schweiger, and Weber, "Cultural Differences and Shareholder Value in Related Mergers," pp. 319–334; D. K. Datta, "Organizational Fit and Acquisition Performance: Effects of Post-Acquisition Integration," *Strategic Management Journal* 12 (1991), pp. 281–297; D. B. Jemison and S. B. Sitkin, "Corporate Acquisitions: A Process Perspective," *Academy of Management Review* 11 (1986), pp. 145–163.

70. T. H. Brush, "Predicted Change in Operational Synergy and Post-Acquisition Performance of Acquired Businesses," *Strategic Management Journal* 17 (1996), pp. 1–24.

71. F. T. Paine and D. J. Power, "Merger Strategy: An Examination of Drucker's Five Rules for Successful Acquisition," *Strategic Management Journal* 5 (1984), pp. 99–110.

72. B. Boyrs and D. B. Jemison, "Hybrid Arrangements as Strategic Alliances: Theoretical Issues in Organizational Combinations," *Academy of Management Review* 14 (1989), pp. 234–249; K. R. Harrigan, "Joint Ventures and Competitive Strategy," *Strategic Management Journal* 9 (1988), pp. 141–158.

73. P. Lorange and J. Roos, "Why Some Strategic Alliances Succeed and Others Fail," *Journal of Business Strategy* (January–February, 1991), p. 25.

74. J. E. Olson and T. A. Cooper, "CEOs On Strategy: Two Companies, Two Strategies," *Journal of Business Strategy* (Summer 1987), p. 53.

75. J. S. Harrison, "Alternatives to Merger—Joint Ventures and Other Strategies," *Long Range Planning* (December 1987), pp. 78–83.

76. C. E. Schillaci, "Designing Successful Joint Ventures," *Journal of Business Strategies* (Fall 1987), pp. 59–63.

77. Schillaci, "Designing Successful Joint Ventures," p. 60. See also J. Hennart, "A Transactions Costs Theory of Equity Joint Ventures," *Strategic Management Journal* 9 (1988), pp. 361–374.

78. L. Doolittle, "Disney Teams with AAA to Provide Multipurpose Rest Area for Travelers," *Orlando Sentinel* (January 25, 1996), p. B1.

79. R. M. Kanter, "Becoming PALS: Pooling, Allying, and Linking Across Companies," *Academy of Management Executive* (August 1989), pp. 183–193.

80. J. Cole, "United Air Orders Airbus Industrie Jets For About $3 Billion, Bypassing Boeing," *Wall Street Journal* (July 9, 1992), p. A3.

81. B. Kogut, "Joint Ventures: Theoretical and Empirical Perspectives," *Strategic Management Journal* 9 (1988), pp. 319–332.

82. M. E. Porter, *The Competitive Advantage of Nations* (New York: The Free Press, 1990); W. Shan and W. Hamilton, "Country-Specific Advantage and International Cooperation," *Strategic Management Journal* 12 (1991), pp. 419–432.

83. Harrigan, "Joint Ventures and Competitive Strategy"; R. N. Osborn and C. C. Baughn, "Forms of Interorganizational Governance for Multinational Alliances," *Academy of Management Journal* 33 (1990), pp. 503–519.

84. D. H. Kent, "Joint Ventures vs. Non-Joint Ventures: An Empirical Investigation," *Strategic Management Journal* 12 (1991), pp. 387–393.

85. J. Koh, "Joint Venture Formations and Stock Market Reactions: An Assessment in the Information Technology Sector," *Academy of Management Journal* 34 (1991), pp. 869–892.

86. Lorange and Roos, "Why Some Strategic Alliances Succeed," pp. 25–30.

87. Schillaci, "Designing Successful Joint Ventures," p. 62.

88. Lorange and Roos, "Why Some Strategic Alliances Succeed," pp. 25–30.

89. Adapted from various sources including: Burrows, "How a Good Partnership Goes Bad"; G. Develin and M. Bleackley, "Strategic Alliances—Guidelines for Success," *Long Range Planning* 21(5) (1988), pp.18–23; Lorange and Roos, "Why Some Strategic Alliances Succeed,"; J. B. Treece, K. Miller, and R. A. Melcher, "The Partners," *Business Week* (February 10, 1992), pp. 102–107.

Portfolio Models for Selection of Businesses and Investment Priorities

Portfolio management refers to managing the mix of businesses in the corporate portfolio. CEOs of large diversified organizations like GE continually face decisions concerning how to divide organizational resources among diversified units and where to invest new capital. Portfolio models are designed to help managers make these types of decisions.

Portfolio planning gained wide acceptance during the 1970s and, by 1979, approximately 45% of the *Fortune 500* companies were using some type of portfolio planning.[1] Monsanto applied portfolio management concepts in restructuring its business portfolio by divesting slow-growing commodity chemical businesses and acquiring faster growing businesses in areas such as biotechnology. Also, at a recent conference, executives from several large corporations, including GE, US West, and Du Pont, indicated that they are still using portfolio management techniques.[2]

In spite of their adoption in many organizations, portfolio management techniques are the subject of a considerable amount of criticism.[3] However, because they are still in wide use, this book would be incomplete without them. Keep in mind that they are not a panacea and should not replace other types of sound strategic analysis.

We begin by describing the simplest and first widely used portfolio model, the Boston Consulting Group Matrix. The model has many shortcomings, stemming mostly from its simplicity. However, most of the other portfolio techniques are adaptations of it, and its simplicity makes it a good starting point. We then describe a more complete model, based on stakeholder analysis.

Boston Consulting Group Matrix

The Boston Consulting Group (BCG) matrix, which is displayed in Figure 7A.1, is based on two factors, business growth rate and relative market share. Business growth rate is the growth rate of the industry in which a particular business unit is involved. Relative market share is calculated as the ratio of the business unit's size to the size of its largest competitor. The two factors are used to plot all of the businesses in which the organization is involved, represented as Stars, Question

Figure 7A.1 *The Boston Consulting Group Matrix*

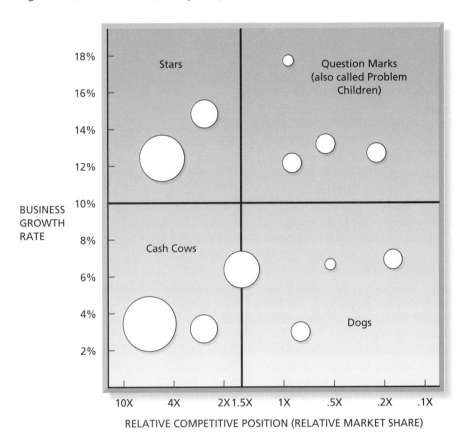

Source: Reprinted from *Long Range Planning,* Vol. 10 (February 1977), B. Hedley, "Strategy and the Business Portfolio," p. 12, copyright © 1977, with permission from Pergamon Press Ltd, Headlington Hill Hall, Oxford OX3 OBW, United Kingdom.

Marks (also called Problem Children), Cash Cows, and Dogs. The size of the circles in Figure 7A.1 represent the size of the various businesses of an organization. Remember that only one organization, comprised of many different business units, is plotted on each matrix.

The BCG matrix is sometimes useful in planning cash flows. Cash Cows tend to generate more cash than they can effectively reinvest, while Question Marks require additional cash to sustain rapid growth and Stars generate about as much cash as they use, on average. According to BCG, Stars and Cash Cows, with their superior market share positions, tend to be the most profitable businesses.

Consequently, the optimal BCG portfolio contains a balance of Stars, Cash Cows, and Question Marks. Stars have the greatest potential for growth and tend to be highly profitable. However, as the industries in which Stars are involved mature and their growth slows, they naturally become Cash Cows. Therefore, Question Marks are important because of their potential role as future Stars in the organization. Dogs are the least attractive types of business. The original prescription was to divest them. However, even Dogs can be maintained in the portfolio as long as they do not become a drain on corporate resources. Also, some organizations are successful at positioning their Dogs in an attractive niche in their industries.

One of the central ideas of the BCG matrix is that high market share leads to high profitability due to learning effects, experience effects, entry barriers, market power, and other influences. In fact, there is evidence, both in the strategic management literature and in the economics literature, that higher market share is associated with higher profitability in some instances. However, some low share businesses enjoy high profitability.[4] The real relationship between market share and profitability depends on many factors, including the nature of the industry and the strategy of the firm. For example, one researcher found that the market share–profitability relationship is stronger in some industries (capital goods) than in others (raw materials). He also discovered that beyond a certain market share, profitability tended to trail off.[5]

One of the shortcomings of the BCG matrix is that it does not allow for changes in strategy due to differing environments. The standard BCG prescription is this: Achieve market share leadership and become a Star or a Cash Cow. The problem with this prescription is that it may only be valid for firms pursuing a low-cost leadership strategy. The use of market share as a measure of competitive strategy carries with it the implicit assumption that size has led to economies of scale and learning effects, and that these effects have resulted in competitive success through the creation of a low-cost position. Differentiation and focus competitive strategies are not incorporated into the model. Also, companies that are successful in pursuing focus strategies (through low cost or differentiation) in low-growth industries may be classified as Dogs even though their profit streams are strong. For example, Rolex would qualify as a Dog.

Other problems with the BCG matrix are related to its simplicity. Only two factors are considered and only two divisions, high and low, are used for each factor. Also, growth rate is inadequate as the only indicator of the attractiveness of an industry. For example, some fast-growing industries have never been particularly profitable. Market share, for all of the reasons stated previously, is also an insufficient indicator of competitive position. Other variables, such as corporate image, cost position, or R&D advantages, are likely to be equally or more important to the competitiveness of a business.

A common criticism that applies to many portfolio models, and especially the BGG matrix, is that they are based on the past instead of the future. Given the rate of change in the current economic and political environments, this criticism is probably valid. Finally, another problem that is inherent in all matrix approaches is that industries are hard to define.

In conclusion, the BCG matrix is only applicable to firms in particular operating environments that are pursuing low-cost leadership strategies based on the experience curve. Nevertheless, the matrix may help firms anticipate cash needs and flows. Numerous organizational managers and business writers have developed portfolio matrices that overcome some of the limitations of the BCG matrix. One of these approaches is described next.

General Electric Business Screen

Virtually any variables or combination of variables of strategic importance can be plotted along the axes of a portfolio matrix. The selection of variables depends on what the organization considers important. Many matrices contain factors that are

Figure 7A.2 *The General Electric Business Screen*

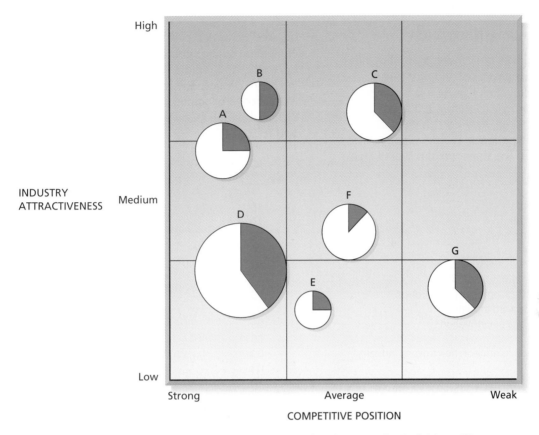

Source: C.W. Hofer and D. Schendel, *Strategy Formulation; Analytical Concepts* (St. Paul, Minn.: West Publishing Company, 1978), p. 32.

composites of several variables. One of the most famous of these, developed at General Electric, is illustrated in Figure 7A.2. The General Electric model is referred to as the G.E. portfolio matrix, the nine-cell grid, or the G.E. business screen.

In the G.E. business screen, the area in the circles represents the size of the industries in which each business competes. The slice out of the circle is the market share of the business unit in each of these industries. The variables that are used to assess industry attractiveness are typically derived from the objectives and characteristics of the organization (e.g., attitude toward growth, profitability, or social responsibility) and the industries themselves. Assessment of competitive position is based on a firm's position with respect to the key success factors in an industry. An organization would like to have all of its businesses in the top left cell. These businesses are called Winners. However, some of these Winners should be established businesses that are not growing rapidly so that a portion of their cash flow can be used to support developing winners.

By applying stakeholder analysis to a portfolio model such as the GE business screen, it may be possible to tap the potential of a business unit as well as its current competitive standing. In this regard, Strategic Applications 7A.1 and 7A.2 contain stakeholder criteria that are relevant in determining the attractiveness of

STRATEGIC APPLICATION 7A.1

ASSESSING INDUSTRY ATTRACTIVENESS

The following factors are among those that influence the attractiveness of an industry (see Chapter 2 for explanations). As a basis for discussion or to create consistency in the way businesses are compared, they can be weighted based on their importance in determining attractiveness (weight). The same weights would then be used across all businesses in which the firm competes. Ratings come from an analysis of the operating and remote environments, as well as industry statistics. The following example is merely illustrative of some of the variables that can be included and the way they might be weighted and ranked.

Criteria	Weight	Rating*	Score
Power of suppliers	.10	4	.40
Power of customers	.10	4	.40
Power of substitute products	.03	2	.06
Height of entry barriers	.10	3	.30
Level of competitive rivalry	.15	2	.30
Amount and type of regulation	.10	1	.10
Attitude and mobilization of activist groups	.03	2	.06
Societal attitude toward industry	.03	2	.06
Speed of technological innovation	.03	5	.15
Unionization	.06	2	.12
Attitude of financial intermediaries toward industry	.03	2	.06
Rate of growth	.04	4	.16
Profitability	.10	4	.40
Performance during economic downturns	.10	5	.50
	1.00		3.07

*5=highly favorable; 1=highly unfavorable.

an industry and the competitive position of a firm in that industry. The lists of variables are not intended to be exhaustive, but merely illustrative of the variables that may be included.

The way an organization allocates its internal resources reconfirms its selection of businesses. For example, business units that are considered critical to the future success of an organization should receive high priority in resource allocation decisions, whereas unimportant businesses may receive only maintenance levels of support. From a portfolio management perspective, businesses that are in a strong competitive position in attractive industries should be given the highest priority.

Summary

In conclusion, while all portfolio management models have weaknesses and limitations, they provide an additional tool to assist managers in anticipating cash flows and making resource allocation decisions. The GE business screen, in particular, is flexible enough to accommodate a wide variety of indicators of industry attractiveness and competitive strength. We now turn our attention to the methods organizations use to diversify their business portfolios.

STRATEGIC APPLICATION 7A.2

ASSESSING COMPETITIVE POSITION

The following factors help determine the competitive position of a firm in a particular industry. As a basis for discussion or to create consistency in the way businesses are compared, they can be weighted based on their importance in determining attractiveness (weight). The same weights would then be applied across all businesses.

Ratings come from an analysis of the operating and remote environments, as well as internal company documents and industry statistics. The following example is merely illustrative of some of the variables that can be included and the way they might be weighted and ranked. The term *firm* refers to a business unit and not the entire organization.

Criteria	Weight	Rating*	Score
Position of firm with respect to suppliers	.04	2	.08
Position of firm with respect to customers	.04	5	.20
Ability of substitute products to erode sales	.02	4	.08
Position of firm with respect to entry barriers	.04	3	.12
Reputation of products/services	.10	2	.20
Political power and contacts	.06	1	.06
Position of firm with respect to activist groups	.02	2	.04
Societal attitude toward firm	.04	2	.08
Strength of R&D program	.10	5	.50
Strength of management	.10	3	.30
Skill levels of employees	.04	4	.16
Effectiveness of training programs	.08	4	.32
Effectiveness of TQM program	.08	3	.24
Strength of marketing program	.04	2	.08
Relationship with unions (give the average rating if there are no unions)	.04	4	.16
Attitude of financial intermediaries toward firm	.02	4	.08
Rate of growth	.04	4	.16
Current profitability	.10	5	.50
	1.00		3.36

*5=highly favorable; 1=highly unfavorable.

References

1. P. Hapeslagh, "Portfolio Planning: Uses and Limitations," *Harvard Business Review* (January–February 1982), pp. 58–73.
2. G. S. Swartz, "Organizing to Become Market-Driven," *Marketing Science Institute Conference Summary* (1990), report 90–123.
3. R. A. Kerin, V. Mahajan, and P. R. Varadarajan, *Strategic Market Planning* (Needham Heights, Mass.: Allyn & Bacon, 1990), p. 94; J.A. Seeger, "Reversing the Images of BCG's Growth Share Matrix," *Strategic Management Journal* 5 (1984), pp. 93–97.
4. R. G. Hammermesh, M. J. Anderson, and J. E. Harris, "Strategies for Low Market Share Businesses," *Harvard Business Review* (May–June 1978), pp. 95–102; C. Y. Woo and A. C. Cooper, "Market Share Leadership—Not Always So Good," *Harvard Business Review* (January–February 1984), pp. 50–54.
5. J. Schwalbach, "Profitability and Market Share: A Reflection on the Functional Relationship," *Strategic Management Journal* 12 (1991), pp. 299–306.

4

part

Strategy Implementation and Control

8

Strategy Implementation

IBM Makes PC Business a Separate Operating Unit

In the early 1990s, IBM announced an extraordinary change in the way it manages its many businesses. IBM makes personal computers, minicomputers, mainframe computers, software, special computer-related services, and semiconductors. Although all of IBM's businesses may be described under the broad topic of "computers," the businesses face different types of demand patterns, customer requirements, and competitor actions.

IBM decided to break off its personal computer business as a separate operating unit, which could eventually become a wholly owned subsidiary. In the old organization structure, one part of the corporation was responsible for marketing while another was responsible for producing the personal computers. The new operating unit has responsibility for developing, manufacturing, distributing, and marketing all personal computers worldwide. About 1,200 employees of the U.S. marketing and sales group were reassigned to the new operating unit.

The purpose of the change in structure was to eliminate bureaucracy in decision making, cut overhead, and improve responsiveness. The restructuring of the personal computer business is part of a long-term plan to decentralize authority and decision making in all of IBM's businesses. Other autonomous operating units will be created around software, semiconductor, hardware, and service businesses. Ultimately, IBM will look much like a holding company with the head of each operating unit functioning as the executive officer, and corporate headquarters serving an advisory function.[1]

Organizations employ a wide variety of tactics to implement their strategies. In this example, IBM used a more decentralized management structure to enhance implementation of its related diversification strategy. Organization structure can have a powerful influence on the execution of strategy.

Strategy implementation typically goes hand in hand with strategy formulation, and we have made no attempt to create an artificial barrier between the two activities. Consequently, much of what you have read in this book pertains to strategy implementation. We presented various international strategies and then immediately discussed the methods firms use to carry them out. In the chapter on corporate-level strategy, we also discussed specific tactics organizations use to implement their corporate-level strategies—internal development, acquisitions, and joint ventures. Earlier, we discussed stakeholder analysis, which is a formulation activity, but quickly moved on to stakeholder management tactics such as creation of alliances and involvement of stakeholders in processes such as product design. Culture and leadership, which are powerful implementation tools, were discussed in the chapter on internal analysis.

Why, then, are you currently reading a chapter called "Strategy Implementation"? In formal written strategic plans, two topics are typically reserved for the section on strategy implementation: (1) functional level strategies and action plans required to implement the strategies and (2) organization structures necessary to focus resources and people on strategies. In this chapter we discuss functional strategies briefly, because business-level strategies are implemented through day-to-day decisions made at the operating level of the firm.[2] We do not provide a full treatment of functional strategies, however, because those topics are thoroughly covered by other courses in your program of study. Instead, we emphasize the stakeholder issues that functional managers face when developing strategies and tactics, and the importance of linking functional activities when pursuing value-creating strategies. We also discuss in this chapter the types of structures that organizations use for single businesses and for multibusiness corporations, as in the IBM example at the beginning of the chapter, and the relationship of those structures to particular strategies. Another important implementation topic, coordination and control, is discussed in the next chapter.

FUNCTIONAL STRATEGIES

Some of the most successful companies of our time are operating in low-growth, moderately profitable industries and are pursuing strategies that are not unique. The reason for their extraordinary success is their attention to the details associated with strategy implementation. Wal-Mart is in the discount retail business, just like K-mart. They offer similar merchandise, with similar prices, in a similar discount store facility. Why has Wal-Mart consistently outperformed K-mart? One reason is the attention to detail. For many years, Wal-Mart had a company policy that when a customer asked a Wal-mart associate where something was, the associate should stop what he or she was doing and escort the customer to the proper aisle. Wal-Mart employees did not necessarily escort customers through the stores because they were nice people. They did it because management believed the gesture was an important element of service, they had established an operating policy that specified this tactic as the preferred way to handle a customer request, and they taught employees to do it and believe in it.

Other examples of attention to detail are easy to find. One reason McDonald's continues to grow and profit at a time when other hamburger chains are suffering is its fast, reliable service, clean restrooms and dining areas, and attentive, polite employees. Although two warehouse-style toy chains, Lionel and Child World, filed for Chapter 11 protection under federal bankruptcy law in recent years, Toys 'R' Us continues to grow and prosper because of its attention to product line and inventory management, store location and appearance, and technological improvements that reduce operating costs. Nucor, a steel company, has been successful in the declining, virtually profitless steel industry in which much larger foreign and domestic competitors have suffered. Year after year, Nucor uses its lean organizational structure, incentive pay systems, and technological investments to keep its costs lower than those of most competitors. In all of the preceding examples, one company has outperformed its competitors primarily on the strength of its strategy implementation.

In most organizations, the interdependent value chain activities we have discussed throughout this book are grouped into functional categories or departments. Marketing departments are responsible for three of the five primary value activities: outgoing logistics, marketing, and sales and service activities. Operations departments usually control the other two primary value activities: incoming logistics and operations. The support value activities are more likely to involve several departments. For example, even though most procurement activities take place within operations, all parts of the organization procure items regularly. Technology development, in particular, involves many departments. Information systems (IS) departments are responsible for designing, planning, and coordinating the organization's use of computer systems. Research and development (R&D) departments have primary responsibility for most product and process design efforts. However, decisions to upgrade to an automated scheduling and inventory system or to install an improved telephone system are technology developments that involve many departments. While all departments manage human resources and finances, human resource and finance departments are created to oversee the formal plans and procedures for managing those essential resources.

Value chain analysis, explained in Chapter 4, is useful in planning the implementation of a strategy. For managers, the key task of strategy implementation is to align or fit the activities and capabilities of the firm with its chosen strategy. For an organization that is pursuing a differentiation strategy, all organizational activities and resources should be focused on creating a product or service difference that has value to customers. The key is to identify how the firm can differentiate its products or services to create more value than the added cost of improvements. Support activities provide a similar opportunity. For example, many companies provide their new employees with extensive, uniform training programs. Some of these programs focus on providing employees with tools and attributes that help them provide outstanding and efficient service to customers. Disney and Federal Express are two examples of companies that use training to create a competitive advantage.

Similarly, if a company is pursuing a low-cost competitive strategy, then all activities and resources should be focused on cost reduction to improve profitability. When purchasing, operations, distribution, marketing, and service decisions all support low costs, as in the case of Nucor, the low-cost mini-mill steel company, then it is likely that low costs will be achieved. However, if the focus on low costs is lost, then the competitive advantage will be lost. Such was the case with People Express, one of the first no-frills, discount fare airlines. With success, People Express began to indulge in activities that undermined their low-cost position, and they ultimately failed. Strategic Application 8.1 shows how the value chain can be used to examine the link between strategy and value activities.

STRATEGIC APPLICATION 8.1

EVALUATING ACTIVITIES USING THE VALUE CHAIN

The value chain below is for a newspaper company ineffectively implementing a low-cost strategy. Cutbacks intended to bring about a low-cost position instead undermined the capabilities of the organization. Layoffs hurt employee morale, reductions in training and consolidations of job functions created a poorly trained workforce and insecure supervisors, and so-called low-cost newspaper delivery arrangements meant some customers did not get their papers until after 9:00 P.M. Rather than an effective low-cost provider strategy, the company succeeded in producing an ineffective, low-service strategy.

Original Value-Added Chain for a Newspaper Company

Support Activities

Top management's lack of effectiveness
Employee turnover is high
Well-defined mission statement
Upper management hierarchy unstable
Union members barred from certain benefits
Human relations poor; neither employees nor the general public are well informed
Supervisor problems in pressroom prevent full utilization of capacity

Incoming Logistics	Operations	Outbound Logistics	Marketing/Sales	Service
News editors unwilling to include fast-breaking news without full facts News department recognized by state awards	Transition made from letterpress to offset press Reduced production staff Never a defined line between supervisors and workers Ineffective supervisory staff in pressroom	Carriers had other jobs and couldn't wait for late papers Delivery based on cost to company and not on customer needs	Ad rates kept low Sales-driven strategies, not market-driven	Didn't respond to late newspaper delivery even though they lost 2,000 subscribers

(continued)

For managers, an understanding of the linkages and interdependencies among the value-adding activities is critical. For example, in a firm pursuing a low-cost strategy, system-wide low costs are the goal. If the firm manages each activity independently, then what may appear to be a proper low-cost decision may, in fact, work to create higher system-wide costs. For example, if the firm purchases raw materials at the lowest possible price, it may actually be creating higher production costs because of the rework and extra handling required to accommodate lower quality materials. In such a case, the decisions within each activity seem to fit the firm's strategy but, collectively, they do not.

Through very effective management of the interdependent value activities, some organizations have leveraged success with a differentiation strategy into a low-cost position as well. For example, several years ago, Kellogg invested in proprietary technology that allowed the company to develop unique cereals and sell them at a premium price in the grocery stores. With its technology, large share of

STRATEGIC APPLICATION 8.1 *(continued)*

The company's strategy implementation efforts were more hurtful than helpful. To rectify the problems, systemwide change was needed. As shown in the new value chain below, new policies and procedures were needed to redirect the efforts of the organization toward low costs and high service.

Improved Value-Added Chain for a Newspaper Company

Support Activities

Establish strategic planning committee
Establish management/union teams to address production
   and morale problems
Maintain up-to-date technology
Provide training for supervisors in the pressroom

Incoming Logistics	Operations	Outbound Logistics	Marketing/Sales	Service
Listen to readers to find out what news focus they want Provide larger news crew Establish small satellite bureaus	Man the presses to constantly ensure quality Install market segmentation technology to target customer groups Train workers on equipment operation and maintenance	Establish full carrier network so that any person anywhere can have A.M. or P.M. paper delivered to his or her homes	Search for customers in a larger market area Assist customers in overall advertising plan, not just selling space	Man the phones during peak delivery times to receive complaints of late or undelivered papers Keep staff available to deliver papers to missed subscribers

Source: S. Poss and P. Shull, Clemson University, 1992.

---

market, fast product development time, and efficient distribution channels, Kellogg was also one of the lowest cost producers in the industry. Rather than make a trade-off between low costs and differentiation, Kellogg made investment and operating decisions that served both causes interdependently. Strategic Insight 8.1 describes the just-in-time (JIT) philosophy as an example of system-wide, interdependent focus in activity management.

The collective pattern of day-to-day decisions made and actions taken by employees responsible for value activities creates **functional strategies** that implement the growth and competitive strategies of the business. In the following sections, we discuss the responsibilities and patterns of decisions made by marketing, operations, R&D, information systems, human resource, and finance functions in organizations. Management's challenge is to ensure that the pattern is consistent with what was intended. Strategic Insight 8.2 describes the experience of Wallace Co., Inc., a former winner of the Malcolm Baldrige Quality Award, when it refocused its marketing, operations, and human resource efforts to align itself with a new strategic direction.

Functional Strategies
Collective patterns of decisions made and actions taken by employees that implement the growth and competitive strategies of the organization.

STRATEGIC INSIGHT 8.1

An Example of Integrated, Interdependent Activity Management: The Just-in-Time Philosophy

Throughout the 1950s and 1960s, U.S. manufacturers were recognized worldwide for their efficient, low-cost production techniques. Purchasing managers were proud of their hard-nosed competitive bid practices and quantity discounts. Production managers maintained high levels of labor productivity by holding large amounts of work-in-process and producing in large batches so that workers would never have to wait for something to work on. Quality was assured by inspecting products before they were shipped to customers.

Unfortunately, many of the practices that seemed to provide for low costs were actually increasing costs. American managers were failing to see the interdependencies that existed among all of their activities. Quantity discounts resulted in high levels of expensive raw material inventories. The high levels of labor productivity were supported by high work-in-process inventories. Batch production techniques intended to reduce setup costs were, instead, creating high levels of inventory and inflexible scheduling. Inspection of end-items meant that quality problems were caught after all of the expensive materials and labor were invested in the product.

In the 1970s, the Japanese approached the cost reduction problem from a system-wide perspective. The Japanese focused on simplifying product designs so that fewer parts were needed, streamlining process flows so that employees had fewer changes to deal with, and shortening setup times so that batch sizes could be reduced dramatically without increasing costs. They aligned with fewer suppliers so that frequent, small quantity delivery arrangements could be negotiated. They trained workers to inspect for quality throughout the process and stop production immediately when a problem was discovered. The resulting production system provided lower inventories, less rework, higher levels of capacity utilization, and shorter production lead times than those of their American competitors, all of which allowed the Japanese to produce higher quality products at lower unit cost.

Marketing Strategy

One of the most critical responsibilities of marketing employees is to span the boundary of the organization and interact with external stakeholders such as customers and competitors. Marketing is responsible for bringing essential stakeholder information about new customer needs, projected future demand, competitor actions, and new business opportunities into the organization as an input to plans for continuous improvements, capacity and workforce expansions, new technologies, and new products and services. In describing how Motorola makes the most of its technology, CEO George Fisher described the essential boundary-spanning role of marketing:

> *Members of our sales force are surrogates for customers. They should be able to reach back into Motorola and pull out technologists and other people they need to solve problems and anticipate customer needs. We want to put the salesperson at the top of the organization. The rest of us then serve the salesperson.*[3]

STRATEGIC INSIGHT 8.2

BUSINESS

STRATEGY

Wallace Co., Inc., Wins Malcolm Baldrige National Quality Award after Redesign of Functional Strategies

Wallace Co., Inc., of Houston, Texas, founded in 1942, was a distributor of pipes, valves, and fittings for the engineering and construction industries. The family-owned firm's nine regional offices employed a staff of 280 and generated sales of around $100 million.

During the mid- and late 1980s, many of Wallace Co.'s customers, suppliers, and competitors were going bankrupt. Even financially healthy customers were downsizing. Low-price import products contributed to price war conditions and employee morale was crippled from recessionary fears. When two direct competitors filed for bankruptcy and were absorbed by other firms, those organizations wrote off millions of dollars worth of inventory, which put Wallace at an even greater price disadvantage. To make things worse, Wallace lost its credit relationships when its bank failed.

Despite extreme financial pressures, the struggling firm decided to invest a major share of its remaining resources in a major organization-wide quality improvement effort. After engaging a quality training firm, the company invested heavily (85% of annual payroll) in leadership development, company-wide training, employee empowerment, systematic benchmarking, and operational procedures such as statistical process control. It shifted its sales and marketing focus from almost total reliance on engineering and construction to a more diversified, less volatile business base including many maintenance, repair, and operations contracts.

The quality strategy led to several new commitments: Know customer needs, exceed customer expectations, compete on the basis of total cost rather than price, build cooperative customer and supplier partnerships, and establish performance measurements leading to zero defects across all levels of the organization.

As a result of its efforts, Wallace Co. not only survived, it flourished. From 1987–1990, sales increased 60%, profits jumped 740%, and market share rose 75%. The firm achieved the industry's highest worker productivity and a 23% increase in on-time deliveries. In 1990, President Bush awarded the firm the coveted Malcolm Baldrige National Quality Award in the small business category.

Ironically, the story does not end there. In the year following their Baldrige Award, the owners and managers were increasingly preoccupied with teaching other small companies how to improve quality. They failed to spend enough time on their marketing strategy to cultivate new business. When the recession deepened in the early 1990s, they fell on hard times again. In March 1993, Wallace Co. was acquired by Wilson Industries, a Texas-based competitor.

Source: "Wallace Co., Inc." *Strengthening America's Competitiveness.* Warner Books on behalf of Connecticut Mutual Life Insurance and the U.S. Chamber of Commerce, 1991), p. 102; Leslie King, "The 1990 Baldrige Winners Look Backward and Forward," *Industrial Engineering* 24 (1992), pp. 14–16; and "Wilson Industries," *The Oil and Gas Journal* 91 (1993), p. 82.

Marketing Strategy
A plan to promote, price, and distribute the products and services of an organization, as well as how to identify and service customer groups.

Marketing strategy evolves from the cumulative pattern of decisions made by the employees who interact with customers and perform marketing activities. To support growth strategies, marketing identifies new customer opportunities, suggests product opportunities, creates advertising and promotional programs, arranges distribution channels, and creates pricing and customer service policies that help position the company's products for the proper customer groups. If a company pursues a stability or retrenchment strategy within one of its businesses, the demands placed on marketing will change. Instead of pursuing growth, marketing may manage a reduction in the number of customer groups, distribution channels, and products in the product line—all in an attempt to focus on the more profitable and promising aspects of the business. Such was the case with Sturm Ruger & Co., a maker of guns for hunters, target shooters, and collectors. Facing a decline in the gun industry, the company decided it could no longer support wholesalers who also sold Smith & Wesson weapons. Fifty percent of its distributors agreed to supply Ruger guns only, which reduced the company's marketing costs and helped create a prestigious, hard-to-find image for its products.[4]

The competitive strategy of the firm also influences marketing decisions. Low-cost competitive strategies require low-cost channels of distribution and low-risk product and market development activities. If demand can be influenced by advertising or price discounts, then marketing may pursue aggressive advertising and promotion programs or deep price discounts to get demand to a level that will support full-capacity utilization and economies of scale within operations, as occurs when the soft drink companies advertise and discount their products.

Differentiation strategies require that marketing identify the attributes of products and services that customers will value, price and distribute the product or service in ways that capitalize on the differentiation, and advertise and promote the image of difference. Logitech, the world's leading producer of the personal computer device called the "mouse," used an aggressive marketing strategy to implement a growth strategy.

> There are three ways to sell a mouse: 1) directly to original computer equipment makers, 2) through distributors to retail outlets, and 3) through mail order. In its early start-up stage, Logitech bypassed the traditional mode of entry through distributors. Instead, the company sold direct to customers by advertising its mouse through personal computer magazines at half the price of the leading model. The interest created by the mail order approach fueled pull-through sales with distributors. Logitech also qualified as a supplier to AT&T. Logitech leveraged its AT&T contact into a European market entry when it won a contract with Olivetti, an AT&T alliance partner.[5]

The many stakeholder interests and the inherent trade-offs that are embedded in decision making make development of marketing strategies difficult and subject to inconsistencies. For example, one large market segment may be very price competitive while a much smaller segment will pay a premium price. Which is more consistent with the firm's strategy? When introducing a new product, is it better to offer the product at a competitive price and grow with the market, or offer the product at a deeply discounted price to gain market share in the early introduction period? Just how high can the price go on a "differentiated" product before the customer is no longer willing to pay the higher price? Is it desirable to participate in sole-supplier arrangements with customers? How marketing handles these types of questions reflects its understanding of stakeholder needs and influences the strategy that is created over time.

Operations Strategy

Operations strategy emerges from the pattern of decisions made within the firm about production or service operations. The task of operations managers is to design and manage an operations organization that can create the products and services the firm must have to compete in the marketplace. An effective operations unit "is not necessarily one that promises the maximum efficiency or engineering perfection, but rather one that fits the needs of the business—that strives for consistency between its capabilities and policies and the competitive advantage being sought."[6]

Operations managers, like marketing managers, must manage multiple stakeholder interests in their daily decision making. The total quality management (TQM) movement is a direct result of operations managers' neglect of their most critical stakeholder—customers. In the 1970s, many operations managers took the position "We made it, now it is up to marketing to sell it." The cavalier attitude toward the concerns of customers led to systemic quality problems that undermined entire industries.

Faced with fundamental change in their industries, many operations organizations implemented extensive TQM and continuous improvement programs to help focus operations decisions on the needs of customers. KL Spring and Stamping Corporation of Chicago, a supplier of parts to General Motors, was under pressure to change from its traditional focus on cost reduction. To implement a new strategy focused on quality, fast delivery, and service, KL Spring formed quality circles, initiated worker cross-training, increased employee involvement, provided quality and productivity incentives, and invested in new capital equipment. The improvement efforts paid off with acknowledgments from customers: a Mark of Excellence Award from GM and a Certified Quality Vendor Award from AT&T.[7] In some organizations, operations managers have enlisted the support of another stakeholder group, suppliers, in their efforts to better serve the needs of customers. Motorola, Xerox, and Ford have very active quality and technology programs in which they train tens of thousands of their suppliers' employees, including CEOs and executive managers.[8]

The interdependencies among stakeholders can create difficulties for operations managers. Employees want good wages and benefits, reasonable work schedules, and a safe and pleasant work environment. Communities want nonpolluting industries that provide stable employment for citizens of the community and add to the tax base. Suppliers want predictable demand for their products and services and a fair price. Customers want excellent quality, prompt delivery, and reasonable prices. However, a change in customer demand can upset schedules with workers and suppliers. A problem with a supplier can create havoc with the schedules and quality levels that are intended to serve the needs of customers. A new labor contract can cause cost structures and, hence, prices to go up. A new product for a customer may require new raw materials, which may, in turn, require new pollution control procedures. In managing these interdependencies, operations managers must be guided by an understanding of business-level strategies.

Every strategy affects operations in ways that have implications for stakeholder interests. For example, growth strategies put pressure on the systems and procedures used to schedule customer orders, plan employee work arrangements, order raw materials, and manage inventories. Retrenchment strategies often target the activities of operations first: Line employees are laid-off, equipment lies idle,

Operations Strategy
A plan to design and manage the processes needed to create the products and services of the organization.

plants (offices and stores) are closed. In implementing a TQM program, an organization may choose to move to sole-supplier arrangements, which will increase dependency on one supplier and sever relationships with others. Differentiation strategies based on flexibility and high-quality service may require a flexible or temporary workforce, special arrangements with suppliers, and very high levels of training for employees. Major capital investments in new equipment depress earnings in the short run, which lowers earnings per share reported to stockholders. How operations handles these types of trade-off decisions can have a substantial influence on the performance of the firm.

Research and Development Strategy

In most organizations, research and development involves four different activities: basic research, applications development, product development, and process development. Depending on the strategy of the firm as well as identification of core competencies and related technologies, some of these research activities may be more important than others. The strategy that emerges from the decisions and actions within R&D, engineering, and technical support activities is the **research and development strategy.**

Research and Development Strategy
A plan that guides basic research of the organization as well as its development of more effective and efficient applications, products, and processes.

Basic research is commonly referred to as the activity associated with pushing back the boundaries of science as we know it. For the most part, government laboratories, universities, and some high-technology companies have the most aggressive programs in basic research. Recombinant DNA technologies, superconductors, and specialty materials are examples of the types of radical findings and inventions that have resulted from pure scientific exploration.

In most companies, R&D efforts are in support of the known strategies of the firm. For example, a firm that is pursuing a market development growth strategy will invest in applications development so that its products can be tested and qualified for more uses. Fabric manufacturers put their industrial fabrics through extensive wear-testing to qualify them for everything from conveyor belts to tents to bandages.

If the firm is pursuing a product development strategy, the engineers and scientists within R&D will modify the product to improve its performance or extend its application to different markets. In some cases, they will develop a line of product variations to serve particular market segments. The widespread use of Dupont's Teflon fibers, coating, films, and membranes in everything from pots and pans to industrial equipment is the result of aggressive product development activities within the company.

Once products and entire product lines begin to mature, the focus of much of the R&D effort often shifts to process development.[9] Although some product changes may still be required, the firm is primarily concerned with reducing its costs of production. Engineers and scientists work to improve processing methods and conditions, and design special-purpose equipment that can efficiently produce the company's products. For example, some of the R&D efforts within many computer and electronics firms have been redirected toward process development as product lines have matured and foreign competitors have achieved lower processing costs.

R&D decisions are also characterized by trade-offs that must be matched with the strategies of the business and the interests of internal and external stakeholders. Should the firm be a leader or a follower in its research and development activities? Which stakeholder interests should take priority in product design decisions—what the customer and marketing want, or what operations can produce? What should be the balance among product, process, and applications development? Should new product modifications be worked on sequentially or worked on by two teams operating in parallel so that new product variations can be introduced more quickly? Under what conditions should the plug be pulled on a new product development project that is not proceeding as planned? When is it no longer profitable or worthwhile to continue to create product variations? As in marketing and operations, the pattern created in deciding among the trade-offs can either work for or against the planned strategy of the firm.

Information Systems Strategy

Since the early 1980s, the role of information systems in organizations has changed fundamentally. Before microcomputers, computer information systems were used primarily for accounting transactions and information record keeping. In the 1980s, computer technology revolutionized the way organizations do business. In some organizations, an information systems department plans computer use organization-wide so that computer resources are compatible and integrated. However, as systems become more user-friendly and decentralized, many information system activities are being managed within other departments.

Organizations regularly make decisions about how to make use of information systems, such as which hardware and software to use, what kind of information and transactions will be available on computer, and how information systems resources will be linked. The pattern of information systems decisions creates an **information systems strategy.** The purpose of the information systems strategy is to provide the organization with the technology and systems which, at a minimum, are necessary for operating, planning, and controlling the business. In some instances, well-designed integrated information systems serve as the foundation for a competitive advantage.

In many organizations, computer information systems affect every aspect of business operations and serve a major role in linking stakeholders. Local-area networks (LANs) and internal webs sometimes called "intranets" link employees and improve communications and decision making.[10] With spreadsheet packages, expert systems, and other decision-support software, employees at the lowest levels of the organization have the information and the tools to make decisions that were once reserved by middle managers. Computer-aided design (CAD) systems help marketing, manufacturing, and R&D employees develop designs faster and with fewer errors. In computer-integrated manufacturing (CIM) environments, product designs and production schedules are linked directly to manufacturing equipment, which increases accuracy, flexibility, and speed in meeting customer orders. Direct linkages with suppliers help in managing JIT delivery arrangements. Real-time inventory systems linked to order-taking systems provide valuable information that improves customer service. Direct computer linkages with customers provide real-time sales data, which the organization can use to plan for the future.

Some organizations have built their entire competitive strategy on effective use of information systems and creation of effective decision support systems (DSSs) that record data and present it in a format that assists managers in their decision making. For example, at Toys 'R' Us, scanners are used to record sales data by product and by store. Store managers use the data to update inventory records and reorder products so they do not run out of stock. The sales data from the hundreds of stores are transmitted daily to the corporate office where they are studied

Information Systems Strategy
A plan to provide the organization with the information technology necessary for the operation, planning, and control of business activities.

by product and by store to determine patterns and trends in customer buying behavior. Toys 'R' Us has made such effective use of its customer buying information that toy manufacturers regularly consult the company before scaling up to manufacture a new product.

Benetton, the largest producer of clothing in Europe, has also made information systems a central part of its strategy. Benetton maintains an integrated production, distribution, and sales communication system which has removed much of the risk in the fashion apparel business. The company subcontracts 80% of its clothing production through a large number of subcontractors and sells through a network of 4,000 franchised shops worldwide. Clothing is designed on computers which create patterns immediately. Patterns can be transferred to subcontractors within a matter of hours. All items are bar-coded which allows shop owners to monitor sales by product and by sales assistant. Orders and customer buying information are transmitted to the headquarters in Italy so that new production lots can be planned.[11]

Human Resources Strategy

As mentioned in Chapter 6, human resources (HR) management can play an important role in the implementation of a firm's strategies.[12] In the not-too-distant past, HR activities were considered to be more administrative than strategic. While some human resources departments are still primarily concerned with avoiding people problems (strikes, turnover, lawsuits, unions), others have evolved to the point where HR managers are actively involved in the formulation of strategies.[13] Human resources managers serve a coordinating role between the organization's management and employees, and between the organization and external stakeholder groups including labor unions and government regulators of labor and safety practices such as the Equal Employment Opportunity Commission and the Occupational Safety and Health Administration.

Human Resources Strategy
A plan that guides the recruiting, hiring, training, and compensating of employees as well as organizational change efforts.

The pattern of decisions about selection, training, rewards, and benefits creates a **human resources strategy.** Different industry environments and organizational strategies tend to reinforce different HR practices. In high-technology and growth organizations, employees are usually hired from outside the organization to fill positions at all levels—entry positions through top-level management. Compensation systems emphasize long-range performance goals, with frequent use of bonus and profit-sharing plans.[14] Therefore, in organizations pursuing growth strategies, like Microsoft in software and Merck in pharmaceuticals, the HR strategy focuses on hiring, training, and placing employees at all levels in the organization, and on developing performance-based compensation strategies.

Mature or cost-oriented businesses usually hire employees at the entry level and promote from within to fill higher level positions. They are more likely to focus rewards on short-range performance goals and to include seniority issues in compensation systems.[15] Firms following retrenchment strategies, such as General Motors, IBM, and Delta Airlines, have to focus their HR priorities on programs for early retirements, structured layoffs, skills retraining, and outplacement services.

The human resources strategies that are in place create a workforce with certain skills and expectations, which then influences the strategy alternatives available for the future.[16] If, throughout the life of a growth organization, salespeople are rewarded for finding new customers, R&D is rewarded for frequent new product variations, and operations is rewarded for maximizing throughput, then a retrenchment strategy that limits customer groups, product lines, and production levels can be very difficult to implement. A change in reward systems must precede or accompany the change in strategy. Because of the potential for conflict between existing HR policies and new organization strategies, HR managers play their most strategic role at the point when a major change in organization strategy is necessary. They must anticipate the change in skills and behavior that will be needed to support the strategy, modify the HR practices, and plan for an orderly, timely transition.

> *Although General Motors has been plagued with labor–management problems throughout its history, much of the success of the company's new Saturn automobile may be attributed to strategic human resource policies. Saturn is the highest quality American-made car, with a J. D. Power and Associate customer satisfaction rating exceeding those of Mercedes, Toyota (not Lexus), and all other American cars. Saturn achieves its extraordinary quality by tying quality objectives to rewards.*
>
> *All employees are on salary, including the workers on the assembly line. Quality, productivity, and profitability are linked to 20% of each employee's pay. Recently, with customer demand at a very high level, Saturn management tried to increase factory output. Because of fears that machine stress and rushing would create quality problems, line workers insisted that output be returned to the original levels that were more compatible with highest quality. The change in rewards created changes in behavior which were completely consistent with the organization's strategy of high quality.*[17]

Another trend that is affecting human resource strategy in many firms is the tactic of outsourcing labor resources, and of outsourcing human resource department activities. For example, some firms keep a relatively low percentage of their direct labor on the full-time payroll. Instead, they keep a pool of temporary, part-time workers who can be called in as needed, or they contract with a temporary services firm that will provide temporary workers as needed. The purpose of this tactic is to reduce the overall cost of human resources by avoiding the payment of benefits and by avoiding the cost of idle labor. The downside of this strategy is that human resources may not develop the skills needed for the job or develop a sense of loyalty to the organization. In addition, some firms are outsourcing their human resource department activities, such as benefits planning and administration. The purpose is to reduce costs, and possibly improve quality, by turning those administrative activities over to external partners who can specialize and operate at large scales.

As companies become more global, the challenges for the HR staff are mounting. In the 1990s, the HR staff will determine what skills are needed to manage people of different cultures, recruit top candidates worldwide, create training programs and experiences that help employees appreciate other cultures, and conduct relocations worldwide.[18] Furthermore, they may need to create compensation strategies for employees who, because of their national culture, value different reward and benefit packages. For example, in cultures that value personal accomplishment, control of one's destiny and independence, such as the United States and Britain, compensation strategies may focus on individual performance. In cultures that value team accomplishment, sacrifice for others, and external control or fate, the rewards may focus on group measures and seniority.[19]

Financial Strategy

The finance and accounting functions play a strategic role within organizations because they control one of the most important resources needed to implement strategies: money. In implementing strategy, two sources of funds are needed: (1) large amounts of capital for growth and maintenance-related objectives and strate-

Financial Strategy
A plan to provide the organization with the capital structure and funds appropriate for implementing growth and competitive strategies.

gies and (2) expense budgets to support the ongoing, daily activities of the business. The primary purpose of a **financial strategy** is to provide the organization with the capital structure and funds that are appropriate for implementing growth and competitive strategies.

In managing the funds of the business, finance is responsible for virtually all contact between the organization and some very influential stakeholders: stockholders, bankers, other investors, the Securities and Exchange Commission, and the Internal Revenue Service. The finance group decides the appropriate levels of debt, equity, and internal financing needed to support strategies by weighing the costs of each alternative, the plans for the funds, and the financial interests of various internal and external stakeholder groups. Finance also determines dividend policies and, through preparation of financial reports, influences how financial performance will be interpreted and presented to stockholders. In fact, financial reports may be the only contact many members of the investment community and most stockholders have with the organization.

Capital and expense budgets are an extremely important means for allocating funds to those departments, projects, and activities that need funds to support strategies. In theory, all expenditures in capital and expense budgets should be linked back to the strategies of the firm. "The structure that a mature enterprise takes on at any point in time essentially represents the accumulation of a long series of prior resource allocation decisions. If a company wants to develop in a specific direction, it must make these resource allocation decisions in an organized fashion."[20]

Unfortunately, the financial policies that many companies have in place work against the "strategic" use of funds. In most firms, proposals for new equipment, new products, and new facilities must be described in terms of projected cash flows, which are then used in a payback or discounted cash flow analysis. Several problems arise with these types of capital budgeting analyses, including the potential for inaccurate numbers, inappropriate assumptions, and trade-offs that undermine the future competitiveness of the company. The problems that underlie capital budgeting techniques are described in more detail in Table 8.1.

The trade-offs that are embedded in financial decisions carry significant implications for strategy implementation. Should the firm pay earnings out in dividends to satisfy stockholders who want a fast return on their investment, or instead invest them back in the company to benefit employees, communities, and stockholders who want a longer term increase in share price? In assessing expenses, investments, and earnings, should long-run or short-run performance be given more emphasis and how should that information be presented to stockholders and the investment community? Which internal stakeholder groups—marketing, operations, R&D, employees—should wield the most influence in capital allocation decisions? As described in Table 8.1, how minimum acceptable rates of return, base comparisons, indirect cost allocation processes, and qualitative issues are handled in investment and budgeting decisions also represent trade-offs. Because American industry is so burdened with obsolete factories and out-of-date equipment, it is worthwhile to consider that our financial policies and capital investment processes may have worked to discourage timely investments in plant and equipment.[21]

Managing Functional Strategies

Organizations are made up of people who interact with each other and with external stakeholders as they perform functions designed to meet the goals of the organization. Several years ago, researchers found that those companies which were most successful in implementing their strategies created a "pervasive strategic vi-

Table 8.1 *Problems with Capital Budgeting Systems*

Inaccurate Cost Data

Traditional management accounting systems compute product costs by adding direct labor and materials to indirect and overhead costs. Typically, overhead and indirect costs are allocated on the basis of direct labor hours. While this procedure made sense years ago, direct labor hours represent such a small proportion (<15%) of production costs in businesses now that the allocation procedure distorts true product costs.

Base Comparisons

When deciding whether to make an investment, many companies assume if no investment is made, business will continue as usual. Unfortunately, the decision to neglect or delay an investment may place the firm at a substantial disadvantage against competitors who did make the investment. The correct base case to have used was a substantial deterioration in position rather than business as usual.

Hurdle Rate

It is very common for firms to set hurdle rates (minimum acceptable return on investment) for capital projects at levels that are well beyond the cost of capital or the firm's current return on investment. Such high hurdle rates are unrealistic and discourage new investment.

Qualitative Factors

Many companies generate cash flows based on what they are sure about: existing customers, competitors, states of technology, and market conditions. Often a new investment—say, in new flexible automation—will open the door to new knowledge and opportunities. It is the difficult-to-quantify opportunities that may provide the greatest future return but are most often omitted in the analysis.

Source: R. Hayes, S. Wheelwright, and K. Clark, *Dynamic Manufacturing* (New York: The Free Press, 1988); R. Johnson and R. Kaplan, *Relevance Lost* (Boston: Harvard Business Press, 1990).

sion" throughout the company, with the full involvement of all employees.[22] In those firms where strategies were implemented effectively, employees worked as a coordinated system with all of their separate but interdependent efforts directed toward the goals of the firm. Consequently, each functional area is one piece of a larger system and coordination among the pieces is essential to successful strategy execution.

Therefore, well-developed functional strategies should have the following characteristics:

1. *Decisions made within each function will be consistent with each other.* For example, if marketing chooses to spend a great deal of money creating a premium brand name for a new product, it should take advantage of distribution channels that allow the product to reach customers who will pay a price premium. If the wrong distribution channels are chosen, then the efforts spent on advertising, promotion, and product placement will be lost. Several years ago, one of the synthetic fiber producers allowed one of its best branded products to become associated with discount, low-quality garments and its investment in the trademark was lost.

2. *Decisions made within one function will be consistent with those made in other functions.* As described earlier, interdependencies and linkages exist among the many activities of a firm. It is common for the decisions made by one department to be inconsistent with those of another department. For example, financial policies may be in conflict with the goals of engineering. Although they are responsible for most of the primary value-adding activities, marketing and

operations frequently advocate very different approaches to the many inter-dependent decisions that exist between them. Left to their own devices, with no guidance from the organization, it is likely that marketing, over time, will make decisions that implement a differentiation strategy while manufacturing, over time, will implement a low-cost strategy. Table 8.2 shows the many areas of potential conflict that exist between marketing and manufacturing groups.

3. *Decisions made within functions will be consistent with the strategies of the business.* It is often difficult to adapt to changes in the competitive environment. Suppose a company is pursuing an aggressive growth strategy in a healthy business environment. Under those conditions, marketing may pursue market share increases and revenue growth as its top priority. If the business environment changes—demand slows down and profits are squeezed—then the focus of marketing may have to change to stability and profit improvement over sales volume increases. Unless prodded by the organization, marketing may be very reluctant to change from its traditional way of doing business.[23]

The rapid success and subsequent decline of People Express Airlines is a good demonstration of what can happen when there is inconsistency in tactical decisions across departments or between a generic strategy and functional strategies.

Following the deregulation of the airlines, Donald Burr started People Express as a low-cost commuter airline. In the beginning, every management decision supported low costs: aircraft were bought second hand, pilots kept planes in the air more hours per day than any other airline, terminal leases were inexpensive, and human resource policies required cross-training, encouraged high productivity, and rewarded employees with profit-sharing plans. In line with its no-frills commuter approach, the company did not book reservations or provide in-flight meals. The airline was extraordinarily successful with its strategy, and achieved the lowest cost position in the industry. However, with success, People Express began to alter its pattern of decisions and, over time, drift from its low cost strategy. It pursued longer routes which pulled it into direct competition with the full service airlines, even though it did not have the elaborate reservation systems and customer services. It contracted more expensive terminal arrangements and purchased new aircraft at market prices. The close-knit, high performance culture which encouraged an extraordinary work pace in exchange for profit-sharing was undermined by rapid growth and too many new faces. Just a few years after its start-up, People Express was in serious financial trouble and was forced to sell out to another airline.

Strategic Application 8.2 provides a summary of the functional strategy decision areas. It may be used as a tool for determining functional strategy needs and critiquing consistency.

STRUCTURING TO SUPPORT STRATEGY

Since so many activities take place within organizations, the activities and people are usually subdivided into departments and groups so that employees can specialize in a limited number of activities and focus on a limited set of responsibilities. The **formal structure** specifies the number and types of departments or groups and provides the formal reporting relationships and lines of communication among internal stakeholders.

Alfred Chandler was the first researcher to recognize the importance of the structure–strategy relationship. According to Chandler, an organization's structure should be designed to support the intended strategy of the firm.[24] The underlying assumption is that a strategy–structure fit will lead to superior organiza-

Formal Structure
The division of activities and employees of the organization into specialized departments or groups.

Table 8.2 *Areas of Interdependency and Potential Conflict between Marketing and Operations*

1. *Facility Size/Process Choice vs. Market Forecasts*
   For a firm to exploit economies of scale and achieve low costs, offer a broad product line, serve a large market region, produce standardized products, or produce customized products, it must have properly sized facilities and appropriate processes. To make correct decisions about size and technology, operations requires information from marketing about expected long-run volume, future product mix, low cost versus responsiveness competitive priorities, and the role of product and service quality. Often, marketing will complain that operations has failed to build enough capacity and properly plan facilities. Operations will, in turn, blame marketing for failing to provide accurate demand forecasts.

2. *Facility Location vs. Market Planning*
   Depending upon the demands of the marketplace, facilities may be located near suppliers, low-cost labor, or customers. To make correct decisions about facility location, operations depends on marketing for information about the relative importance of low costs, responsiveness, and delivery speed, as well as the location of current and future customers and the demand patterns expected for each product and market region.

3. *Production Schedules vs. Forecasts, Orders, and Promotions*
   Production schedules determine inventory levels, sourcing arrangements, labor utilization, capacity utilization, delivery performance, and cost structures. In making production scheduling decisions, operations depends on marketing for short-run demand forecasts and promotion plans by product and by market, firm customer commitments whenever possible, and guidance about the relative importance of low costs and delivery performance. When operations is unable to meet demand in the short run, marketing complains about flexibility and commitment to the needs of customers. Operations, in turn, blames marketing for failing to provide good forecasts and arrange for longer lead times on orders.

4. *Operating Policies*
   On a daily basis, operations management makes decisions about the focus of continuous improvement activities and whether to schedule overtime, disrupt production schedules to meet the special requests of customers, stop shipment of marginal quality goods, or build inventory in anticipation of demand. Many of these decisions embody trade-offs. For example, it is difficult to maintain low costs if high stock levels are required to service unexpected demand. In all cases, those decisions are influenced by information from marketing about demand patterns and competitive priorities.

tion performance, which seems logical but has not been proven conclusively. Several principles or dimensions can be used to characterize an organization's structure. The dimensions, described in Table 8.3, capture the formal arrangements of people, activities, and decision-making authority.

When making decisions about how to structure an organization, it is important to remember the following:

1. Structure is not an end, it is a means to an end. The "end" is successful organizational performance.
2. There is no single best structure. A change in organization strategy may require a corresponding change in structure to avoid administrative inefficiencies, but the organization's size, strategies, external environment, stakeholder relationships, and management style all influence the appropriateness of a given structure. All structures embody trade-offs.[25]

CONDUCTING A FUNCTIONAL STRATEGY AUDIT

The functional strategy audit is a procedure for systematically reviewing the decisions in each of the functional areas to determine which ones should be changed to support the new strategy and needs of stakeholders. The format for the audit is shown.

Marketing Strategy Decisions	Current	Change Needed
Target customers (few vs. many, what groups, what regions)		
Product positioning (premium, commodity, multi-use, specialty use)		
Product line mix (a mix of complementary products)		
Product line breadth (a full-line offering of products)		
Pricing strategies (discount, moderate, premium prices)		
Promotion practices (direct sales, advertising, direct mail)		
Distribution channels (few or many, sole contract relationships)		
Customer service policies (flexibility, responsiveness, quality)		
Product/service image (premium quality, good price, reliable)		
Market research (accuracy and frequency of information on customers and competitors)		

Operations Strategy Decision Areas		
Capacity planning (lead demand to ensure availability or lag demand to achieve capacity utilization)		
Facility location (locate near suppliers, customers, labor, natural resources, transportation)		
Facility layout (continuous or intermittent flow)		
Technology and equipment choices (degree of automation, computerization)		
Sourcing arrangements (cooperative relationships with a few vs. competitive bid)		
Planning and scheduling (make to stock, make to order, flexibility to customer requests)		
Quality assurance (acceptance sampling, process control, standards)		
Workforce policies (training levels, cross-training, reward systems)		
Hardware (LAN, mainframe, minicomputer, internal systems)		

(continued)

Information Systems Strategy Decision Areas	Current	Change Needed

Software
   (data processing, decision support, CAD, CIM, JIT)
Information security
   (hardware, software, physical layout)
Disaster recovery
   (off-site processing, backup procedures)
Business intelligence
   (management support, marketing, accounting, operations,
   R&D, human resources, finance)

R&D/Technology Strategy Decision Areas

Research focus
   (product, process, applications)
Orientation
   (leader vs. follower)
Project priorities
   (budget, quality, creativity, time)
Linkages with external research organizations

Human Resources Strategy Decision Areas

Recruitment
   (entry level vs. experienced employees)
Selection
   (selection criteria and methods)
Performance appraisal
   (appraisal methods, frequency)
Salary and wages
   (relationship to performance, competitiveness)
Benefits
   (bonuses, stock ownership programs, other benefits)
Personnel actions
   (disciplinary plans, outplacement, early retirements)
Training
   (types of training, availability to all employees)

Financial Strategy Decision Areas

Capital
   (debt vs. equity vs. internal financing)
Financial reporting to stockholders
Minimum return on investment levels
   (relationship to cost of capital)
Basis for allocating overhead costs
   (direct labor, machine use, sales volume, activity)

Evaluation of Consistency

Are all of the marketing decisions internally consistent?
   Operations decisions? R&D decisions? Human resource
   decisions? Financial decisions?
Are the decisions in each function consistent with decisions
   in other functions?
Are the functional decisions consistent with the planned strategy
   of the firm and the expectations of stakeholders?

Table 8.3 *Dimensions of Formal Structure*

1. *Hierarchy of authority* refers to the formal reporting relationships as shown by the vertical lines on an organization chart. It also describes the span of control or number of employees reporting to each supervisor. Some organizations have tall, narrow structures while others have short, wide structures. The number of levels and the span of control frequently are associated with the type of industry a firm is in and its chosen strategy.

2. *Degree of centralization* refers to where in the organization structure decision-making authority resides. In centralized organizations, top managers make most of the important decisions. In decentralized organizations, lower level managers have the authority to make important decisions. Centralized structures are typically associated with more stable environments. Decentralized structures are more often associated with highly competitive environments where lack of time prevents a problem from making it to the top of the organization for a decision.

3. *Complexity* describes the number of levels, number of departments or job types, and number of market regions within an organization. An organization's structure becomes more complex with increasing numbers of levels, departments, and regions.

4. *Specialization* refers to the degree to which the various organization activities are divided into separate jobs. If specialization is high, then employees perform only a few activites. If specialization is low, employees are expected to perform many activities.

5. *Formality* describes the degree to which the structure is supported by written documentation such as an official organization chart, job descriptions, and policy manuals. Formality also describes the degree to which those written, formal documents are followed by employees. Typically, large organizations have more written documentation of jobs and structure than small organizations. In some organizations, large and small, the formal, documented lines of communication and job descriptions are not followed because an informal structure has evolved over time that better serves the needs of organization members.

Source: Adapted from R. L. Daft, *Organization Theory and Design,* 3rd ed. (St. Paul, Minn.: West Publishing Company, 1989).

3. Once in place, the new structure becomes a characteristic of the organization that will serve as a constraint on future strategic choices.
4. Administrative inefficiencies, poor service to customers, communication problems, or employee frustrations may indicate a strategy–structure mismatch.

Strategic Insight 8.3 describes the structure problems at TransAmerica Telemarketing which hurt productivity and customer service. To implement their strategy as intended, they reorganized departments and responsibilities.

Business-Level Structures

Managers typically use one of four organization structures when grouping the activities of a single business or division: functional, product or market group, project matrix, or network. Each of the four structures has important strengths and weaknesses that must be considered when making organization design decisions. The attributes of the four structures are summarized in Table 8.4.

Functional Structure
The division of an organization into groups based on a specific activity, such as accounting, marketing, R&D, etc.

Functional Structure. A **functional structure** is organized around the inputs or activities that are required to produce products and services, such as marketing, operations, finance, and R&D.[26] Organizations that are functionally structured usually have marketing, operations, finance, and R&D departments. The structure is centralized, highly specialized, and most appropriate when a limited product line

STRATEGIC INSIGHT 8.3

BUSINESS

STRATEGY

A Change in Organizational Structure at TransAmerica Telemarketing, Inc., Improves Customer Service

When TransAmerica Telemarketing, Inc., was founded in 1985, it had two separate offices: one in Washington, D.C., and the other in Harrisonburg, Virginia. The telemarketing and direct mail services firm housed its administrative offices, marketing, sales, and account services departments in Washington. The operations center was in Harrisonburg. As the company grew, the Washington office, located a two-hour drive from Harrisonburg, proved to be a highly ineffective location for servicing accounts.

Over time, the Harrisonburg operations center began assuming many of the account staff's duties because it had quick answers to clients' questions. Lack of communication caused mass confusion between the two offices and among clients. In addition, several people performed the same tasks, thus duplicating effort and wasting valuable time. The disorganization was so apparent, TransAmerica Telemarketing lost the business of a large client.

To rectify the situation, the company redefined the duties of each member. The account service staff moved to Harrisonburg, where it could maintain constant and direct communications with the operations managers. The marketing/sales people and the account services staff began weekly meetings to ensure that the lines of communication were always open. Now, instead of hiring from outside the company, accounts services recruits from within the operating center, bringing special hands-on knowledge to every position.

Today, the marketing staff is able to allocate 100% of its time to sales. Customer service has improved. Projects are managed more efficiently and the account team handles a 30% greater client load. Billings have increased and money is being saved in areas which previously lost money.

Source: "TransAmerica Telemarketing, Inc." *Strengthening America's Competitiveness* (Warner Books on behalf of Connecticut Mutual Life Insurance and the U.S. Chamber of Commerce, 1991), p. 28.

is offered to a particular market segment and the needs of external stakeholders are relatively stable. The functional structure is oriented toward internal efficiency and encourages functional expertise. It is particularly appropriate in organizations that want to exploit economies of scale and learning effects from focused activities. Small and start-up businesses often employ functional structures very effectively (see Figure 8.1). A functional structure can also be effective for a firm pursuing a market penetration strategy because organization scope (i.e., number of products and markets) and stakeholder requirements will be relatively stable over time.

The functional structure is not appropriate in an environment where stakeholder needs are diverse or changing, such as when a firm is trying to provide many products or services to many different customer groups. The functional structure may undermine the interdependency among internal stakeholders that is so essential to effective strategy implementation and hurt the ability of the organization to respond quickly to changes in customer needs. Over time, the different departments may become insular and focus on departmental goals at the expense

Table 8.4 *Attributes of Business-Level Structure*

	Functional	Product/Market	Project Matrix	Network
Organizing Framework	Inputs	Outputs	Inputs and outputs	Outputs
Degree of Centralization	Centralized	Decentralized	Decentralized with sharing	Very decentralized
Competitive Environment	Stable	Dynamic with external market pressures	Dynamic with external market pressures and internal technical pressures	Competitive conditions differ from region to region
Growth Strategy	Market penetration	Market and/or product development	Frequent new product/ market development managed as project teams	Market penetration and market development

of overall organizational goals. In the late 1970s, the functionally organized maintenance activities of the U.S. Air Force's Tactical Air Command experienced just such a problem:

> *In 1978, The U.S. Air Force's Tactical Air Command was responsible for a $25 billion fleet of planes, only half of which were capable of flying at any given time. Because of the aircraft shortage, TAC pilots were not getting enough flying time to keep their skill levels up. The accident rate was increasing and frustrated pilots (trained at a cost of almost $1 million each) were leaving the service in frustration.*
>
> *When General W. L. Creech took command of TAC in 1978, he attributed many of the maintenance problems to the functionally structured, centralized maintenance unit. When a fighter plane needed repairs, the crew chief inspected the plane, then called a centralized maintenance unit to report the problem. If an electrical problem was suspected, then the central maintenance unit dispatched an electrician to the flight line. If the electrician discovered that a panel needed to be removed to repair the electrical problem, the electrician called the central maintenance unit to request someone from the mechanical group. If additional skills were needed, the procedure was repeated. It often took hours for all of the necessary people to arrive on the site, with expensive planes and frustrated pilots sitting idle the entire time.*[27]

Product or Market Group Structure
The division of an organization into groups focused on a specific output or distribution strategy, such as products, customer groups, or geographical regions.

Product/Market Structure. A **product** or **market group structure** organizes activities around the outputs of the organization system, such as products, customers, or geographical regions.[28] When a business pursues a product or market development strategy, it adds products to its product line and interacts with more stakeholder groups, which may lead to administrative inefficiencies and confusion unless the organization structure is modified. It may be necessary to form smaller, more decentralized market groups or divisions to handle the broader scope of activities and to be more responsive to the diverse needs of customers. A firm that expands its business from a regional market base to a national market base may form new units around geographical market segments. For example, a restaurant chain or retail toy chain may be divided into units responsible for Eastern and Western regions (see Figure 8.2a).

Some firms that pursue growth through market development seek out new customer groups and new product applications. If sales to a particular new type of customer reach sufficient volume, the organization may reorganize around cus-

Figure 8.1 *The Functional Structure*

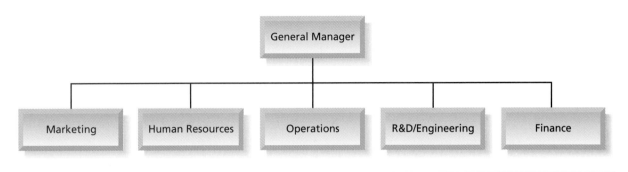

tomer groups. For example, a soft drink company may divide its business into "fountain" and "retail" segments, with the fountain unit targeting its marketing and sales efforts to restaurants and theaters and the retail unit focusing on grocery and convenience stores. Similarly, a microcomputer company might organize its business around home user, business, academic, and mail-order customer groups. An architectural firm might organize around commercial, military, and residential projects. When a business organizes around geographical regions or type of customer, it may continue to centralize its production or service operations in one area if economies of scale are significant (see Figure 8.2b). If not, then each geographical region or market unit may have its own operations facilities (as in Figure 8.2a). To correct the maintenance inefficiencies described earlier, Tactical Air Command's maintenance group was reorganized around a decentralized market structure.

> *General Creech restructured TAC around the 24-plane squadron. Technicians from each maintenance area were assigned directly to a squadron and worked only on those aircraft. Rather than operating out of a central dispatching area, all members of maintenance stayed on the flight line. Soon squadrons began to develop strong identities. The maintenance technicians became very loyal and personally interested in the condition of the aircraft and safety of the pilots in their squadron.*
>
> *Six years after the organization change, 85% of planes were mission capable compared to less than 50% in 1977. The crash rate dropped from one every 13,000 flight hours to one every 50,000 hours. Crashes from faulty maintenance were almost nonexistent.*[29]

Organizations that structure around markets or geographical regions have the opportunity to tailor their strategy to the needs of the local customer. As illustrated in the TAC example, decentralized market activities can lead to improved service, responsiveness, and customer awareness. However, structuring around markets can lead to some complications. There is potential for duplication of staff resources, which can be expensive. Also, if the market regions or groups cultivate different strategies to serve their customers, a lack of overall organizational identity may result, with different segments trying to pull the organization in different directions.

A product group or division is often appropriate when a business pursues growth through product or service development. As a firm pursues product development, its product line increases and often, as a result, its number and type of

Figure 8.2 *Types of Product/Market Structures*

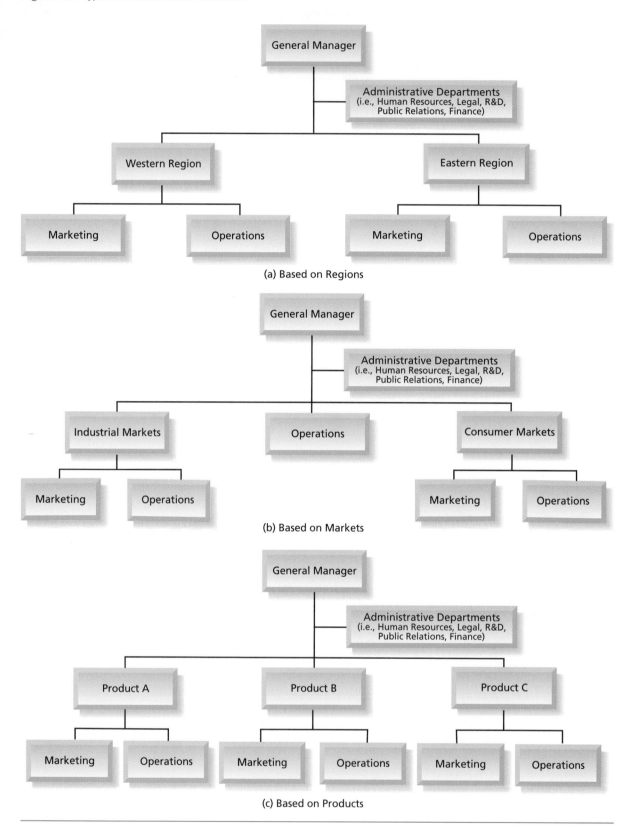

(a) Based on Regions

(b) Based on Markets

(c) Based on Products

customer groups increases. A pharmaceutical company that pursues product development may eventually form one unit for cardiovascular drugs and another for cancer drugs. A bank may form separate units for personal accounts, mortgage loans, and bank cards (see Figure 8.2c). In all cases, the new organization units are intended to improve the organization's ability to respond to internal and external stakeholder demands in a more timely and efficient manner.

The product structure has some of the advantages and disadvantages of the market and functional structures. With the product structure, the organization specializes in one product or one part of the product line, which encourages expertise and learning in product development and operations, but may undermine economies of scale and contribute to a duplication of marketing resources.

Project Matrix Structure. A hybrid structure that combines some elements of both functional and product/market forms is called a **project matrix structure**. The project matrix structure is viewed by some as a transitional stage between a functional form and a product/market group structure and by others as a complex form necessary for complex environments.[30] Either way, the many stakeholder influences that simultaneously pull an organization toward functional forms and the more diverse market/product forms reach an equilibrium in the matrix structure. Project matrix structures are most common in turbulent or uncertain competitive environments where internal stakeholders are highly interdependent, and external stakeholder demands are diverse and changing.[31] Matrix structures can improve communications between groups, increase the amount of information the organization can handle, and allow more flexible use of people and equipment.[32]

In a matrix structure, the organization is simultaneously functional and either product, market, or project oriented (see Figure 8.3). Fluor Daniel, one of the world's largest engineering design and construction companies, employs a matrix structure.

> At Fluor Daniel, it is very common for design engineers to report to two or more managers: the project manager on a particular contract and the functional manager of their particular design area, such as electrical or mechanical systems. The dual reporting relationships of the matrix structure emphasize the equal importance of functional design performance and service on the particular project. The functional dimension encourages employees to share technical information from one project to the next (learning) and helps avoid unnecessary duplication of skills. The project dimension allows the organization to focus on serving the needs of the customer while simultaneously encouraging cooperation and coordination among the different interdependent functions.

Unfortunately, matrix structures can be disconcerting for employees because of the "too many bosses" problem. It is difficult to balance the needs of the different lines of authority and coordinate among the many people and schedules. The overall complexity of the structure can create ambiguity and conflict between functional and product managers and between individuals. The sheer number of people that must be involved in decision making can slow decision processes and add administrative costs.[33]

Network Structure. Some organizations, particularly large integrated service organizations, use the network, or "spider's web" structure.[34] The **network structure** is very decentralized and organized around customer groups or geographical regions. As shown in Figure 8.4, a network structure represents a web of independent units, with little or no formal hierarchy to organize and control their relationship. The independent units are loosely organized to capture and share useful

Project Matrix Structure
A complex form of organizational structure that divides organization functions by both product/market group and functional activities.

Network Structure
A large, integrated organization with divisions, organized loosely around customer groups or geographical regions.

Figure 8.3 *The Project Matrix Structure*

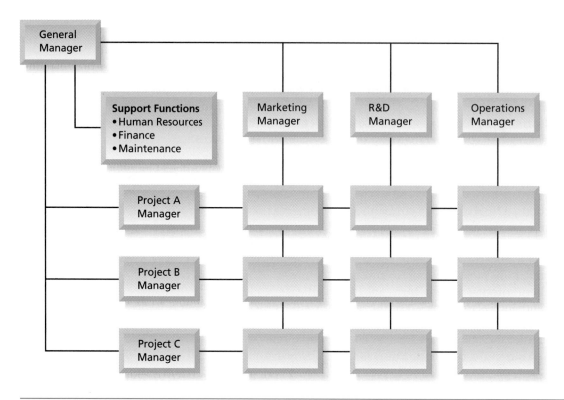

information. Other than information sharing, however, there is little formal contact among operating units. When formal contact is needed, committees and task forces are created on an ad hoc basis. The network structure is particularly appropriate in knowledge-intensive industries where decentralization and duplication of resources are required to service the market, yet there are no manufacturing or technology economies of scale to drive centralization.

> *Arthur Anderson & Co. is an accounting firm with 243 offices managed by over 2000 partners in 54 countries. Using a CD-ROM system, the company links its highly independent offices so they can share information. It maintains worldwide customer reference files and up-to-date resource information on taxes rules, customers, court rulings, and professional standards. The files are updated regularly and distributed to each office.[35]*

A network structure may not be appropriate when high levels of coordination and resource sharing are required. The network structure is an extreme form of decentralization, with executive-level management serving primarily an advisory function and lower level managers controlling most decisions. The weaknesses of the network structure include the potential for lost control of the autonomous units and high costs from the extensive duplication of resources. Network structures may be appropriate for universities, large medical and legal practices, investment banking, global distribution firms, consulting services, and charitable organizations such as United Way and Girl Scouts of America.

Figure 8.4 *The Network Structure*

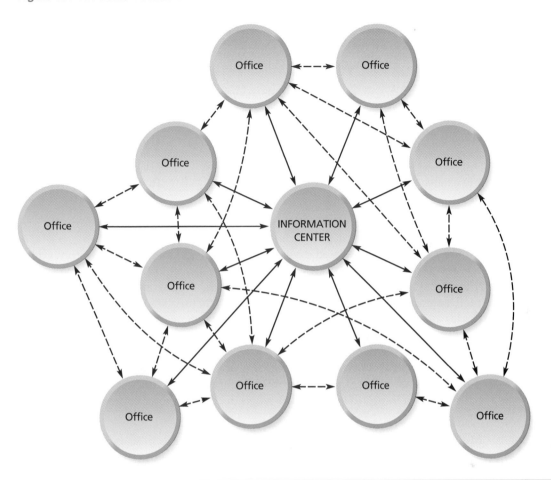

Corporate-Level Structures

As in business-level structuring decisions, the principles of corporate organization find their roots in the work of Alfred Chandler.[36] As organizations grow and pursue different business opportunities, administrative problems and complexity create pressures to break the organization into more manageable units. As part of the process of corporate strategy implementation, managers must structure and align the different business units. Earlier we discussed structuring *within* a business. In this section we are concerned with structuring relationships *among* an organization's businesses.

Depending on the strategies that are being pursued, management may be interested in cultivating independence or interdependence among business units. **Independence** among units requires an organization structure that encourages separation and autonomy, and coordinating mechanisms that achieve hierarchical (between business units and top management) rather than lateral (among business units) coordination. An independent structure is appropriate when businesses are unrelated and managers seek only financial synergies.

Independence
An organizational structure that encourages separation and autonomy among business units but has hierarchical coordination with top management.

Table 8.5 *Making the Corporate Structure Choice*

	Number of Businesses	Relatedness	Need for Coordination	Expected Synergy
Divisional	Few	Moderate/low	Moderate/low	Financial; limited operational
SBU	Many	Groups of related businesses	Moderate within SBU; low between SBUs	Limited operational within SBU; financial among SBUs
Corporate Matrix	Few or many	High	Very high	High operational synergies: costs, access, or innovation
Transnational	Many, in different nations	High	Very high	High operational synergies: cost, access, or innovation

When pursuing a related diversification strategy, managers try to convert the theoretical relatedness and fit of multibusiness strategies and strategic alliances into true synergistic relationships that benefit the organization as a whole. To exploit operational synergies, managers must structure relationships among businesses and partners in ways that encourage **interdependence,** and manage them over time with shared goals, shared information, resource sharing, and cooperative program development.[37]

Four general types of structures are used by multibusiness organizations: multidivisional, strategic business unit, corporate matrix, and transnational. Table 8.5 shows the issues that are raised when deciding among corporate-level structures.

Multidivisional. If an organization has a few businesses in its portfolio, management may choose a line-of-business or **multidivisional structure,** with each business existing as a separate unit. For example, a multidivisional organization may have an agricultural chemicals division, industrial chemicals division, and pharmaceuticals division. In this type of structure, a general manager—usually referred to as a divisional vice-president—heads up each of the three divisions. Each division has its own support activities, including sales, accounting/finance, personnel, and research and development. Services that are common to all three businesses are housed at the corporate level, such as legal services, public relations, and corporate research.

International strategies are often implemented through multidivisional structures. If an organization chooses to produce and sell its products in Europe, management may form an International Division to house those activities. If a firm pursues a multidomestic strategy that involves it in several independent national or regional businesses, management may form a separate division for each business. The multidivisional structure is appropriate when management of the different businesses does not require sharing of employees, marketing resources, or operations facilities.

The multidivisional structure, shown in Figure 8.5, has several advantages. By existing as a separate unit, each business is better able to focus its efforts on the needs of its particular stakeholders, without being distracted by the problems of other businesses. Corporate-level management is freed from day-to-day issues

Interdependence
Structures among businesses and partners that encourage the sharing of information and resources, as well as cooperative program development.

Multidivisional Structure
Organizational structure in which each business exists as a separate unit.

Figure 8.5 *The Multidivisional Structure*

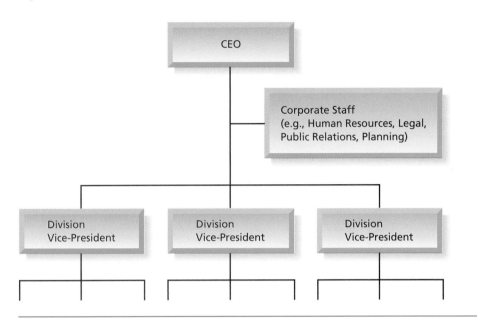

and is instead able to take a long-term, integrative view of the collection of businesses. Corporate executives may monitor the performance of each division separately and allocate corporate resources for specific activities that show promise.

With the multidivisional structure, it is often difficult to decide which activities will be performed at the corporate level and which ones will be held within each division. Competition for corporate resources (R&D, legal, investment funds) may create coordination difficulties among divisions. Also, organizational efforts may be duplicated, particularly when the different businesses within the corporate portfolio are highly related. It may be that shared distribution channels or common process development could save costs for the two businesses, yet separation in the organization structure discourages cooperation. Although many firms use multidivisional structures when configuring the relationships between related businesses, the structure makes resource sharing and cooperation difficult. Unfortunately, resource sharing and cooperation are necessary for synergy. Therefore, multidivisional corporate structures may hinder the creation of synergies within organizations.

Strategic Business Unit. When an organization is broadly diversified with several businesses in its portfolio, it becomes difficult for top management to keep track of and understand the many different industry environments and business conditions. Management may choose to form **strategic business units (SBUs)** with each SBU incorporating a few closely related businesses and operating as a profit center. Each SBU is composed of related divisions, with divisional vice-presidents reporting to an SBU or group vice-president. If an organization becomes very large, it may combine strategic business units into groups or sectors, thus adding another level of management. An example of a SBU structure is shown in Figure 8.6.

The SBU structure makes it possible for top management to keep track of many businesses at one time. It allows decentralization around dimensions that

Strategic Business Units (SBUs)
Organizational structure in which closely related businesses are grouped together for purposes of management and control.

Figure 8.6 *The Strategic Business Unit (SBU) Structure*

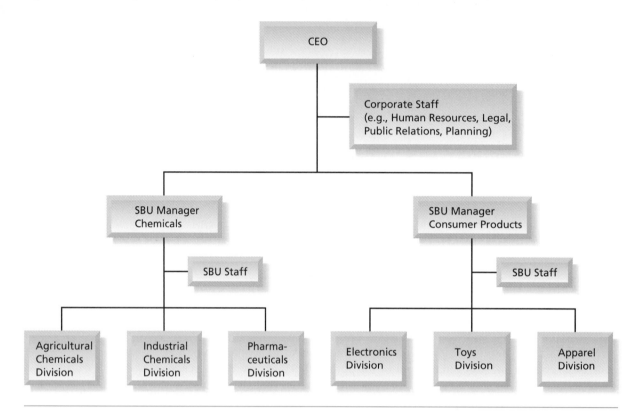

are meaningful to the business, such as markets or technologies. SBU vice-presidents can encourage the members of the SBU to coordinate activities and share information. The intent of the structure is to provide top management with a manageable number of units to keep track of and to force responsibility for decision making lower in the organization, near the important internal and external stakeholders.

The difficulty of the SBU structure is that operating units and, therefore, the customer are even further removed from top management than in the multidivisional form. As with the multidivisional form, there is competition for corporate financial and staff resources which may create conflicts and coordination problems. It is important to assign specific job responsibilities and expectations to business vice-presidents, SBU vice-presidents, and the corporate president, or conflicts may occur. Strategic Insight 8.4 describes the SBU structure used by Johnson & Johnson.

Corporate Matrix
Organizational structure used to decentralize units closer to market and technological trends while at the same time maintaining centralized control to bring about economies of scope and shared learning.

Corporate Matrix. The **corporate matrix** is the corporate-level counterpart to the project matrix structure described earlier. It is a way to achieve a high degree of coordination among several related businesses. Corporate matrix structures are used when the individual businesses within a corporation's portfolio need to take advantage of resource, information, or technology sharing in order to succeed in their industries. The corporate matrix structure tries to reach a balance between pressures to decentralize units closer to market and technological trends, and pressures to maintain centralized control to bring about economies of scope and shared learning.

STRATEGIC INSIGHT 8.4

BUSINESS

STRATEGY

Strategic Business Unit Structure at Johnson & Johnson

Johnson & Johnson Corporation employs an SBU-like structure in the management of its many health care businesses. The corporation has 166 separate operating companies. The operating companies are grouped into nineteen units. The nineteen units are formed into sectors which represent different markets: pharmaceutical, consumer, and professional. A few of the 166 operating companies are:

Johnson & Johnson Consumer Products, which makes Johnson's Baby Oil, Baby Powder, Baby Shampoo, Reach Toothbrushes, and Band-Aids

McNeil Consumer Products, which makes over-the-counter medicines such as Tylenol pain reliever and cold products

Ortho Pharmaceuticals, which makes several prescription medicines

Ethicon, which makes surgical products for sale to hospitals

By keeping operating units small and focused, employees and managers have a sense of ownership and control over their businesses. J&J believes small decentralized units are easier to manage and faster to react to changing markets and technologies. However, such a high degree of decentralization means that there is considerable duplication in overhead functions and sales. For example, dozens of sales representatives from the autonomous J&J companies call on big customers such as Wal-Mart and K-mart.

The J&J structure seems to be particularly appropriate for fast growth and new product development. When new products are developed, they are spun off as free-standing companies. The structure, however, does not lend itself to coordination across operating units. In 1989, one of J&J's pharmaceutical operating companies, Janssen, introduced a new antihistamine. When a J&J executive noticed that another pharmaceutical operating company, McNeil, had some extra salespeople, McNeil's salespeople helped promote the Janssen antihistamine to doctors. However, the arrangements were made with a formal contract specifying payment terms.

Source: Johnson & Johnson Company *Annual Reports,* 1990–1991; Joseph Weber, "A Big Company That Works," *Business Week* (May 4, 1992), pp. 124–132.

3M is a global company with twenty-three business units producing 60,000 products in fifty-five countries. To interact with the many stakeholder groups in the different nations, 3M must have a flexible, responsive organizational structure. Harry Hammerly, executive vice-president of international operations, describes the 3M structure this way:

When people ask how we structure a corporation with such a disparate lot of variables, I begin by discussing 3M's matrix management structure. One side of the matrix represents the company's product divisions. Along the other axis are the international subsidiaries. For any business in an international subsidiary, responsibility is shared by the managing director of the subsidiary (who reports through area or regional vice-presidents to me as head of International Operations) and the product manager (who reports to the vice-president of his or her division).[38]

The corporate matrix structure is particularly appropriate for related diversification strategies and global strategies. For example, a consumer products firm that has businesses in beverages, snack foods, and packaged foods may use a matrix structure to capitalize on economies of scale and capture synergies in marketing and distribution, as shown in Figure 8.7. Ideally, the corporate matrix structure improves coordination among different internal stakeholders by forcing managers within related businesses to maintain close contact with each other. It can help the organization become more flexible and responsive to changes in the business environment and can encourage teamwork and participation.[39]

The corporate matrix form may also be effective in structuring an organization that produces several products that are all sold in several nations. A multinational organization may create a matrix structure that groups all products under each national manager and simultaneously groups all nations under each product manager. This type of matrix structure allows the firm to achieve national focus in its marketing and distribution practices and encourages synergies through economies of scale and shared information within each product category. The corporate matrix structure applied to a multinational organization is shown in Figure 8.7b.

Transnational. A more complex version of the corporate matrix structure is the **transnational structure.**[40] Whereas the global matrix structure organizes businesses along two dimensions, the transnational structure organizes businesses along three dimensions: nation or region, product, and function. The transnational form is an attempt to achieve integration within product categories, within nations, and within functions while simultaneously achieving coordination across all of those activities. As shown in Figure 8.8, the transnational form requires three types of managers who serve integrating roles: (1) country or region managers who oversee all products and functions performed in their area to maintain a focal point for customers, (2) functional managers who oversee the activities of a particular function (technology, marketing, or manufacturing) for all products in all nations, and (3) product or business managers who oversee all functions and markets supported by a particular product or product group.[41] Organizations that employ transnational structures can build three capabilities: responsiveness and flexibility at the national level, global scale economies, and experience that transcends national, functional, and product boundaries.[42] Many large multiproduct global organizations, in industries ranging from computers to consumer products, are making the transition to a transnational structure. Xerox uses a transnational structure, as described by Chairman and CEO Paul Allaire:

> We have created an organization that by its very design forces managers to confront—and manage–the necessary tensions between autonomy and integration. . . . In a sense, we have turned the traditional vertically organized company on its side. At one end is technology, and we have retained an integrated corporate research and technology organization. At the other end is the customer. We have organized our sales and service people into three geographic customer-operations divisions, so that we can keep a common face to the customer. Between these two poles are the new business divisions. Their purpose is to create some suction on technology and pull it into the marketplace.[43]

The corporate matrix and transnational structures are plagued by one serious difficulty: Sheer complexity may interfere with what they are designed to accomplish. It is difficult to balance the needs of the different functional, national, and product stakeholders. The unusual command structure can create an atmosphere of ambiguity, conflict, and mixed loyalties. The overall complexity and bureau-

Transnational Structure
A complex corporate matrix structure that organizes businesses along national or regional, product, and function dimensions.

Figure 8.7 *Types of Corporate Matrix Structures*

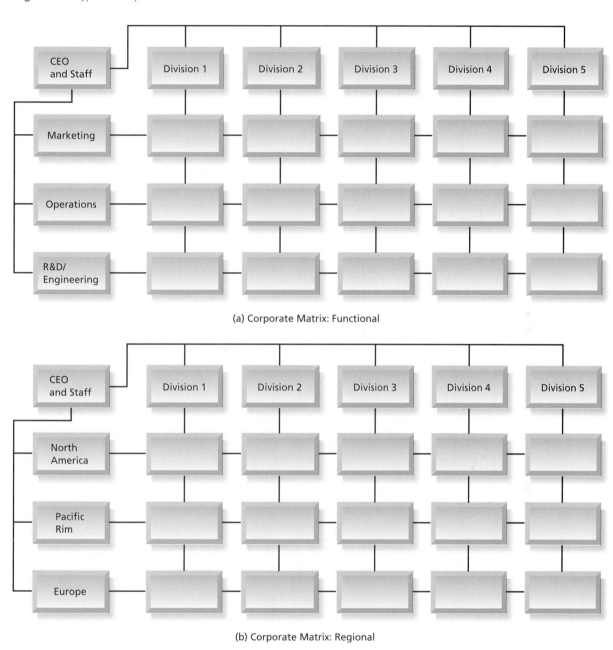

(a) Corporate Matrix: Functional

(b) Corporate Matrix: Regional

cracy of the structure may stifle creativity and slow decision making because of the sheer number of people that must be involved. Furthermore, the administrative costs associated with decision delays and extra management may overwhelm the benefits of coordination.[44] To derive the benefits of any of the corporate-level or business-level structures, but especially those that are more complex, managers must take extra steps to ensure coordination. Coordination is discussed in the next chapter on strategic control.

Figure 8.8 *The Transnational Structure*

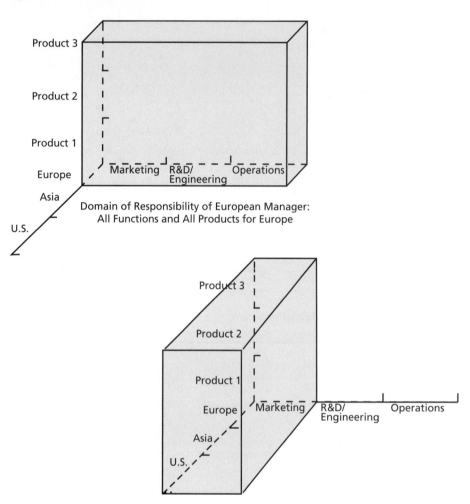

Domain of Responsibility of European Manager:
All Functions and All Products for Europe

Domain of Responsibility of Marketing Manager:
Marketing for All Regions and All Products

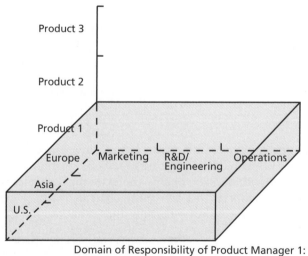

Domain of Responsibility of Product Manager 1:
All Functions and All Regions for Product 1

Summary

In this chapter, we described the functional strategies and organization structures that are used in implementing strategies. Strategies are implemented through the day-to-day decisions and actions of employees throughout the organization. Management's challenge is to create a pattern of integrated, coordinated decisions that meets the needs of stakeholders and fulfills the planned strategy of the organization.

The primary and supporting value activities of a firm are accounted for by departments or functional areas: marketing, operations, research and development, information systems, human resources, and finance. In each area, employees interact with different stakeholder groups and manage conflicting expectations. The pattern of decisions made by employees in these functional areas creates functional strategies. In managing functional strategies, managers must ensure that decisions within each area are consistent over time, with other functions, and with the stated strategies of the firm.

In configuring the relationships among departments in a single business, organizations usually employ one of the following structures: functional, product/market group, project matrix, or network. Each of the structures exhibits strengths, weaknesses, and fits with particular strategic choices. The functional structure encourages functional specialization and focus but discourages coordination between functions or departments. The product/market group form segments products and markets into smaller, more manageable subunits that may improve service to customers or economies of scale but result in resource duplication. The project matrix structure employs a dual-reporting relationship that is intended to balance functional focus and expertise required for learning with responsiveness to customer needs. However, it may create ambiguity and slow decision making if managed improperly. The network structure is a very decentralized form that is particularly well suited to geographically dispersed offices, stores, or units that, except for some sharing of information and operating policies, operate independently. The network structure may result in extreme resource duplication and missed opportunities for sharing and learning.

In structuring relationships among multiple business units, managers attempt to create independence so that organizations are free and unencumbered, or interdependence to exploit operating synergies. Multidivisional and strategic business unit structures divide businesses into divisions. While these structures focus the organization on the needs of its stakeholders, they make coordination and resource sharing among businesses, which are necessary to exploit operating synergies, very difficult. Corporate matrix and transnational structures are intended to exploit economies, learning, and resource sharing across businesses; however, they require extra measures of coordination to avoid divided loyalties, slow decision making, and management conflicts.

Discussion Questions

1. For each of the following departments, discuss the role organization members play in managing multiple stakeholder interests: marketing, operations, R&D, information systems, finance, and human resources.
2. Discuss the strengths and weaknesses of each of the structures presented in this chapter and the strategic choices for which each structure is most appropriate.
3. Use the resources of your college library and selected interviews in your community to determine the organization structures of each of the following types of businesses: a bank, a department store, and a small manufacturer. How and why do the structures differ?
4. What is the primary difference between the functional structure and the product/market structure? How is a project matrix structure a combination of the two?
5. How are the multidivisional and SBU structures the same? How are they different? When would one structure be more appropriate than the other?
6. How are the corporate matrix and transnational structures the same? How are they different? When would one structure be more appropriate than the other?

References

1. Developed from J. W. Verity, T. Peterson, D. Depke, and E. Schwartz,"The New IBM," *Business Week* (December 16, 1991), pp. 112–118; L. Hooper, "IBM to Unveil New Structure of PC Business," *Wall Street Journal* (September 3, 1992), p. A3.

2. L. G. Hrebiniak and W. F. Joyce, *Implementing Strategy* (New York: Macmillan, 1984).

3. B. Avishai and W. Taylor, "Customers Drive a Technology-Driven Company: An Interview with George Fisher," *Harvard Business Review* 67(6) (November–December 1989), pp. 107–108.

4. J. Millman, "Steady Finger on the Trigger," *Forbes* (November 9, 1992), pp. 188–189.

5. V. K. Jolly and K. A. Bechler, "Logitech: The Mouse That Roared," *Planning Review* (November–December 1992), pp. 20–32.

6. R. Hayes and S. Wheelwright, *Restoring our Competitive Edge: Competing Through Manufacturing* (New York: John Wiley & Sons, 1984), p. 30.

7. "KL Spring & Stamping Corporation," *Strengthening America's Competitiveness* (Warner Books for Connecticut Mutual Life Insurance Company and the U.S. Chamber of Commerce, 1991), p. 91.

8. J. Welch, L. Cook, and J. Blackburn, "The Bridge to Competitiveness—Building Supplier-Customer Linkages," *Target* (November–December 1992), pp. 17–29.

9. W. J. Abernathy and P. L. Townsend, "Technology, Productivity, and Process Change," *Technological Forecasting and Social Change* 7(4) (1975), pp. 379–396.

10. A. Cortese, "Here Comes the Intranet," *Business Week* (February 26, 1996), pp. 76–80; A. L. Sprout, "The Internet Inside Your Company," *Fortune* (November 27, 1995), pp. 161–168.

11. E. Sutherland and Y. Morieux, *Business Strategy and Information Technology* (New York: Routledge, Chapman and Hall, 1991), p. 118.

12. W. E. Fulmer, "Human Resources Management: The Right Hand of Strategy Implementation," *Human Resource Planning* 12(4) (February 1990), pp. 1–10.

13. Fulmer, "Human Resource Management."

14. C. Fisher, "Current and Recurrent Challenges in HRM," *Journal of Management* 15(2) (1989), pp. 157–180.

15. Fisher, "Current and Recurrent Challenges in HRM."

16. C. A. Lengnick-Hall and M. L. Lengnick-Hall, "Strategic Human Resource Management: A Review of the Literature and a Proposed Typology," *Academy of Management Review* 13(3) (1988), pp. 466–467.

17. D. Woodruff, J. B. Treece, Sunita Wadekar Bhargava, and Karen Lowry Miller, "Saturn," *Business Week* (August 17, 1992), pp. 86–91.

18. N. M. Tichy, "Setting the Global Human Resource Management Agenda for the 1990s," *Human Resource Management* 27(1) (Spring 1988), pp. 1–18.

19. L. R. Gomez-Mejia and T. Welbourne, "Compensation Strategies in a Global Context," *Human Resource Planning* 14(1) (Spring 1992), pp. 29–41.

20. R. H. Hayes, S. C. Wheelwright, and K. B. Clark, *Dynamic Manufacturing* (New York: The Free Press, 1988) p. 61.

21. Hayes, Wheelwright, and Clark, *Dynamic Manufacturing*.

22. F. W. Gluck, S. D. Kaufman, and A. S. Walleck, "Strategic Management for Competitive Advantage," *Harvard Business Review* (July–August 1980), pp. 154–161.

23. Hayes and Wheelwright, *Restoring our Competitive Edge*.

24. A. D. Chandler, *Strategy and Structure: Chapters in the History of the American Industrial Enterprise* (Cambridge, Mass.: The MIT Press, 1962).

25. P. R. Lawrence and J. W. Lorsch, *Organization and Environment* (Homewood, Ill.: Irwin, 1969), pp. 23–39.

26. A. C. Hax and N. S. Majluf, *The Strategy Concept and Process: A Pragmatic Approach* (Englewood Cliffs, N.J.: Prentice-Hall, 1991).

27. J. Finegan, "Four Star Management," *Inc.* (January 1987), pp. 42–51.

28. Hax and Majluf, *The Strategy Concept and Process*.

29. Finegan, "Four Star Management."

30. J. R. Galbraith and R. K. Kazanjian, *Strategy Implementation: Structure, Systems, and Processes*, 2nd ed. (St. Paul, Minn.: West Publishing Co., 1986).

31. R. L. Daft, *Organization Theory and Design*, 3rd ed. (St. Paul, Minn.: West Publishing Co., 1989), p. 240.

32. R. C. Ford and W. A. Randolph, "Cross-Functional Structures: A Review and Integration of Matrix Organization and Project Management," *Journal of Management* 18(2) (1992), pp. 267–294.

33. Ford and Randolph, "Cross-Functional Structures."

34. J. B. Quinn, *Intelligent Enterprise* (New York: The Free Press, 1992).

35. Quinn, *Intelligent Enterprise*.

36. Chandler, *Strategy and Structure*.

37. C. W. L. Hill, M. A. Hitt, and R. E. Hoskisson, "Cooperative Versus Competitive Structures in Related and Unrelated Diversified Firms," *Organization Science* 3(4), (November 1992), pp. 501–521.

38. H. Hammerly, "Matching Global Strategies with National Responses," *The Journal of Business Strategy* (March–April 1992), p. 10.

39. Ford and Randolph, "Cross-Functional Structures."

40. C. A. Bartlett and S. Ghoshal, *Managing Across Borders: The Transnational Solution* (Boston, Mass.: Harvard Business School Press, 1989).

41. C. A. Bartlett and S. Ghoshal, "The New Global Manager," *Harvard Business Review* (September–October 1992), pp. 124–132.

42. Bartlett and Ghoshal, "The New Global Manager."

43. R. Howard, "The CEO as Organizational Architect: An Interview with Xerox's Paul Allaire," *Harvard Business Review* (September–October 1992), p. 112.

44. Ford and Randolph, "Cross Functional Structures.

chapter

9

Strategic Control

A Security Company That Was Out of Control

In 1992, Pinkerton's Inc., one of the world's largest security companies, was out of control. In the first six months, operating expenses rose 36%, accompanied by a drop in earnings of 41%. All the time executives were telling investors that business was booming. As a result, a group of shareholders filed a legal suit charging that executives misled them so that they could sell some of their shares at an inflated price. The stock price fell from $36 at the beginning of 1992 to around $15 in September.

In an effort to increase revenues, Pinkerton's engaged in a major acquisition program in 1991. They bought a host of small security guard contracting firms with the intention of making the combined businesses more efficient through economies of scale. Instead, costs increased dramatically and the recession hurt profit margins, but no one at Pinkerton's had any idea what was happening. Investment manager James Ruf, president of Ruf Investment Group, explained, "The real fault with the company was not having stronger financial controls."

Thomas Wathen, CEO of Pinkerton's, is tightening those controls, reducing overhead and cutting costs. In particular, he purchased a new computer system and hired a new financial officer to keep tabs on operations. He also consolidated offices to reduce expenses and canceled a planned expansion into alarm systems. Concerning his too rosy financial forecast, he claims, "I probably won't ever make another projection in my life."[1]

How can a large security company with experienced managers end up in such an undesirable situation by surprise? The answer is that top executives were not adequately keeping track of organizational progress. Wathen led Pinkerton's in an ambitious external growth strategy without checking to see what effect the acquisitions were having on financial performance. Now he must scramble to recoup his lost credibility as a manager. Unfortunately, the extreme measures taken to regain control may be harmful to the long-term health of the company, since they could jeopardize the satisfaction of some customers.

Welcome to the complex world of control. From the perspective of top executives, a **strategic control system** is "a system to support managers in assessing the relevance of the organization's strategy to its progress in the accomplishment of its goals, and when discrepancies exist, to support areas needing attention."[2] A basic strategic control model is displayed in Figure 9.1. It illustrates three different types of control: feedforward, concurrent, and feedback. **Feedforward control** helps managers anticipate changes in the external and internal environments, based on analysis of inputs from stakeholders and the remote environment. **Concurrent control**, in some cases, provides managers with real-time information about processes and activities, and, in other cases, acts to influence actions and behavior as it is occurring. **Feedback control** provides managers with information concerning outcomes from organizational activities. With feedback control, managers establish targets (sometimes called objectives or key result areas), then measure performance some time later to determine deviation from expectations.

The purpose of all control systems is to provide information that is critical to decision making. If a control system reveals that something has changed or deviated from expectation, the managers must assess cause and effect in an effort to learn why. The following example illustrates the roles of feedforward, concurrent, and feedback controls, and the importance of understanding cause and effect. Assume that a passenger airline has established an operating target that its planes should be 80% full over the next three months, plus or minus 5%. At the end of the first month, performance is at 70%, which causes enough concern that managers initiate an investigation (feedback control). Managers review the daily customer service, baggage handling, and delivery performance records (concurrent control) and find that all operating process controls were within an acceptable range during the month. They then check their assumptions about the health of the economy and the behavior of competitors, both of which would influence ticket demand for this airline, and discover that early indicators suggest a slowdown in the economy. The airline uses this information to revise its performance targets to 70% full (feedforward control).

The learning processes associated with feedforward, concurrent, and feedback control form the basis for changes in strategic direction, strategies, implementation plans, or even the targets themselves, if they are deemed to be unreasonable given current conditions. In addition to the traditional measuring and monitoring functions, a recent study found that top managers use control systems to overcome resistance to change, communicate new strategic agendas, ensure continuing attention to new strategic initiatives, formalize beliefs, set boundaries on acceptable strategic behavior, and motivate discussion and debate about strategic uncertainties.[3] Control systems become the "tools of strategy implementation."[4]

With this basic control model as a foundation, the strategic control process is now developed in more detail. The next section begins with a brief narrative of the history of strategic control systems in the United States. Understanding the history

Strategic Control System
Organizational system by which top management can evaluate the progress of the organization in accomplishing its goals, as well as point out areas in need of attention.

Feedforward Control
Analysis of inputs from stakeholders and the remote environment that helps management anticipate changes in the external and internal environments of the organization.

Concurrent Control
Organizational control system that provides managers with real-time information about processes and activities, and, in other cases, acts to influence actions and behavior as they are occurring.

Feedback Control
Information concerning outcomes of organizational activities that assess the progress of the organization in meeting its goals.

Figure 9.1 *The Strategic Control Process*

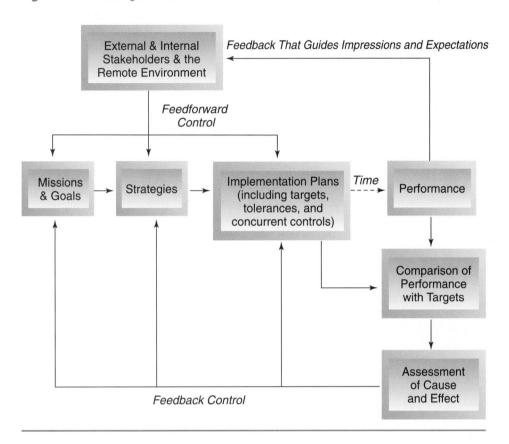

of control is important to comprehending why many of the widely used control systems, based primarily on accounting data, are no longer as relevant as they were in the past. The chapter then turns to a discussion of the processes associated with creating an effective strategic control system, followed by specifics about the types of feedforward, concurrent, and feedback controls that shape a strategic control system. The chapter closes with a section on crisis prevention and management.

DEVELOPMENT OF STRATEGIC CONTROL SYSTEMS

Early in this century, the increase in diversified and vertically integrated organizations created the demand for systems that could help top managers allocate time, capital, and human resources where they were most needed. E.I. DuPont de Nemours Powder Company, formed from a combination of previously independent companies, was one of the early innovators in this area.[5] DuPont created one of the most enduring systems for controlling diversified businesses. The system was based on return on investment (ROI), which was defined as the operating ratio (return on sales) times the stockturn (sales to assets).[6] Using this summary measure of performance for each division, top managers could identify problem areas and allocate capital to the most successful operations and divisions.

Because financial reporting requirements included figures for income, assets, and sales, managers could easily calculate ROI or related measures from existing data. As the multidivisional form of organization proliferated after 1950, the use of financial measures such as ROI gained wide acceptance and application.[7] In many organizations they became the only important measure of success. In the words of Roger Smith, past CEO of General Motors, "I look at the bottom line. It tells me what to do."[8]

Unfortunately, according to some control experts, accounting-based measures are "too late, too aggregated, and too distorted to be relevant for managers' planning and control decisions."[9] Lateness refers to the long lag times between the organizational transactions themselves and the dates when financial reports are ready. For example, Pinkerton's did not know they were in trouble until so much time had passed that the problem became very large. The aggregation problem simply means that accounting measures do not contain the detail that is necessary to make meaningful improvements to organizational processes. Finally, distortions associated with accounting information are well documented. Distortion is especially evident in the way inventories, plant, and equipment are valued and in the way overhead costs are allocated to various departments and divisions.

In addition, accounting-based financial measures can prompt managers to behave in ways that are counterproductive over the long run. For example, financial measures such as ROI discourage investments in long-term research and development projects because expenses must be paid out immediately while benefits may not accrue until many financial periods later.[10] Also, managers may shut down lines or cancel services that appear to be too costly, placing an emphasis on products and services that are most efficiently produced. These types of decisions are fine as long as customers do not prefer the more costly products and services. However, the end result is often that the overproduced "efficient" goods and services have to be sold at a discount to stimulate customer interest. Consequently, profit margins are eroded and the organization would have been better off keeping the lines or services that were dropped.

Trade loading is a good example of a harmful behavior that is induced by an inappropriate focus on accounting-based control:

> . . . a crazy, addictive, and surprisingly common management practice called trade loading runs entirely counter to the corporate crusade to become lean and flexible. Manufacturers—of cars, computers, cigarettes, colas, and many other products—"load" by inducing their wholesale and retail customers, known as the trade, to buy more product than they can promptly resell. Manufacturers begin loading because they are hungry for market share or hell-bent on hitting quarterly profit targets. The short-term high is this: You ship enough extra products to reach your financial goals and maybe goose the stock.
>
> Even as you feel good inside, financial health can deteriorate. Particularly in today's slow-growing markets, you find that to pump up the volume, or even maintain it, you must offer increasingly lucrative discounts and deals. During each load-in, you overwork your system: whipsaw production, crank distribution, stress your sales and marketing people. Costs rise. Inventories build. And build.[11]

Some companies, most notably Procter & Gamble, are now attempting to fix this problem, which costs American consumers an estimated $20 billion annually. Edwin Artzt, CEO of P&G, calls the situation a "monstrosity."[12]

The traditional and perhaps outdated top-down control cycle is depicted in Figure 9.2. Since control information tends to be collected at the top of the organization, top executives possess all of the power to control organizational processes. These managers analyze the information and provide instructions to subordinates

Figure 9.2 *The Top-Down Control Cycle*

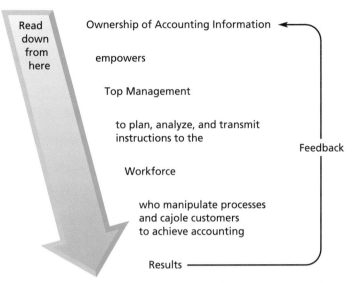

Source: Adapted with the permission of The Free Press, a Division of Simon & Schuster, from *Relevance Regained: From Top-Down Control to Bottom-up Empowerment* by H. Thomas Johnson. Copyright © 1992 by H. Thomas Johnson, p. x.

concerning expected levels of performance. Subordinates then attempt to meet top management expectations through whatever means are available to them. This type of system assumes that organizational learning occurs at the top of the organization. Unfortunately, most top managers are too distant from the value-creating activities of their companies to understand or learn what needs to be done to improve long-run performance. This type of management is known as "management by remote control."[13] As a control specialist put it:

> The chief problem with using accounting information to control operations—managing by remote control—is the tendency for businesses to lose sight of the processes by which people and customers make a company competitive and profitable. What I believe has happened in American businesses since the 1950s is that managers and operating personnel at all levels have lost sight of people, customers, and processes as top management has turned everyone's attention to accounting results.[14]

Competitive forces in the global economy have led to the need for a "grass-roots" approach to control, as depicted in Figure 9.3. According to this model, customers themselves have substantial power due to readily available information about products, services, and prices. Consequently, organizations must be much more responsive to the desires of customers. For this system to work, feedback from customers must be available to the workforce so that they can make the adjustments that are required for continuous improvement to organizational activities.

Regarding global organizations, control systems that take a "bottom-up" approach overcome many of the difficulties that are encountered when organizations attempt to control international operations with a standardized "top-down" approach. Bottom-up approaches are, by their nature, flexible and adaptable to the

Figure 9.3 *The Bottom-Up Empowerment Cycle*

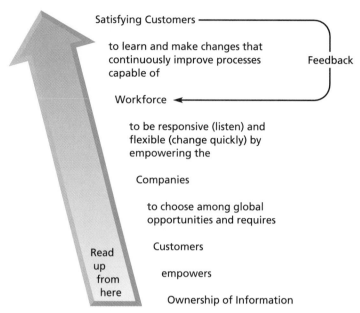

Satisfying Customers

to learn and make changes that continuously improve processes capable of

Feedback

Workforce

to be responsive (listen) and flexible (change quickly) by empowering the

Companies

to choose among global opportunities and requires

Customers

empowers

Ownership of Information

Read up from here

Source: Adapted with the permission of The Free Press, a Division of Simon & Schuster, from *Relevance Regained: From Top-Down Control to Bottom-up Empowerment* by H. Thomas Johnson. Copyright © 1992 by H. Thomas Johnson, p. ix.

peculiarities of particular systems. Consequently, the processes that an organization employs to *develop* a grassroots control system in Brazil will be similar to the processes employed in the United States, although the resulting systems themselves are likely to be different due to differences in culture, training, systems, materials, or technology.

The extreme case of grassroots control is a situation in which customers actually control the activities of the companies from which they are buying. For example, Ito-Yokado Co., a company that manages 7-Eleven stores in Japan, controls the product mix, the manufacturing schedule, and the delivery of its most important supplies. "The moment a 7-Eleven customer in Japan buys a soft drink or a can of beer, the information goes directly to bottler or brewery. It immediately becomes both production schedule and delivery schedule, actually specifying the hour when the new supply has to be delivered and to which of the 4,300 stores."[15] This concurrent control process eliminates five or six wholesale levels. A little closer to home, Wal-Mart has similar practices with many of its suppliers. According to Peter Drucker, a well-known business writer, these trends are a result of the availability of better information, "Now that we have real-time information on what goes on in the marketplace, decisions will increasingly be based on what goes on where the ultimate customers, whether housewives or hospitals, take *buying* action."

In summary, top-down, accounting-based feedback control systems were originally developed in an effort to help managers allocate their time and organizational resources across multiple business units. These types of systems were widely applied in larger organizations by the middle of the twentieth century. The main problem with top-down control systems as a primary basis for control is that high-level managers typically do not have an adequate understanding of what must be done to improve value-adding activities within the organization. Furthermore, top-down controls sometimes result in behavior that leads to higher short-run profits but is not in the best interests of an organization over the long term. Finally, top-down control systems put most of the information that is necessary to control organizational processes in the hands of top managers, who are too far away from the customer to use it effectively. We now describe strategic control systems.

Designing a Strategic Control System

Although the traditional approach to control is top down, the current thinking is that control systems should be comprehensive and designed to include input from internal and external stakeholders and from organizational processes. The processes associated with developing strategic control systems include determining what factors need to be controlled, identifying appropriate measures of the factors, and integrating information from all levels and all areas of the organization into a system that makes sense. Strategic Insight 9.1 contains an example of a small business that used a comprehensive strategic control system to overcome a difficult situation.

Determination of Control Factors

The first step in developing a strategic control system is determining what needs to be controlled. The stakeholder view of organizations provides an integrative view of control. By considering organization performance from a variety of stakeholder perspectives, key indicators of success can be derived from activities that lead to the satisfaction of stakeholders such as customers, employees, and shareholders.

Robert Kaplan and David Norton have developed a comprehensive approach to designing strategic control systems that considers organizational performance from four perspectives: (1) financial, (2) customer, (3) internal business, and (4) innovation and learning.[16] Each of these performance perspectives has its own set of feedback controls and is linked to particular stakeholder groups. For example, those stakeholders who evaluate an organization's performance using financial targets will typically look to return on investment, cash flow, stock price, and stability of earnings. Customers, on the other hand, evaluate other types of information: pricing, innovation, quality, value, and customer service. From an internal stakeholder and processes perspective, another set of "performance" indicators becomes important, such as cost controls, skill levels and capabilities, product line breadth, safety, on-time delivery, quality, and many others. From an innovation and learning perspective, an organization may consider the foundation it is building for the future, such as workforce morale, innovation, investments in R&D, and progress in continuous improvement.

According to Kaplan and Norton, an organization should ask itself the following question: "If we achieve our vision, how will we differ?" The "differences" should then be expressed from each of the four perspectives. The specifics of the differences that the firm expects to see are tied to the strategies that it intends to follow, and become the strategic goals or overall control targets. For example, suppose a firm has a vision to become the dominant shareholder in its industry (vision) through superior quality and service (business strategy). The specifics of that vision can be expressed as future changes in financial performance (e.g., increased

STRATEGIC INSIGHT 9.1

BUSINESS

STRATEGY

Lifeline Systems Implements TQM

Established in 1974, Lifeline Systems, Inc., manufactures and provides personal response services and equipment. The personal response industry services individuals who require emergency assistance due to health problems or security needs. Lifeline's customers wear a small call button that enables them to send a signal to its monitoring headquarters where appropriate help is summoned. The personal response industry grew slowly in the 1970s and early 1980s. In the mid-1980s changes in health care resulted in early patient discharge, which expanded the need for outpatient and home care services. Because Lifeline's service allows individuals to return home and still be protected in the event of a medical emergency, these changes provided the company with an excellent chance to increase business.

The aging of the baby boom generation represents another area of growth. In the year 2010, more than 50 million people in the United States will be age 65 and over. This age group is the personal response industry's main customer base. Up until 1987, Lifeline was not fully positioned to take advantage of these opportunities. Although it was producing constant revenue growth with increased market penetration, Lifeline's earnings were erratic and it suffered from a host of problems, including poor customer service and low employee morale.

To rectify the situation, Lifeline's senior management team, led by company president Arthur R. Phipps, implemented a TQM program. The new focus was on continuous improvement and a belief that all errors are preventable. Quality committees were created such as (1) the quality assurance committee, headed by the president; (2) a zero defects committee in manufacturing; (3) an out-of-box failure committee analyzing problems in the field; and (4) a service subcommittee focusing on customer satisfaction. A corporate-wide vendor certification program was implemented and quality cost programs were used to control costs and improve decision making. The company also used quality function deployment, which coordinated company objectives with customer satisfaction. Finally, concurrent engineering was used to minimize materials, production, and quality control costs. An example is the manufacture of a main Lifeline unit and its remote button at the same time on the same board.

As part of the success of the TQM program, Lifeline established a corporate culture stressing quality while encouraging innovation and entrepreneurship. The financial results speak for themselves. In a three-year period annual sales rose 53% to $30 million, the number of people using Lifeline's services increased from 190,000 to 275,000, and its stock price more than doubled.

Source: Adapted from "Lifeline Systems, Inc.," *Strengthening America's Competitiveness: The Blue Chip Enterprise Initiative* (Warner Books on behalf of Connecticut Mutual Life Insurance Company and the U.S. Chamber of Commerce, 1991), pp. 76–77.

STRATEGIC APPLICATION 9.1

A SAMPLE SCORECARD FOR "KEEPING SCORE WITH STAKEHOLDERS"

Stakeholder Category	Possible Near-Term Measures	Possible Long-Term Measures
Customers	Sales ($ and volume) New customers Number of new customer needs met ("Tries")	Growth in sales Turnover of customer base Ability to control price
Suppliers	Cost of raw material Delivery time Inventory Availability of raw material	Growth rates of 　raw material costs 　delivery time 　inventory New ideas from suppliers
Financial Community	EPS Stock price Number of "buy" lists ROE etc.	Ability to convince Wall 　Street of strategy Growth in ROE 　etc.
Employees	Number of suggestions Productivity Number of grievances	Number of internal 　promotions Turnover
Congress	Number of new pieces of 　legislation that affect the firm Access to key members and staff	Number of new regulations 　that affect industry Ratio of "cooperative" vs. "competitive" 　encounters
Consumer Advocate	Number of meetings Number of "hostile" encounters Number of times coalitions formed Number of legal actions	Number of changes in 　policy due to CA Number of CA-initiated "calls for help"
Environmentalists	Number of meetings Number of hostile encounters Number of times coalitions formed Number of EPA complaints Number of legal actions	Number of changes in 　policy due to environmentalists Number of environmentalist "calls 　for help"

Source: R. E. Freeman, *Strategic Management: A Stakeholder Approach* (Boston: Pittman, 1984), p. 179. Reprinted with permission of the author.

ROI), customer perceptions and behavior (e.g., perceived improved quality and reputation), and internal skills and capabilities (e.g., improved sales activity, higher quality standards and outputs), all of which are goals.

The next step in the process is to identify those **critical result areas** that are key to ensuring that the organization accomplishes its goals and, ultimately, its vision. In the preceding example, some critical result areas might be (1) improvement in worker skill levels (human resources training), (2) product redesign (engineering), (3) creation of new quality specifications and process control systems (operations management), (4) purchase of higher quality raw materials (purchasing), (5) new marketing programs that promote and position the improved quality (marketing), (6) improved packaging to resist shipment damage (engineering), (7) changes in

Critical Result Areas Organizational areas that are key to ensuring that the organization accomplishes its goals and its vision; examples are improving worker skills, product redesign, and creation of new process control systems.

performance evaluation and rewards to encourage a high-quality culture (operations and human resource management), and (8) improved product margins from increased volume, decreased costs, and increased price.

Once identified and linked specifically to financial, customer, internal process, and learning outcomes, *the critical result areas become the objectives and targets that pace strategy implementation.* As time passes and objectives are met, the broader goals (ROI, reputation, etc.) will be met as well, and ultimately the vision will be realized. By specifically linking financial, customer, internal, and learning performance targets to the vision, the firm can structure a control system that is strategically relevant.

Some advocates of stakeholder management believe that performance should be evaluated and controlled from an even broader base of perspectives, including that of suppliers, consumer groups, and environmentalists. For example, an organization may choose to set a performance target with respect to its involvement and reputation in the community, or in its partnerships with suppliers. Since the things that get measured are often the things that receive attention in organizations, managers need to be sensitive to the needs of stakeholders and make sure that the set of critical result areas reflects the priorities that have been established concerning satisfaction of various stakeholder needs and interests. Strategic Application 9.1 shows some examples of the types of information that might be monitored as part of a broad perspective strategic control system.

ELEMENTS OF A STRATEGIC CONTROL SYSTEM

Once the goals and critical results areas are determined, systems for monitoring progress must be put in place. A well-developed strategic control system will include feedforward, concurrent, and feedback control elements, each of which attacks a different part of the overall control process. The role of each type of control element is discussed in the following paragraphs.

Feedforward Controls

Environmental Discontinuities
Major unexpected changes in the social, economic, technological, and political environments that necessitate change within the organization.

Good feedforward control systems are important because of **environmental discontinuities,** which are major, unexpected changes in the social, economic, technological, and political environments that necessitate change within organizations.[17] Those environmental discontinuities can also arise from inside the organization, such as the unplanned development of a new product or a problem with labor turnover. Environmental discontinuities introduce changes to the assumptions that underlie the organizational vision, goals, strategies, and, in some cases, organization structure and technology. For example, a merger between two competitors would cause a firm to reevaluate its goals and strategies. A serious problem with labor turnover might cause a firm to improve its wage and benefits plans, which would affect its cost structure. New industry regulations could influence new product development plans. A shortage of skilled labor could force a firm to consider investments in automation or relocation of its factories. Even in stable environments, where environmental discontinuities play a minor role (e.g., production of commodities), feedforward control systems are essential to learning processes that allow organizations to move toward the accomplishment of their goals. Feedforward control systems compare information collected through business intelligence systems to the premises, or assumptions, that underlie organization vision, goals, and strategy.

Premise Control. Strategic direction and strategies are established based on premises about the organization and its external environment. These **premises** are assumptions about what will happen in the future, based on current conditions. For example, an organization may plan to expand its manufacturing facilities over a period of five years based on the assumption that interest rates will remain approximately the same. If interest rates change dramatically, it could make the planned expansion unprofitable. These types of situations demonstrate the need for premise control. **Premise control** helps organizations avoid situations in which their established strategies and goals are no longer appropriate.

> Premise control has been designed to check systematically and continuously whether or not the premises set during the planning and implementation process are still valid. Accordingly, premise control is to be organized along these premises. The premises should be listed and then assigned to persons or departments who are qualified sources of information. The sales force, for instance, may be a valuable source for monitoring the expected price policy of the major competitors.[18]

Business Intelligence and Strategic Surveillance. In feedforward control systems, information is collected from the internal and external environments, compiled in a usable form, then compared to the premises or assumptions made by the organization. The information collected from the broad, operating, and internal environments becomes part of the **business intelligence** of the firm. Business intelligence can be defined as "the collection and analysis of information on markets, new technologies, customers, competitors, and broad social trends."[19] Therefore, all organizations have a business intelligence system, although some systems are elaborate and formal while others may be simple and informal. In many small businesses, the business intelligence system consists of the information absorbed by the owner/manager.

Preliminary efforts to develop business intelligence systems include the creation of management information systems (MIS), decision support systems (DSS), and group decision support systems (GDSS). An MIS requires collection and use of information about products, services, costs, and quality that is typically gathered from internal sources. Accounting information systems are a type of MIS. DSS goes one step further in allowing individual or multiple managers to tap into databases and ask novel questions that are not answered through standard reports.[20] For example, Frito-Lay has an enormous DSS, which collects sales information from 10,000 salespeople on a daily basis. The system is used by managers to fine-tune product/market decisions.[21]

Full-scale business intelligence systems are similar to decision support systems, except that their scope is comprehensive. They perform the functions of supporting the strategic decision-making and control processes of the organization, providing early warning signals of threats and opportunities, and tracking the actions and reactions of competitors.[22] Table 9.1 provides some examples of the types of information organizations collect to support their business intelligence efforts.

Figure 9.4 demonstrates the importance of a well-developed business intelligence system as a part of the strategic management process. Information in the system helps managers to identify strengths, weaknesses, opportunities, and threats. Also, the business intelligence system is central to the development and application of organizational resources, which can help an organization develop competencies leading to a competitive advantage. The system is also central to the strategic management activities of establishing strategic direction, developing strategies, and implementing those strategies.

Premises
Assumptions about what will happen in the future, based on current conditions.

Premise Control
System that evaluates whether information used to establish strategies and goals is still valid given the organization's current internal and external environments.

Business Intelligence
Information on markets, new technologies, customers, competitors, and broad social trends.

Table 9.1 *Examples of Information That Should Be Collected Regularly*

Group or Segment	Examples of Useful Information
Internal Stakeholders	
Employees	Satisfaction with working conditions
	Special skills and education
Owners	Names and characteristics of large stockholders
	Business relationships with other stakeholders (e.g., suppliers, competitors)
Managers	Compensation relative to managers in rival firms
	Experience within firm and in previous firms
External Stakeholders	
Competitors	Product features
	Background of key executives
Customers	Customer satisfaction
	Unmet customer desires
Creditors	Competing organizations
	Other clients who may also be stakeholders (e.g., suppliers, competitors)
Activists	Size and strength of organizations
	Political agendas
Venture Partners	Other ventures
	Distinctive competencies
Suppliers	Sales and profitability
	Other important customers
Unions	Labor contracts in other firms
	Background of officers
Government	Bills under consideration
	Background of officials within relevant regulatory offices
Local Communities	Local problems
	Workforce projections
Broad Environment	
Technology Leaders	Technological advancements
	Key research institutions and researchers
Society	Demographic trends
	Social issues
Global Economy	Projected growth
	Interest rate movements

The development of a business intelligence system is a complex and difficult task, even for companies that have limited their activities to highly industrialized countries such as Japan, Germany, or the United States. However, this task is even more difficult in developing countries, where accurate information is often not readily available. Organizations have to learn to derive their information according to circumstances, relying on line managers in-house for much of what is collected. The sales force can still gather information about competitors' products and can establish informally the level of competitors' sales. Accountants may be able to get some information through the strength of their contacts with banks. In general, successful strategic planning in developing countries relies more on fast feedback than precision of information.[23]

Figure 9.4 *Business Intelligence and the Strategic Management Process*

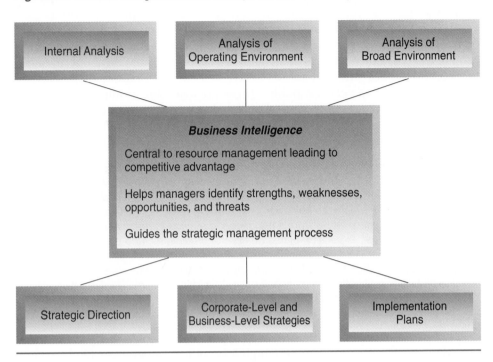

Ethical Implications of Business Intelligence. The collection and dissemination of intelligence is loaded with ethical implications. People associate intelligence-gathering activities with spying. In fact, "spying" agencies such as the Central Intelligence Agency and the Soviet KGB developed some of the most comprehensive and sophisticated information management systems in the world. Clearly, organizations should always abide by the laws preventing surreptitious activities. But even when laws are not broken, scouting out information on competitors and customers can be laden with ethical implications. Effective information management often means organizing and making good use of available information rather than going to extreme lengths to find confidential information.

The stakeholder management approach described in this book presents special challenges for managers in their collection and use of stakeholder information. As organizations form tighter relationships with their external stakeholders, they typically share more information and coordinate their plans, which can increase the likelihood of a confidentiality breach. For example, as organizations form tighter relationships with their suppliers, they typically coordinate their plans for capacity expansion and product development. Each organization then has in its possession sensitive confidential information about the other—information that could be used by a competitor in a negative way. This need for critical information exchange between stakeholders heightens the need for guidelines and rules for handling information. Organizations should develop specific policies and procedures for intelligence gathering and information management. These policies and procedures should be communicated to all employees who use the system, with instructions that divulging stakeholder secrets is tantamount to revealing the organization's secrets. Furthermore, security systems should be put in place to ensure that only certain individuals have access to sensitive information.

Responsibility for Intelligence Management. Responsibility for collecting and disseminating intelligence information should be assigned in a very deliberate fashion to the appropriate levels, areas, and individuals within the firm. For example, marketing departments are typically responsible for collecting information on consumer tastes and preferences, sales departments manage most of the interactions with customers, middle managers can collect information about union activities, and public relations departments typically deal with the media, special interest groups, and the general public. These are just a few examples of possible assignments. If responsibility for the collection and analysis of pertinent information is not assigned, something important may be overlooked, as the following example demonstrates:

> *It came as a nasty shock for a large U.S. manufacturer of medical supplies: An important Japanese competitor, Kokoku Rubber Industry, was greatly boosting output at a new plant in Kentucky. The U.S. outfit, caught by surprise, had to cut prices drastically as it struggled to hold market share. Yet details of Kokoku's move had been available years earlier from a hodgepodge of easy-to-reach sources.*
>
> *The plant's cost, expansion plans, number of employees, and product line had been reported in the Lexington* Herald-Leader *in 1987—three years before the plant geared up. Some of the U.S. company's employees almost certainly knew of Kokoku's plans—but the company had no system for passing along information, so senior management remained in the dark. Stupid? No less a strategist than Frederick the Great said, "It is pardonable to be defeated, but never to be surprised."*[24]

Many firms have created a very high level officer sometimes called the chief information officer (CIO) to oversee the collection, analysis, and dissemination of information. Also, many leading-edge corporations are also experimenting with the creation of special units within their organizations, called environmental scanning, or analysis, units. These units play a variety of different roles in the organization:

1. *Public policy role.* These units are assigned the tasks of scanning the environment for early detection of emerging issues that are suspected to be harbingers of widespread shifts in societal attitudes, laws, or social norms. Examples of these shifts are urban decay and women's rights.
2. *Strategic planning integrated role.* These units play an integral role in the corporate-wide strategic planning process. The focus is on both the operating and broad environments. Typically these units are required to prepare an environmental forecast and analysis for the entire corporation, to be distributed to line and/or staff executives during various stages in the planning cycle.
3. *Function-oriented role.* The function-oriented role is just the opposite of the public policy role. While the public policy role means that scanning units search for broad issues, the function-oriented role focuses on only those aspects of the environment that impinge directly on the activities of one function, such as product development or public relations. These units are typically housed within the functional departments of an organization.[25]

In conclusion, feedforward control systems take information collected through the business intelligence system and compare it to the premises, or assumptions, that the organization is using in its strategic management activities. Top managers are already involved in a continuous process of collecting information, assessing key stakeholders, devising strategies that will satisfy their needs and desires, and delegating duties for stakeholder analysis and management. A good business intelligence system can assist top management in these processes and in identifying emerging environmental discontinuities that will affect the organization.

Feedback Control Systems

Feedback control systems perform several important functions in organizations.[26] First, creating specific objectives or targets ensures that managers at various levels and areas in the organization understand the plans and strategies that guide organizational decisions. Second, feedback control systems motivate managers to pursue organizational interests as opposed to purely personal interests, because they know they will be held accountable for the results of their actions. This alignment of interests reduces some of the agency problems discussed in Chapter 4. Finally, feedback control systems help managers decide when and how to intervene in organizational processes by identifying areas that require further attention. Without good control systems, managers can fall into the trap of spending too much time dealing with issues and problems that are not particularly important to the future of the organization.

Any time goals or objectives are established and are measured against actual results, a feedback control system exists. The terms *key result areas, objectives,* and *goals* all capture the same basic concept: They each represent a performance target for an individual, a department, a division, a business, or a corporation.

Goals are established at all levels in the organization. At the corporate level, goals are broad enough to encompass the entire organization. At the business level, goals focus on the performance of a particular business unit. Goals are also developed at the functional level, where they provide functional specialists with specific targets.

One of the keys to effective goal setting is that they must be well integrated from level to level. In some organizations, the functional areas establish goals, which form the basis for business-level goals. The business-level goals of the various divisions are then summed to form corporate-level goals. This is a **bottom-up approach** to goal setting. Even with a bottom-up approach, however, the organizational vision guides the development of goals. Business-level managers decide how best to accomplish that vision. In a **top-down approach,** the order is reversed, with the corporate level essentially dictating what lower level goals should be. As mentioned previously, this type of approach is not very effective when it is used to the exclusion of bottom-up input. Most organizations use a combination of the two approaches, based on negotiation between the levels. Figure 9.5 illustrates these points in a hypothetical organization with two operating divisions that are of approximately equal size. Notice that the marketing departments in the two divisions have different perspectives on the goals that will be necessary to achieve their overall sales goals.

Specific operating goals are established in an effort to bring the concepts found in the mission and vision statements to life—to a level that managers and employees can influence and control. Vision and mission statements often include broad organizational goals that are lofty ideals which embrace the values of the organization. These ideals can provide motivation to employees and managers. However, these broad goals typically provide general, not specific, direction. Unlike the broad goals contained in vision statements, operating goals in key result areas provide specific guidance concerning desired outcomes. Consequently, they are an important part of strategy implementation. Effective operating goals should have the following characteristics:

Bottom-Up Approach
Goal setting begins in functional areas, which translates into business-level goals of the various divisions that are combined to form the corporate-level goals.

Top-Down Approach
The corporate level essentially determines and then dictates what lower-level goals should be.

Figure 9.5 *Integration of Goals*

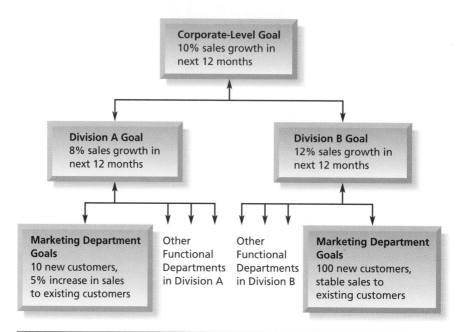

1. *They are high enough to be motivating.* If goals are set too low, employees will quickly achieve them and then spend too much time pursuing their own interests on company time.
2. *They are realistic.* If employees believe that goals are too high, they will become discouraged, which will reduce their motivation.
3. *They are specific.* Goals should be established for specific areas of the organization. In other words, broad goals should be divided into smaller goals, which become the responsibility of specific departments and operating units. If specific responsibilities are not assigned, goals are unlikely to be accomplished.
4. *They are measurable.* Although missions are more or less a permanent statement of organizational purpose, goals can actually be obtained. Once they are achieved (or not achieved), it is the responsibility of management to reestablish, alter, or discard them. A goal such as, "The organization will be innovative," is not measurable. A better goal would be, "The organization will patent five new products in the next fiscal year."
5. *They cover a specific time period.* Time periods are an essential factor in all good strategic planning.
6. *They are understood by all affected employees.* If employees do not understand a goal, it is just as if they never heard it. Effective communication of goals is essential to their attainment.
7. *They are set through participative processes.* If managers and employees who are affected by the goals participate in their creation, they will be more committed to them.
8. *Feedback on performance is a part of the process.* When goals are set and then forgotten, organizational members soon learn that they have no meaning.[27]

Several specific types of feedback control are available that can provide information for those stakeholders who are interested in a financial perspective.

Budgets, for example, provide revenue and expense targets. Managers and employees are held responsible for variations that are greater than established tolerances. Sometimes tolerances are not stated, but are implied or are understood due to past budgeting processes. Budgets may also be used to evaluate the performance of managers; however, this procedure can be problematic because it may discourage investments in training, R&D, or new capital equipment due to their short-term impact on expense accounts. If a budget is used to evaluate managerial performance, organizations should consider adding back these types of investments before evaluation. Another alternative is to create separate accounts for longer term investment programs that are independent of the rest of the budget.

Financial ratios are also used to control organizational processes and behavior. Ratios such as ROI or a current ratio are measured against targets that are established on the basis of past performance or in comparison with competing firms. As mentioned previously, overdependence on this type of control, which is often top down in nature, can be dangerous to the long-term performance of firms. However, the real problems manifest themselves when top-down ratio analysis is used as the primary method for controlling organizational processes. A financial ratio such as the current ratio is important to managing working capital and a debt-to-equity ratio can tell an organization whether it is assuming too much financial risk.

It is also common for corporate-level managers to use ratios such as ROI to evaluate the performance of managers of individual business units. As in the case of using budgets to evaluate managerial performance, organizations should consider adding back long-term investments before calculating ROIs. However, another important issue concerns whether this type of measure is even appropriate after it is adjusted. In related diversified firms, ROI-based rewards systems (financial controls) may be inappropriate because they encourage competition among business units instead of the cooperation that is necessary to achieve synergy. Also, since the operations of the various business units should be highly interconnected, it is hard to determine which unit is really most responsible for success. Therefore, in the case of a related diversified firm, business unit ROI is probably an ineffective control measure as it relates to the rewards system.

In related diversified firms, top managers probably should rely more on what are referred to in the field as "strategic controls," which means that business units are evaluated based on more subjective measures of their contributions to the overall strategy of the company. The top managers in these companies have to stay current on what is happening in each of the related business units or "strategic controls" will fail.

However, in an unrelated diversified firm, financial performance ratios may be appropriate for determining the performance of business unit managers. In this situation, organizational managers should be held accountable only for their own financial performance because linkages with other firms in the portfolio are uncommon. Consequently, ROI (after adjustments) may be an appropriate gauge of the performance of business unit managers in unrelated diversified organizations.[28]

Audits are also a type of feedback control system. Audits can provide information to support financial, customer, or internal perspectives, depending on the purpose and design of the audit process. The idea behind an audit is that firm conduct and outcomes are measured against established guidelines and are often performed by independent auditors. Financial audits control accuracy within accounting systems, based on standard, generally accepted accounting principles

Budgets
Feedback controls that provide revenue and expense targets.

Financial Ratios
Feedback controls used to control organizational processes and behavior. Examples are the current ratio, which is important to managing working capital, and the debt-to-equity ratio, which can tell an organization whether it is assuming too much financial risk.

Audits
A type of feedback control system used to provide information to support financial, customer, or internal perspectives. Firm conduct and outcomes are measured against established guidelines.

(GAAP). Social audits control ethical behavior, based on criteria that are established either totally in-house or in conjunction with activist groups, regulatory
agencies, or editors of magazines that compile this sort of information (e.g.,
Business and Society Review).

Customer Surveys
A type of feedback control system used to measure how well established standards for customer satisfaction are being met.

Customer surveys are also used to generate feedback for control. Many companies include customer comment cards inside product cartons or call their customers a few weeks after the purchase. Restaurant chains often leave feedback
cards by their cash registers. In addition, some marketing research firms specialize
in collecting information on customer satisfaction. *Consumer Reports* is one example. As with other control systems, organizations establish standards for customer
satisfaction and then compare the actual to the standard to determine if problems
exist. Sales growth and number of repeat customers are indicators of customer satisfaction as well and can be used as feedback control indicators.

These are only a few examples of an almost limitless number of possible feedback control systems. As information technologies improve, firms are combining
concurrent controls with their traditional systems of feedback controls. Concurrent controls are the topic of the next section.

Concurrent Controls

Concurrent controls are very similar to feedback controls, except that the time
horizon is shortened to "real time." For example, the warning systems that are
built into navigational equipment on an aircraft tell the pilot immediately if the aircraft has fallen below an acceptable altitude. It does not just feed back an aggregate
report at the end of the flight telling the pilot how many times the aircraft fell below acceptable standards. That aggregate feedback information might be important for some uses, such as designing new navigational systems, but it would not
be useful for the pilot. Within a business environment, real-time feedback is also
useful in some instances, but would be a disadvantage in others. Real-time financial feedback, for example, would make managing a business much like operating
on the floor of the stock market—frenetic. On the other hand, real-time controls in
service delivery environments and in production environments can be very useful.

Process Controls. Some of the most common types of concurrent controls are those
associated with production and service processes and with quality standards.
Statistical process control involves setting performance standards for specific
work activities. The employees performing the activities monitor their own performance and the "outputs" of their efforts. If their work is out of specification,
they fix it before handing it off to someone else. In those cases, real-time controls
work to encourage autonomy and improve quality and efficiency.

Other types of concurrent controls are those associated with inventory levels
and order taking. For example, the more successful mail-order firms have real-
time inventory systems that allow them to know when stock is low for a particular item so that a new order can be sent to their manufacturers as soon as needed.
They also use the real-time inventory controls to give customers specific information about what items will be shipped, on what day, and when the customer will
receive them.

Behavioral Controls. Another category of concurrent controls is associated with
control of employee behavior. Within an organization, managers must depend on
employees to perform their duties properly, even when management is not
around. Behavioral controls work to encourage employees to comply with organizational norms and procedures. They are "real time" in that they influence the em-

ployee as the job is being performed. These systems are sometimes referred to as **behavioral controls**.[29] Among the most important of these systems are bureaucratic controls, clan control, and human resources systems.

Bureaucratic control systems consist of rules, procedures, and policies that guide the behavior of organizational members. They are especially appropriate where consistency between employees is important. For example, in an effort to guarantee quality, McDonald's has established standard ways of doing everything from frying french fries to assembling orders.

Rules and procedures outline specific steps for an employee to follow in a particular situation. When a particular problem is routine or arises often, a rule or procedure may be developed so that every employee handles it in a way that is consistent with the organization strategy. Since rules and procedures outline detailed actions, they are usually relevant for very specific situations. Unusual situations and quickly changing business conditions can make an existing procedure obsolete or ineffective.

A **policy** is a more general guide to action. Some policies are stated in very broad terms and communicate the organization's commitment to a guiding principle. They serve to guide behavior in a general sense only (e.g., equal opportunity employer), with specific procedures needed to translate that commitment into action. Other policies are more specific. For example, human resource policies may specify which employees are eligible for training programs or what employee behaviors deserve disciplinary actions. A marketing policy may specify which customers are to get priority order handling, and an operations policy may describe under what conditions an order of raw materials will be rejected. The procedures and policies that most companies employ to govern daily activities such as check approval, returns, bid negotiations, overtime, maintenance, and customer service are all a form of concurrent control, and are intended to ensure consistency of action.

Unfortunately, many companies do not see everyday rules, procedures, and policies as "strategic." However, since they guide the decisions and actions of employees, they are a major determinant of how well strategies are implemented. For example, one of the most successful retailers in the United States, The Gap, makes extensive use of detailed procedures. The Gap replaces most of its merchandise in stores every two months. At that time, all store managers receive a book of detailed instructions specifying exactly where every item of clothing will be displayed. Company procedures also require that white walls be touched up once a week, and wood floors polished every three to four days.[30] Gap management believes this level of procedural detail is necessary to achieve consistency and high levels of performance.

It is also possible for policies and procedures to encourage behavior that works against the strategies of the firm. For example, rules and procedures may stifle employees from improving processes because they feel "rule bound." Merchandise return policies that alienate customers can undermine any attempt at a customer service advantage. Purchasing policies that require bids to be awarded on the basis of price can erode quality. Frequently, reward policies create tensions among interdependent stakeholder groups.

Several years ago, a large chemical company was pursuing an important project: a multimillion dollar process improvement and equipment modification. The upgrade did not involve making a new product, but was initiated by engineering as a way to improve productivity and, ultimately, quality. The new process development

Behavioral Controls
Systems, including bureaucratic control systems, clan control, and human resource systems, that influence the behavior of organizational members.

Bureaucratic Control Systems
Rules, policies, guidelines, and procedures that guide the behavior of organizational members.

Rules and Procedures
Specific steps of actions for an employee to follow in a particular situation.

Policy
A general guideline for employee or organizational actions.

required around-the-clock activity by R&D and plant engineering for many months. When the product was finally commercialized, the improved product quality allowed the sales department to identify new markets and charge higher prices. After a record sales year, the marketing department, as part of a bonus reward policy, was treated to a weekend planning session at an ocean resort with plenty of golf and tennis. The engineers and production employees who had worked around the clock were not included. The undermining of trust and respect among departments was tremendous. The success of the new process was clearly a team effort and required a team reward.

An expert on Japanese management provided the following description of control within Japanese firms:

Japanese firms rely to a great extent upon hiring inexperienced workers, socializing them to accept the company's goals as their own, and compensating them according to length of service, number of dependents, and other nonperformance criteria. It is not necessary for these organizations to measure performance to control or direct their employees, since the employees' natural (socialized) inclination is to do what is best for the firm.[31]

Clan Control
Socialization processes that dictate the type of behavior appropriate in the organization.

According to this description, **clan control** is based on socialization processes through which an individual comes to appreciate the values, abilities, and expected behaviors of an organization.[32] Socialization also makes organizational members more inclined to see things the same way, by espousing common beliefs and assumptions, which, in turn, shape their perceptions. Socialization processes for existing employees take the form of intensive training, mentoring relationships and role models, and formal organizational communications including the vision, mission, and values statements. Clan control is closely linked to the concepts of culture and ethics that were discussed in earlier chapters.

Organizations that want to create, preserve, or alter their organization's culture and ethics often make use of formal and informal orientation programs, mentoring programs, rigorous selection procedures, skills and communications training, and other methods of socialization to instill commitment to organization values. The first step is to define those behaviors that the organization finds important and then stress them in selection, orientation, and training procedures. Some organizations select employees on the basis of their existing personal work-related values. Other organizations prefer to hire young people and then socialize them toward a required set of values that will support the culture of the organization. Either way, human resource management systems play an important role in controlling organizational behavior.

Combining Control Elements

Numerous control systems at multiple levels are necessary to keep an organization and its component parts headed in the right directions. However, they should be integrated in such a way that information can be shared. In other words, information from all parts of the organization should be accessible when and where it is needed to improve organizational processes.

To enhance the quantity and quality of organizational learning, comprehensive organizational control systems should have the following characteristics:

1. Information generated by the control systems should be an important and recurring item to be addressed by the highest levels of management.
2. The control process should also be given frequent and regular attention from operating managers at all levels of the organization.

3. Data from the system should be interpreted and discussed in face-to-face meetings among superiors and subordinates.
4. The success of the control process relies on the continual challenge and debate of underlying data, assumptions, and strategies.[33]

A well-designed strategic control system should provide feedback for ongoing, iterative adjustments in direction, resources allocations, and management priorities. When performance suffers, a strategic control system may provide early warnings of performance problems, but it cannot prevent them. Unfortunately some managers find, through their control systems or too late, that their organization's performance does not fit with their expectations, or the expectations of their interested stakeholders.

With the concepts and processes of control behind us, we are now in a position to discuss a special type of control that is specifically designed to prevent major disasters.

CRISIS PREVENTION AND MANAGEMENT

Organizational crises are critical situations that threaten high-priority organizational goals, impose a severe restriction on the amount of time in which key members of the organization can respond, and contain elements of surprise.[34] While crises such as natural disasters can sometimes be avoided, they are hard to control. On the other hand, managers have more control over the incidence and resolution of human-induced organizational crises. Examples of these crises include the explosion of the space shuttle *Challenger*, the injection of cyanide into Tylenol pain capsules, and the explosion of the Chernobyl nuclear reactor in the Soviet Union.

Figure 9.6 contains a model of the five phases of crisis management. Organizations that ignore crises until they are involved in one will spend most of their time in the containment and recovery stages, essentially mopping up the damage. On the other hand, crisis-prepared organizations establish early detection systems and prepare for or even prevent crises from occurring (left side of the model). The learning processes depicted at the bottom of the model are similar to the cause-and-effect processes in the broad model of control introduced at the beginning of this chapter. An organization that learns from crises can improve its ability to prevent, detect, or recover from them.

Studies conducted at the University of Southern California Center for Crisis Management have identified crisis-prone organizations as those having the following characteristics:

1. If these organizations prepare at all, they prepare for only a few of the possible types of crises. Furthermore, their preparations are fragmented and compartmentalized.
2. They focus on only one aspect of a crisis, and only after it has already occurred.
3. They only consider technical factors (as opposed to human or social) in the cause or prevention of crises.
4. They consider few, if any, stakeholders in an explicit fashion.[35]

With regard to stakeholders, the key questions organizations should ask are "Who are the individuals, organizations, groups and institutions that can affect as well as be affected by CM (crisis management)? Can the stakeholders who will be involved in any crisis be analyzed systematically?"[36] As in other types of stakeholder management, open communication with important stakeholders is essential to success.

Organizational Crises
Critical situations that threaten high-priority organizational goals, impose a severe restriction on the amount of time in which key members of the organization can respond, and contain elements of surprise.

Figure 9.6 *The Five Phases of Crisis Management*

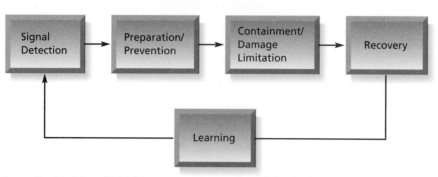

Source: Reprinted from "Crisis Management: Cutting Through the Confusion," by I. I. Mitroff, *Sloan Management Review* (Winter 1988), p. 19, by permission of publisher. Copyright © 1988 by the Sloan Management Review Association. All rights reserved.

Organizations can take steps to control organizational crises. These activities fall into the categories of strategic actions, technical and structural actions, evaluation and diagnostic actions, communication actions, and psychological and cultural actions (see Strategic Application 9.2).

In summary, organizational crises have the potential to thwart organizational efforts toward the accomplishment of goals. However, the Japanese symbol for crisis is made up of two characters. One elaborate character symbolizes threats, and one simple character symbolizes opportunities. Crisis prevention and management programs represent yet another opportunity for organizations to develop distinctive competencies. Distinctive competencies in these areas may be hard to detect, because it is hard to measure, in financial terms, savings from a disaster that does not occur or whose negative effects are reduced. However, as more and more organizations suffer blows from large-scale crises, it is evident that effective crisis prevention and management is critical to steady long-term performance.

Summary

Strategic controls consist of systems to support managers in tracking progress toward organizational vision and goals and ensuring that organizational processes and the behavior of organizational members are consistent with those goals.

Feedforward control helps managers anticipate changes in the external and internal environments, based on analysis of inputs from stakeholders and the remote environment. Feedback control provides managers with information concerning outcomes from organizational activities, which is then used as a basis for comparison with the targets that have been established. Concurrent controls, including process and behavior controls, provide real-time interaction and guidance. The learning processes associated with all three types of control form the basis for changes to strategic direction, strategies, implementation plans, or even the targets themselves, if they are deemed to be unreasonable given current conditions. Control systems are developed at the corporate, business, functional, and operating levels in an organization.

Development of an integrated strategic control system entails determining which factors require control, identifying appropriate measures on which to determine success or failure, and integrating and interpreting intelligence information. The factors that are to be controlled should reflect the interests of various stakeholder groups inside and outside of the organization.

STRATEGIC APPLICATION 9.2

CRISIS MANAGEMENT STRATEGIC CHECKLIST

Strategic Actions

1. Integrate crisis management (CM) into strategic planning processes.
2. Integrate CM into statements of corporate excellence.
3. Include outsiders on the board and on CM teams.
4. Provide training and workshops in CM.
5. Expose organizational members to crisis simulations.
6. Create a diversity or portfolio of CM strategies.

Technical and Structural Actions

1. Create a CM team.
2. Dedicate budget expenditures for CM.
3. Establish accountabilities for updating emergency policies/manuals.
4. Computerize inventories of CM resources (e.g., employee skills).
5. Designate an emergency command control room.
6. Assure technological redundancy in vital areas (e.g., computer systems).
7. Establish working relationships with outside experts in CM.

Evaluation and Diagnostic Actions

1. Conduct legal and financial audit of threats and liabilities.
2. Modify insurance coverage to match CM contingencies.
3. Conduct environmental impact studies.

4. Prioritize activities necessary for daily operations.
5. Establish tracking system for early warning signals.
6. Establish tracking system to follow up past crises or near crises.

Communication Actions

1. Provide training for dealing with the media regarding CM.
2. Improve communication lines with local communities.
3. Improve communication with intervening stakeholders (e.g., police).

Psychological and Cultural Actions

1. Increase visibility of strong top management commitment to CM.
2. Improve relationships with activist groups.
3. Improve upward communication (including "whistleblowers")
4. Improve downward communication regarding CM programs/accountabilities
5. Provide training regarding human and emotional impacts of crises.
6. Provide psychological support services (e.g., stress/anxiety management)
7. Reinforce symbolic recall/corporate memory of past crises/dangers.

Source: I.I. Mitroff and C. Pearson, "From Crisis Prone to Crisis Prepared: A Systematic and Integrative Framework for Crisis Management," *Academy of Management Executive* (February 1993), p. 58. Used with permission.

Crisis prevention and management systems are a special type of control specifically designed to prevent major disasters. Organizational crises are critical situations that threaten high-priority organizational goals, impose a severe restriction on the amount of time in which key members of the organization can respond, and contain elements of surprise. Organizations can take steps to control organizational crises. Crisis prevention and management activities fall into the general categories of strategic actions, technical and structural actions, evaluation and diagnostic actions, communication actions, and psychological and cultural actions. While the potential for a crisis is a threat to an organization, it may also represent an opportunity to develop a distinctive competence.

Discussion Questions

1. Describe the problems associated with traditional top-down accounting-based controls. Are they ever appropriate? In what circumstances?

2. What is a control system? What is the difference between feedback, feedforward, and concurrent control? Give examples of each type.

3. In what ways does a business intelligence system support feedforward premise control? Give an example of how a university might develop a system for premise control.

4. Describe the steps associated with developing a strategic control system. Use a university as your example.

5. Name at least five of the most important factors that require control in organizations, including the stakeholder perspectives they represent. Include ideas concerning possible control measures or processes for each one.

6. Define bureaucratic control and clan control. Can these types of behavioral control exist in organizations with more formal control systems? Is it possible for bureaucratic and clan controls to be operating as planned while financial feedback performance measures are out of control? Give an example.

7. What are the characteristics of accident-prone organizations? Name ten things organizations can do to control organizational crises. Using library resources, research a recent crisis. Did the organization experiencing the crisis attempt any of the ten?

References

1. A. Barrett, "Feeling a Bit Insecure: Overexpansion and Too Rosy Forecast Plague Pinkerton," *Business Week* (September 28, 1992), pp. 69–72; "Bogie's Men: Pinkerton," *The Economist* (October 5, 1991), p. 73; "Pinkerton's Reports Earnings Pressures, Revises 1992 Earnings Expectations," *Newswire* (June 19, 1992), p. 0618A1456; "Two Investors Charge Pinkerton's Misled Them to Inflate Stock," *Wall Street Journal* (June 26, 1992), p. A7.

2. P. Lorange, M. F. Scott Morton, and S. Ghoshal, *Strategic Control* (St. Paul, Minn.: West Publishing Company, 1986), p. 10.

3. R. Simons, "How New Top Managers Use Control Systems As Levers of Strategic Renewal," *Strategic Management Journal* 15 (1994), pp. 169–189.

4. R. Simons, "Strategic Orientation and Management Attention to Control Systems," *Strategic Management Journal* 12 (1991), pp. 49-62.

5. H. T. Johnson and R. S. Kaplan, *Relevance Lost: The Rise and Fall of Management Accounting* (Boston, Mass.: Harvard Business School Press, 1987), pp. 10–18.

6. J. F. Weston and E. F. Brigham, *Essentials of Managerial Finance*, 7th ed. (Hinsdale, Ill.: The Dryden Press, 1985), p. 154.

7. O. E. Williamson, *Markets and Hierarchies: Analysis and Antitrust Applications* (New York: The Free Press, 1975).

8. A. Lee, *Call Me Roger* (Chicago: Contemporary Books, 1988), p. 110.

9. Johnson and Kaplan, *Relevance Lost*, p. 1.

10. R. E. Hoskisson and M. A. Hitt, "Strategic Control and Relative R&D Investment in Large Multiproduct Firm," *Strategic Management Journal* 6 (1988), pp. 605–622.

11. P. Sellers, "The Dumbest Marketing Ploy," *Fortune* (October 5, 1992), pp. 88–89.

12. Sellers, "The Dumbest," p. 88.

13. R. H. Hayes and W. J. Abernathy, "Managing Our Way to Economic Decline," *Harvard Business Review* (July–August 1980), pp. 67–77; H. T. Johnson, "Managing by Remote Control: Recent Management Accounting Practice in Historical Perspective," in P. Temin, ed., *Inside the Business Enterprise: Historical Perspectives on the Use of Information* (Chicago: The University of Chicago Press, 1991), pp. 41–66.

14. H. T. Johnson, *Relevance Regained: From Top-Down Control to Bottom-up Empowerment* (New York: The Free Press, 1990), p. 30.

15. This entire paragraph is based on P. F. Drucker, "The Economy's Power Shift," *The Wall Street Journal* (September 24, 1992).

16. R. S. Kaplan and D. P. Norton, "Putting the Balanced Scoreboard to Work," *Harvard Business Review* (September–October 1993), 134–147.

17. Lorange, Scott Morton, and Ghoshal, *Strategic Control*, pp. 2–8.

18. G. Schreyogg and H. Steinmann, "Strategic Control: A New Perspective," *Academy of Management Review* 12 (1987), p. 96.

19. S. Ghoshal and S. K. Kim, "Building Effective Intelligence Systems for Competitive Advantage," *Sloan Management Review* (Fall 1986), p. 49.

20. J. P. Stamen, "Decision Support Systems Help Planners Hit Their Targets," *The Journal of Business Strategy* (March–April 1990), pp. 30–33.

21. J. Rothfeder, J. Bartimo, and L. Therrien, "How Software Is Making Food Sales a Piece of Cake," *Business Week* (July 2, 1990), pp. 54–55.

22. J. P. Herring, "Building a Business Intelligence System," *Journal of Business Strategy* (May–June 1988), pp. 4–9.

23. W. R. Haines, "Making Corporate Planning Work in Developing Countries," *Long Range Planning* (April 1988), pp. 91–96.

24. R. S. Teitelbaum, "The New Race for Intelligence," *Fortune* (November 2, 1992), p. 104.

25. R. T. Lenz and J. L. Engledow, "Environmental Analysis Units and Strategic Decision-making: A Field Study of Selected "Leading-Edge" Corporations," *Strategic Management Journal* 7 (1986), pp. 69–89.

26. M. Goold and J. J. Quinn, "The Paradox of Strategic Controls," *Strategic Management Journal* 11 (1990), pp. 43–57.

27. G. P. Latham and E. A. Locke, "Goal Setting—A Motivational Technique That Works," *Organizational Dynamics* (Autumn 1979), pp. 68–80; M. D. Richards, *Setting Strategic Goals and Objectives,* 2nd ed. (St. Paul, Minn.: West Publishing, 1986); M. E. Tubbs, "Goal Setting: A Meta-Analytic Examination of Empirical Evidence," *Journal of Applied Psychology* 3 (1986), pp. 474–475.

28. C. W. L. Hill and R. E. Hoskisson, "Strategy and Structure in the Multiproduct Firm," *Academy of Management Review* 12 (1987), pp. 331–341.

29. V. Govindarajan and J. Fisher, "Strategy, Control Systems, and Resource Sharing: Effects on Business Unit Performance," *Academy of Management Journal* 33 (1990), pp. 259–285.

30. R. Mitchell, "Inside the Gap," *Business Week* (March 9, 1992), pp. 58–64.

31. W. G. Ouchi, "Markets, Bureaucracies and Clans," *Administrative Science Quarterly* 25 (1992), pp. 129–141.

32. P. McDonald and J. Gandz, "Getting Value from Shared Values, " *Organization Dynamics* (Winter 1992), pp. 60–71.

33. R. Simons, "Strategic Orientation," p. 50.

34. C. F. Hermann, ed., *International Crises: Insights from Behavioral Research* (New York: The Free Press, 1972).

35. I. I. Mitroff and C. Pearson, "From Crisis Prone to Crisis Prepared: A Systematic and Integrative Framework for Crisis Management" *Academy of Management Executive* (February 1993), pp. 48–59.

36. Mitroff and Pearson, "From Crisis Prone to Crisis Prepared."

10

Corporate Restructuring

The World's Biggest Company Is in Trouble

Does the world's biggest company have a future? Some seasoned analysts see Mitsubishi Corp. of Tokyo as a "lumbering, prehistoric beast that has outlived its epoch" and "should roll over and die." Although harsh, these doomsday analysts have a point. The core business that built the trading company—hauling raw materials into Japan and speeding finished goods out into the world—has been declining for more than a decade.

Mitsubishi's annual revenues of $176 billion are indeed gigantic. Mitsubishi's revenues are bigger than those of AT&T, DuPont, Citicorp, and Procter & Gamble combined. In serving its 45,000 customers, Mitsubishi moves as many as 100,000 products, from kernels of corn to huge power generators, around the world. Among the dozens of properties it owns outright are all or parts of cattle feedlots and coal mines in Australia, pulp mills and iron ore mines in Canada, copper mines in Chile, a resort in Hawaii, and the liquefied natural gas fields off the coast of Brunei that have made the sultan of that tiny state one of the world's richest men. The sultan may be thriving, but Mitsubishi is scraping by on meager earnings of $219 million. That translates into a pintsize profit margin of just 12%.

Minoru Makihara, chief executive since 1992, is keenly aware of Mitsubishi's difficult plight. His challenge: to persuade subordinates, who may have become too comfortable, that the need for transformation is urgent. "We have to change the contents of our business," says Makihara. "But in order to change the business, I have to create a sense of crisis. If you are running IBM, you can create a sense of crisis by firing people. Tradition won't allow me to do that here." Makihara believes he must impress on his troops how vital it is to become truly global, to invest in faraway businesses that have no ties to Japan. He also believes the company should have a major place in the multimedia business.[1]

No strategy or organizational design works indefinitely. If a firm is successful with its strategies, that success *alone* will create a need for change, because the increases in sales volume and organization size will demand different management methods and organization structures. What is just as typical, however, is for customers, competitors, and technologies to interact to create a changing business environment, which will require that the organization make changes also. Unless a firm is the permanent sole participant in a no-growth industry (which is extremely unlikely), change is constant and should be assumed. The iterative, ongoing strategic management process described in this book, with its continuous scanning of the internal and external environments and its reevaluation of strategies and implementation methods, is all about the management of change over time.

Researchers have observed that as organizations evolve over time they tend to move through a period of convergence, followed by a period of reorientation or radical adjustment, with a continuation of the convergence–reorientation cycle over time.[2] During the convergence stage, the organization makes minor adapative changes to strategies, but for the most part follows a consistent approach. During this time, the structure and systems are more or less stable and performance is acceptable.

For many organizations, the successes reinforce a certain way of doing business. During the convergence stage, managers develop certain mental models, or mind-sets, about how the industry and the organization work. **Mental models** represent the knowledge managers have about the industry and the organization, and how specific actions relate to desired outcomes.[3] It is what they understand to be true about the organization and its industry. The mental models are derived from experiences, with past successes and failures contributing to the overall picture. As long as the premises that underlie these mental models do not change, the mental models represent useful experience that *should* be brought to bear on decisions. When premises do change, however, the established mental models may prevent the executives, managers, and employees from recognizing the *need* for change at all.

A few well-known examples will illustrate this point. In the automotive industry several years ago and in the minicomputer industry more recently, established management mental models contributed to a sluggish response to industry change.[4] In both industries, the established competitors had achieved extraordinary, sustained success. They had effective strategies, useful structures, and strong cultures. When the assumptions underlying their industries changed, the existing competitors were slow to recognize what was happening. In the automotive industry, competitors failed to recognize the demographic, economic, and social trends driving demand for fuel-efficient economy cars, or the potential competitive threat from German and Japanese automakers. In the minicomputer industry, competitors failed to recognize that networked microcomputers would take the place of minicomputers.

Not only were they slow to recognize the need for change, they were also slow to make changes once the need was recognized. In other words, the out-of-sync mental models combined with established organizational structures, resources, and processes to create high levels of inertia, or reluctance to change course.

You should be asking yourself, "What about the feedforward control systems we read about in the last chapter? Why didn't these firms use the information that was available to them to question their own premises?" The answer is, for the most part, we don't know. Managers in these firms did not recognize and respond to change until firm performance began to suffer. One of the limitations of human de-

Mental Models
The knowledge managers have about the industry and the organization, and how specific actions relate to desired outcomes.

cision making is that often we succumb to perceptual distortion. The information that does not fit our preconceived mental model is just not seen at all. As one researcher recently described it, "The writing on the wall cannot be read. . . ."[5]

A period of convergence can continue indefinitely, as long as the industry conditions and organization characteristics are not significantly out of alignment.[6] However, when gradual drift results in a substantial misalignment or an environmental discontinuity occurs, the organization will be forced to reorient itself. A **reorientation** is a significant realignment of organization strategies, structure, and processes with the new environmental realities.[7] Transformation, renewal, reorientation, and restructuring are all words that describe the same general phenomenon: a radical change in how business is conducted. In the next section, we discuss some of the restructuring tactics that managers employ.

Reorientation
A significant realignment of organization strategies, structure, and processes with the new environmental realities.

REORIENTATION THROUGH RESTRUCTURING

Restructuring has become commonplace in recent years.[8] Many large companies like Mitsubishi are experiencing performance declines that are causing corporate-level managers to rethink their organizations. Apple Computer, once described as the "Magic Kingdom" during the mid-1980s, is now cutting product lines and approaching new markets in an attempt to survive.[9] Even David Glass, CEO of Wal-Mart, is rethinking his company's strategy. The discount retailing giant, after a string of ninety-nine straight quarters of growth in earnings, recently experienced its first decline.[10]

Disgruntled stakeholders are often the force that causes corporate-level managers to consider restructuring. For example, stockholders may be dissatisfied with their financial returns or debt rating agencies such as Standard and Poor's may devalue firm securities due to high risk. If an organization has spent many years diversifying in various and sundry directions, top managers may feel as though the organization is "out of control." This feeling of loss of control is also related to organizational size. In the largest organizations, top managers may even be unfamiliar with some of the businesses in their portfolios. Also, many organizations have acquired high levels of debt, often associated with acquisitions. For these companies, even small economic downturns can be a rude awakening to the risks associated with high leverage.[11]

On the other hand, some authors suggest that restructuring should be a continuous process.[12] Changes in global markets and technology have created a permanent need for firms to focus on what they do best and divest any parts of their organizations that are no longer contributing to their missions or long-term goals.

Regardless of reason, restructuring typically involves a renewed emphasis on the things an organization does well, combined with a variety of tactics to revitalize the organization and strengthen its competitive position. Popular restructuring tactics include refocusing corporate assets on distinctive competencies, retrenchment, Chapter XI reorganization, leveraged buyouts, and organizational changes. Organizations may use any one or a combination of these strategies in restructuring efforts.

Refocusing Corporate Assets

Refocusing activities are generally viewed favorably by external stakeholders such as the financial community.[13] Refocusing entails trimming businesses that are not consistent with the strategic direction of the organization. This type of refocusing is often called downscoping. **Downscoping** involves reducing diversification by

Downscoping
Reducing diversification by selling nonessential businesses not related to the organization's major businesses.

selling off nonessential businesses that are not related to the organization's core competencies and capabilities.[14]

Researchers have discovered that most restructuring companies are moving in the direction of reducing their diversification as opposed to increasing it. Furthermore, they discovered an increase in research associated with this type of restructuring. You may recall from Chapter 7 that this is the opposite of the impact acquisitions can have in reducing innovative activity.[15]

On the other hand, sell-offs that do not improve the strategic focus of the organization may signal failure or market retreat, which can cause concern among stakeholders such as owners, debt holders, and the financial community. For instance, the stock market tends to react positively to divestitures linked to corporate-level or business-level strategies and negatively to divestitures that are portrayed as simply getting rid of unwanted assets.[16]

Divestiture
The sale of a business unit—a reverse acquisition.

A **divestiture** is a reverse acquisition. One type of divestiture is a sell-off, in which a business unit is sold to another firm or, in the case of a leveraged buyout, to the business unit's managers. For example, Chrysler agreed to sell most of its aerospace and defense holdings to Raytheon, and Mobil is planning to sell its real-estate development arm to an investment fund.[17] In another move in the aerospace industry, Rockwell sold its aerospace and defense assets to Boeing.

Another form of divestiture is the spin-off, which means that current shareholders are issued a proportional number of shares in the spun-off business. For example, if a shareholder owns 100 shares of XYZ company and the company spins off business unit J, the shareholder would then own 100 shares of XYZ company and 100 shares of an independently operated company called J. The key advantage of a spin-off relative to other divestiture options is that shareholders still have the option of retaining ownership in the spun-off business. General Motors spun off EDS, but kept a ten-year contract in which EDS will continue to provide computer services to GM. Also, Corning, unable to sell its $1.6 billion laboratory-testing business, spun it off to shareholders.[18]

The businesses that should be divested during a restructuring include those that have little to do with the distinctive competencies of the organization. An obvious example is when Johnson & Johnson, the consumer-oriented drug and toiletry giant, sold their sausage casings company.[19] Also, W. R. Grace, one of the largest chemical companies, refocused its efforts away from basic chemistry and toward chemical conversion processes. Grace has already sold several companies and will have sold off 43% of its business portfolio when restructuring is completed, representing sales of nearly $3 billion.[20] Other examples include General Mills's departure from retailing, Sears's withdrawal from mail-order catalogs, and Xerox's retreat from financial services.[21]

Refocusing may also involve new acquisitions or new ventures to round out a corporate portfolio or add more strength in an area that is essential to corporate distinctive competencies.[22] For instance, Grand Metropolitan bought Pillsbury and simultaneously sold Bennigans and Steak & Ale restaurants in an effort to redefine its domain in the food processing industry.[23] Also, American Airlines, tired of losses in its airline segment, is headed in the direction of diversifying away from flying.[24]

Retrenchment

Retrenchment
A turnaround strategy that may involve selling or liquidating unprofitable business units, workforce reductions, tighter cost or quality controls, or new emphasis on quality or efficiency.

Retrenchment is a turnaround strategy. It can involve such tactics as workforce reductions, closing unprofitable plants, outsourcing unprofitable activities, implementation of tighter cost or quality controls, or new policies that emphasize quality or efficiency. Chrysler Corporation, under the leadership of Lee Iacocca, combined many of these tactics in its amazing recovery more than a decade ago. Chrysler cut the workforce and emphasized quality, which included a five-year, 50,000-mile warranty on its automobiles. Lee Iacocca used a variety of tools, including media releases, television commercials, and speeches, to convince the American public of the "New Chrysler Corporation."

Nabisco, currently involved in a major retrenchment program, plans to cut 4,200 jobs and eliminate slower selling products. ConAgra, the food processing giant, will eliminate 6,500 jobs and close or reconfigure twenty-nine production plants.[25] In the early 1990s, Amoco, one of the largest oil companies in the United States, set out on a retrenchment strategy of major proportions:

> *Amoco Corp. undertook a restructuring that included cutting 8,500 jobs, or 16% of its work force, and taking an $800 million charge. The charge covered the costs of selling and abandoning oil and gas fields, disposing of various chemical operations at a loss, the write-down of a number of assets, and the expenses associated with the job reductions. "The human impact of our decisions is very real and very painful," said H. Laurance Fuller, Amoco's chairman. Mr. Fuller wrote a letter to all employees in April that Amoco needed to make "an extraordinary effort to identify and eliminate unnecessary costs" and that layoffs were inevitable.[26]*

Workforce reductions, sometimes called downsizing, have become commonplace in organizations in the United States, as a response to the burgeoning bureaucracies in the post–WWII era. Even the military has a new focus on a "lighter fighter" division that can respond faster to combat situations. The great mystery is that some companies continue to lay off employees in spite of record profits. For example, in 1995 Mobil posted "soaring" first quarter earnings and then announced plans to cut 4,700 jobs.[27]

The evidence is mounting that "downsizing does not reduce expenses as much as desired, and that sometimes expenses may actually increase."[28] Certainly, severance packages are one reason for the increase. Nabisco will take a $300 million charge to cover its restructuring, while ConAgra will spend $505 million. Also, a study of "white-collar" layoffs in the U.S. automobile industry found that most companies experienced problems such as a reduction in quality, a loss in productivity, decreased effectiveness, lost trust, increased conflict, and low morale.[29] Strategic Insight 10.1 contains comments from middle managers that provide evidence of many of these problems associated not only with layoffs, but with retrenchment activities in general.

Many organizations cut muscle, as well as fat, through layoffs. One reason the muscle is cut is that some of the best employees leave, either because of attractive severance packages or fear of future job loss. Because the best employees can usually get new jobs fairly easily, they may decide to leave while all of their options are open to them. Also, studies have shown that the "surviving" employees experience feelings of guilt and fear, which may hurt productivity or organizational loyalty.[30] It is not surprising, then, that the stock market often reacts unfavorably to announcements of major layoffs.[31]

A survey by the American Management Association of 1,142 companies that had been involved in workforce reductions indicates that about half of these companies were poorly prepared for these activities.[32] One of the keys to successful downsizing, then, may be sufficient preparation with regard to outplacement, new reporting relationships, and training.

Of course, another important element in all successful restructuring activities, especially workforce reductions, is effective communication with and examination

STRATEGIC INSIGHT 10.1

BUSINESS

STRATEGY

Voices of Survivors: Words That Downsizing CEOs Should Hear

Middle managers play a crucial role in corporate downsizing and restructuring as they evaluate and implement a strategy that is emotionally demanding and non-traditional. The following statements are from middle managers who, for the time being, have survived layoffs in their companies. They demonstrate a full range of emotions, most of which are potentially damaging to the organization.

Anger

> *Stop blaming us! We've been loyal to the company. We've worked hard, and did everything we were told. We've moved for the company; we've traveled for the company; and we've taken on extra work for the company. And now you say we did wrong. You told us to do it. Management told us to do it! And the company did pretty well while we did it. Stop blaming us!*

Anxiety/Confusion

> *Who are we? The company used to stand for something. We all wore our company pins proudly. But now, I don't know who we are anymore. I've got a notion that we're meaner and leaner—but isn't everybody else? And is that who we want to be. . . ?*

Cynicism

> *I understand that these are hard times. But how come we are the worst? Everyone in the industry is going through a downturn, but not everyone is feeling the heat the way we are. We've downsized more, but our stock and credit rating is still bad. What happened to make us the worst?*

Resentment

> *There's a double standard here. We lined up everything that needed to be cut. We set priorities. We participated. Did the executive dining room go? No! Did the corporate helicopter go? No! Who's kidding whom?*

Retribution

> *Why don't you leave? Get out, and let us get on with the business. Leave the company, and let us build a new one.*

Hope

> *We want to be the best. Lead us there!*
> *Give us a mission, a vision. . . .*

Source: Adapted from H.M. O'Neill and D.J. Lenn, "Voices of Survivors: Words that Downsizing CEOs Should Hear," *Academy of Management Executive* (November 1995), pp. 23–33. Used with permission.

of the needs of key stakeholders.[33] Managers anticipating layoffs should combine caring with cost consciousness and "humanize" their approaches to workforce reductions.[34] Many organizations are avoiding layoffs through hiring freezes, restricting overtime, retraining and redeploying workers, switching workers to part time, starting job-sharing programs, giving unpaid vacations, shortening the workweek, or reducing pay.[35]

Chapter XI Reorganization

An organization that is in serious financial trouble can voluntarily file for Chapter XI protection under the Federal Bankruptcy Code: "Chapter XI provides a proceeding for an organization to work out a plan or arrangement for solving its financial problems under the supervision of a federal court. It is intended primarily for debtors who feel they can solve their financial problems on their own if given sufficient time, and if relieved of some pressure."[36] Strategic Insight 10.2 describes a company that was able to turn things around after filing Chapter XI.

One of the major disadvantages of Chapter XI is that, after filing, all subsequent managerial decisions of substance must be approved by a court. Thus, managerial discretion and flexibility are reduced. One organizational response to this problem is the **prepackaged reorganization strategy.** Firms using this strategy negotiate a reorganization plan with creditors *before* filing Chapter XI. Consequently, the courts stay out of the picture until after a tentative agreement is reached. Two attorneys who specialize in prepackaged reorganizations list four ingredients for success:

Prepackaged Reorganization Strategy Reorganization plan negotiated with creditors before a firm files Chapter XI.

1. A realistic assessment of financial problems by management.
2. Willingness and ability of management to incur the professional fees that are necessary to carry out the prepackaged reorganization. Lawyers, accountants, investment bankers, and others are necessary to work out the details. Organizations will either have to pay the costs now or later—they are not avoidable.
3. Formulation of a reorganization plan that is acceptable to most of the organization's creditors. Also, if there are too many creditors, negotiations may not be feasible.
4. A creditor group that is willing to negotiate. Some creditors insist on litigation instead of negotiation.[37]

Although Chapter XI, if executed properly, can provide firms with time and protection as they attempt to reorganize, it is not a panacea for firms with financial problems. Also, researchers do not agree on the potential for successful reorganization. Some researchers have argued that it is in the best interests of organizations that are facing high amounts of adversity to quickly select Chapter XI (instead of having it imposed on them), unless they have high levels of organizational slack.[38] On the other hand, in a recent study of firms that had voluntarily filed for Chapter XI protection, only a little over half of the firms were "nominally successful in reorganizing," and "two-thirds of those retained less than 50 percent of their assets on completion of the reorganization process."[39] While larger firms had a better chance of successfully reorganizing, Chapter XI should probably still be used as a strategy of last resort.

Leveraged Buyouts

Leveraged buyouts (LBOs) involve private purchase of a business unit by managers, employees, unions, or private investors. They are called *leveraged* because

STRATEGIC INSIGHT 10.2

BUSINESS

STRATEGY

FM Corporation Survives Chapter XI

The FM Corporation of Rogers, Arkansas, manufactures custom molded structural plastics. In late 1984, FM was on the verge of financial collapse after auditors found a loss of $3 million due to inventory problems. Their banks promptly lowered FM's credit limit and demanded they settle all accounts while the board of directors called for completely new management. Employee morale bottomed out because job security was uncertain. The corporation was finally forced to file for Chapter XI protection.

To tackle its inventory problems, FM Corporation's management team implemented a total review of the costing system to confirm all costs—direct and indirect. Materials were identified and tracked through production and a physical inventory was taken every month.

Understanding the urgency of the situation, all associates pulled together to save the corporation and their jobs. A profit-sharing plan and other benefits were introduced to reward and retain good employees. Training and improved management techniques were employed, including the use of some outside consultants.

The final step in saving FM Corporation was to implement a revamped marketing program. Rather than competing with larger, stronger firms on high-volume business, they focused instead on providing value-added services to current customers. Computerized production schedule and inventory transactions provided more reliable data in a format that allowed better control and this, in turn, meant faster, more reliable service for its customers.

FM Corporation was able to find new investors willing to provide the cash that permitted the managers more time to reorganize and develop a plan to remain on sound financial ground. In December 1986, the court approved a plan allowing the corporation's successful emergence from Chapter XI, a feat achieved by only 20% of the companies that file for it.

The FM Corporation is now a reliable supplier with an excellent reputation. It was named supplier of the year in 1989 and 1990 by its largest customer. Remarkably, its market position has been greatly enhanced during an economic period that saw many of its competitors lose business. Its dedication to customer satisfaction has even resulted in FM being asked to participate, through early supplier involvement, in the engineering and manufacture of new products for many *Fortune* 500 companies.

Source: Adapted from "FM Corporation," *Strengthening America's Competitiveness: The Blue Chip Enterprise Initiative* (Warner Books on behalf of Connecticut Mutual Life Insurance Company and the U.S. Chamber of Commerce, 1991), pp. 89–90.

much of the money that is used to purchase the business unit is borrowed from financial intermediaries (often at higher-than-normal interest rates). Because of high leverage, LBOs are often accompanied by selling off assets to repay debt. Consequently, organizations typically become smaller and more focused after an LBO. Strategic Insight 10.3 describes a highly successful LBO.

During the late 1970s and early 1980s, LBOs gained a good reputation as a means of turning around failing divisions. For instance, Hart Ski, once a subsidiary

STRATEGIC INSIGHT 10.3

BUSINESS

STRATEGY

Kelly Truck Line—A Small LBO That Worked

Kelly Truck Line, Inc., located in Pittsburg, Kansas, has 185 employees. Founded in 1957, the trucking company has bases in Kansas, Missouri, Texas, Ohio, and Arkansas.

When Michael Kelly entered into a leveraged buyout of the existing business, things were looking pretty grim. At the same time its new insurance carrier, after a 300% rate increase, went into receivership while holding $143,000 of the company's money in deposit. The company had negative net worth. Also, its aging truck fleet's newest vehicle was four years old and the newest trailer was five years old. To survive, Kelly Truck Line had to take some drastic steps.

Kelly decided to specialize in one area of business, selling off all trailer types except the flatbeds. Proceeds were used to reduce debt. Kelly then hired an outside sales staff and implemented an incentive program for salespersons, customer service department dispatchers, and their drivers. The company systematically replaced its aging fleet with new trucks and trailers while tripling its size. A new computer system relieved paper congestion and allowed the company to communicate with customers through electronic data interchange.

During a span of five years, Kelly Truck Line retired all of its debt from the leveraged buyout and completed replacement of its aging fleet. It has grown from a $5.5 million a year company to $14 million and has been able to attract major corporations as clients throughout the country.

Source: Adapted from "Kelly Truck Line, Inc.," *Strengthening America's Competitiveness: The Blue Chip Enterprise Initiative* (Warner Books on behalf of Connecticut Mutual Life Insurance Company and the U.S. Chamber of Commerce, 1991), p. 152.

of Beatrice, was revived through an LBO led by the son of one of its founders. Also, managers and the union joined forces to turn around American Safety Razor, a failing division of Philip Morris. These LBOs benefited many of these organizations' stakeholders, including employees and local communities.[40]

However, some researchers have discovered that LBOs stifle innovation and research and development, similar to mergers and acquisitions.[41] Others have found that LBO firms have comparatively slower growth in sales and employees and that they tend to divest a larger proportion of both noncore and core businesses, compared to firms that remained public.[42] Also, some executives who initiate LBOs seem to receive an excessive return. For example, John Kluge made a $3 billion profit in two years by dismantling Metromedia following an LBO.[43] Consequently, some businesspeople are starting to wonder if LBOs are really in the best interests of all stakeholders. Plant closings, relocations, and workforce reductions are all common results from LBOs. Some LBOs are accomplished, as in the case of Metromedia, primarily to gain a short-term profit, regardless of the consequences. It is the responsibility of the board of directors to ensure that stakeholder interests are considered prior to approving an LBO:

When considering a leveraged buyout, board members must treat fairly not only shareholders but other stakeholders as well. Corporate groups—employees, cred-

itors, customers, suppliers, and local communities—claim the right to object to leveraged buyouts on the ground that they have made a larger investment in and have a more enduring relationship with the corporation than do persons who trade share certificates daily on the stock exchanges. . . . Similarly, if short-run profit is at the expense of and violates the expectations of employees, customers, communities, or suppliers, companies will find themselves unable to do business. The better employees will leave. Customers will stop buying. Communities will refuse to extend services. Suppliers will minimize their exposure.[44]

Not surprisingly, reports of failed LBOs are becoming more common. Successful LBOs require buying a company at the right price with the right financing, combined with outstanding management and fair treatment of stakeholders.[45]

Changes to Organizational Design

Organizational design, which was discussed in detail in Chapter 8, can be a potent force in restructuring efforts. As organizations diversify, top managers have a more difficult time processing the vast amounts of diverse information that are needed to control each business appropriately. Their span of control is too large. Consequently, an organization that is functionally structured may move to a more decentralized product/market or divisional structure. The end result is more managers with smaller spans of control and a greater capacity to understand each of their respective business areas.

In an effort to increase control, some organizations are actually splitting their operations into multiple, public corporations. An extreme case of the spin-off tactic described earlier, this restructuring strategy might be called the "break-up." For example, AT&T is splitting into three independent, publicly traded operating companies. One unit, their computer business, is what is left from the acquisition of NCR. Another unit is a strong equipment business. The final unit is the communications mainstay for which AT&T is best known. The purpose of the split is to allow AT&T to compete better against the Bell operating companies.[46] Hanson, PLC, the British Conglomerate, is also splitting up. The result will be four companies— Chemicals, Tobacco, Energy, and Building Materials and Equipment. These units have revenues of more than $3 billion.[47]

On the other hand, some organizations restructure by becoming more centralized. For instance, British Petroleum collapsed its structure to save costs. According to Robert Horton, former chairman and CEO of British Petroleum:

Excessive differentiation and decentralization in the past has been a terrible mistake. We now run our European division from Brussels. We have one office and we run the whole of Europe from there. Now it has been a hell of a fight and you know Paris did not like it, and Hamburg did not like it, and Vienna did not like it, and I have to tell you London did not like it either. I mean, I run the corporation worldwide from London, but the operations for continental Europe are now run from Brussels. But of course, the savings are enormous. Instead of having twelve head offices, you just have one. Instead of having twelve research centers, you have one.[48]

In a similar move, Philip Morris is merging its Kraft and General Foods units into one company. "An executive familiar with the reorganization said Kraft and General Foods will consolidate corporate staffs and fully combine their sales forces, which together number 3,500. Executives expect Kraft to cut 100 corporate jobs right away and trim the sales force later on."[49]

Closely linked to changes in organizational structure are adjustments to the culture of the organization, the unseen glue that holds the structure together. The successful turnaround of Chrysler, described earlier, was accompanied by a dramatic change in culture that led to a leaner, meaner, and more focused organization.

If restructuring activities are precipitated by unusually poor economic or competitive conditions, a strong strategy-supportive culture can be undermined by the actions taken during the restructuring. For decades, Delta Airlines, traditionally one of the most respected and financially secure of all airlines, has maintained a very strong organizational culture focused on friendly, customer service. Delta has fallen on hard times in the last several years because of the recession, fare wars, and the company's expensive acquisition of Pan Am Corp.'s European routes. To combat the recent performance downturn, the company has fired thousands of temporary workers, stopped all new hiring, cut benefits, and cut some employee work days down to six hours:

> *These and other cost-cutting moves reflect a huge change in corporate culture for the industry's Southern gentlemen, who went out of their way to take care of employees and counted on job security to translate into hospitality for passengers.*[50]

In other retrenchment situations, the existing culture may be part of the problem: too little focus on quality, too little learning and sharing, a poor attitude toward customers, or lack of innovation. If the culture is part of the problem, then the restructuring effort has to address the necessary changes in culture. It is very difficult for an organization to throw off its old way of doing business. Following a hostile takeover, Linda Wachner, CEO of Warnaco, says she had to instill a new, hardworking "do it now" culture to improve the organization's performance:

> *Don't get me wrong, getting these successes hasn't been easy. And some people felt that the pressure to succeed was too great. Some people left. So we said, 'Okay, if you can't meet the goal or if you can't get under the limbo rack, good-bye, and we don't hold it against you.' But of the 100 people we put in equity (ownership positions in the company) almost seven years ago, 86 are still here and have a major financial stake in the company.*[51]

Combined Restructuring Approaches

Organizations sometimes combine restructuring tactics in an effort to turn their organizations around.

> *When J. F. (Jack) Welch, Jr., took over General Electric in 1981, it was a different company from the one we know today. Between 1981 and 1989 Welch divested about $9 billion in assets, while acquiring $12 billion. He also squeezed 350 product lines into 13 large businesses, each in first or second place within its industry, while flattening the GE management hierarchy. In so doing, he moved the corporation from eleventh place ($12 billion) in 1980 to second place ($73 billion) among U.S. corporations in stock market value by the end of 1992.*[52]

As the GE example demonstrates, restructuring can take time and often involves several restructuring approaches. Navistar's (International Harvester) restructuring, featured in Strategic Insight 10.4, also took place over most of a decade and utilized several of the techniques discussed in this chapter.

The successful Navistar turnaround demonstrates an important point—it is not enough to simply sell off unwanted business units or restructure debt. Permanent organizational changes are required if an organization is going to emerge from a restructuring with increased competitiveness. These changes often include a renewed emphasis on research and development, better development of

STRATEGIC INSIGHT 10.4

BUSINESS

STRATEGY

International Harvester's Restructuring Process

International Harvester (IH), an industry leader in the manufacture of trucks, engines, and agricultural and construction products, nearly went bankrupt in the early 1980s. Problems stemmed from two decades of complacency and mismanagement, combined with several external events. By 1984, the company had lost in excess of $3 billion. The company responded by negotiating debt restructuring agreements with its more than 200 lenders; however, IH's problems required much more than just debt restructuring.

In response to persistent problems, IH developed a complete restructuring plan which included plant closings, layoffs, and the sale of many large business units, including its construction equipment business and its solar turbine division. Even more painful, in November 1984 the company sold its International Harvester agricultural equipment operations to Tenneco and, by virtue of the sale agreement, changed its name to Navistar. These divestitures resulted in a reduction from forty-two facilities worldwide to seven. Employment went from 95,000 to 13,000.

Navistar management recognized the need to create permanent changes within the organization. They worked to develop a more competitive organization by decentralizing decision-making authority, creating a culture that centered on a set of "corporate values" that were developed jointly with operating managers within the company, and establishing permanent continuous improvement teams that were responsible for corporate renewal.

Source: C. Borucki and C.K. Barnett, "Restructuring for Survival—The Navistar Case," *Academy of Management Executive* (February 1990), pp. 36–49. Used with permission.

human capital through training and development, and the creation of an effective corporate culture that encourages entrepreneurial activity, high quality, and a global, long-term perspective.[53]

Stakeholders should also be considered when an organization is contemplating a program of restructuring, since such programs are so ethically laden. Poorly executed restructurings can damage trust and thus long-term relationships. Even in the best planned restructurings, some stakeholders are likely to be upset; however, if organizational managers make decisions in light of the needs of stakeholders, the negative effects can be reduced. Also, the organization will be able to anticipate and prepare a strategy for dealing with objections. Strategic Application 10.1 contains a tool that is useful in evaluating potential restructuring strategies in light of stakeholder needs and demands.

REORIENTATION THROUGH CONTINUOUS LEARNING

Efforts to fundamentally restructure organizations do not have an attractive success rate, unfortunately. Some are very successful, some are dismal failures, but most merely create minor improvements in the overall, sustained health of the organization.[54] Quite often the morale problems that follow a radical restructuring

STRATEGIC APPLICATION 10.1

RESTRUCTURING IMPACT ANALYSIS FOR A LARGE, DIVERSIFIED FIRM

The following chart can help you determine the impact on and reaction of key stakeholders to various restructuring moves by the firm:

Step 1: Determine the objectives of the restructuring (e.g., debt reduction, refocus on distinctive competencies, greater efficiency)

Step 2: Create a chart for the organization with the columns and rows labeled as shown below. Leave plenty of room between columns and stakeholders. List specific alternatives (e.g., retrenchment, Chapter XI restructuring, LBO, etc.) and describe them in detail.

Also, make sure to list specific, not general, stakeholders under each broad heading. If the organization is already involved in multiple environments through its business units, list only the stakeholders that are likely to be affected by this particular decision. Members of the remote environment (e.g., societal groups, the media) can also be listed if they are considered relevant to the analysis.

Step 3: Based on theory and models found in earlier chapters, assign a priority level to each stakeholder. Generally, the levels of high, moderate, and low are adequate for this kind of analysis.

Step 4: Describe the impact of each of the restructuring strategies on each of the stakeholders. In particular, which of the strategies is likely to be favored by each stakeholder? Which of the strategies is likely to be resisted by each stakeholder? What will be the nature of the resistance (e.g., legal suits, battle with regulators, unfavorable press releases, strikes, boycott, etc.).

Step 5: Carefully weigh the trade-offs and the priorities and decide.

Desired Outcome from Restructuring:

		Impact Analysis		
Stakeholder	Priority	Restructuring Option A	Restructuring Option B	Restructuring Option C
Top Management				
Other Managers				
Employees				
Board of Directors				
Owners/Share- holders				
Customers				
Suppliers				
Competitors				
Potential Competitors				
Government Regulators				
Local Communities				
Activist Groups				
Unions				
Creditors				

are so severe that it takes years for the organization to gain momentum in the new direction.

Some organizations try to preempt the seemingly inevitable need for fundamental restructuring by instilling a commitment to continuous learning and strategic change. Top managers, who are responsible for shaping the vision and purpose that lead to focus and stability, must also serve a disruptive role.[55] Bill Gates of Microsoft recently demonstrated he had not succumbed to a rigid mental model of the evolution of information and computing systems when he stopped work on some projects and made a substantial new commitment to the Internet. As Yoshio Maruta of Japan's second largest diversified cosmetics and computer firm describes it:

> *Past wisdom must not be a constraint but something to be challenged. Yesterday's success formula is often today's obsolete dogma. My challenge is to have the organization continually questioning the past so we can renew ourselves every day.*[56]

To encourage questioning, learning, and renewal, executives use different disruption tactics. At 3M, an organization with a reputation for continuous learning, the CEO set a new "stretch" goal for new product introductions. Formerly, the target was that 20% of sales had to come from products less than four years old—an extremely challenging target by most companies' standards. In 1993, CEO Livio DeSimone raised the target to 30%.[57]

Rather than use regular meetings for budget and strategy review, some executives are using regular meetings for hypothetical contingency planning. By proposing a series of "what if" questions about the environment, the executives are attempting to keep mental models of industry and organization practice from becoming too rigid. This process of regular self-examination and forced disruptive thinking helps organizations avoid "business as usual." [58] Strategic Insight 10.5 provides a profile of a learning organization, Knight-Ridder, Inc.

To maintain an adaptive, learning atmosphere at all organizational levels, many firms have created self-managed work teams and cross-functional product development teams, so that multiple perspectives will be brought to problem solving. When a significant new idea is needed, or a particularly difficult problem solved, some of the more progressive organizations will create special task forces modeled after the Lockheed "Skunkworks" product design teams. These special teams, which were common in the early years of the microcomputer industry, are free from virtually all organizational requirements and boundaries. They have full authority and autonomy to create ideas and solutions. Increasingly, these types of autonomous, entrepreneurial teams are needed to prevent the lethargy and inertia that can plague large organizations.

THE CHALLENGE OF THE FUTURE

Without question, the greatest managerial challenges lie ahead. It is hard to predict with precision the kind of business environment the next generation of managers will face; however, judging from the recent past, it will probably be associated with increasing global complexity and interconnectedness. Table 10.1 contains a few of the characteristics we expect to find in the business environment of the early twenty-first century.

What kind of leaders will be needed to navigate through the business environment of the future? In a *Fortune* article titled "Leaders of Corporate Change,"

STRATEGIC INSIGHT 10.5

BUSINESS

STRATEGY

Learning Profile of a Learning Organization

Knight-Ridder, Inc., is the second largest newspaper company in the United States, with twenty-nine daily newspapers. Knight-Ridder has a strong reputation within the newspaper industry, having won a record sixty-two Pulitzer Prizes and enjoyed steady growth in revenues and profits for more than a decade. In the 1970s, Knight-Ridder anticipated the leveling off or decline of the newspaper industry and began diversification into related businesses. First, the firm purchased three television stations, and then formed a joint venture with AT&T to create a videotext service. None of these ventures was successful. In 1979, Knight-Ridder entered the on-line business information services industry, creating a Business Information Services (BIS) Division. Until the late 1980s, however, Knight-Ridder was a minor player in business information services.

In the late 1980s, Knight-Ridder initiated a major change—the acquisition of Dialog Information Services, which doubled the size of the BIS Division and provided Knight-Ridder with the world's largest full-text information collection. To instill a commitment to change, management at Knight-Ridder had to build a shared vision of the industry and Knight-Ridder's role in it.

In building a shared vision, CEO James Batten presented the new identity as an expression rather than as a fundamental change of scope. Knight-Ridder was now a "deliverer of information services" rather than a newspaper company: "If the customer wants information, we ought to be prepared to deliver it whether it be by fax, satellite, land lines, free standing machines, networks, audiotext, hardcopy, or anything." By positioning the Dialog acquisition within this context, management was able to show how Dialog fit within Knight-Ridder's existing mission and values. ". . . we mapped what Dialog said it was about against what Knight-Ridder believed it was about."

Knight-Ridder had two other characteristics that helped it successfully create change: relevant experience and inclusive decision processes. Because of its previous acquisitions of smaller information services firms, the management at Knight-Ridder had prepared itself for its big acquisition of Dialog. Although no one acquisition had created real financial risk for the company, each acquisition had provided management with valuable experiences in the information services industry and in the management of acquisitions. Also, management at Knight-Ridder formed teams to collect information and address implementation issues. Management emphasized extensive information collection and quantitative analysis, what they called "due diligence." They insisted on the airing of diverse opinions, but put in the time to build consensus. Over time, management and employees evolved new mental models about how customers want to receive information, what constitutes successful information delivery, and how Knight-Ridder would participate in the information industry with Dialog.

Source: N.A. Wishart, J.J. Elam, and D. Robey, "Redrawing the Portrait of a Learning Organization: Inside Knight-Ridder, Inc.," *Academy of Management Executive* 10 (February 1996), pp. 7–20.

Table 10.1 *Strategic Management for the Twenty-First Century*

Increasing levels of global trade and global awareness
Global and domestic social turbulence
Increased sensitivity to ethical issues and environmental concerns
Rapidly advancing technology, especially in communications
Continued erosion of buying power in the United States
Continued development of third world economies
Increases in U.S. and global strategic alliances
Revolution in the U.S. health industry

four CEOs of *Fortune* 500 companies—Stanley Gault of Goodyear Tire and Rubber, Linda Wachner of Warnaco, Mike Walsh of Tenneco, and David Johnson of Campbell Soup—discussed their responsibilities in restructuring and reorienting an organization during difficult times.[59] In addition to providing a direction or strategy, each executive mentioned the importance of instilling commitment to the new strategy, setting new and challenging expectations, getting people to rethink what they do and improve on it, and creating a high-performance culture. In each case, the executive was describing transformational leadership: creating a new vision, instilling commitment to the new vision and way of doing business, and mobilizing change through new structure and systems.[60] Every year, thousands of organizations face severe threats to their survival and need the help of transformational leaders who can provide a new approach.

In other firms where business is more usual, leaders perform the same activities but not on as sweeping a scale. They communicate the vision of the organization to internal and external stakeholders, modify organization structures to better align with internal and external environments, negotiate external alliances, make executive staffing decisions, and sustain the organizational culture.

The tools, theories and techniques found in this book can help you become an effective leader for the next century. We encourage you to apply what you have learned to current and future business situations in which you and your organizations are found.

Summary

As a result of performance problems and/or pressure from stakeholders, many firms are now restructuring. The restructuring techniques that were described in this chapter included refocusing assets, retrenchment, Chapter XI reorganization, leveraged buyouts, and changes to organization structure. These methods can also be used in combination. Since restructuring has such a large impact on so many stakeholders, organizations should devote special attention to analyzing the needs of stakeholders prior to restructuring and should practice effective stakeholder management afterward.

The business environment of the future will undeniably be more complex than what we know today. However, transformational leaders can help their organizations succeed in the twenty-first century. These leaders know how to create a new vision, instill commitment to that vision and a way of accomplishing it, and mobilize change through new structure and systems. Even in more stable and predictable environments, effective leaders know how to communicate the vision of the organization to internal and external stakeholders, modify organization structures to better align with internal and external environments, negotiate external alliances, make executive staffing decisions, and sustain the organizational culture.

Discussion Questions

1. Describe each of the major techniques for restructuring.
2. In your opinion, which one of the major restructuring strategies entails the greatest risks? Which one of them is the most ethically laden? Defend your answers.
3. Which of the major restructuring techniques is most likely to provide rapid results? Defend your answer.
4. What are some of the ill effects from layoffs? How can an organization avoid layoffs and still reduce labor costs?
5. Is it possible for an organization to pursue more than one restructuring strategy at the same time? Can you think of an organization (not mentioned in the book) that is pursuing more than one strategy? Please describe the restructuring approach of this organization.
6. What will the business environment of the future be like? What kind of leaders will be needed to manage the organization of the future?

References

1. Adapted from L. Smith, "Does the World's Biggest Company Have a Future?" *Fortune* (August 7, 1995), p. 124.
2. C. J. Gersick, "Revolutionary Change Theories: A Multi-Level Exploration of the Punctuated Equilibrium Paradigm," *Academy of Management Review* 16 (1991), pp. 10–37; M. I. Tushman and E. Romanelli, "Organizational Evolution: A Metamorphosis Model of Convergence and Reorientation," in E. E. Cummings and B. M. Staw, eds., *Research in Organization Behavior* (Greenwich, Conn.: JAI Press, 1985), pp. 171–222.
3. N. A. Wishart, J. J. Elam, and D. Robey, "Redrawing the Portrait of a Learning Organization: Inside Knight-Ridder, Inc.," *Academy of Management Executive* 10 (February 1996), pp. 7–20; J. P. Walsh, "Managerial and Organizational Cognition," *Organization Science* 6 (1995), pp. 280–321.
4. A. Saxenian, *Culture and Competition in Silicon Valley and Route 128* (Cambridge, Mass: Harvard University Press, 1994).
5. Gersick, "Revolutionary Change Theories," p. 22.
6. Gersick, "Revolutionary Change Theories"; Tushman and Romanelli, "Organizational Evolution."
7. Gersick, "Revolutionary Change Theories"; Tushman and Romanelli, "Organizational Evolution."
8. R. E. Hoskisson and R. A. Johnson, "Corporate Restructuring and Strategic Change: The Effect on Diversification Strategy and R&D Intensity," *Strategic Management Journal* 13 (1992), pp. 625–634.
9. J. Carlton, "Apple CEO Outlines Survival Strategy," *Wall Street Journal* (May 14, 1996), pp. A2, A22; K. Rebello and P. Burrows, "The Fall of an American Icon," *Business Week* (February 5, 1996), pp. 34–42.
10. P. Sellers, "Can Wal-Mart Get Back the Magic?" *Fortune* (April 29, 1996), pp. 130–136,
11. These arguments are outlined in M. A. Hitt, R. E. Hoskisson, and J. S. Harrison, "Strategic Competitiveness in the 1990s: Challenges and Opportunities for U.S. Executives," *Academy of Management Executive* (May 1991), pp. 7–22.
12. J. F. Bandnowski, "Restructuring Is a Continuous Process," *Long Range Planning* (January 1991), pp. 10–14.
13. C. Markides, "Consequences of Corporate Refocusing: Ex

Ante Evidence," *Academy of Management Journal* 35 (1992), pp. 398–412.
14. Hitt, Hoskisson, and Harrison, "Strategic Competitiveness in the 1990s"; R. E. Hoskisson and M. A. Hitt, *Downscoping: How to Tame the Diversified Firm* (New York: Oxford University Press, 1994), p. 3.
15. Hoskisson and Johnson, "Corporate Restructuring and Strategic Change"; Hoskisson and Hitt, *Downscoping.*
16. C. A. Montgomery, A. R. Thomas, and R. Kammath, "Divestiture, Market Valuation, and Strategy," *Academy of Management Journal* 27 (1984), pp. 830–840.
17. J. Cole, "Chrysler Agrees to Sell to Raytheon Co. Bulk of Its Aerospace, Defense Holdings," *Wall Street Journal* (April 8, 1996), p. A3; *Wall Street Journal*, "Business and Finance" (June 10, 1996), p. A1.
18. W. Bounds, "Corning Will Spin Off Its Lab-Testing Division," *Wall Street Journal* (May 15, 1996), p. B4; *Wall Street Journal*, "Business and Finance" (April 2, 1996), p. A1.
19. J. Weber, "A Big Company that Works," *Business Week* (May 4, 1992), p. 125.
20. D. Hunter, "Grace Sharpens Its Focus," *Chemical Week* (April 1, 1992), p. 15.
21. T. Smart, "So Much for Diversification," *Business Week* (February 1, 1993), p. 31; P. Yoshihashi, "Unocal Corp. Will Revamp into Two Units," *Wall Street Journal* (July 9, 1992), p. A4.
22. M. A. Hitt, R. E. Hoskisson, and J. S. Harrison, "Strategic Competitiveness in the 1990s," pp. 7–21.
23. R. L. Daft, *Organization Theory and Design*, 4th ed. (St. Paul, Minn.: West Publishing Company, 1992), p. 94.
24. B. O'Brian, "Tired of Airline Losses, AMR Pushes its Bid to Diversify Businesses," *Wall Street Journal* (February 18, 1993), p. A1.
25. J. Baily and R. Gibson, "ConAgra to Cut 6,500 Jobs, Close Plants," *Wall Street Journal* (May 15, 1996), pp. A3, A8; Y. Ono, "Nabisco to Cut 4,200 Jobs in Restructuring," *Wall Street Journal* (June 25, 1996), pp. A3, A6.
26. Adapted from C. Solomon, "Amoco to Cut 8,500 Workers, or 16% of Force," *Wall Street Journal* (July 9, 1992), p. A3.
27. M. Murray, "Amid Record Profits, Companies Continue to

Lay Off Employees," *Wall Street Journal* (May 4, 1995), pp. A1, A6.

28. W. McKinley, C. M. Sanchez, and A. G. Schick, "Organizational Downsizing: Constraining, Cloning, Learning," *Academy of Management Executive* (August 1995), p. 32.

29. K. S. Cameron, S. J. Freeman, and Aneil K. Mishra, "Best Practices in White-Collar Downsizing: Managing Contradictions," *Academy of Management Executive* (August 1991), pp. 57–73.

30. J. Brockner, S. Grover, T. Reed, R. DeWitt, and M. O'Malley, "Survivors' Reactions to Layoffs: We Get By With a Little Help From Our Friends," *Administrative Science Quarterly* 32 (1987), pp. 526–541.

31. D. L. Worrell, W. N. Davidson III, and V. M. Sharma, "Layoff Announcements and Stockholder Wealth," *Academy of Management Journal* 34 (1991), pp. 662–678.

32. D. A. Heenan, "The Downside of Downsizing," *Journal of Business Strategy* (November–December 1989), p. 18.

33. If you would like to read some of this literature, you can start with Brockner *et al.,* "Survivors' Reactions to Layoffs" and C. Hardy, "Investing in Retrenchment: Avoiding the Hidden Costs," *California Management Review* 29 (1987), pp. 111–125.

34. M. Settles, "Human Downsizing: Can It Be Done?" *Journal of Business Ethics* 7 (1988), pp. 961–963; Worrell, Davidson, and Sharma, "Layoff Announcements and Stockholder Wealth."

35. E. Faltermeyer, "Is This Layoff Necessary?" *Fortune* (June 1, 1992), pp. 71–86.

36. D. M. Flynn and M. Farid, "The Intentional Use of Chapter XI: Lingering Versus Immediate Filing," *Strategic Management Journal* 12 (1991), pp. 63–64.

37. Based on T. J. Salerno and C. D. Hansen, "A Prepackaged Bankruptcy Strategy," *Journal of Business Strategy* (January–February 1991), pp. 36–41.

38. Flynn and Farid, "The Intentional Use of Chapter XI."

39. W. N. Moulton, "Bankruptcy as a Deliberate Strategy: Theoretical Considerations and Empirical Evidence," *Strategic Management Journal* 14 (1993), p. 130.

40. K. M. Davidson, "Another Look at LBOs," *Journal of Business Strategies* (January–February 1988), pp. 44–47.

41. A good review of these studies, of which there are seven, is found in S.A. Zahra and M. Fescina, "Will Leveraged Buyouts Kill U.S. Corporate Research and Development,"

Academy of Management Executive (November 1991), pp. 7–21.

42. M. F. Wiersema and J. P. Liebeskind, "The Effects of Leveraged Buyouts on Corporate Growth and Diversification in Large Firms," *Strategic Management Journal* 16 (1995), pp. 447–460.

43. K. M. Davidson, "Another Look at LBOs," *Journal of Business Strategies* (January–February 1988), pp. 44–47.

44. Davidson, "Another Look at LBOs," pp. 44–45.

45. M. Schwarz and E. A. Weinstein, "So You Want to Do a Leveraged Buyout," *Journal of Business Strategies* (January–February 1989), pp. 10–15.

46. J. J. Keller, "Defying Merger Trend, AT&T Plans to Split Into Three Companies," *Wall Street Journal* (September 21, 1995), pp. A1, A14.

47. R. Bonte-Friedheim and J. Guyon, "Hanson to Divide into Four Businesses," *Wall Street Journal* (January 31, 1996), pp. A3, A16.

48. R. Calori and B. Dufour, "Management European Style," *Academy of Management Executive* (August 1995), p. 67.

49. S. L. Hwang, "Philip Morris to Reorganize Food Operation," *Wall Street Journal* (January 4, 1995), pp. A3, A4.

50. B. O'Brian, "Delta Air Makes Painful Cuts in Effort to Stem Red Ink," *Wall Street Journal* (September 10, 1992), p.B4.

51. Graves, "Leaders of Corporate Change," p. 113.

52. Hoskisson and Hitt, *Downscoping.*

53. Hitt, Hoskisson and Harrison, "Strategic Competitiveness in the 1990s."

54. J. P. Kotter, "Leading Change: Why Transformation Efforts Fail," *Harvard Business Review* (March–April 1995), pp. 59–67.

55. S. Ghoshal and C. A. Bartlett, "Changing the Role of Top Management: Beyond Structure to Process," *Harvard Business Review* 73 (January–February 1995), pp. 86–96.

56. Ghoshal and Bartlett, "Changing the Role of Top Management," p. 94.

57. Ghoshal and Bartlett, "Changing the Role of Top Management."

58. Wishart, Elam, and Robey, "Redrawing the Portrait of a Learning Organization."

59. J. M. Graves, "Leaders of Corporate Change."

60. R. L. Daft, *Organization Theory and Design,* 3rd ed., (St. Paul, Minn.: West Publishing Co., 1989).

CASE NOTE

Preparing a Case Analysis

Strategic management is an iterative, ongoing process designed to position a firm for competitive advantage in its ever-changing environment. To manage an organization strategically, a manager must understand and appreciate the desires of key organizational stakeholders, the industry environment, and the firm's position relative to its stakeholders and industry. This knowledge allows a manager to set goals and direct the organization's resources in a way that corrects weaknesses, overcomes threats, takes advantage of strengths and opportunities, and, ultimately, satisfies stakeholders. The first ten chapters of this book contain a foundation for understanding these strategic management processes.

With case analysis, you can practice some of the techniques of strategic management. Case analysis, to some extent, mirrors the processes managers use to make real strategic decisions. The main advantages managers have over students who analyze cases are that they have more information and more experience. For example, managers have ongoing relationships with internal and external stakeholders, from whom information can be gathered. They may also have a business intelligence system and staff to help them make decisions. In addition, managers usually have substantial experience in the industry and company. Nevertheless, managers must still make decisions without full information. Like students, they never have all of the facts or the time and resources to gather them. In case analysis, you must sort accurate, relevant information from that which is inaccurate or irrelevant.

The authors of cases have attempted to capture as much information as possible. They typically conducted extensive interviews with managers and employees and gathered information from public sources such as annual reports and business magazines. Many cases include a detailed description of the industry and competitors as well as an extensive profile of one organization. You can supplement this information through your own library research, if your instructor thinks this is appropriate.

Case analysis typically begins with a brief introduction of the company. The introduction, which sets the stage for the rest of the case, should include a brief description of the defining characteristics of the firm, including some of its outstanding qualities, past successes and failures, and products or services. The industries in which the firm is involved are also identified.

The next section of a case analysis can be either an environmental analysis or an internal analysis. Opportunities are defined as conditions in the broad and operating *environments* that allow a firm to take advantage of *organizational* strengths, overcome *organizational* weaknesses or neutralize *environmental* threats. Consequently, both environmental and organizational analyses are required before all of the organization's opportunities can be identified. We have chosen to treat environmental analysis first because it establishes the context in which firm strategies and resources can be understood. However, reversing the order of analysis would not be incorrect and is even preferred by many strategic management scholars.

Environmental analysis is an examination of the external environment, including external stakeholders, the competition, and the broad environment. Systematic external analysis will help you draw conclusions about the potential for growth and profit in the industry and determine keys to survival and success in the industry.

An organizational analysis, which follows the external analysis, is designed to evaluate the organization's strategic direction, business- and corporate-level strategies, resources, capabilities, and relationships with internal and external stakeholders, and then determine the strengths, weaknesses, vulnerabilities, and sources of competitive advantage exhibited by the firm. These determinations must be made against a background of knowledge about the external environment so that the full range of opportunities and threats can also be identified.

STRUCTURING AN ENVIRONMENTAL ANALYSIS

An analysis of the external environment includes an industry analysis and an examination of key external stakeholders and the broad environment. Findings are then summarized, with an emphasis on identifying industry growth and profit potential and the keys to survival and success in the industry. Some organizations are involved in more than one industry. Consequently, a separate industry analysis is done for each of the industries in which a firm is involved.

Industry Analysis

Environmental analysis should begin with an industry analysis. The first step in industry analysis is to provide a basic description of the industry and the competitive forces that dominate it. Porter's Five Forces are evaluated, along with other relevant issues.

1. What is the product or service? What function does it serve? What are the channels of distribution?
2. What is the industry size in units and dollars? How fast is it growing? Are products differentiated? Are there high exit barriers? Are there high fixed costs? These are some of the forces that determine the strength of competition among existing competitors.
3. Who are the major competitors? What are their market shares? In other words, is the industry consolidated or fragmented?
4. Who are the major customers of the industry? Are they powerful? What gives them power?
5. Who are the major suppliers to the industry? Are they powerful? What gives them power?
6. Do significant entry barriers exist? What are they? Are they effective in protecting existing competitors, thus enhancing profits?
7. Are there any close substitutes for industry products and services? Do they provide pressure on prices charged in this industry?
8. What are the basic strategies of competitors? How successful are they?
9. To what extent is the industry global? Are there any apparent advantages to being involved in more than one country?
10. Is the industry regulated? What influence do regulations have on industry competitiveness?

External Stakeholders and the Broad Environment

A complete environmental analysis also includes an assessment of external stakeholders and the broad environment. The identity and power of competitors, suppliers, and customers was already established during the industry analysis. At this stage of the analysis, other important stakeholders also should be identified and their influence on the industry determined (see Chapter 3). If any of the external stakeholders poses a threat or opportunity, this also should be identified. One of the outcomes of this part of the analysis should be the establishment of priorities for each external stakeholder group. High-priority stakeholders will receive greater attention during the development of the strategic plan.

The broad environment should also be evaluated. Four of the most important factors are current social forces, global economic forces, global political forces, and technological innovations. Remember that each of these forces is evaluated only as it relates to the industry in question. Forces in the broad environment may also pose threats or provide opportunities.

After describing the industry as it exists now, it is important to capture the underlying dynamics that will create industry change and require new strategic approaches. One useful way to accomplish this is to group factors that influence the industry into two categories: those that create and influence industry demand and those that create and influence industry cost structures and profit potential. The findings of this part of the analysis will help you decide whether the industry is "attractive" (growing and profitable) and worthy of further investment (i.e., time, money, resources). It will also help you identify areas in which the firm may be able to excel in an effort to create a competitive advantage.

Factors That Influence Demand. Many industry factors and stakeholder actions create and influence demand for products and services. Some of the factors are part of the broad environment of the firm, such as the state of the economy. Other factors are part of the operating environment, most of which are related to the actions of two key stakeholder groups: customers and competitors. If the underlying factors that create demand are changing, then it is likely that demand patterns will change. For example, demand for washing machines is a function of household formations and replacements. To predict future demand, you would study the numbers of people in the household-forming age bracket, durability of washers, and economic conditions.

Some of the industry factors and stakeholder actions that create and influence demand and growth prospects in an industry include:

1. The function(s) served by the product.
2. The stage of the product life cycle (i.e., degree of market penetration already experienced).
3. Economic trends, including income levels and economic cycles (i.e., recession, boom)
4. Demographic trends (part of social trend analysis) such as population and age.
5. Other societal/cultural trends, including fads and commonly held values and beliefs.
6. Political trends, which may include protectionist legislation such as trade barriers.
7. Technological trends, including new applications, new markets, and cost savings that make prices more competitive.

8. Programs developed by firms in the industry, such as new product introductions, new marketing programs, new distribution channels, and new functions served.
9. Strong brand recognition, domestically or worldwide.
10. Pricing actions that stimulate demand.

After analyzing the factors that create and influence demand, you should be able to draw some conclusions about industry growth prospects for the industry and firm. Since you can never be certain about the timetable and ultimate outcome of a trend that, by definition, is changing over time, one technique that may be useful is to develop alternative demand scenarios. For example, if the health of the economy is a major driver of a product's demand, you could consider the upside and downside of an economic recovery using the following type of format: "If the economy recovers within six months, then industry demand for the product could be the highest in five years. If the recovery does not materialize, then demand might linger at last year's levels."

Factors that Influence Cost Structures. After determining growth prospects for the industry, you will want to determine the cost structure and profit potential of the industry. As with demand, various factors and stakeholder actions create and influence cost/profit structures in an industry. Among these factors are:

1. Stage of the product life cycle. In the early stages of the life cycle, firms have large investments in product development, distribution channel development, new plant and equipment, and workforce training. In the latter stages, investments are more incremental.
2. Capital intensity. Large investments in fixed costs such as plants and equipment make firms very sensitive to fluctuations in demand—high levels of capacity utilization are needed to cover or "spread" fixed costs. Industries that have a lower relative fixed cost investment but higher variable costs are able to control their costs more readily in turbulent demand periods.
3. Economies of scale.
4. Learning/experience effects.
5. The power of customers, suppliers, competitive rivalry, substitutes, and entry barriers. Powerful customers, suppliers, competitive rivalry, substitutes, or low entry barriers can erode profit potential.
6. The influence of other stakeholders, such as powerful foreign governments, joint venture partners, powerful unions, strong creditors, etc.
7. Technological changes that provide opportunities to reduce costs through investing in new equipment, new products, and new processes or that alter the balance of investments between fixed and variable costs.

After systematically profiling the factors and stakeholder actions that influence cost structures and profits, you should be able to draw conclusions about industry profit potential. After the basic environmental analysis is complete, the next step is to perform a more detailed examination of the major strategic issues facing the industry.

Strategic Issues Facing the Industry

A thorough environmental analysis provides the information needed to identify factors and forces that are important to the industry in which your organization is involved and, therefore, your organization. These factors and forces may be categorized as follows:

1. Driving forces in the industry, which are trends that are so significant that they are creating fundamental industry change, such as the opening up of Eastern Europe or networked computer communications. Of course, each industry will have its own unique set of driving forces.
2. Threats, defined as noteworthy trends or changes that threaten growth prospects, profit potential, and traditional ways of doing business.
3. Opportunities, which are important trends, changes, or ideas that provide new opportunities for growth or profits.
4. Requirements for survival, identified as resources and capabilities that all firms must possess to survive in the industry. An example in the pharmaceutical industry is "product purity." These factors do not command a premium price. They are necessary, but not sufficient to be successful.
5. Key success factors, which are factors firms typically should possess if they desire to be successful in the industry. An example in the pharmaceutical industry is the ability to create products with new therapeutic qualities. This ability may lead to high performance.

Having completed an analysis of the external environment, you are ready to conduct a more specific analysis of the internal organization.

STRUCTURING AN ORGANIZATIONAL ANALYSIS

Understanding industry trends, growth prospects, profit potential, and key strategic issues can help you critique an organization's strategies and evaluate its strengths and weaknesses. For example, what might qualify as a strength in one industry may be an ordinary characteristic or a weakness in another industry. A good organizational analysis should begin with a general evaluation of the internal organization.

Evaluation of the Internal Environment

The following questions are useful in assessing the internal organization:

1. What is the company's strategic direction, including its vision, business definition, enterprise strategy (e.g., which stakeholder groups does it appear to give priority), long-term goals, and attitude toward global expansion. If some of these factors are contained in a formal mission, share it.
2. How has the strategic direction changed over time? In what way? Has the evolution been consistent with the organization's capabilities and planned strategies?
3. Who are the principal internal stakeholders? In particular, who are the key managers and what is their background? What are their strengths and weaknesses? Are they authoritarian or participative in their management style? Is this appropriate for the situation? What seems to drive their actions?
4. Who owns the organization? Is it a publicly traded company with a board of directors? If there is a board and you know who is on it, is the composition of the board appropriate? Is there an individual or group with a controlling interest? Is there evidence of agency problems? How active are the owners and what do they value?
5. What are the operating characteristics of the company, including its size in sales, assets, and employees, its age, and its geographical locations (including international operations)?
6. Are employees highly trained? If a union is present, how are relations with the union?

7.   How would you describe the organization's culture? Is it a high performing culture? Is it supportive of the firm's strategies?

Most instructors also require a financial analysis both to identify financial strengths and weaknesses and to evaluate performance. A financial analysis should include a comparison of ratios and financial figures with major competitors or the industry in which the organization competes (cross-sectional) as well as an analysis of trends in these ratios over several years (longitudinal). Some commonly used financial ratios are specified in Chapter 4 (Table 4.4).

Financial ratio analysis can provide an indication as to whether the firm is pursuing an appropriate strategic direction, with appropriate strategies that are well executed. Poor financial trends are sometimes symptoms of greater problems. For example, a firm may discover that administrative costs are increasing at a faster rate than sales. This could be an indication of diseconomies of scale or the need for tighter controls on overhead costs. Financial analysis is also used to indicate the ability of the firm to finance growth. For example, managers of a firm that has very high leverage (long-term debt) may have to be less ambitious in their strategies for taking advantage of opportunities. On the other hand, an organization with a strong balance sheet is well poised to pursue a wide range of opportunities. Strong financial resources are often hard to imitate in the short term.

When superficially analyzed, ratios can be more misleading than informative. For example, in comparing return-on-assets for two firms in the same industry, the one with the higher ratio could have superior earnings or devalued assets from too little investment. Two firms can differ in return-on-equity because of different debt-equity financing policies rather than from true performance reasons. When accurately interpreted and considered in the larger organization context, the analysis may also uncover strengths, weaknesses, or symptoms of larger organizational problems.

Identification of Resources and Capabilities

The foregoing analysis of the internal environment provides an excellent starting point for identifying key resources and capabilities. For example, outstanding resources and capabilities may result from (1) superior management, (2) well-trained employees, (3) an excellent board of directors, (4) a high performance culture, (5) superior financial resources, or (6) the appropriate level and type of international involvement. However, these potential sources of competitive advantage barely scratch the organizational surface.

You also should evaluate the organization's primary value chain activities to identify resources and capabilities. These activities include its (7) inbound logistics, (8) operations, (9) outbound logistics, (10) marketing and sales, and (11) service, as well as the support activities of (12) procurement, (13) technology development, (14) human resource management, and (15) administration. Chapter 6 provides an in-depth description of how to use the value chain.

In addition, an organization may have (16) an excellent reputation, (17) a strong brand name, (18) patents and secrets, (19) excellent locations, or (20) strong or valuable ties (i.e., alliances, joint ventures, contracts, cooperation) with one or more external stakeholders. All of these potential resources and capabilities (and many others) have been discussed in this book. They form a starting point that you can use to help identify the potential sources of competitive advantage. Each company will have its own unique list.

Performance Evaluation

The next step in internal analysis is to describe and critique the organization's past strategies. In critiquing strategies, you will need to describe them in detail, discuss whether they have been successful, and then *evaluate whether they fit with the industry environment and the resources and capabilities of the organization.*

1. What is the company's pattern of past strategies (corporate level, business level, international)?
2. How successful has the company been in the past with its chosen strategies? How successful is the company now?
3. For each strategy, what explains success or failure? (Use your environmental and organizational analyses to support your answer.)

Many instructors require their students to evaluate the success of an organization on the basis of both qualitative and quantitative (financial) measures. The financial measures were developed during your financial analysis, so you only need to make reference to them here. Some common qualitative measures include product or service quality, productivity, responsiveness to industry change, innovation, reputation, and other measures that indicate key stakeholder satisfaction (i.e., employees, customers, managers, regulatory bodies, society).

Sources of Competitive Advantage

You are now ready to consolidate your internal and external analyses into lists of strengths and weaknesses, and to expand and revise your lists of opportunities and threats. In Chapter 1, strengths were defined as firm resources and capabilities that can lead to a competitive advantage. Weaknesses, on the other hand, were described as resources and capabilities that the firm does not possess, resulting in a competitive disadvantage. Consequently, each of the resources and capabilities identified during the organizational analysis should be measured against the factors identified in the environmental analysis. The next paragraph describes how this is to be done.

Resources and capabilities become strengths if they have the potential to lead to a competitive advantage. This happens when (1) they are valuable, which means that they allow the firm to exploit opportunities and/or neutralize threats arising from the external environment and (2) they are unique, meaning that only a few firms possess the resource or capability. Using these criteria, a list of strengths should be assembled. If a strength is also hard to imitate, then it can lead to a *sustainable* competitive advantage; consequently, these types of strengths should be highlighted. Finally, if a resource or capability could have broad application to many business areas, it is a core competence or capability.

Weaknesses also should be listed. These are resources and capabilities the firm does not possess that, according to your environmental analysis, lead to a competitive disadvantage.

Opportunities are conditions in the external environment that allow a firm to take advantage of organizational strengths, overcome organizational weaknesses or neutralize environmental threats. Consequently, now that the organizational analysis is complete, you should reevaluate your list of opportunities to determine whether they apply to your organization. You should also evaluate threats to make sure they are applicable to your firm. Threats are conditions in the broad and operating environments that may stand in the way of organizational competitiveness or the achievement of stakeholder satisfaction.

At this point, you may also want to add to your list of opportunities some of the potential linkages and alliances that the firm could develop with external stakeholders. For example, if your company is strong in production but weak in foreign marketing, you may see an opportunity to enter a new foreign market through a joint venture with a strong marketing company. Another example may involve neutralizing a threat of new government regulation by forming an alliance with competitors to influence the regulating body.

DEVELOPING A STRATEGIC PLAN

Your environmental and organizational analyses helped you to evaluate the past strategies and strategic direction of the firm, as well as develop a list of strengths, weaknesses, opportunities, and threats. The next step is to make recommendations concerning the strategies the firm may want to pursue in the future. If the firm is not a stellar performer, this should be an easy task. However, even firms that have been highly successful in the past should consider taking advantage of opportunities and should respond to threats. History has taught us that firms that are unwilling to progress eventually decline.

Strategic Direction and Major Strategies

You should probably begin your strategic recommendations by focusing on the strategic direction and major strategies of the firm. Based on your earlier analyses, you may want to consider adjustments to the mission of the firm, including its vision, business definition, or enterprise strategy. Of course, the business definition also helps identify the corporate-level strategy (concentration, vertical integration, related or unrelated diversification). Determine whether your corporate-level strategy is still appropriate, given your environmental analysis. Is your dominant industry stagnant? Is it overregulated? Is competition hurting profitability? Should you consider investing in other industries? If so, what are their defining characteristics? What core competencies and capabilities could be applied elsewhere? What opportunities could be explored that relate to the corporate-level strategy?

The business-level strategy should also be considered. If you determined earlier that the business-level strategy is not as successful as it should be, what adjustments should be made? Could the company have more success by focusing on one segment of the market? Or if the company is pursuing a focus strategy, would broadening the target market be appropriate? If the company is pursuing cost leadership, would a differentiation strategy work better? If differentiation does not seem to be working very well, would a cost leadership strategy be better? Finally, would a best cost strategy be the most appropriate?

It is possible that you may want to leave the strategic direction and major strategies alone, especially if the organization has enjoyed recent success. Regardless of whether you altered the direction and strategies, at this point you have now established what you think they should be. The direction and corporate- and business-level strategies provide guidance for fine-tuning an organization's strategies. Each of the recommendations you make from this point on should be consistent with the strategic direction and major strategies of the organization. At this point, it is time to explore strategic opportunities further.

Evaluation of Opportunities and Recommendations

Using the strategic direction and corporate- and business-level strategies as guides, strategic opportunities should be evaluated further. These alternatives were generated during earlier analyses. They include:

1. Opportunities that allow a firm to take advantage of organizational strengths. These opportunities may involve alternatives such as better promotion of current products and services, new products or services, new applications for existing products and services within existing markets, exploring new domestic or foreign markets, diversifying into areas in which strengths can be applied, or creation of joint ventures with companies with complementary strengths. These are only a few examples.

2. Opportunities for the firm to overcome organizational weaknesses. Do any of the organizational weaknesses relate to an area that you described in your industry analysis as essential for survival? Do any of the weaknesses relate to key success factors? Firms can overcome their weaknesses through strategies such as learning from joint venture partners, creating new alliances with organizations that are strong where the organization is weak, or fixing problems internally through R&D, better controls, efficiency programs, IT, TAM, and so on. Again, these are only a few examples.

3. Opportunities for the firm to neutralize environmental threats. These often involve creation of strategic alliances to offset the influence of a powerful stakeholder such as a government regulator, a strong union, a powerful competitor, or an influential special interest group. The firm may form an alliance *with* the powerful stakeholder or with other stakeholders in an effort to balance the power. Firms may also form alliances to help cope with threats emerging from the broad environment.

Evaluation of opportunities means much more than simply accepting them on the basis of earlier environmental and organizational analyses. They should also be evaluated based on factors such as the following:

1. *Cost–benefit analysis.* Do the financial benefits of pursuing the opportunity appear to outweigh the financial costs?

2. *Ethical analysis.* Is pursuit of this strategy consistent with the enterprise strategy of the organization? Could there be any negative effects on the reputation of the organization?

3. *Protection of other strengths.* Does pursuit of this opportunity in any way detract from or weaken other strengths? For example, could it damage a brand name? Could it weaken a strong financial position?

4. *Implementation ability.* Will implementation of this strategy be easy or difficult? In other words, does the strategy "fit" the capabilities, structure, systems, processes, and culture of the organization?

5. *Stakeholder analysis.* How will this strategy affect key stakeholders? Which ones are likely to support it? Are they high priority? Which ones are likely to oppose it? Are they high priority? What are the strategic ramifications of their support or opposition?

6. *Future position.* Will the strategy continue to be viable as the industry and the broad environment undergo their expected changes? Will it provide a foundation for survival or competitive success?

The result of this analysis should be a recommendation or recommendations that the organization should pursue. Many evaluation tools can facilitate the eval-

STRATEGIC APPLICATION A.1

A PAYOFF MATRIX APPROACH TO EVALUATING OPPORTUNITIES

Instructions: Establish which opportunities you are going to evaluate. List them down the left column. Then identify which criteria you will use to evaluate your alternatives. Place these criteria along the top. Evaluate each of your alternatives on the basis of each of your criteria and assign a numerical (e.g., 1 to 5, 1 to 3, −2 to +2) or non-numerical (+/− or pro/con, etc.) score based on your analysis. Total your scores to arrive at a recommendation.

Criteria

	Criterion 1	Criterion 2	Criterion 3	Total	
Opportunity 1	−2	1	2	1	
Opportunity 2	2	1	−1	2	
Opportunity 3	1	2	1	4	

Note: In this example matrix, −2 means that the opportunity is very weak based on the criterion, −1 means weak, 0 means that the opportunity is neither weak nor strong, 1 means it is strong and 2 means very strong.

uation process, such as the payoff matrix illustrated in Strategic Application A.1. However, the tools should never act as substitutes for in-depth analysis of the alternatives themselves. In other words, even if a numeric score-keeping system is used, the numbers should be explained based on detailed strategic analysis.

You may not be required by your instructor to conduct a formal analysis of alternatives based on a standard set of criteria; however, you should still make recommendations concerning changes the organization should make to remain or become competitive and satisfy its stakeholders. Through this entire process, remember that many companies identify areas of strength that are no longer capable of giving the company a competitive edge. What was a key to success yesterday may be a requirement for survival today.

Implementation and Control

Recommendations should always be accompanied by an implementation plan and basic controls. The following are major questions that should be addressed during this section of a case analysis. Items 7 and 8 relate specifically to control.

1. How do the recommendations specifically address concerns that were identified during the analysis?
2. What will be the roles and responsibilities of key internal and external stakeholders in carrying out the recommendations and how are they expected to respond? What actions should be taken to smooth out the transition period or avoid stakeholder discontent?
3. Does the organization have the resources (funds, people, skills) to carry out the recommendations? If not, how should the organization proceed in developing or acquiring those resources?

4. Does the organization have the appropriate systems, structures, and processes to carry out the recommendations? If not, how should the organization proceed in creating the appropriate systems, structures, and processes?

5. What is the appropriate time horizon for implementing recommendations? What should the organization and its managers do immediately, in one month, in six months, in a year, and so on?

6. What are the roadblocks the organization could encounter while implementing the recommendations (e.g., financing, skilled labor shortages)? How can the organization overcome these roadblocks?

7. What are the desired outcomes or changes the organization should expect once the recommendations have been implemented? How will the organization know if the recommendations have been successful? In other words, what are the objectives associated with your recommendations?

8. What were some of the major assumptions you made with regard to the external environment? Which of these factors, if different from expected, would require an adjustment to your recommendations?

Following the implementation section, you may want to update your audience (your instructor or other students) concerning actions the firm has taken since the case was written. If a case update is required, it should center on actions that pertain to the focus of your case analysis. If you do an update, remember that what the organization did, even if it appears to have been successful, may not have been the optimal solution.

GLOSSARY

Acquisitions Occur when one organization buys a controlling interest in the stock of another corporation or buys it outright from its owner.

Adaptation The process of responding to the environment.

Administration General management activities of the firm, such as planning and accounting.

Agency Costs Costs such as salaries, insurance, perks, and other expenses associated with boards of directors that corporations pay to ensure that managers act in the best interests of shareholders.

Agency Problem Occurs when managers maximize their own self-interests at the expense of shareholders.

Agents Individuals with a fiduciary duty to act in the best interests of other groups or individuals; for example, managers are agents when ownership and management responsibilities are separated.

Analyzers Organizations that attempt to maintain existing market positions while still locating conservative growth opportunities.

Antitrust Laws Established to prevent an organization from getting large enough to engage in monopoly pricing or other noncompetitive or illegal behavior.

Audits A type of feedback control system used to provide information to support financial, customer, or internal perspectives. Firm conduct and outcomes are measured against established guidelines.

Basic Innovation An invention that impacts more than one product category or industry.

Behavioral Controls Systems, including bureaucratic control systems, clan control, and human resource systems, that influence the behavior of organizational members.

Bottom-Up Approach Goal setting begins in functional areas, which translates into business-level goals of the various divisions that are combined to form the corporate-level goals.

Bridging Stakeholder management techniques that build on interdependencies rather than buffer them.

Broad Environment Socio-cultural forces, global economic forces, technological change, and global political/legal forces.

Budgets Feedback controls that provide revenue and expense targets.

Buffering Stakeholder management techniques of planning for and adapting to the environment so that the needs and demands of critical stakeholders are met.

Bureaucratic Control Systems Rules, policies, guidelines, and procedures that guide the behavior of organizational members.

Business Intelligence Information on markets, new technologies, customers, competitors, and broad social trends.

Business-level Strategy Formulation How organizations will compete in the areas they have selected.

Capacity Utilization Higher levels of capacity utilization spread fixed expenses, leading to lower unit costs.

Chief Executive Officer Highest ranking officer in an organization with primary responsibility for setting the firm's strategic direction.

Clan Control Socialization processes that dictate the type of behavior appropriate in the organization.

Collusion Formal price-setting cooperation within an industry.

Commodity (or Decline) Stage Demand for product either declines as it is outdated or is replaced, or it becomes a basic part of consumers' lives.

Competitive Benchmarking A tool in which management uses the best practices of competitors in setting objectives to encourage improvement in organizational performance.

Competitive Shakeout When market growth slows, weaker competitors can no longer generate enough sales or profits and drop out of the market.

Concentration Corporate-level strategy in which the organization produces a single or small group of products or services.

Concurrent Control Organizational control system that provides managers with real-time information about processes and activities, and, in other cases, acts to influence actions and behavior as they are occurring.

Conglomerates Large, unrelated diversified firms.

Core Competency (or Core Capability) A resource or capability that is valuable, unique, hard to imitate, and can be applied to more than one business area.

Corporate Matrix Organizational structure used to decentralize units closer to market and technological trends while at the same time maintaining centralized control to bring about economies of scope and shared learning.

Corporate Raiders   Organizations or individuals who engage in acquisitions, often against the wishes of the managers of the target companies.

Corporate-level Strategy Formulation   Selection of business areas in which the organization will compete.

Critical Result Areas   Organizational areas that are key to ensuring that the organization accomplishes its goals and its vision; examples are improving worker skills, product redesign, and creation of new process control systems.

Customer Surveys   A type of feedback control system used to measure how well established standards for customer satisfaction are being met.

Defenders   Organizations with a strategy that protects their current position and which engage in little or no new product/market development.

Deliberate Strategy   An intended strategic course planned and pursued by managers.

Diseconomies of Scale   Per-unit cost savings are overwhelmed by administrative and other costs associated with a larger production facility.

Divestiture   The sale of a business unit—a reverse acquisition.

Domestic Stage   The organization focuses its efforts on domestic operations but begins to export its products and services.

Dominant Logic   The way managers deal with managerial tasks, the things they value, and their general approach to running their businesses.

Downscoping   Reducing diversification by selling nonessential businesses not related to the organization's major businesses.

Economies of Scale   Per-unit cost reductions associated with a larger production facility.

Economies of Technology   Technological improvements that result in lower total unit costs.

Emergent Strategy   A strategy not planned or intended, but which emerges from a stream of managerial decisions.

Enactment   The process of influencing the environment to make it less hostile and more conducive to organizational success.

Enterprise Strategy   The organization's best possible reason for the actions it takes; it represents the joining of ethical and strategic thinking about the organization.

Entry Barriers   Forces such as economies of scale, capital requirements, product differentiation, governmental policy or regulation, access to distribution channels, and other factors that keep potential competitors out of the market.

Environment   Groups, individuals, and forces outside of the traditional boundaries of the organization that are significantly influenced by or have a major impact on the organization.

Environmental Determinism   The view that good management is associated with determining which strategy will best fit environmental, technical, and human forces at a particular point in time and then working to carry it out.

Environmental Discontinuities   Major unexpected changes in the social, economic, technological, and political environments that necessitate change within the organization.

Environmental Uncertainty   Organizations' uncertainties regarding factors such as economic cycles, social trends, their ability to secure adequate resources, future government regulations, and the actions of external stakeholders—all adding to the difficulty of managerial decision making.

Ethics   A personal value system used in determining what is right or good.

Exit Barriers   Occur when the capital equipment and skills of an organization are not applicable to other businesses or when there are other significant costs associated with exiting a business area or market.

Experience Effects   Time required to complete indirect labor tasks decreases as a predictable function of the number of times the tasks are repeated.

Feedback Control   Information concerning outcomes of organizational activities that assess the progress of the organization in meeting its goals.

Feedforward Control   Analysis of inputs from stakeholders and the remote environment that helps management anticipate changes in the external and internal environments of the organization.

Financial Ratios   Feedback controls used to control organizational processes and behavior. Examples are the current ratio, which is important to managing working capital, and the debt-to-equity ratio, which can tell an organization whether it is assuming too much financial risk.

Financial Strategy   A plan to provide the organization with the capital structure and funds appropriate for implementing growth and competitive strategies.

Formal Structure   The division of activities and employees of the organization into specialized departments or groups.

Functional Strategies Collective patterns of decisions made and actions taken by employees that implement the growth and competitive strategies of the organization.

Functional Structure The division of an organization into groups based on a specific activity, such as accounting, marketing, R&D, etc.

Functional-level Strategy Formulation How an organization's functional areas should work together to achieve the business-level strategy.

Functions The specific needs of consumers that are being satisfied by an organization's products or services.

Global Stage The organization is no longer associated primarily with any one country.

Global Product/Market Strategy Organizations design, produce, and market a product in the same fashion throughout the world.

Growth Stage Product experiences a large increase in demand; often attracts new competitors.

Hostile Acquisition An acquisition that is against the wishes of the management of the target company.

Human Resource Management Human-based activities of the organization such as recruiting, hiring, training, and compensation.

Human Resources Strategy A plan that guides the recruiting, hiring, training, and compensating of employees as well as organizational change efforts.

Hypercompetition A condition of rapidly escalating competition based on price, quality, first mover actions, defensive moves to protect markets, formation of strategic alliances, and reliance on wealthy parent companies.

Inbound Logistics Activities associated with acquiring inputs used in the product.

Independence An organizational structure that encourages separation and autonomy among business units but has hierarchical coordination with top management.

Industries Groups of organizations who compete directly with each other for market share.

Industry Life Cycle How sales volume for a product-market area changes over its lifetime.

Industry Supply Chain Represents the flow of goods in an industry from their crudest forms to their final, consumable forms.

Information Systems Strategy A plan to provide the organization with the information technology necessary for the operation, planning, and control of business activities.

Innovation An invention that can be replicated reliably on a meaningful scale.

Intangible Relatedness Occurs when skills developed in one area of the organization can be applied to another area.

Interdependence Structures among businesses and partners that encourage the sharing of information and resources, as well as cooperative program development.

Interlocking Directorates Occur when the CEO of one company sits on the board of another company.

International Stage Export becomes an important part of the organization's strategy.

Introduction Stage Initial offering and gradually building of sales for a product as consumers come to understand the product and its uses.

Invention A new idea or technology proven to work in the laboratory.

Joint Venture An alliance formed by two or more organizations to pursue activities of mutual benefit or interest, which may include entering new markets, developing new products, or improving existing technologies.

Keiretsu Cooperative alliances of manufacturers, suppliers, and finance companies in Japan that often own stock in each other and lead to greater efficiency for their members.

Learning Effects Time required to complete a production task decreases as a predictable function of the number of times the task is repeated.

Market Development Broadening an organization's definition of its markets by seeking new market segments or new applications of its products.

Market Failure Occurs when transaction costs are high enough to encourage an organization to produce a good or service in-house instead of buying it from the open market.

Market Penetration Investing in advertising, expanding capacity, and/or increasing sales force in order to increase market share in the current business.

Marketing and Sales Processes through which the customer is induced to and is able to purchase the product.

Marketing Strategy A plan to promote, price, and distribute the products and services of an organization, as well as how to identify and service customer groups.

Markets Consumer groups that an organization attempts to satisfy through its products or services.

Maturity Stage Sales growth of a product levels off.

Mental Models The knowledge managers have about the industry and the organization, and how specific actions relate to desired outcomes.

Mergers   Occur any time two organizations combine to form one.

Mission Statement   Statement describing the organization's overall purpose, broad goals, and the scope of its operations.

Multidivisional Structure   Organizational structure in which each business exists as a separate unit.

Multidomestic Product/Market Strategy   Organizations handle product design, production, and marketing on a country-by-country basis determined by individual market needs.

Multinational Stage   The organization has marketing and production facilities throughout the world, with over one-third of sales from overseas operations.

Network Structure   A large, integrated organization's divisions, organized loosely around customer groups or geographical regions.

Operating Environment   An organization's external stakeholders: competitors, customers, suppliers, financial intermediaries, local communities, unions, activist groups, and government agencies and administrators.

Operations   Activities that transform inputs into the final product.

Operations Strategy   A plan to design and manage the processes needed to create the products and services of the organization.

Opportunities   Conditions in the broad and operating environments that allow a firm to take advantage of organizational strengths, overcome organizational weaknesses, and/or neutralize environmental threats.

Organization   All of the stakeholders, resources, and processes that exist within the boundaries of the firm.

Organizational Crises   Critical situations that threaten high-priority organizational goals, impose a severe restriction on the amount of time in which key members of the organization can respond, and contain elements of surprise.

Organizational Ethics   A value system widely adopted by members of an organization.

Organizational Fit   Occurs when two organizations or business units have similar management processes, cultures, systems, and structures.

Outbound Logistics   Activities related to storing and physically distributing the product to customers.

Partnership   Two or more owners share management and responsibility for the activities and liabilities of an organization.

Policy   A general guideline for employee or organizational actions.

Political Strategy   All of an organization's strategies that have as an objective the creation of a friendlier political climate for the organization.

Portfolio Management   Managing the mix of businesses in the corporate portfolio.

Premise Control   System that evaluates whether information used to establish strategies and goals is still valid given the organization's current internal and external environments.

Premises   Assumptions about what will happen in the future, based on current conditions.

Prepackaged Reorganization Strategy   Reorganization plan negotiated with creditors before a firm files Chapter XI.

Procurement   The actual purchase of inputs at any stage of the value chain.

Product or Market Group Structure   The division of an organization into groups focused on a specific output or distribution strategy, such as products, customer groups, or geographical regions.

Product/Service Development   Modifying existing products or developing new products/services for the purpose of selling more to existing customers or creating new market segments.

Products or Services   The actual output an organization provides in an attempt to satisfy consumers' needs.

Project Matrix Structure   A complex form of organizational structure that divides organization functions by both product/market group and functional activities.

Prospectors   Organizations that aggressively seek new market opportunities and are willing to take risks.

Public Interest Groups   Activist groups that represent the position of a broad cross-section of society on such issues as pollution, fair hiring practices, safety, and waste management.

Quasi Integration   Occurs when a firm purchases most of what it needs of a particular product or service from a firm in which it holds an ownership stake.

Reactors   Organizations with no distinct strategy except to respond to environmental situations.

Related Diversification   Organization's involvement in other businesses or activities related to its core business.

Reorientation   A significant realignment of organization strategies, structure, and processes with the new environmental realities.

Research and Development Strategy   A plan that guides basic research of the organization as well as its development of more effective and efficient applications, products, and processes.

Resource Conversion Processes and Capabilities The manufacturing or service processes and capabilities an organization uses to satisfy consumers' needs.

Resource-based View of the Firm   A perspective on strategy development that views the organization as a bundle of financial, physical, human, and general organizational resources.

Restructuring   Streamlining and reorienting an organization's current format of operations to place it in a position in which it is better able to compete; often involves reducing the scope of the business at the corporate level combined with refocusing efforts on the things the organization does well.

Retrenchment   A turnaround strategy that may involve selling or liquidating unprofitable business units, work force reductions, tighter cost or quality controls, or new emphasis on quality or efficiency.

Rules and Procedures   Specific steps of actions for an employee to follow in a particular situation.

Scope   The breadth of an organization's activities across markets, functions, resource conversion processes, and products or services.

"Semistrong" Market Efficiency   The idea that information about the value of a financial security is quickly assimilated by the market and absorbed into the price of the security.

Service   Activities that enhance or maintain the product's value to the customer.

Situation Analysis   Analyzing the internal and external environments of the organization to arrive at organizational strengths, weaknesses, opportunities, and threats (SWOT).

Sole Proprietorship   Business run by a single owner/manager who is personally responsible for its activities, debts, liabilities, taxes, and profits.

Special Interest Groups   Activist groups that represent the views of smaller subgroups in society.

Stakeholder Analysis   Identifying and prioritizing key stakeholders, assessing their needs, collecting ideas from them, and integrating this knowledge into strategic management processes.

Stakeholder Management   Communicating, negotiating, contracting, and managing relationships with stakeholders and motivating them to behave in ways that are beneficial to the organization and its other stakeholders.

Stakeholders   Groups or individuals who can significantly affect or be affected by an organization's activities.

Strategic Alliances   Formed by two or more organizations to develop new products or services, enter new markets, or improve resource conversion processes.

Strategic Business Units (SBUs)   Organizational structure in which closely related businesses are grouped together for purposes of management and control.

Strategic Control   Ongoing evaluation and appropriate adjustments of the mission, goals, strategies, or implementation plan.

Strategic Control System   Organizational system by which top management can evaluate the progress of the organization in accomplishing its goals, as well as point out areas in need of attention.

Strategic Fit   The effective matching of strategic organizational capabilities.

Strategic Group Map   Tracking of strategies of competing firms by plotting two or more important strategic dimensions of the industry.

Strategic Management   The process through which organizations analyze and learn from their internal and external environments, establish long- and short-term goals, create strategies that are intended to help achieve established goals, and execute those strategies, all in an effort to satisfy key organizational stakeholders.

Strategy   An organizational plan of action intended to move an organization toward the achievement of its goals and mission.

Strategy Implementation   Creating the functional strategies, systems, structures, and processes needed by the organization to achieve strategic goals.

Strengths   A firm's resources and capabilities that can lead to a competitive advantage.

Structural Inertia   Forces within the organization that work to maintain the status quo.

Sustainable Competitive Advantage   An advantage that is difficult to imitate by competitors, leading to higher-than-average organizational performance over a long time period.

Tangible Relatedness   An organization may use the same physical resources for multiple purposes.

Taper Integration   Occurs when an organization produces part of its requirements in-house and buys the rest of what it needs on the open market.

Technology   Human knowledge about products and services and the ways they are made and delivered.

Technology Development   Learning processes that

result in improvements in the way organizational functions are performed.

Threats Conditions in the broad and operating environments that may stand in the way of organizational competitiveness or the achievement of stakeholder satisfaction.

Top Management Team A group of high-ranking officers within an organization who make the important strategic and operating decisions.

Top-Down Approach The corporate level essentially determines and then dictates what lower-level goals should be.

Transaction Cost Economics The study of economic transactions and their costs.

Transnational Product/Market Strategy Organizations seek both global efficiency and local responsiveness by establishing an integrated network with shared vision and resources but individual decision making to adapt to local needs.

Transnational Structure A complex corporate matrix structure that organizes businesses along national or regional, product, and function dimensions.

Unrelated Diversification Organization's involvement in businesses or activities not related to its core business.

Value Chain Distinct organizational processes that create value for the customer.

Vertical Integration The extent to which a firm is involved in several stages of the industry supply chain.

Vision Statement Statement expressing management's view of what the organization can or should become in the future.

Weaknesses Resources and capabilities that the firm needs but does not possess, resulting in a competitive disadvantage.

INDEX